PHILIP'S

MODERN SCHOOL ATLAS

95TH EDITION

IN ASSOCIATION WITH
THE ROYAL GEOGRAPHICAL SOCIETY
WITH THE INSTITUTE OF BRITISH GEOGRAPHERS

CONTENTS

Published in Great Britain in 2006 by Philip's,
a division of Octopus Publishing Group Limited,
2–4 Heron Quays, London E14 4JP
www.octopusbooks.co.uk

An Hachette Livre UK Company
www.hachettelivre.co.uk

Cartography by Philip's
Ninety-fifth edition

Copyright © 2006 Philip's
Revised reprint 2008

ISBN 978-0-540-08746-4 (PAPERBACK EDITION)

ISBN 978-0-540-08745-7 (HARDBACK EDITION)

Details of other Philip's titles and services
can be found on our website at:
www.philips-maps.co.uk

Printed in Hong Kong

Philip's World Atlases are published in association with The Royal Geographical
Society (with The Institute of British Geographers).

The Society was founded in 1830 and given a Royal Charter in 1859 for
'the advancement of geographical science'. Today it is a leading world centre
for geographical learning – supporting education, teaching, research and
expeditions, and promoting public understanding of the subject.

Further information about the Society and how to join may be found on its
website at: **www.rgs.org**

PHOTOGRAPHIC ACKNOWLEDGEMENTS
All satellite images in the atlas are courtesy of NPA Group, Edenbridge, Kent
(www.satmaps.com), with the exception of the following: p. 17 M-SAT Ltd/Science
Photo Library; p. 49 PLI/Science Photo Library; p. 134 NASA/GSFC.

SUBJECT LIST

MAP SYMBOLS

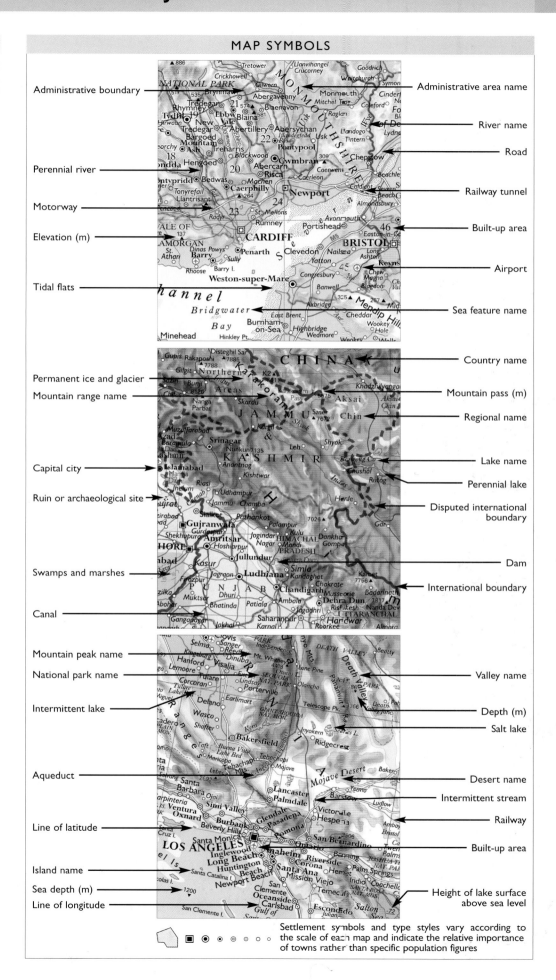

Administrative boundary — Administrative area name — River name — Road — Railway tunnel — Built-up area — Airport — Sea feature name

Perennial river

Motorway

Elevation (m)

Tidal flats

Permanent ice and glacier — Country name

Mountain range name — Mountain pass (m) — Regional name

Capital city — Lake name — Perennial lake

Ruin or archaeological site — Disputed international boundary

Swamps and marshes — Dam — International boundary

Canal

Mountain peak name — Valley name

National park name

Intermittent lake — Depth (m) — Salt lake

Aqueduct — Desert name — Intermittent stream — Railway

Line of latitude — Built-up area

Island name

Sea depth (m) — Height of lake surface above sea level

Line of longitude

Settlement symbols and type styles vary according to the scale of each map and indicate the relative importance of towns rather than specific population figures

SCALE

The scale of a map is the relationship of the distance between two points shown on the map and the distance between the same two points on the Earth's surface. For instance, 1 inch on the map represents 1 mile on the ground, or 10 kilometres on the ground is represented by 1 centimetre on the map.

Instead of saying 1 centimetre represents 10 kilometres, we could say that 1 centimetre represents 1 000 000 centimetres on the map. If the scale is stated so that the same unit of measurement is used on both the map and the ground, then the proportion will hold for any unit of measurement. Therefore, the scale is usually written 1:1 000 000. This is called a 'representative fraction' and usually appears at the top of the map page, above the scale bar.

Calculations can easily be made in centimetres and kilometres by dividing the second figure in the representative fraction by 100 000 (i.e. by deleting the last five zeros). Thus at a scale of 1:5 000 000, 1 cm on the map represents 50 km on the ground. This is called a 'scale statement'. The calculation for inches and miles is more laborious, but 1 000 000 divided by 63 360 (the number of inches in a mile) shows that 1:1 000 000 can be stated as 1 inch on the map represents approximately 16 miles on the ground.

Many of the maps in this atlas feature a scale bar. This is a bar divided into the units of the map – miles and kilometres – so that a map distance can be measured with a ruler, dividers or a piece of paper, then placed along the scale bar, and the distance read off. To the left of the zero on the scale bar there are usually more divisions. By placing the ruler or dividers on the nearest rounded figure to the right of the zero, the smaller units can be counted off to the left.

The map extracts to the right show Los Angeles and its surrounding area at six different scales. The representative fraction, scale statement and scale bar are positioned above each map. Map 1 is at 1:27 000 and is the largest scale extract shown. Many of the individual buildings are identified and most of the streets are named, but at this scale only part of central Los Angeles can be shown within the given area. Map 2 is much smaller in scale at 1:250 000. Only a few important buildings and streets can be named, but the whole of central Los Angeles is shown. Maps 3, 4 and 5 show how greater areas can be depicted as the map scale decreases, down to Map 6 at 1:35 000 000. At this small scale, the entire Los Angeles conurbation is depicted by a single town symbol and a large part of the south-western USA and part of Mexico is shown.

The scales of maps must be used with care since large distances on small-scale maps can be represented by one or two centimetres. On certain projections scale is only correct along certain lines, parallels or meridians. As a general rule, the larger the map scale, the more accurate and reliable will be the distance measured.

LATITUDE AND LONGITUDE

Accurate positioning of individual points on the Earth's surface is made possible by reference to the geometric system of latitude and longitude.

Latitude is the distance of a point north or south of the Equator measured at an angle with the centre of the Earth, whereby the Equator is latitude 0 degrees,

1 1 : 27 000 — 1 cm on the map represents 0.27 km on the ground

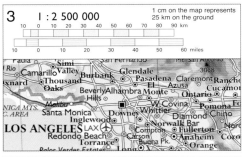

2 1 : 250 000 — 1 cm on the map represents 2.5 km on the ground

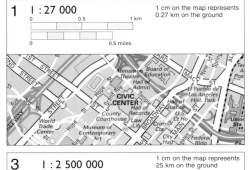

3 1 : 2 500 000 — 1 cm on the map represents 25 km on the ground

4 1 : 6 000 000 — 1 cm on the map represents 60 km on the ground

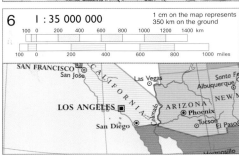

5 1 : 12 000 000 — 1 cm on the map represents 120 km on the ground

6 1 : 35 000 000 — 1 cm on the map represents 350 km on the ground

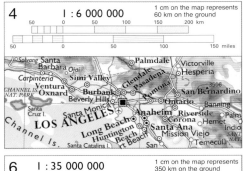

the North Pole is 90 degrees north and the South Pole 90 degrees south. Latitude parallels are drawn west–east around the Earth, parallel to the Equator, decreasing in diameter from the Equator until they become a point at the poles. On the maps in this atlas the lines of latitude are represented by blue lines running across the map in smooth curves, with the degree figures in blue at the sides of the maps. The degree interval depends on the scale of the map.

Lines of longitude are meridians drawn north–south, cutting the lines of latitude at right angles on the Earth's surface and intersecting with one another at the poles. Longitude is measured by an angle at the centre of the Earth from the prime meridian (0 degrees), which passes through Greenwich in London. It is given as a measurement east or west of the Greenwich Meridian from 0 to 180 degrees. The meridians are normally drawn north–south vertically down the map, with the degree figures

in blue in the top and bottom margins of the map.

In the index each place name is followed by its latitude and longitude, and then its map page number and letter-figure grid reference. The unit of measurement is the degree, which is subdivided into 60 minutes. An index entry states the position of a place in degrees and minutes. The latitude is followed by N(orth) or S(outh) and the longitude E(ast) or W(est).

For example:
Helston, U.K.   50°7N 5°17W   **27** G3
Helston is 50 degrees 7 minutes north of the Equator and 5 degrees 17 minutes west of Greenwich, and is on map page 27, in grid square G3.

McKinley, Mt., U.S.A.   63°4N 151°0W   **108** C4
Mount McKinley is 63 degrees 4 minutes north of the Equator and 151 degrees west of Greenwich, and is on map page 108, in grid square C4.

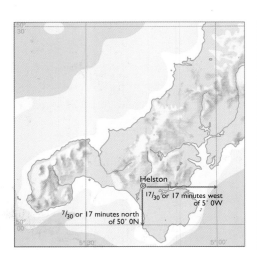

How to locate a place or feature

The two diagrams (*left*) show how to estimate the required distance from the nearest line of latitude or longitude on the map page, in order to locate a place or feature listed in the index (such as Helston in the UK and Mount McKinley in the USA, as detailed in the above example).

In the left-hand diagram there are 30 minutes between the lines and so to find the position of Helston an estimate has to be made: 7 parts of the 30 degrees north of the 50 0N latitude line, and 17 parts of the 30 degrees west of the 5 0W longitude line.

In the right-hand diagram it is more difficult to estimate because there is an interval of 10 degrees between the lines. In the example of Mount McKinley, the reader has to estimate 3 degrees 4 minutes north of 60 0N and 1 degree west of 150 0W.

MAP PROJECTIONS

A map projection is the systematic depiction of the imaginary grid of lines of latitude and longitude from a globe on to a flat surface. The grid of lines is called the 'graticule' and it can be constructed either by graphical means or by mathematical formulae to form the basis of a map. As a globe is three dimensional, it is not possible to depict its surface on a flat map without some form of distortion. Preservation of one of the basic properties listed below can only be secured at the expense of the others and thus the choice of projection is often a compromise solution.

Correct area

In these projections the areas from the globe are to scale on the map. This is particularly useful in the mapping of densities and distributions. Projections with this property are termed 'equal area', 'equivalent' or 'homolographic'.

Correct distance

In these projections the scale is correct along the meridians, or, in the case of the 'azimuthal equidistant', scale is true along any line drawn from the centre of the projection. They are called 'equidistant'.

Correct shape

This property can only be true within small areas as it is achieved only by having a uniform scale distortion along both the 'x' and 'y' axes of the projection. The projections are called 'conformal' or 'orthomorphic'.

Map projections can be divided into three broad categories – 'azimuthal', 'conic' and 'cylindrical'. Cartographers use different projections from these categories depending on the map scale, the size of the area to be mapped, and what they want the map to show.

AZIMUTHAL OR ZENITHAL PROJECTIONS

These are constructed by the projection of part of the graticule from the globe on to a plane tangential to any single point on it. This plane may be tangential to the equator (equatorial case), the poles (polar case) or any other point (oblique case). Any straight line drawn from the point at which the plane touches the globe is the shortest distance from that point and is known as a 'great circle'. In its 'gnomonic' construction any straight line on the map is a great circle, but there is great exaggeration towards the edges and this reduces its general uses. There are five different ways of transferring the graticule on to the plane and these are shown below. The diagrams below also show how the graticules vary, using the polar case as the example.

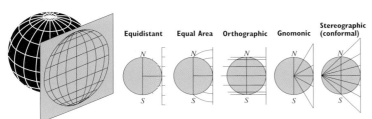

Equidistant   Equal Area   Orthographic   Gnomonic   Stereographic (conformal)

Polar case

The polar case is the simplest to construct and the diagram on the right shows the differing effects of all five methods of construction, comparing their coverage, distortion, etc, using North America as the example.

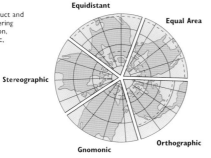

Equidistant
Equal Area
Stereographic
Gnomonic
Orthographic

Oblique case

The plane touches the globe at any point between the Equator and poles. The oblique orthographic uses the distortion in azimuthal projections away from the centre to give a graphic depiction of the Earth as seen from any desired point in space.

Equatorial case

The example shown here is Lambert's Equivalent Azimuthal. It is the only projection which is both equal area and where bearing is true from the centre.

CONICAL PROJECTIONS

These use the projection of the graticule from the globe on to a cone which is tangential to a line of latitude (termed the 'standard parallel'). This line is always an arc and scale is always true along it. Because of its method of construction, it is used mainly for depicting the temperate latitudes around the standard parallel, i.e. where there is least distortion. To reduce the distortion and include a larger range of latitudes, the projection may be constructed with the cone bisecting the surface of the globe so that there are two standard parallels, each of which is true to scale. The distortion is thus spread more evenly between the two chosen parallels.

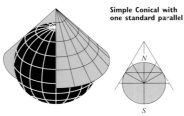

Simple Conical with one standard parallel

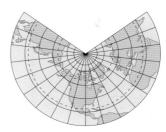

Bonne

This is a modification of the simple conic, whereby the true scale along the meridians is sacrificed to enable the accurate representation of areas. However, scale is true along each parallel but shapes are distorted at the edges.

Albers Conical Equal Area

This projection uses two standard parallels. The selection of these relative to the land area to be mapped is very important. It is equal area and is especially useful for large land masses oriented east–west, such as the USA.

CYLINDRICAL AND OTHER WORLD PROJECTIONS

This group of projections are those which permit the whole of the Earth's surface to be depicted on one map. They are a very large group of projections and the following are only a few of them. Cylindrical projections are constructed by the projection of the graticule from the globe on to a cylinder tangential to the globe. Although cylindrical projections can depict all the main land masses, there is considerable distortion of shape and area towards the poles. One cylindrical projection, Mercator, overcomes this shortcoming by possessing the unique navigational property that any straight line drawn on it is a line of constant bearing ('loxodrome'). It is used for maps and charts between 15° either side of the Equator. Beyond this, enlargement of area is a serious drawback, although it is used for navigational charts at all latitudes.

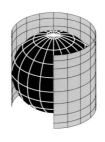

Simple Cylindrical

Cylindrical with two standard parallels

Mercator

Eckert IV
(pseudo-cylindrical equal area)

Hammer
(polyconic equal area)

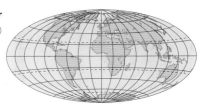

The first satellite to monitor our environment systematically was launched as long ago as April 1961. It was called TIROS-1 and was designed specifically to record atmospheric change. The first of the generation of Earth resources satellites was Landsat-1, launched in July 1972.

The succeeding decades have seen a revolution in our ability to survey and map our global environment. Digital sensors mounted on satellites now scan vast areas of the Earth's surface day and night. They collect and relay back to Earth huge volumes of geographical data which is processed and stored by computers.

Satellite imagery and remote sensing

Continuous development and refinement, and freedom from national access restrictions, have meant that sensors on these satellite platforms are increasingly replacing surface and airborne data-gathering techniques. Twenty-four hours a day, satellites are scanning and measuring the Earth's surface and atmosphere, adding to an ever-expanding range of geographic and geophysical data available to help us identify and manage the problems of our human and physical environments. Remote sensing is the science of extracting information from such images.

Satellite orbits

Most Earth-observation satellites (such as the Landsat, SPOT and IRS series) are in a near-polar, Sun-synchronous orbit (*see diagram opposite*). At altitudes of around 700–900 km the satellites revolve around the Earth approximately every 100 minutes and on each orbit cross a particular line of latitude at the same local (solar) time. This ensures that the satellite can obtain coverage of most of the globe, replicating the coverage typically within 2–3 weeks. In more recent satellites, sensors can be pointed sideways from the orbital path, and 'revisit' times with high-resolution frames can thus be reduced to a few days.

Exceptions to these Sun-synchronous orbits include the geostationary meteorological satellites, such as Meteosat. These have a 36,000 km high orbit and rotate around the Earth every 24 hours, thus remaining above the same point on the Equator.

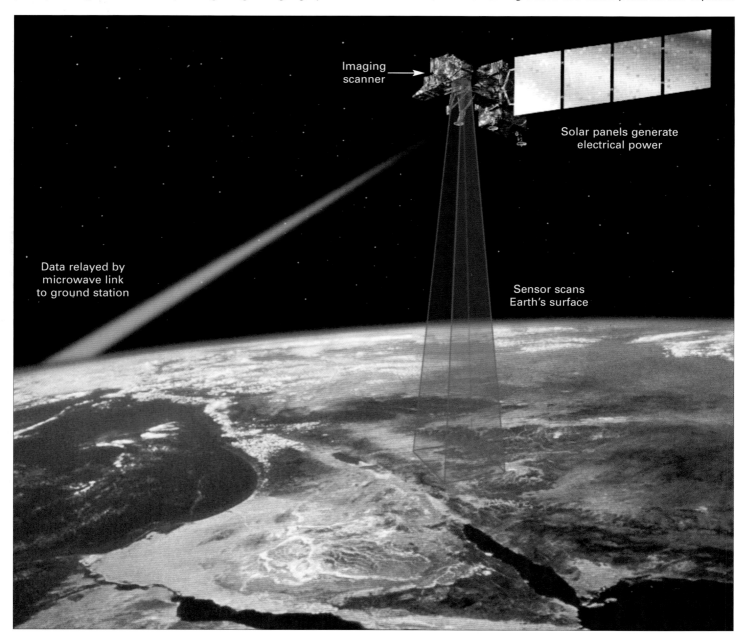

Imaging scanner

Solar panels generate electrical power

Data relayed by microwave link to ground station

Sensor scans Earth's surface

Landsat-7
This is the latest addition to the Landsat Earth-observation satellite programme, orbiting at 705 km above the Earth. With onboard recorders, the satellite can store data until it passes within range of a ground station. Basic geometric and radiometric corrections are then applied before distribution of the imagery to users.

These satellites acquire frequent images showing cloud and atmospheric moisture movements for almost a full hemisphere.

In addition, there is the Global Positioning System (GPS) satellite 'constellation', which orbits at a height of 20,200 km, consisting of 24 satellites. These circle the Earth in six different orbital planes, enabling us to fix our position on the Earth's surface to an accuracy of a few centimetres. Although developed for military use, this system is now available to individuals through hand-held receivers and in-car navigation systems. The other principal commercial uses are for surveying and air and sea navigation.

Digital sensors

Early satellite designs involved images being exposed to photographic film and returned to Earth by capsule for processing, a technique still sometimes used today. However, even the first commercial satellite imagery, from Landsat-1, used digital imaging sensors and transmitted the data back to ground stations (*see diagram opposite*).

Passive, or optical, sensors record the radiation reflected from the Earth for specific wavebands. Active sensors transmit their own microwave radiation, which is reflected from the Earth's surface back to the satellite and recorded. The SAR (Synthetic Aperture Radar) Radarsat images on page 15 are examples of the latter.

Whichever scanning method is used, each satellite records image data of constant width but potentially several thousand kilometres in length. Once the data has been received on Earth, it is usually split into approximately square sections or 'scenes' for distribution.

Spectral resolution, wavebands and false-colour composites

Satellites can record data from many sections of the electromagnetic spectrum (wavebands) simultaneously. Since we can only see images made from the three primary colours (red, green and blue), a selection of any three wavebands needs to be made in order to form a picture that will enable visual interpretation of the scene to be made. When any combination other than the visible bands are used, such as near or middle infrared, the resulting image is termed a 'false-colour composite'. An example of this is shown on page 8.

The selection of these wavebands depends on the purpose of the final image – geology, hydrology, agronomy and environmental requirements each have their own optimum waveband combinations.

GEOGRAPHIC INFORMATION SYSTEMS

A Geographic Information System (GIS) enables any available geospatial data to be compiled, presented and analysed using specialized computer software.

Many aspects of our lives now benefit from the use of GIS – from the management and maintenance of the networks of pipelines and cables that supply our homes, to the exploitation or protection of the natural resources that we use. Much of this is at a regional or national scale and the data collected from satellites form an important part of our interpretation and understanding of the world around us.

GIS systems are used for many aspects of central planning and modern life, such as defence, land use, reclamation, telecommunications and the deployment of emergency services. Commercial companies can use demographic and infrastructure data within a GIS to plan marketing strategies, identifying where their services would be most needed, and thus decide where best to locate their businesses. Insurance companies use GIS to determine premiums based on population distribution, crime figures and the likelihood of natural disasters, such as flooding or subsidence.

Whatever the application, all the geographically related information that is available can be input and prepared in a GIS, so that a user can display the specific information of interest, or combine data to produce further information which might answer or help resolve a specific problem. From analysis of the data that has been acquired, it is often possible to use a GIS to generate a 'model' of possible future situations and to see what impact might result from decisions and actions taken. A GIS can also monitor change over time, to aid the observation and interpretation of long-term change.

A GIS can utilize a satellite image to extract useful information and map large areas, which would otherwise take many man-years of labour to achieve on the ground. For industrial applications, including hydrocarbon and mineral exploration, forestry, agriculture, environmental monitoring and urban development, such dramatic and beneficial increases in efficiency have made it possible to evaluate and undertake projects and studies in parts of the world that were previously considered inaccessible, and on a scale that would not have been possible before.

SELECTED REMOTE SENSING SATELLITES			
Year Launched	**Satellite**	**Country**	**Pixel Size (Resolution)**
Passive Sensors (Optical)			
1972	Landsat-1 MSS	USA	80 m
1975	Landsat-2 MSS	USA	80 m
1978	Landsat-3 MSS	USA	80 m
1978	NOAA AVHRR	USA	1.1 km
1981	Cosmos TK-350	Russia	10 m
1982	Landsat-4 TM	USA	30 m
1984	Landsat-5 TM	USA	30 m
1986	SPOT-1	France	10 / 20 m
1988	IRS-1A	India	36 / 72 m
1988	SPOT-2	France	10 / 20 m
1989	Cosmos KVR-1000	Russia	2 m
1991	IRS-1B	India	36 / 72 m
1992	SPOT-3	France	10 / 20 m
1995	IRS-1C	India	5.8 / 23.5 m
1997	IRS-1D	India	5.8 / 23.5 m
1998	SPOT-4	France	10 / 20 m
1999	Landsat-7 ETM	USA	15 / 30 m
1999	UoSAT-12	UK	10 / 32 m
1999	IKONOS-2	USA	1.0 / 4 m
1999	ASTER	USA	15 m
2000	Hyperion	USA	30 m
2000	EROS-A1	International	1.8 m
2001	Quickbird	USA	0.61 / 2.4 m
2002	SPOT-5	France	2.5 / 5 / 10 m
2002	DMC AlSat-1	Algeria (UK)	32 m
2003	DMC UK	UK	32 m
2003	DMC NigeriaSat-1	Nigeria (UK)	32 m
2003	DMC BilSat	Turkey (UK)	32 m
2003	OrbView-3	USA	1.0 / 4 m
2004	Formosat-2	Taiwan	2.0 / 8 m
2004	KOMPSAT-2	South Korea	1.0 / 4 m
Active Sensors (Synthetic Aperture Radar)			
1991	ERS-1	Europe	25 m
1992	JERS-1	Japan	18 m
1995	ERS-2	Europe	25 m
1995	Radarsat	Canada	8–100 m
2002	ENVISAT	Europe	25 m

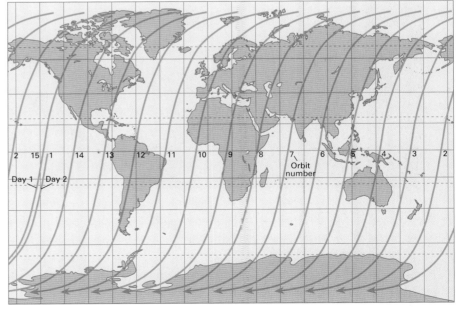

Satellite orbits
Landsat-7 makes over 14 orbits per day in its Sun-synchronous orbit. During the full 16 days of a repeat cycle, coverage of the areas between those shown is achieved.

Natural-colour and false-colour composites
These images show the salt ponds at the southern end of San Francisco Bay, which now form the San Francisco Bay National Wildlife Refuge. They demonstrate the difference between 'natural colour' (*top*) and 'false colour' (*bottom*) composites.

The top image is made from visible red, green and blue wavelengths. The colours correspond closely to those one would observe from an aircraft. The salt ponds appear green or orange-red due to the colour of the sediments they contain. The urban areas appear grey and vegetation is either dark green (trees) or light brown (dry grass).

The bottom image is made up of near-infrared, visible red and visible green wavelengths. These wavebands are represented here in red, green and blue, respectively. Since chlorophyll in healthy vegetation strongly reflects near-infrared light, this is clearly visible as red in the image.

False-colour composite imagery is therefore very sensitive to the presence of healthy vegetation. The bottom image thus shows better discrimination between the 'leafy' residential urban areas, such as Palo Alto (south-west of the Bay) from other urban areas by the 'redness' of the trees. The high chlorophyll content of watered urban grass areas shows as bright red, contrasting with the dark red of trees and the brown of natural, dry grass. *(EROS)*

Western Grand Canyon, Arizona, USA

This false-colour image shows in bright red the sparse vegetation on the limestone plateau, including sage, mesquite and grasses. Imagery such as this is used to monitor this and similar fragile environments. The sediment-laden river, shown as blue-green, can be seen dispersing into Lake Mead to the north-west. Side canyons cross the main canyon in straight lines, showing where erosion along weakened fault lines has occurred. *(EROS)*

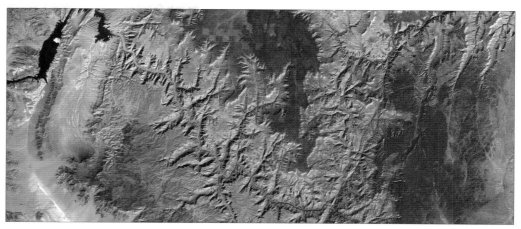

Ayers Rock and Mt Olga, Northern Territory, Australia

These two huge outliers are the remnants of Precambrian mountain ranges created some 500 million years ago and then eroded away. Ayers Rock (*seen at right*) rises 345 m above the surrounding land and has been a part of Aboriginal life for over 10,000 years. Their dramatic coloration, caused by oxidized iron in the sandstone, attracts visitors from around the world. *(EROS)*

Mount St Helens, Washington, USA

A massive volcanic eruption on 18 May 1980 killed 60 people and devastated around 400 sq km of forest within minutes. The blast reduced the mountain peak by 400 m to its current height of 2,550 m, and volcanic ash rose some 25 km into the atmosphere. The image shows Mount St Helens eight years after the eruption in 1988. The characteristic volcanic cone has collapsed in the north, resulting in the devastating 'liquid' flow of mud and rock. *(EROS)*

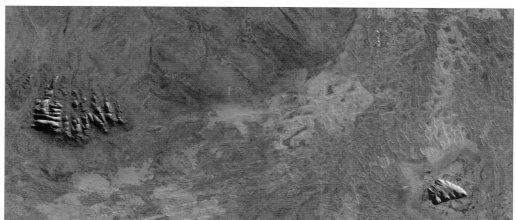

Niger Delta, West Africa

The River Niger is the third longest river in Africa after the Nile and Congo. Deltas are by nature constantly evolving sedimentary features and often contain many ecosystems within them. In the case of the Niger Delta, there are also vast hydro-carbon reserves beneath it with associated wells and pipelines. Satellite imagery helps to plan activity and monitor this fragile and changing environment. *(EROS)*

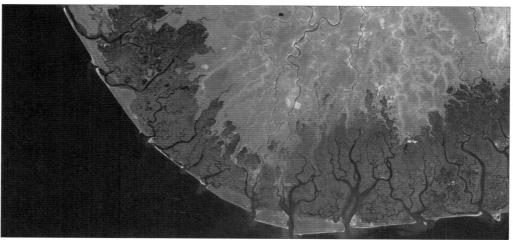

Europe at night

This image was derived as part of the Defense Meteorological Satellite Program. The sensor recorded all the emissions of near-infrared radiation at night, mainly the lights from cities, towns and villages. Note also the 'lights' in the North Sea from the flares of the oil production platforms. This project was the first systematic attempt to record human settlement on a global scale using remote sensing. *(NOAA)*

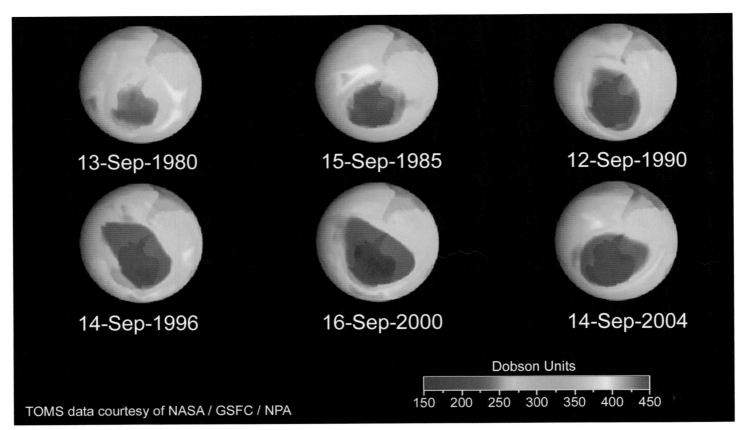

Antarctic ozone depletion

The Total Ozone Mapping Spectrometer (TOMS) instruments, first launched in 1978, can measure a range of atmospheric trace constituents, in particular global ozone distributions. Environmental and public health authorities need this up-to-date information to alert people to health risks. For example, low ozone levels result in increased UV-B radiation, which is harmful and can cause cancers, cataracts and impact the human immune system. 'Dobson Units' indicate the level of ozone depletion (normal levels are around 280DU).

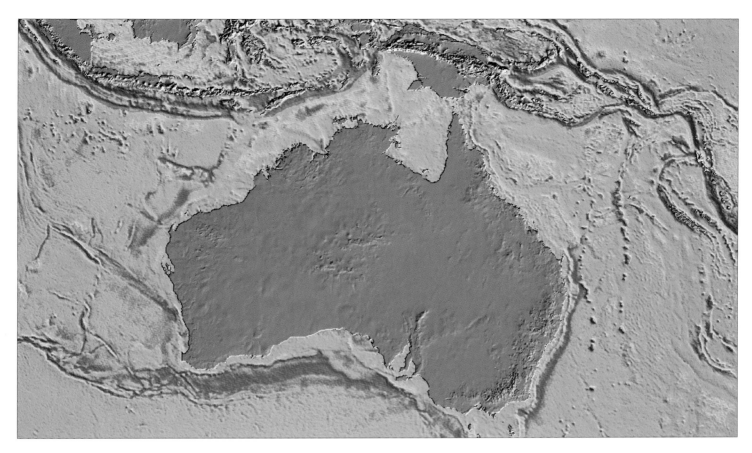

Gravitational fields

The strength of the Earth's gravitational field at its surface varies according to the ocean depth and the density of local rocks. This causes local variations in the sea level. Satellites orbiting in precisely determined orbits are able to measure the sea level to an accuracy of a few centimetres. These variations give us a better understanding of the geological structure of the sea floor. Information from these sensors can also be used to determine ocean wave heights, which relate to surface wind speed, and are therefore useful in meteorological forecasting. *(NPA)*

Weather monitoring

Geostationary and polar orbiting satellites monitor the Earth's cloud and atmospheric moisture movements, giving us an insight into the global workings of the atmosphere and permitting us to predict weather change.

Hurricane Katrina

Making landfall along the US Gulf coast on 29 August 2005, Hurricane Katrina became the most expensive natural disaster ever to strike the USA. Its path was tracked by images such as this. *(NASA/J. Schmaltz, MODIS Land Rapid Response Team)*

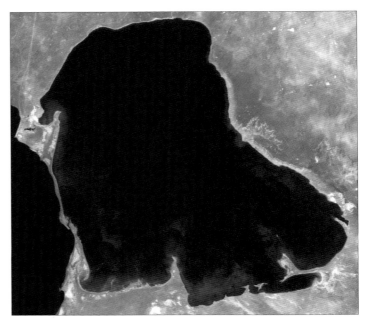

Kara-Bogaz-Gol, Turkmenistan

The Kara-Bogaz-Gol (*above, left and right*) is a large, shallow lagoon joined by a narrow, steep-sided strait to the Caspian Sea. Evaporation makes it one of the most saline bodies of water in the world. Believing the Caspian sea level was falling, the strait was dammed by the Soviet Union in 1980 with the intention of conserving the water to sustain the salt industry. However, by 1983 it had dried up completely (*above left*), leading to widespread wind-blown salt, soil poisoning and health problems downwind to the east. In 1992 the Turkmenistan government began to demolish the dam to re-establish the flow of water from the Caspian Sea (*above right*). Satellite imagery has helped to monitor and map the Kara-Bogaz-Gol as it has fluctuated in size. *(EROS)*

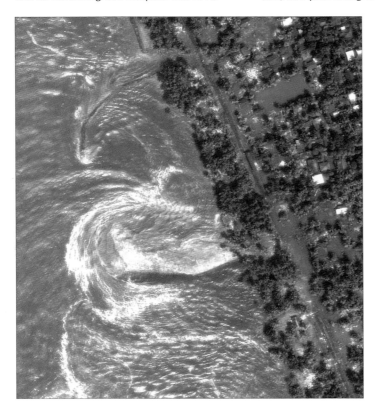

Southern Asia tsunami, Sri Lanka

The turbulent receding waters of the Southern Asia tsunami on 26 December 2004 can clearly be seen in this high-resolution imagery collected by the QuickBird satellite. The area shown here is the holiday resort of Kalutara on the west coast of Sri Lanka, to the south of Colombo. Such imagery enabled rescuers to assess the worst affected areas and direct the overstretched emergency services where most needed. *(DigitalGlobe)*

Lake Amadeus, Northern Territory, Australia

This saline lake system is an important wetland environment situated at the heart of one of the most arid areas in Australia. It supports a wide range of complex habitats and owes its existence to seepage from the central groundwater system. Changes in its extent in an otherwise remote site can be monitored using satellite imagery such as this Landsat ETM scene. *(EROS)*

New Orleans, Louisiana, USA
These two images show the area around the New Orleans Superdome before *(top)* and after *(below)* Hurricane Katrina struck in August 2005. In the lower image, damage to the dome roof can be clearly seen, and the darker areas surrounding the buildings are streets inundated by floodwaters. In the aftermath of the hurricane, satellite imagery played a key role in the assessment of the damage caused and the deployment of emergency services. *(DigitalGlobe)*

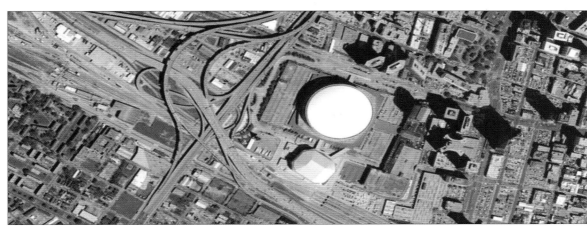

Larsen B ice shelf, Antarctica
Between January and March 2002, the 3,250 km² Larsen B ice shelf on the Antarctic Peninsula collapsed. The upper right-hand image shows its area in December 2001 before the collapse, while the lower image shows the area in December 2002 after the collapse. The 200 m thick ice sheet had been retreating before this date, but over 500 billion tonnes of ice collapsed in under a month. This was due to rising temperatures of 0.5°C per year in this part of Antarctica. Satellite imagery is the only way for scientists to monitor fragile environments, such as this, in inaccessible areas of the world.

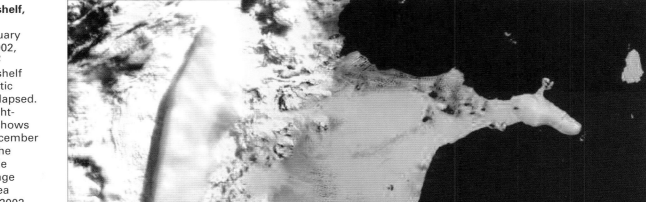

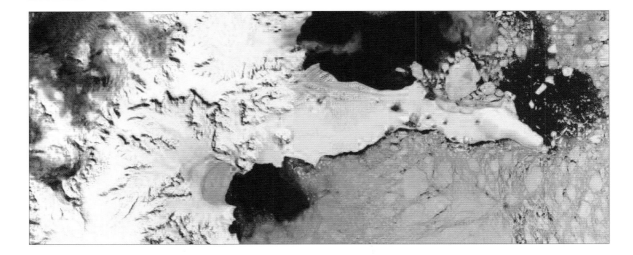

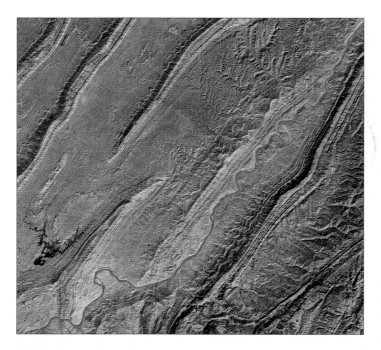

Sichuan Basin, China

The north-east/south-west trending ridges in this image are anticlinal folds developed in the Earth's crust as a result of plate collision and compression. Geologists map these folds and the lowlands between them formed by synclinal folds, as they are often the areas where oil or gas are found in commercial quantities. The river shown in this image is the Yangtze, near Chongqing. *(China RSGS)*

North Anatolian Fault, Turkey

The east–west trending valley running through the centre of this image is formed by the North Anatolian wrench fault. It is the result of Arabia colliding with southern Eurasia, forcing most of Turkey westwards towards Greece. The valley was created by the Kelkit river removing the loosened rock formed by the two tectonic plates grinding together. This active fault has also caused considerable damage further east in the Gulf of Izmit. *(EROS)*

Wadi Hadhramaut, Yemen

Yemen is extremely arid – however, in the past it was more humid and wet, enabling large river systems to carve out the deep and spectacular gorges and dried-out river beds (*wadis*) seen in this image. The erosion has revealed many contrasting rock types. The image has been processed to exaggerate this effect, producing many shades of red, pink and purple, which make geological mapping easier and more cost-effective. *(EROS)*

Zagros Mountains, Iran

These mountains were formed as Arabia collided with Southern Eurasia. The upper half of this colour-enhanced image shows an anticline that runs east–west. The dark grey features are called *diapirs*, which are bodies of viscous rock salt that are very buoyant and sometimes rise to the surface, spilling and spreading out like a glacier. The presence of salt in the region is important as it stops oil escaping to the surface. *(EROS)*

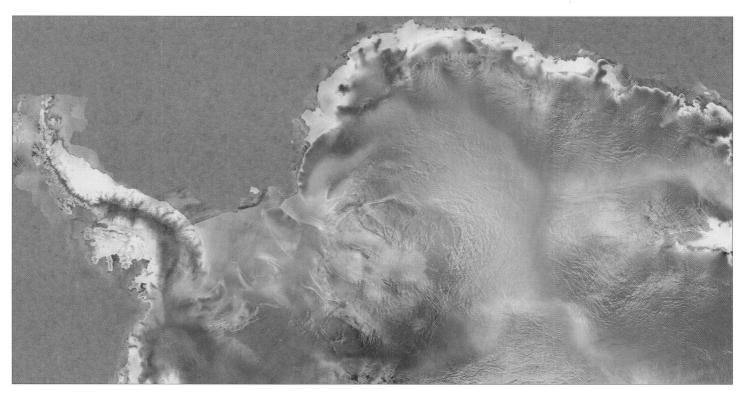

Antarctic Peninsula

Synthetic Aperture Radar (SAR) image brightness is dependent on surface texture. This image of part of Antarctica clearly shows the ice tongues projecting from the Wilkins and George VI Ice Shelves at the south-west end of the peninsula, as well as other coastal ice features. Images can be received, even during the winter 'night', and over a period of time form a valuable resource in our ability to monitor the recession of the ice. (Radarsat,

Montserrat, Caribbean Sea

SAR sensors send out a microwave signal and create an image from the radiation reflected back. The signal penetrates cloud cover and does not need any solar illumination. This image of Montserrat shows how the island can still be seen, despite clouds and the continuing eruption of the Soufrière volcano in the south. The delta visible in the sea to the east is being formed by lava flows pouring down the Tar River Valley. (Radarsat)

Las Vegas, Nevada, USA

Two satellite images viewing the same area of ground from different orbits can be used to compile a Digital Elevation Model (DEM) of the Earth's surface. A computer compares the images and calculates the ground surface elevation to a vertical precision of 8–15 m, preparing this for thousands of square kilometres in just a few minutes. Overlaying a colour satellite image on to a DEM produced the picture of Las Vegas shown here. *(NPA)*

London, United Kingdom

Lasers based on aircraft or satellites can be used to scan surface elevations to an accuracy of a few centimetres. This extract from a survey of the whole of London shows the City of London (from St Paul's Cathedral in the north-west to the Tower of London and Tower Bridge in the south-east. The very narrow and deep urban canyons and atriums in this area clearly demonstrate the advantages of airborne laser scanning (Lidar), which only requires a single line-of-sight to obtain precise measurements. A basic variant of this technology has been used for several years from satellites to acquire elevation profiles of the surface of Mars. Sensors capable of more detailed scanning are currently under development for Earth-orbiting satellites. *(Precision Terrain Surveys Ltd – www.precisionterrain.com)*

SHETLAND ISLANDS
on same scale

Muckle Flugga
Herma Ness
Haroldswick
Balta
Bluemull Sd.
Unst
Whale Firth
Baltasound
Cullivoe
Gutcher
Uyeasound
Mu Ness
Belmont
Ramna Stacks
Pt. of Fethaland
Fetlar
The Faither
North Roe
Ronas Hill ▲453
Mid Yell
Yell
The Snap
Esha Ness
Hillswick
Ulsta
Burravoe
St. Magnus Bay
Sullom
Lunna Ness
Out Skerries
Muckle Roe
Brae
SHETLAND
Skaw Taing
Papa Stour
Vidlin
Whalsay
Sandness
Aith
Voe
Symbister
South Nesting B.
Sd. of Papa
Dury Voe
Walls
Vaila
Easter Skeld
Score Hd.
Bressay
Gruting Voe
Lerwick
I. of Noss
Scalloway
293
Hamnavoe
West Burra
Bard Hd.
Kettla Ness
Bressay Sd.
Helli Ness
Hoswick
Mousa
St. Ninian's I.
Northpunds
Scousburgh
Boddam
Fitful Hd.
B. of Quendale
Sumburgh Hd.

Fair Isle

Scale bars
ft m
3000 1000
2250 750
1500 500
1200 400
600 200
300 100
0 0
20 60
50 150
100 300
200 600
m ft

Projection : Conical with two standard parallels
West from Greenwich

C. Wrath
L. Inchard
Kinlochber
L. Laxford
Handa I.
Laxford Bridge
Scourie
Butt of Lewis (Rubha Robhanais)
Port of Ness (Port Nis)
Eddrachillis Bay
Kylestrome
South Dell
Pt. of Stoer
Drumbeg
Unapool
Borve
Cellar Hd.
Assynt
Ness
Barvas (Barabhas)
North Tolsta
Tolsta Hd.
Stoer
L. Assynt
Shawbost
Lochinver
Inverkirkaig
Carloway (Carlabhagh)
Ben Mholach ▲291
Back
Broad Bay
Tiumpan Hd.
Rubha Coigeach
167
Reiff
Enard B.
Newmarket
Portaguiran
Gallan Hd.
Great Bernera
Stornoway (Steornabhaigh)
Melbost
Eye Peninsula
Summer Is.
Elphin
Uig
Callanish
Gorynahine
Bayble
Chicken Hd.
Achiltibuie
L. Lurgainn
Cronn Hills
Lewis
Coigach
L. Roag
Aird Brenish
575
Gisla
Balallan
L. Erisort
Cromore
Greenstone Pt.
Strathcan
Brenish
L. Langavat
Kintarvie
Gruinard B.
L. Broom
Scarp
North Harris
Ardvourlie
Seaforth
L. Shell
Lemreway
Kebock Hd.
Mellon Charles
Ullapool
Gasker
Husinish (Haisinis)
789
Clisham
Beinn Mhor ▲571
WESTERN
Gruinard
Aultbea
Ardessie
Husinish Pt.
Ardcharnich
West L. Tarbert
Ardhasig
An Teallach ▲1062
L. na Sealga
Taransay
Tarbert (Tairbeart)
East L. Tarbert
Scalpay
Sd. of Shiant
Shiant Is.
Braemore
Sd. of Taransay
Mellon
Toe Hd.
Scarastavore
HARRIS
Melvaig
Pabbay
South Harris
Leverburgh (An T-ob)
Rubha Hunish
L. Ewe
Poolewe
Fionn L.
Sd. of Pabbay
Berneray
Rodel (Roghadal)
Renish Pt.
Kilmaluag
Longa I.
179 L. Gairloch
Gairloch
Kerrysdale
Haskeir Is.
ISLES
Rubha Coigeach
Staffa
Port Henderson
L. Maree
Griminish Pt.
Red Point
981
Sollas
Vaternish Pt.
Uig
L. Torridon
Diabaig
Slioch
Kinlochewe
Lochmaddy (Loch Nam Madadh)
L. Snizort
Trotternish
Rona
Liathach 1053
Achnasheen
North Uist
L. Maddy
Dunvegan Hd.
Stein
The Storr 719 ▲
Sound of Raasay
Fasag
Torridon
Shieldaig
Monach Is.
Paible
Clachan
L. Eport
Lusta
316
Applecross Forest
Coulags
Achnashellach
Baleshare
Carinish
347
Eaval
Ronay
194
Milovaig
Lephin
Dunvegan
Roskhill
Carbost
Portree
Raasay
Applecross
Carron
Strathcon
Monar Forest
Grimsay
Gramsdale
Wiay
Neist Pt.
488
Healaval Bheag
Bracadale
Toscaig
L. Kishorn
Lochcarron
1052
L. Mone
Benbecula
Ardivachar Pt.
Bagh nam Faoileann
Coillore
Fernilea
L. Harport
Scanser
Scalpay
Stromeferry
Plockton
Strome
Sgurr na Lapaich 1150
Howmore
Creagory
Ben Mhor
Carbost
Drynoch
776
Glamaig
Kyle of Lochalsh
Auchtertyre
Ling
Mullardoch
L. Bee
Hecla 605
Minginish
Sligachan
Bla Bheinn 928
Breakish
L. Alsh
Dornie
Carn Eige 1182
Rubha Ardvule
South Uist
620
Ben Mhor
Glenbrittle
Cuillin Hills 1009
Broadford
Kylerhea
Glenelg
A'Chralaig 1120
Daliburgh
L. Eynort
Rubh' an Dunain
Soay Sd.
Soay
L. Scavaig
Elgol
Kyleakin
Shiel Bridge
Five Sisters 1068
L. Affric
Lochboisdale (Loch Baghasdail)
L. Boisdale
L. Eishort
Eilean Iarmain
Teangue
The Saddle 1012
Arnisdale
L. Chuanie
Kilbride
Sd. of Eriskay
Eriskay
Cuillin Sd.
Armadale
Ardvasar
Sd. of Sleat
Ladhar Bheinn 1019
Glen Shiel
L. Hourn
L. Quoich
Loyne
Tomdoun
Sea of
Canna
183
Tarskavaig
Knoydart
L. Nevis
Inverie
1040
Sgurr na Ciche
Glen Gar
Greian Hd.
Sanday
Pt. of Sleat
Mallaig
Morar
Tarbet
L. Arkaig
Barra
Castlebay
Heaval 384
Bruernish Pt.
Kinloch
Rhum (Rum)
810
Sd. of Rhum
Arisaig
L. Morar
983
Culvain
Gairloch
Vatersay
the
Eigg
310
Lochailort
Glenfinnan
Kinlocheil
Corpach
Sandray
Pabbay
394
Sd. of Eigg
Rhois-Bheinn 882
Mingulay
Berneray
Muck
Moidart
L. Moidart
Kinlochmoidart
L. Shiel
L. Eil
Fort William
Ben Ne
Barra Hd.
124
Ardgour
Ardnamurchan
Moidart
Sunart
Acharacle
268
Pt. of Ardnamurchan
Kilchoan
Ben Hiant 527
Salen
L. Sunart
888
Strontian
Corran
Kinloche
L. Leven
Coll
Clabhach
Sorisdale
Mingary
Drimnin
Ballachulish
Glen
Arinagour
Caliach Pt.
Caliach
Tobermory
1148
Bidean nam E

Outer Hebrides
Inner Hebrides
Hebrides
Little Minch
North Minch
Sd. of Canna
HIGHLAND
HIGHL

ORKNEY ISLANDS
on same scale

I : I 000 000

COPYRIGHT PHILIP'S

Projection : Conical with two standard parallels

West from Greenwich

14 See pages 44-45 for names of Unitary Authorities.

Elevation scale (ft / m):
3000 / 1000
2250 / 750
1500 / 500
1200 / 400
600 / 200
300 / 100
0 / 0
60 / 20
150 / 50
300 / 100
600 / 200

Place names

Highland / North area:
Moidart, L. Moidart, Shona I., Kinlochmoidart, Loch Shiel, Fort William, 1342, L. Treig, Ben Alder 1148, L. Ericht, L. Errochty, Tummel, Kinloch Rannoch, Pt. of Ardnamurchan, Ardnamurchan, Kilchoan, Ben Hiant 527, Mingary, Acharacle, Salen, Sunart, Ardgour, Corran, Onich, Kinlochleven, HIGHLAND, Glencoe, Glen Coe, Blackwater Res., Rannoch Station, Kinloch Rannoch, Tummel, L. Rannoch, Schiehallion 1081, Keltneyburn, Coll, Clabhach, Sorisdale, Dervaig, Drimnin, L. Sunart, Strontian 888, L. Leven, Ballachulish, Bidean nam Bian 1148, Clach Leathad 1098, Rannoch Moor, Rannoch, L. Laidon, L. Rannoch, Glen Lyon, Fearnan

Tiree, Caoles, Caliach Pt., Tobermory, Calgary, Morvern, Kingairloch, Loch Linnhe, Appin, Portnacroish, Glen Etive, Clach Leathad, Bridge of Orchy, Ben Dorain 1074, Ben Lui 1130, Ben Lawers 1214, Lawers, Breadalbane

Scarinish, Hynish B., Hynish, Treshnish Is., L. Frisa, Oskamull, Ulva, Gometra, Staffa, Salen, L. na Keal, Ben More 966, Lochdon, Kerrera, Oban, Taynuilt, Connel, Ben Cruachan 1126, Loch Etive, Ben Lui, Dalmally, Ben More 1174, Crianlarich, Lochearnhead, L. Earn, St. Fillans

Iona, Fionnphort, Bunessan, Ross of Mull, L. Scridain, Seil, Balvicar, L. Avich, ARGYLL, Lorn, Kilninver, Kilchrenan, Cladich, Loch Awe, Inveraray, Cairndow, L. Voil, Balquhidder, Ben Vorlich 983, Strathyre, Ben Venue 729, The Trossachs, L. Katrine, LOCH LOMOND & THE TROSSACHS NATIONAL PARK, Stronachlachar, Aberfoyle, STIRLING, Doune, Callander

Dubh Artach, Torran Rocks, Colonsay, Scalasaig, Oronsay, G. of Corryvreckan, Kinuachdrachd, Garvellachs, Scarba, Luing, L. Melfort, Kilmelford, Ford, Kilmartin, L. Craignish, Kilmichael, Furnace, Strachur, Lochgoilhead, L. Goil, L. Long, Arrochar, Tarbet, Luss, Ben Ime 1011, L. Eck, Garelochhead, Faslane, Gare L., Helensburgh, Bonhill, Renton, Campsie Fells, Lennox Hills, 520, 578, Lennoxtown, Killearn, Balfron, Drymen, Buchlyvie, Kippen, Forth, Balloch

Ardlussa, Lochgilphead, Crinan Canal, Crinan, Ardrishaig, Loch Fyne, Knapdale, Otter Ferry, Dunans, Cowal, Cove, Coulport, Ardentinny, Dunoon, Gourock, Greenock, Port Glasgow, Erskine, Dumbarton, Milngavie, Bearsden, Clydebank, GLASGOW, Bishopbriggs, Kilsyth

Jura, Paps of Jura 784, Feolin Ferry, Craighouse, Sd. of Jura, L. Tarbert, Rubh a' Mhail, Ardnave Pt., Lagg, Keillmore, L. Sween, L. Caolisport, Kilberry, W. L. Tarbert, West Tarbert, Tarbert, Tighnabruaich, Kames, Colintraive, Kyles of Bute, Port Bannatyne, Rothesay, Kilfinan, Skelmorlie, Wemyss Bay, Largs, NORTH AYRSHIRE, Lochwinnoch, Kilbirnie, Beith, Johnstone, Barrhead, Paisley, Rutherglen, East Kilbride, Hamilton

Islay, Port Askaig, Ballygrant, Bridgend, Bowmore, Coul Pt., Bruichladdich, Port Charlotte, L. Indaal, Ben Bheigeir 490, Ardmore Pt., Gigha, Whitehouse, Inchmarnock, Clachan, Skipness, Claonaig, Bute, Kingarth, Sd. of Bute, Millport, Great Cumbrae Is., Fairlie, Hunterston, West Kilbride, Ardrossan, Saltcoats, Stevenston, Irvine, Dreghorn, Kilwinning, Stewarton, Dunlop, Lugton, Eaglesham, Neilston, Fenwick, 376, Kilmaurs, Kilmarnock, Darvel, Newmilns, Greenholm, Galston, Strathaven, Stonehouse

Portnahaven, Rhinns Pt., Laggan B., Port Ellen, Ardbeg, The Oa, Mull of Oa, 522, Kintyre, Tayinloan, Killean, 165, Lochranza, Pirnmill, Corrie, Goat Fell 874, Arran, Brodick, Lamlash, Holy I., Glenbarr, Carradale, Saddell, Kilchenzie, Blackwaterfoot, Dippen, Pladda, Troon, Monkton, Prestwick, Barassie, Kyle, EAST AYRSHIRE, Tarbolton, Mauchline, Sorn, Catrine, Auchinleck, Muirkirk

Machrihanish Bay, Machrihanish, Campbeltown, Earadale Pt., Choc Moy 446, Johnston's Pt., Southend, Heads of Ayr, Dunure, Ayr, Coylton, Drongan, Ochiltree, Cumnock, New Cumnock, AYRSHIRE, SOUTH AYRSHIRE, Dalrymple, Patna, Connel Park, Dalmellington, 700, Bellsbank

Ireland / Northern Ireland:
IRELAND, Glengad Hd., Culdaff, Inishowen Hd., The Skerries, Rathlin I., Giants Causeway, Benbane Hd., Ballintoy, Ballycastle B., Ballycastle, Fair Hd., Ballyvoy, Runabay Hd., Mull of Kintyre, Sanda I., Ailsa Craig 334, North Channel, Firth of Clyde, Girvan, SOUTH AYRSHIRE, Dailly, Crosshill, Maybole, Kirkoswald, Turnberry, Doon, Straiton, 781, Carrick, Barr, 796

Greencastle, Moville, Carrowkeel, Lough Foyle, Magilligan Pt., Portstewart, Portrush, Bushmills, Ballintoy, Ballybogy, Derrykeighan, Armoy, Knocklayd 517, Cushendun, Red B., Cushendall, Garron Pt., Carnlough, Lendalfoot, Bennane Hd., Colmonel, Ballantrae, Barrhill, 844, Merrick, Rhinns of Kells, Glentrool Village, 781, Beneraird 439, DUMFRIES

Coleraine, Ballymoney, Magilligan, Downhill, Ballykelly, Limavady, Ringsend, Crossgare, Macosquin, Ballymena, Mountains of Antrim, Glenariff, Trostan 554, GLENARIFF NAT. PARK, Carnlough, Glenarm, Corsewall Pt., Kirkcolm, Cairnryan, Milleur Pt., 123, Loch Ryan, Leswalt, Stranraer, Lochans, New Luce, Newton Stewart, Minnigaff, 710, Cairnsmore of Fleet, New Galloway, L. Ken, Creetown, Gatehouse of Fleet, Ringford, Clatteringshaws L., Galloway, Dalry

LONDONDERRY, Claudy, Dungiven, Feeny, Garvagh, Kilrea, Swatragh, Maghera, Rasharkin, Clogh, Braughshane, Broughshane, Sperrin Mts., Sawel Mt. 683, 554, NORTHERN IRELAND, ANTRIM, Ballymena, Cullybackey, Ahoghill, Glenarm, Agnews Hill 476, Larne Lough, Larne, Ulster, Draperstown, Desertmartin, Magherafelt, Castledawson, Portglenone, Randalstown, Antrim, Moorfields, Kells, Glenoe, I. Magee, Black Hd., 269, Portpatrick, Port Logan, Drummore, Luce Bay, Sandhead, Stoneykirk, Port William, The Machars, Whauphill, Wigtown, Sorbie, Garlieston, Wigtown B., Kirkcudbright

Cookstown, Coagh, TYRONE, Carrickmore, Pomeroy, Tullaghoge, Ballinderry, Moneymore, The Loup, Ballyronan, Maghera, L. Beg, Main, Toome, M2, Ballyclare, Ballynure, Eden, Whitehead, Carrickfergus, Belfast Lough, Copeland I., Groomsport, Donaghadee, Millisle, Mull of Galloway, Burrow Hd., Isle of Whithorn, Whithorn, Port Logan

Creggan, Rousky, Drapperstown, Desertmartin, Magherafelt, Castledawson, Lough Neagh, Crumlin, Glenavy, Templepatrick, Newtownabbey, Greenisland, Glengormley, Holywood, Bangor, BELFAST, BFS, Crumlin, Ballyclare

Sperrin Mts., Sawel Mt., Maghera, IRELAND, Moorfields, Kells, Glenoe, Larne, Ballygowan

NORTH

SEA

1:1 000 000

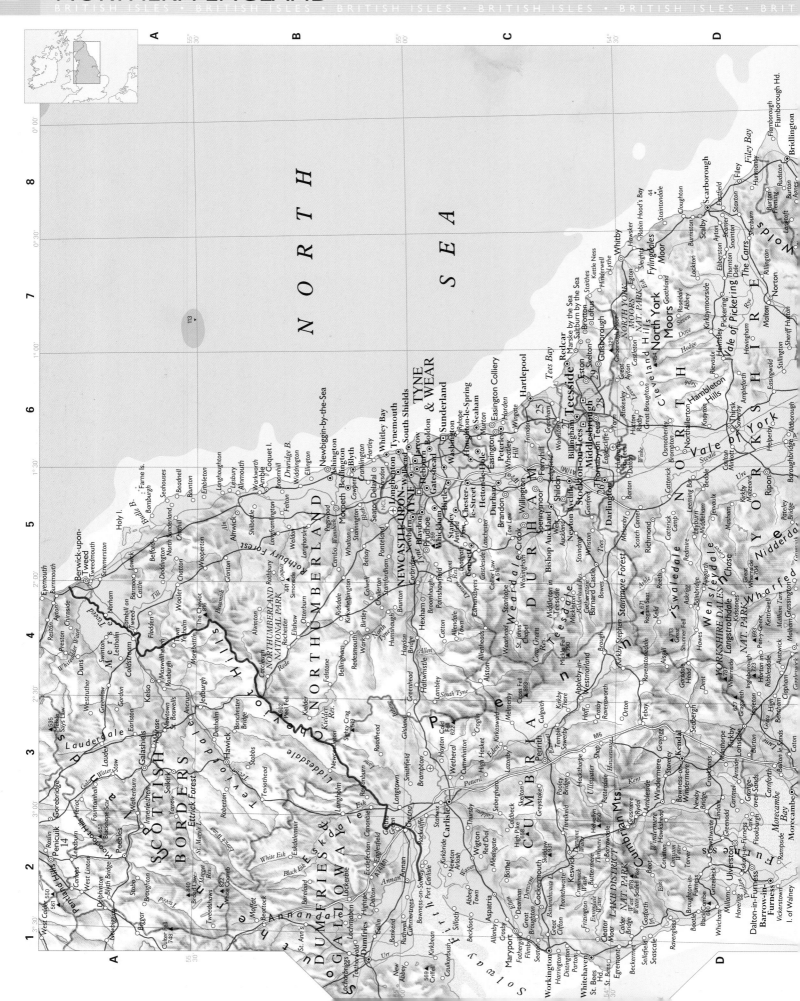

1:1 000 000

36   See pages 44-45 for names of Unitary Authorities.

Projection: Conical with two standard parallels

West from Greenwich

BRITISH ISLES • BRITISH ISLES • BRITISH ISLES • BRITISH ISLES • BRIT

STAFFORDSHIRE

SHROPSHIRE

WOLVERHAMPTON

WEST MIDLANDS

BIRMINGHAM

COVENTRY

LEICESTER

POWYS

HEREFORDSHIRE

WORCESTERSHIRE

WARWICKSHIRE

NORTHA...

CARMARTHEN SHIRE

MONMOUTHSHIRE

GLOUCESTERSHIRE

OXFORDSHIRE

Black Mountains

BRECON BEACONS NATIONAL PARK

Mynydd Du (Black Mt.) Fforest Fawr

Cotswold Hills

Vale of White Horse

Berkshire Downs

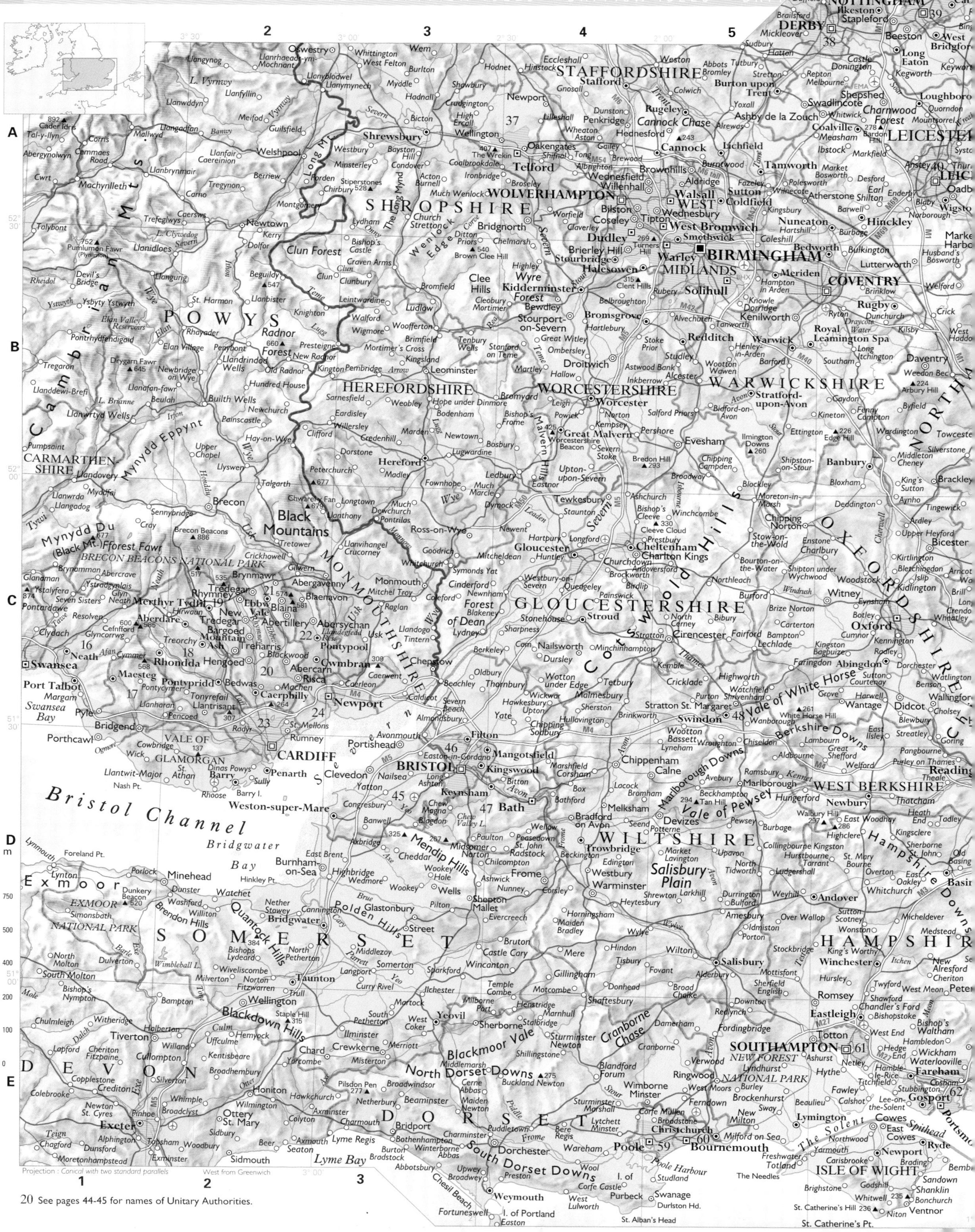

Swansea

Port Talbot

CARDIFF

Newport

BRISTOL

Bath

WEST BERKSHIRE

Reading

Swindon

Marlborough Downs

Vale of Pewsey

WILTSHIRE

Salisbury Plain

HAMPSHIRE

Hampshire Downs

Bristol Channel

Bridgwater Bay

Exmoor

EXMOOR NATIONAL PARK

Quantock Hills

Brendon Hills

Polden Hills

Mendip Hills

Blackdown Hills

SOMERSET

Cranborne Chase

Blackmoor Vale

North Dorset Downs

DORSET

DEVON

Exeter

Taunton

Yeovil

Salisbury

Winchester

SOUTHAMPTON

New Forest

LYNDHURST NATIONAL PARK

Bournemouth

Poole

South Dorset Downs

Chesil Beach

Lyme Bay

I. of Portland

ISLE OF WIGHT

The Needles

The Solent

Bristol Channel

Projection : Conical with two standard parallels

West from Greenwich

Map: South-East England

Counties / Regions:

LINCOLNSHIRE · NORFOLK · CAMBRIDGESHIRE · SUFFOLK · BEDFORDSHIRE · HERTFORDSHIRE · ESSEX · BUCKINGHAMSHIRE · GREATER LONDON · SURREY · KENT · WEST SUSSEX · EAST SUSSEX · NORTHAMPTONSHIRE

Water features: The Wash · The Wensum · The Fens · Great Ouse · Thames · Thames Estuary · Strait of Dover · NORFOLK BROADS · Breckland · The Weald · North Downs · South Downs · Ashdown Forest · Rye Bay · Pegwell Bay · Romney Marsh

Major towns: Grantham · Stamford · Peterborough · King's Lynn · Norwich · Great Yarmouth · Lowestoft · Cromer · Thetford · Bury St. Edmunds · Ipswich · Cambridge · Bedford · Northampton · Milton Keynes · Luton · Stevenage · Colchester · Harwich · Felixstowe · Chelmsford · Southend-on-Sea · LONDON · Watford · Basildon · Brentwood · Guildford · Reigate · Crawley · Brighton · Hove · Worthing · Eastbourne · Hastings · Maidstone · Canterbury · Dover · Folkestone · Ashford · Tonbridge · Royal Tunbridge Wells · Margate · Ramsgate · Broadstairs · Deal

France: Calais · Boulogne-sur-Mer · C. Gris-Nez · Sangatte · Guînes · Marquise · Wimereux · Wimille · Rinxent · Le Portel · Outreau · St-Étienne-au-Mont · Desvres · Samer

East from Greenwich

COPYRIGHT PHILIP'S

Scale 1:1 000 000

km: 5 0 10 20 30 40 50 km

miles: 5 0 5 10 15 20 25 30 35 miles

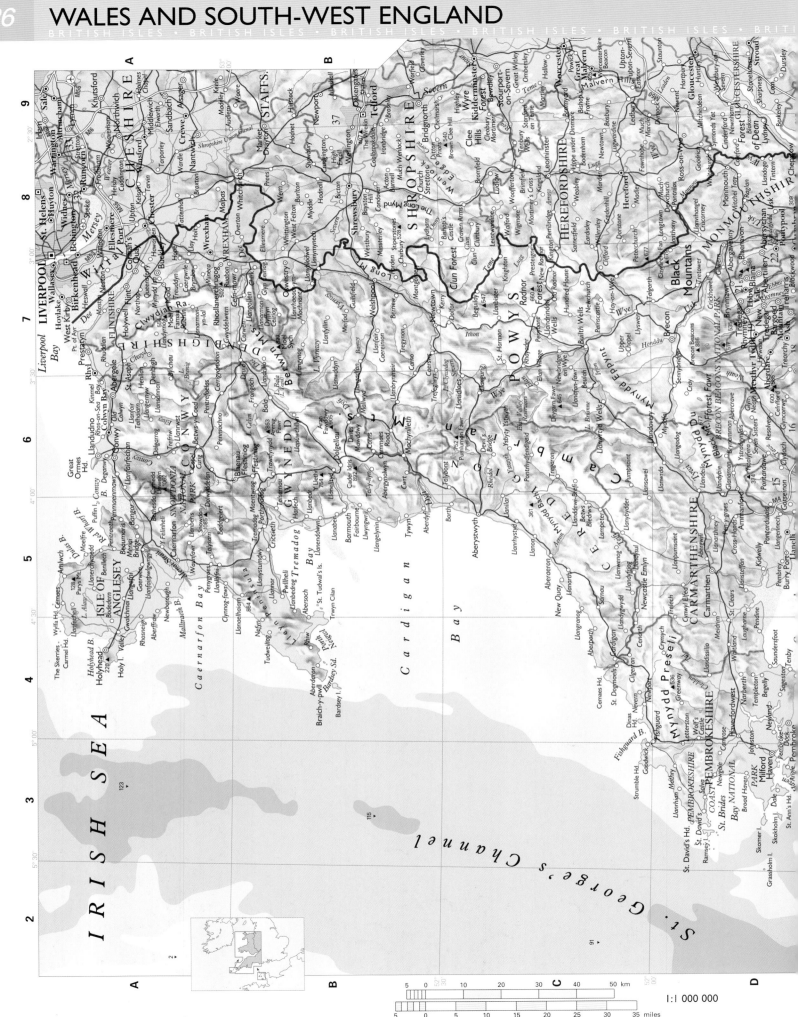

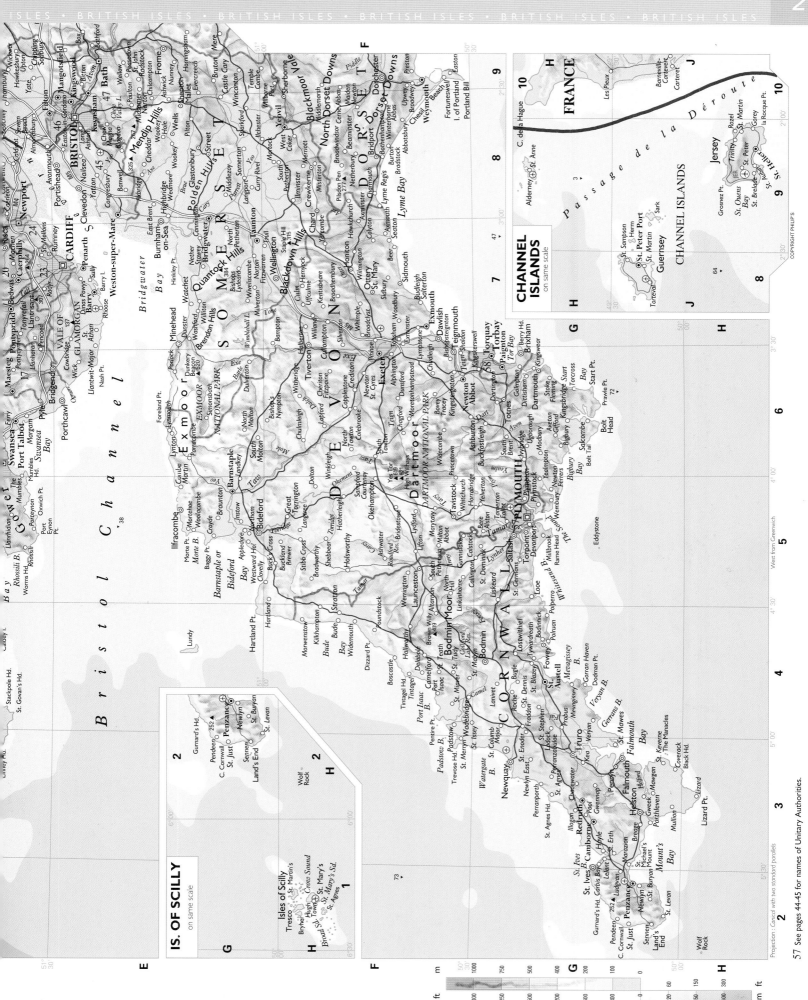

CHANNEL ISLANDS
on same scale

FRANCE

Passage de la Déroute

CHANNEL ISLANDS

Jersey

Guernsey

Alderney

Sark

Herm

COPYRIGHT PHILIP'S

IS. OF SCILLY
on same scale

Isles of Scilly

Tresco
St. Mary's
St. Agnes

Bristol Channel

Projection: Conical with two standard parallels

57 See pages 44-45 for names of Unitary Authorities.

West from Greenwich

ft
3000
2250
1500
1200
600
300
0

m
900
600
400
200
100
50
0

m
1000
750
500
400
200
100
0

ft
300
150
60
0

Projection : Conical with two standard parallels

West from Greenwich

7   **8**   **9**   **10**   **11**   **12**   **13**

Inishtrahull

Glengad Hd.

ARGYLL AND BUTE

Machrihanish
Machrihanish Bay
Earadale Pt.

Kilchenzie
Campbeltown

Arran

Dippen
Pladda

Heads of Ayr
Dunure

Ayr
Coylton

Ochiltree

EAST
Cumnock
New Cumnock

Malin
Culdaff
Gleneely
Greencastle
Moville

Glengad Hd.
Inishowen Hd.
The Skerries

446
Cnoc Moy

Kintyre

Southend

Johnston's Pt.

Sanda I.

Mull of Kintyre

North Channel

Ailsa Craig
334

Girvan

Maybole
Turnberry

Kirkeswald
Dalrymple
Patna

Crosshill

Drongan

SOUTH
AYRSHIRE

Dalmellington

Connel Park
700

AYRSHIRE
Carrick

Magilligan Pt.
Portstewart

Giants Causeway
Bushmills

Benbane Hd.
Ballintoy
Ballycastle B.
Fair Hd.

Rathlin I.

Barr
Sinclair
Lendalfoot
Bennane Hd.

781
Drumjohn

The Glenkens

Lough
Carrowkeel
Foyle

Magilligan
Downhill
Portrush
Coleraine

Ballybogy
Derrykeighan
Ballymoney

Ballyvoy
Knocklayd
517

Runabay Hd.

Cushendun

123

Colmonel

Pinwherry
Ballantrae

Barrhill

844
Merrick
796

Carsphairn

Rhinns
of Kells

Dalry

Muff
Eglinton
Ballykelly
Limavady

Bellarena
Macosquin
Ringsend

Armoy
Dunloy

Glenariff
NAT. PARK
554
Trostan

Cushendall
Red B.
Garron Pt.

Corsewall Pt.
Milleur Pt.

Beneraird
439

Glentrool
Village

Clatteringshaws L.

710
Cairnsmore
of Fleet

LONDONDERRY

Claudy

Dungiven

Kilrea

Swatragh
Inishrush

Crommelin
Newtown
436

Mountains of Antrim

Glenarm

Kirkcolm
Leswalt

Lochans
Stranraer

New Luce

DUMFRIES &
GALLOWAY

Newton
Stewart

Minnigaff
Creetown

Gatehouse
of Fleet

Feeny

Garvagh
Maghera

Bellaghy

Clogh
Rasharkin

Carnlough

269

Stranraer

Kirkcowan

Wigtown

Kirkinner

SPERRIN MTS.
554
683
Sawel Hill

Draperstown
Desertmartin
Magherafelt

L. Beg

Ballymena

Moorfields

Broughshane
Agnews Hill
476

Larne
Glenoe

Larne Lough

Portpatrick

Stoneykirk
Sandhead

The Machars

Whauphill

Sorbie

Garlieston

Wigtown B.

Plumbridge
Gortin

Rousky
Beragh
Seskinore

Tobermore
Moneymore
The Loup

Maghera
Ballyronan

Main
Randalstown
Antrim

Kells
Ballyclare
Ballynure

Eden

Greenisland

I. Magee
Black Hd.
Whitehead

Port Logan

Drummore

Luce
Bay

Port William

Isle of Whithorn
Whithorn

23

Burrow Hd.

THERN IRELAND

TYRONE

Carrickmore
Sixmilecross
Donaghmore

Cookstown
Coagh
Coalisland

Ballinderry

Templepatrick

Crumlin

BFS

Newtownabbey

Belfast Lough
Glengormley

Carrickfergus

Copeland I.
Groomsport
Donaghadee
Millisle

Mull of
Galloway

Mountfield
Creggan
Pomeroy

Dungannon

Lough
Neagh

Aghalee

Glenavy

Legoniel

BELFAST

Dunmurry
Lisburn

Holywood
Dundonald

Bangor

Newtownards

Comber

Greyabbey
Ballywalter

Beragh
Ballygawley

Moy
Charlemont
Portadown

Craigavon
Lurgan
Moira

Drumbeg
Hillsborough

Carryduff

Saintfield

Ballyhalbert

Ardglass

Portavogie

Auger
Clogher

Benburb
Aughnacloy

Ulster

Caledon

ARMAGH

Armagh
Middletown

Keady

Tandragee
Gilford

Loughbrickland
Banbridge

Dromore

Ballynahinch

Killyleagh
Crossgar

Portaferry
Strangford

Ballyquintin Pt.
Killard Pt.

miletown
383
Slieve Beagh
372
Tedavnet

Glaslough

Markethill
Mountnorris

Katesbridge
Ballyroney

DOWN

Downpatrick

Ardglass

rosslea
Monaghan

Smithborough

MONAGHAN

Newbliss

Ballybay

Drum
Rockcorry
Cootehill

Newtown
Hamilton
Bessbrook

Cullyhanna
577
Slieve Gullion

Crossmaglen

Forkhill

Poyntz Pass

Rathfriland
Hilltown

Mayobridge

Newry

Warrenpoint

Rostrevor

Mourne Mts.
852
Slieve Donard

744

Kilcoo
Castlewellan

Kilcurry

Slieve Foye
590

Greenore
Carlingford

Cranfield Pt.

Kilkeel

Annalong

Newcastle

Dundrum
B.

Killough
17
St. John's Pt.

125

ISLE OF MAN

Pt. of Ayre
Bride
Andreas

Ballaugh
Sulby

Ramsey B.
Ramsey

Maughold
Maughold Hd.

Kirk Michael

Snaefell
620

Laxey

VAN
Stradone

Clones
Finn

Shercock
Carrickmacross

Kingscourt

Inishkeen

Louth

Dundalk
(Dún Dealgan)

Dromiskin

Castlebellingham
Annagassan

Dunany Pt.

164

Peel
Glenmaye

St. John's
Onchan

Foxdale
483
South
Barrule

Douglas

Ballasalla

45

Bailieborough
Ballyjamesduff

Virginia

Nobber
Mullagh

Drumcondra

Ardee
Dee
Dunleer

LOUTH

Clogherhead
Clogher Hd.
Termonfeckin

Bradda Hd.
Port Erin

Colby
Castletown
Langness

Port
St. Mary

Oldcastle
261
278
Carnbane East

Crossakiel

Ceanannus Mor
(Kells)
Rathkenny

Slane

Newtown
Monasterboice

Drogheda
(Droichead Atha)

Mornington
Laytown
Julianstown

Calf of Man

IRISH SEA

EATH
Cloghan

Killucan

MEATH

Athboy

An Uaimh
(Navan)

Boyne

Duleek

Balbriggan

Skerries

The Downs
Royal Canal
Kinnegad

Ballivor

Trim

Dunshaughlin

Ratoath

Ballyboghil

Ardcath

Naul

Lusk
Rush

Lambay I.

Derravaragh
Delvin

Rathmolyon

Summerhill

Ashbourne

Swords
Cloghran

Donabate
Portmarnock

Ireland's Eye
Malahide

The Skerries
Carmel Hd.

Wylfa Hd.
Cemaes
Llanfechell

Amlwch

Llanerchymedd

 Clonard
Enfield

Moyvalley

Dunboyne

Kilcock
Cloncurry

Clonee
Maynooth

Leixlip
Lucan

Ward

DUB

DUBLIN

Glasnevin
Finglas

Baldoyle
Clontarf

Howth
Howth Hd.

Anglesey
Holyhead B.
Holyhead

128
Parys Mt.

L. Alaw

ISLE OF
ANGLESEY

Bodedern

Llangefni

chforthbridge
Edenderry

Killane
Daingean

Carbury
Timahoe

Johnstown Bridge

Allenwood

Kilcloon

Celbridge
Clane

Rathcoole

Clondalkin
Dundrum

Tallaght

DUBLIN
(Baile Atha Cliath)

Blackrock

Dun Laoghaire (Dúnleary)

Holy I.
Valley

220

Gwalchmai

Bodedern

7   **8**   **9**   **10**   **11**   **12**   **13**

A
B
C
D
E

50 km
35 miles
1:1 000 000

2   3   4   5   6

ATLANTIC

OCEAN

MAYO

GALWAY

CONNEMARA

Inishshark
Inishbofin
Cleggan
Tully Cross
Letterfrack
Leenaun
683
Lough Mask
Ballinrobe
Kilmaine
Milltown
Dunmore
Glennamaddy
Roscommon
Fuerty
Ballymurray
Keenagh
Lough Ree

CONNEMARA NAT. PARK
730
Benbaun
Maumturk Mts.
Joyce Country
Maum
Clonbur
Shrule
Kilbennan Church
Tuam
Barnaderg
Maylough
Ballinamore Bridge
Kiltoom
Athleague
Mount Talbot
Tang

Clifden B.
Clifden
Recess
660
Maam Cross
Oughterard
Rosscahill
Belclare
Newbridge
Castleblakeney
Glentane
Mount Bellew Bridge
Thomas Street
Ahascragh
ROS-COMMON

Ballyconneely
Toombeola
Slyne Hd.
Roundstone
Derryrush
Glinsk
Screeb
Moycullen
Clare
Monivea
Castlegar
Ballinasloe
Aughrim
Suck
Shannonbridge
Ferbane
Athlone

Ballyconneely B.
Bertraghboy Bay
Kilkieran
Carna
Lettermore
Costelloe
Rossaveel
Spiddal
Barna
Salthill
Claregalway
Athenry
Oranmore
Clarinbridge
Craughwell
Killtullagh
Killconnell
Laurencetown
Eyrecourt
Cloghan

119

Gorumna
Lettermullan
Inveran
Galway (Gaillimh)
Kilcolgan
Ardrahan
Loughrea
Mullagh
Ballydavid
Killimor
Banagher
Five Alley

North Sound
Cashla B.
Galway Bay
Kinvarra
Laban
Peterswell
L. Rea
Tynagh
Portumna
Birr

B

Inishmore
Kilmurvy
Kilronan
Black Hd.
Murroogh
Burren
Gort
Abbey
Slieve Aughty
Woodford
Carrigahorig
Crinkill
Clareen
Boheraphuc

Aran Is.
Inishmaan
South Sd.
Inisheer
Ballyvaghan
Sl. Elva
345
358
Derrybrien
207
Shinrone
Modreeny
Roscrea

BURREN NAT. PARK
Lisdoonvarna
Kilfenora
Aughrim
L. Graney
L. Cutra
379
Whitegate
Terryglass
Ballingarry
Borrisokane
Cloghjordan
Moneygall

53° 00'

Cliffs of Moher
Hags Hd.
Liscannor
Corrofin
Ennistimon
Crusheen
Feakle
Scariff
CLARE
Tuamgraney
Tulla
Kilkishen
Bodyke
Portroe
Nenagh
Toomyvara
Devilsbit Mountain
482

79

Liscannor Bay
Lehinch
Inagh
Feakle
533
Arra Mts.
Ballina
Silvermines
Dolla
Templemore

Spanish Pt.
Mal Bay
Mutton I.
Milltown Malbay
391
Slievecallan
Kilmaley
Ennis
Clarecastle
Quin
Broadford
Killaloe
Keeper Hill
694
Silvermine Mts.
Loughmoe

C

Quilty
Kilmurry
Darragh
Newmarket-on-Fergus
O'Briensbridge
Castleconnell
Newport
Borrisoleigh
Bouladuff
Thurles

124

Donegal Pt.
Creegh
Liscasey
Ballynacally
Sixmilebridge
Slievefelim
465
Upperchurch
TIPPER

Doonbeg
Kilmihil
Doonbeg
Killadysert
Shannon Airport
Limerick (Luimneach)
Cappamore
Golden Vale

Kilkee
Moyasta
Labasheeda
Foynes
Pallaskenry
Kildimo
Askeaton
Patrickswell
Caherconlish
Pallas Green
Dundrum
Ballinur

Kilrush
Carrigaholt
Astee
Tarbert
Glin
Shanagolden
Creeves
Newbridge
Rathkeale
Adare
Croom
Fedamore
Herbertstown
Emly
Limerick Junction
Cashel
Golden

Loop Hd.
Kilbaha
Scattery I.
Ballylongford
Ballyhahill
LIMERICK
Bruff
Hospital
Tipperary
Rose
Newinn

Shannon
Mouth of the Shannon
Lisselton
Gale
Athea
Ardagh
Ballingarry
Rockhill
Bruree
Kilmallock
Galbally
Galty Mts.
920
Galtymore
Caher

Ballybunion
Ballyduff
Listowel
Newcastle West
Kilmeedy
Rath Luirc (Charleville)
Kilfinnane
Ballylanders
Kilbeheny
Knocklofty

Kerry Hd.
Causeway
Lixnaw
Feale
Munster
Abbeyfeale
Broadford
Newtownshandrum
Ballyhoura Mts.
519
Mitchelstown
Ballylooby
Ardfinnane

D

Seven Hogs
Ballyheige
Lerrig
Abbeydorney
Stacks Mts.
357
334
Mullaghareirk Mts.
409
Milford
Liscarroll
Buttevant
Kildorrery
302
Kilworth Mts.
Clogheen
Knockmealdown Mts.
795

Brandon B.
Brandon Pt.
Rough Pt.
Tralee B.
Ardfert
Fenit
Tralee
Glanaruddery Mts.
Newmarket
Doneraile
Rockmills
Araglin
Tar
Knockmealdown
Mt.

Ballydavid Hd.
953
Brandon Mt.
Stradbally
927
Castlegregory
Castleisland
Feale
Kanturk
Castletownroche
Glanworth
Kilworth
Ballyduff

Smerwick Harbour
Sybil Pt.
Ballydavid
853
Slieve Mish
Castlemaine Maine
Farranfore
Kishkeam
Mallow
Killavullen
Fermoy
Lismore
W

Inishtooskert
Ventry
Dingle
Anascaul
Inch
Milltown
Rathmore
Blackwater
Banteer
Ballynamona
Nagles Mts.
429
Knocknaskagh
Blackwater
Curraglass
Tallowbridge

Great Blasket I.
Sea Hd.
Castlemaine Harbour
Killorglin
KERRY
Killarney
Millstreet
Donoughmore
Rathcormack
Conna
Tallow

E

Inishvickillane
Dingle Bay
46
Glenbeigh
L. Caragh
Laune
L. Leane
The Paps
696
Boggeragh Mts.
646
Carrignavar
Watergrasshill

Doulus Hd.
Valencia Harbour
775
Teermoyle Mt.
Carrauntoohill
1041
835
KILLARNEY NAT. PARK
Flesk
Derrynasaggart Mts.
650
Bride
Dungourney
Killeagh
Youghal

Valencia I.
Cahersiveen
Lissatinnig Bridge
Macgillycuddy's Reeks
Mangerton Mt.
840
Ballyvourney
CORK
Blarney
Cork (Corcaigh)
Midleton
Castlemartyr
You

Bray Hd.
Portmagee
New Chapel Cross
Derriana
Kenmare
Kilgarvan
Macroom
Coachford
Inniscarra Res.
Carrigtohill
Ballynacorra
Cloyne

Puffin I.
St. Finan's Bay
Waterville
Sneem
Parknasilla
Templenoe
Ballingeary
Lee
Carrigadrohid Res.
Ballincollig
Passage West
Great
Whitegate
Ballycotton

Great Skellig
Ardkearagh
L. Currane
Bunaw
Inchigeelagh
Kilmichael
Crookstown
Ballinhassig
Cóbh
38

Scariff I.
Bolus Hd.
Ballinskelligs B.
Hog's Hd.
Lamb's Hd.
Kenmare River
Caha Mts.
Glengarriff
Knockboy
707
575
Shehy Mts.
Dunmanway
Bandon
Kinsale
Carrigaline
Crosshaven
Cork Harbour

E

73
Lauragh
Ardgroom
Kealkill
537
Nowen Hill
Kilpatrick
Inishannon
Belgooly

Valencia Harbour
Adrigole
Hungry Hill
686
Bantry
Kilcrohane
Ballineen
Enniskean
Bandon
Kilbrittain
Timoleague
Courtmacsherry
Old Head of Kinsale

Cods Hd.
Coulagh B.
Slieve Miskish
Castletown Bearhaven
Whiddy I.
Bantry Bay
Drimoleague
Clonakilty
Ross Carbery
Barry's Pt.
Seven Heads

Dursey I.
Allihies
Cahermore
Bear I.
Durrus
Ballydehob
Kilcoe
Leap
Glandore
Clonakilty B.
Kinsale Harbour
66

Dursey Hd.
Crow Hd.
Sheeps Hd.
Dunmanus B.
Skull
Castletownshend
Galley Hd.
Glandore Harbour

F

Goleen
Mizen Hd.
Long I.
Roaringwater B.
Sherkin I.
Baltimore
Toe Hd.
Skibbereen

152
C. Clear
Clear I.

Projection : Conical with two standard parallels
West from Greenwich

1   2   3   4   5   6

ft m ft m
2250 750
1500 500
1200 400
600   200
300   100
0   0
20   60
50   150
100 300

WESTMEATH

MEATH

OFFALY Bog of Allen

Leinster

LAOIS

KILDARE

WICKLOW

CARLOW

KILKENNY

WEXFORD

DUBLIN
(Baile Átha Cliath)

Dun Laoghaire (Dúnleary)

WICKLOW MTS.
NATIONAL PARK

Wicklow Mountains

IRISH

SEA

St. George's Channel

CELTIC

SEA

PEMBROKESHIRE

COAST

NATIONAL

PARK

Milford Haven

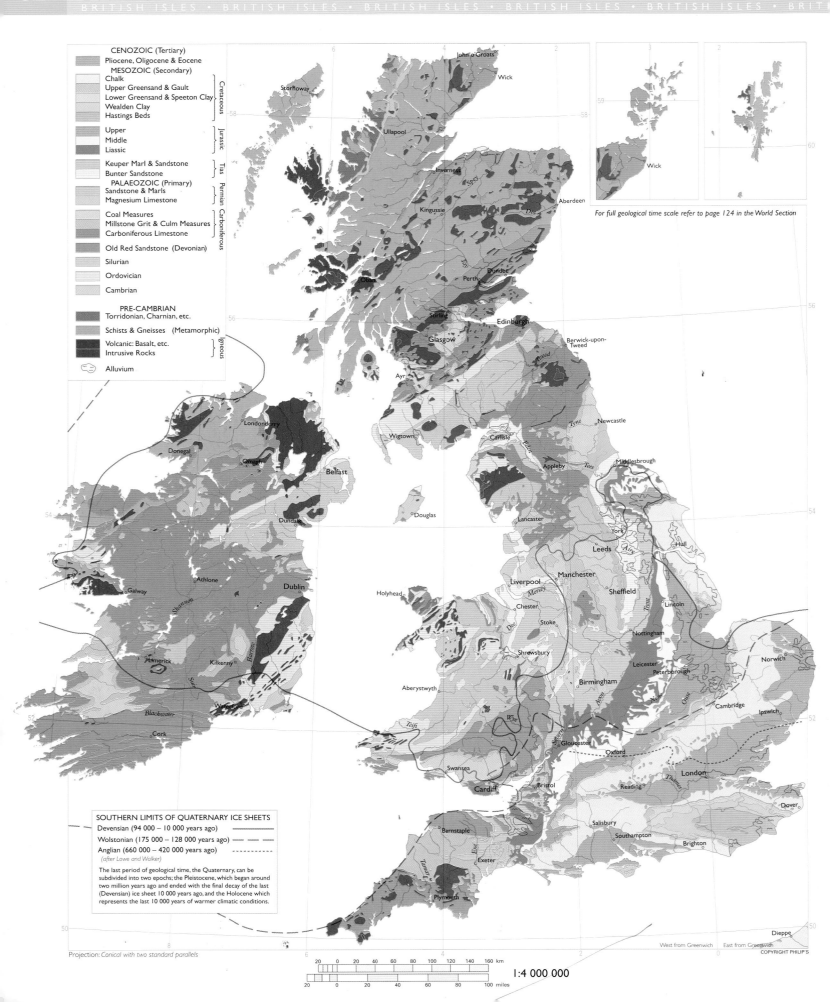

CENOZOIC (Tertiary)
Pliocene, Oligocene & Eocene

MESOZOIC (Secondary)
Chalk
Upper Greensand & Gault   Cretaceous
Lower Greensand & Speeton Clay
Wealden Clay
Hastings Beds

Upper   Jurassic
Middle
Liassic

Keuper Marl & Sandstone   Trias
Bunter Sandstone

PALAEOZOIC (Primary)
Sandstone & Marls   Permian
Magnesium Limestone

Coal Measures   Carboniferous
Millstone Grit & Culm Measures
Carboniferous Limestone

Old Red Sandstone (Devonian)

Silurian

Ordovician

Cambrian

PRE-CAMBRIAN
Torridonian, Charnian, etc.

Schists & Gneisses (Metamorphic)

Volcanic: Basalt, etc.   Igneous
Intrusive Rocks

Alluvium

For full geological time scale refer to page 124 in the World Section

SOUTHERN LIMITS OF QUATERNARY ICE SHEETS

Devensian (94 000 – 10 000 years ago) ————

Wolstonian (175 000 – 128 000 years ago) — — —

Anglian (660 000 – 420 000 years ago) - - - - - - -
(after Lowe and Walker)

The last period of geological time, the Quaternary, can be subdivided into two epochs; the Pleistocene, which began around two million years ago and ended with the final decay of the last (Devensian) ice sheet 10 000 years ago, and the Holocene which represents the last 10 000 years of warmer climatic conditions.

Projection: Conical with two standard parallels

1:4 000 000

West from Greenwich   East from Greenwich
COPYRIGHT PHILIP'S

Projection: Conical with two standard parallels

COPYRIGHT PHILIP'S

1:4 000 000

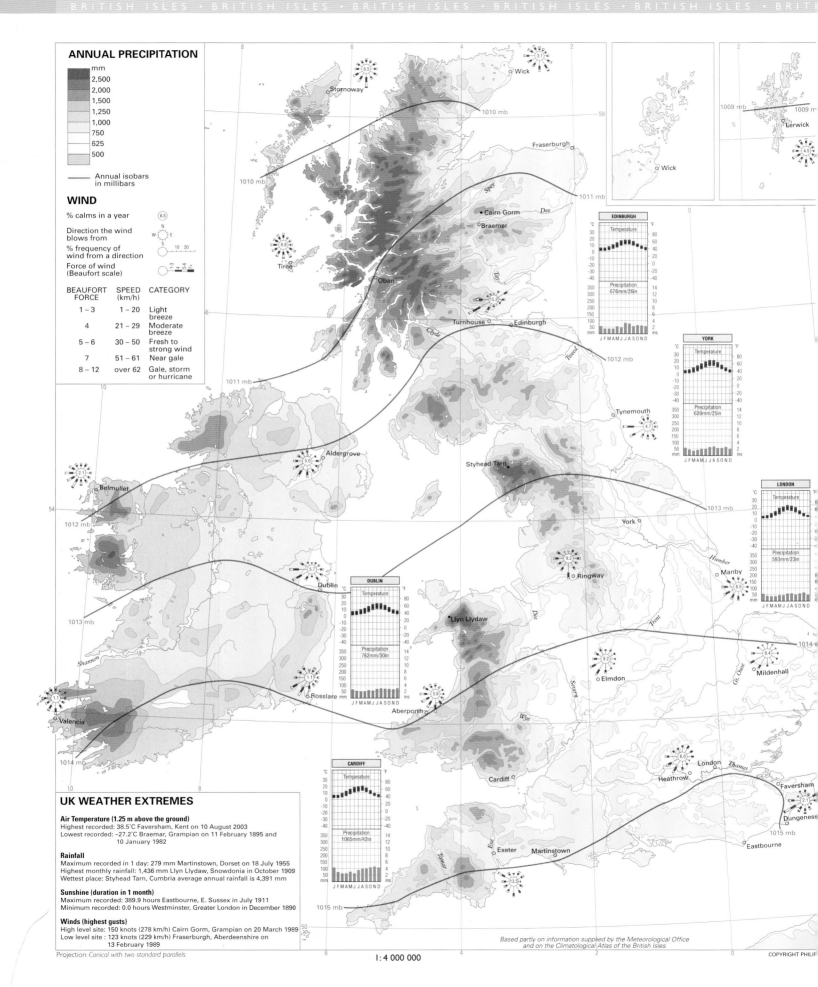

ANNUAL PRECIPITATION

mm
2,500
2,000
1,500
1,250
1,000
750
625
500

—— Annual isobars
in millibars

WIND

% calms in a year

Direction the wind
blows from

% frequency of
wind from a direction

Force of wind
(Beaufort scale)

BEAUFORT FORCE	SPEED (km/h)	CATEGORY
1 – 3	1 – 20	Light breeze
4	21 – 29	Moderate breeze
5 – 6	30 – 50	Fresh to strong wind
7	51 – 61	Near gale
8 – 12	over 62	Gale, storm or hurricane

UK WEATHER EXTREMES

Air Temperature (1.25 m above the ground)
Highest recorded: 38.5°C Faversham, Kent on 10 August 2003
Lowest recorded: –27.2°C Braemar, Grampian on 11 February 1895 and 10 January 1982

Rainfall
Maximum recorded in 1 day: 279 mm Martinstown, Dorset on 18 July 1955
Highest monthly rainfall: 1,436 mm Llyn Llydaw, Snowdonia in October 1909
Wettest place: Styhead Tarn, Cumbria average annual rainfall is 4,391 mm

Sunshine (duration in 1 month)
Maximum recorded: 389.9 hours Eastbourne, E. Sussex in July 1911
Minimum recorded: 0.0 hours Westminster, Greater London in December 1890

Winds (highest gusts)
High level site: 150 knots (278 km/h) Cairn Gorm, Grampian on 20 March 1989
Low level site : 123 knots (229 km/h) Fraserburgh, Aberdeenshire on 13 February 1989

Projection: *Conical with two standard parallels*

1 : 4 000 000

Based partly on information supplied by the Meteorological Office
and on the *Climatological Atlas of the British Isles*

COPYRIGHT PHILIP

CLIMATE GRAPHS

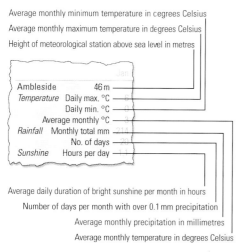

Average monthly minimum temperature in degrees Celsius

Average monthly maximum temperature in degrees Celsius

Height of meteorological station above sea level in metres

Ambleside	46 m
Temperature	Daily max. °C
	Daily min. °C
	Average monthly °C
Rainfall	Monthly total mm
	No. of days
Sunshine	Hours per day

Average daily duration of bright sunshine per month in hours

Number of days per month with over 0.1 mm precipitation

Average monthly precipitation in millimetres

Average monthly temperature in degrees Celsius

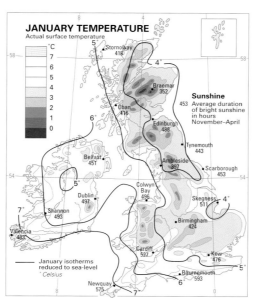

JANUARY TEMPERATURE
Actual surface temperature

°C
7
6
5
4
3
2
1
0

Sunshine
453 Average duration of bright sunshine in hours November–April

Stornoway 418
Braemar 352
Oban 416
Edinburgh 488
Tynemouth 443
Belfast 451
Ambleside 397
Scarborough 453
Colwyn Bay 496
Skegness 511
Dublin 497
Shannon 493
Birmingham 424
Valencia 483
Cardiff 527
Kew 476
Bournemouth 593
Newquay 575

— January isotherms reduced to sea-level
° Celsius

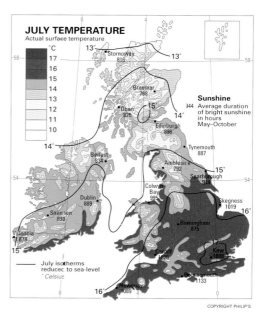

JULY TEMPERATURE
Actual surface temperature

°C
17
16
15
14
13
12
11
10

Sunshine
944 Average duration of bright sunshine in hours May–October

Stornoway 816
Braemar 768
Oban 825
Edinburgh 896
Tynemouth 887
Belfast 834
Ambleside 792
Scarborough 941
Colwyn Bay 995
Skegness 1019
Dublin 889
Shannon 893
Birmingham 875
Valencia 878
Cardiff 998
Kew 1038
Bournemouth 1133
Newquay 1089

— July isotherms reduced to sea-level
° Celsius

COPYRIGHT PHILIP'S

Ambleside 46 m	Jan	Feb	Mar	Apr	May	June	July	Aug	Sept	Oct	Nov	Dec	Year
Temperature Daily max. °C	6	7	9	12	16	19	20	19	17	13	9	7	13
Daily min. °C	0	0	2	4	6	9	11	11	9	6	3	1	5
Average monthly °C	3	4	6	8	11	14	15	15	13	10	6	4	9
Rainfall Monthly total mm	214	146	112	101	90	111	134	139	184	196	209	215	1,851
No. of days	20	17	15	15	14	15	18	17	18	19	19	21	208
Sunshine Hours per day	1.1	2	3.2	4.5	6	5.7	4.5	4.2	3.3	2.2	1.4	1	3.3

Belfast 4 m	Jan	Feb	Mar	Apr	May	June	July	Aug	Sept	Oct	Nov	Dec	Year
Temperature Daily max. °C	6	7	9	12	15	18	18	18	16	13	9	7	12
Daily min. °C	2	2	3	4	6	9	11	11	9	7	4	3	6
Average monthly °C	4	4	6	8	11	13	15	15	13	10	7	5	9
Rainfall Monthly total mm	80	52	50	48	52	68	94	77	80	83	72	90	845
No. of days	20	17	16	16	15	16	19	17	18	19	19	21	213
Sunshine Hours per day	1.5	2.3	3.4	5	6.3	6	4.4	4.4	3.6	2.6	1.8	1.1	3.5

Birkenhead 60 m	Jan	Feb	Mar	Apr	May	June	July	Aug	Sept	Oct	Nov	Dec	Year
Temperature Daily max. °C	6	6	9	11	15	18	19	19	16	13	9	7	12
Daily min. °C	2	2	3	5	8	11	13	13	11	8	5	3	7
Average monthly °C	4	4	6	8	11	14	16	16	14	10	7	5	10
Rainfall Monthly total mm	64	46	40	41	55	55	67	80	66	71	76	65	726
No. of days	18	13	13	13	13	13	15	15	15	17	17	19	181
Sunshine Hours per day	1.6	2.4	3.5	5.3	6.3	6.7	5.7	5.4	4.2	2.9	1.8	1.3	3.9

Birmingham 163 m	Jan	Feb	Mar	Apr	May	June	July	Aug	Sept	Oct	Nov	Dec	Year
Temperature Daily max. °C	5	6	9	12	16	19	20	20	17	13	9	6	13
Daily min. °C	2	2	3	5	7	10	12	12	10	7	5	3	7
Average monthly °C	3	4	6	8	11	15	16	16	14	10	7	5	10
Rainfall Monthly total mm	74	54	50	53	64	50	69	69	61	69	84	67	764
No. of days	17	15	13	13	14	13	15	14	14	15	17	18	178
Sunshine Hours per day	1.4	2.1	3.2	4.6	5.4	6	5.4	5.1	3.9	2.8	1.6	1.2	3.6

Cambridge 12 m	Jan	Feb	Mar	Apr	May	June	July	Aug	Sept	Oct	Nov	Dec	Year
Temperature Daily max. °C	6	7	11	14	17	21	22	22	19	15	10	7	14
Daily min. °C	1	1	2	4	7	10	12	12	10	6	4	2	6
Average monthly °C	3	4	6	9	12	15	17	17	14	10	7	5	10
Rainfall Monthly total mm	49	35	36	37	45	45	58	55	51	51	54	41	558
No. of days	15	13	10	11	11	11	12	12	11	13	14	14	147
Sunshine Hours per day	1.7	2.5	3.8	5.1	6.2	6.7	6	5.7	4.6	3.4	1.9	1.4	4.1

Craibstone 91 m	Jan	Feb	Mar	Apr	May	June	July	Aug	Sept	Oct	Nov	Dec	Year
Temperature Daily max. °C	5	6	8	10	13	16	18	17	15	12	8	6	11
Daily min. °C	0	0	2	3	5	8	10	10	8	6	3	1	5
Average monthly °C	3	3	5	7	9	12	14	13	12	9	6	4	8
Rainfall Monthly total mm	78	55	53	51	63	54	95	75	67	92	93	80	856
No. of days	19	16	15	15	14	14	18	15	16	18	19	18	197
Sunshine Hours per day	1.8	2.9	3.5	4.9	5.9	6.1	5.1	4.8	4.3	3..1	2	1.5	3.8

Durham 102 m	Jan	Feb	Mar	Apr	May	June	July	Aug	Sept	Oct	Nov	Dec	Year
Temperature Daily max. °C	6	6	9	12	15	18	20	19	17	13	9	7	13
Daily min. °C	0	0	1	3	6	9	11	10	9	6	3	2	5
Average monthly °C	3	3	5	7	10	13	15	15	13	9	6	4	9
Rainfall Monthly total mm	59	51	38	38	51	49	61	67	60	63	66	55	658
No. of days	17	15	14	13	13	14	15	14	14	16	17	17	179
Sunshine Hours per day	1.7	2.5	3.3	4.6	5.4	6	5.1	4.8	4.1	3	1.9	1.4	3.6

Lerwick 82 m	Jan	Feb	Mar	Apr	May	June	July	Aug	Sept	Oct	Nov	Dec	Year
Temperature Daily max. °C	5	5	6	8	11	13	14	14	13	10	8	6	9
Daily min. °C	1	1	2	3	5	7	10	10	8	6	4	3	5
Average monthly °C	3	3	4	5	8	10	12	12	11	8	6	4	7
Rainfall Monthly total mm	109	87	69	68	52	55	72	71	87	104	111	118	1,003
No. of days	25	22	20	21	15	15	17	17	19	23	24	25	243
Sunshine Hours per day	0.8	1.8	2.9	4.4	5.3	5.3	4	3.8	3.5	2.2	2.2	0.5	3

Plymouth 27 m	Jan	Feb	Mar	Apr	May	June	July	Aug	Sept	Oct	Nov	Dec	Year
Temperature Daily max. °C	8	8	10	12	15	18	19	19	18	15	11	9	14
Daily min. °C	4	4	5	6	8	11	13	13	12	9	7	5	8
Average monthly °C	6	6	7	9	12	15	16	16	15	12	9	7	11
Rainfall Monthly total mm	99	74	69	53	63	53	70	77	78	91	113	110	950
No. of days	19	15	14	12	12	12	14	14	15	16	17	18	178
Sunshine Hours per day	1.9	2.9	4.3	6.1	7.1	7.4	6.4	6.4	5.1	3.7	2.2	1.7	4.6

Renfrew 6 m	Jan	Feb	Mar	Apr	May	June	July	Aug	Sept	Oct	Nov	Dec	Year
Temperature Daily max. °C	5	7	9	12	15	18	19	19	16	13	9	7	12
Daily min. °C	1	1	2	4	6	9	11	11	9	6	4	2	6
Average monthly °C	3	4	6	8	11	14	15	15	13	9	7	4	9
Rainfall Monthly total mm	111	85	69	67	63	70	97	93	102	119	106	127	1,109
No. of days	19	16	15	15	14	15	17	17	18	18	18	20	201
Sunshine Hours per day	1.1	2.1	2.9	4.7	6	6.1	5.1	4.4	3.7	2.3	1.4	0.8	3.4

St Mary's 50 m	Jan	Feb	Mar	Apr	May	June	July	Aug	Sept	Oct	Nov	Dec	Year
Temperature Daily max. °C	9	9	11	12	14	17	19	19	18	15	12	10	14
Daily min. °C	6	6	7	7	9	12	13	14	13	11	9	7	9
Average monthly °C	8	7	9	10	12	14	16	16	15	13	10	9	12
Rainfall Monthly total mm	91	71	69	46	56	49	61	64	67	80	96	94	844
No. of days	22	17	16	13	14	14	16	15	16	17	19	21	200
Sunshine Hours per day	2	2.9	4.2	6.4	7.6	7.6	6.7	6.7	5.2	3.9	2.5	1.8	4.8

Southampton 20 m	Jan	Feb	Mar	Apr	May	June	July	Aug	Sept	Oct	Nov	Dec	Year
Temperature Daily max. °C	7	8	11	14	17	20	22	22	19	15	11	8	15
Daily min. °C	2	2	3	5	8	11	13	13	11	7	5	3	7
Average monthly °C	5	5	7	10	12	16	17	17	15	11	8	6	11
Rainfall Monthly total mm	83	56	52	45	56	49	60	69	70	86	94	84	804
No. of days	17	13	13	12	12	12	13	13	14	14	16	17	166
Sunshine Hours per day	1.8	2.6	4	5.7	6.7	7.2	6.5	6.4	4.9	3.6	2.2	1.6	4.5

Tiree 9 m	Jan	Feb	Mar	Apr	May	June	July	Aug	Sept	Oct	Nov	Dec	Year
Temperature Daily Max. °C	7	7	9	10	13	15	16	16	15	12	10	8	12
Daily Min. °C	4	3	4	5	7	10	11	11	10	8	6	5	7
Average Monthly °C	5	5	6	8	10	12	14	14	13	10	8	6	9
Rainfall Monthly Total mm	117	77	67	64	55	70	91	90	118	129	122	128	1,128
No. of Days	23	19	17	17	15	16	20	18	20	23	22	24	234
Sunshine Hours per Day	1.3	2.6	3.7	5.7	7.5	6.8	5.2	5.3	4.2	2.6	1.6	0.9	4

Valencia 9 m	Jan	Feb	Mar	Apr	May	June	July	Aug	Sept	Oct	Nov	Dec	Year
Temperature Daily max. °C	9	9	11	13	15	17	18	18	17	14	12	10	14
Daily min. °C	5	4	5	6	8	11	12	13	11	9	7	6	8
Average monthly °C	7	7	8	9	11	14	15	15	14	12	9	8	11
Rainfall Monthly total mm	165	107	103	75	86	81	107	95	122	140	151	168	1,400
No. of days	20	15	14	13	13	13	15	16	17	18	18	21	190
Sunshine Hours per day	1.6	2.5	3.5	5.2	3.5	5.9	4.7	4.9	3.8	2.8	2	1.3	3.7

36 **BRITISH ISLES** *WATER RESOURCES*

BRITISH ISLES • BRITISH ISLES • BRITISH ISLES • BRITISH ISLES • BRITISH ISLES • BRIT!

WATER SUPPLY

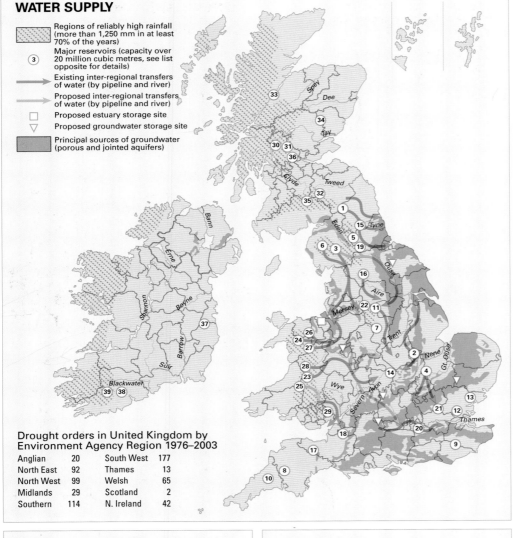

- Regions of reliably high rainfall (more than 1,250 mm at least 70% of the years)
- ③ Major reservoirs (capacity over 20 million cubic metres, see list opposite for details)
- Existing inter-regional transfers of water (by pipeline and river)
- Proposed inter-regional transfers of water (by pipeline and river)
- □ Proposed estuary storage site
- ▽ Proposed groundwater storage site
- Principal sources of groundwater (porous and jointed aquifers)

Drought orders in United Kingdom by Environment Agency Region 1976–2003

Anglian	20	South West	177
North East	92	Thames	13
North West	99	Welsh	65
Midlands	29	Scotland	2
Southern	114	N. Ireland	42

MAJOR RESERVOIRS (with capacity in million m³

England
1	Kielder Res.	198
2	Rutland Water	123
3	Haweswater	85
4	Grafham Water	59
5	Cow Green Res.	41
6	Thirlmere	41
7	Carsington Res.	36
8	Roadford Res.	35
9	Bewl Water Res.	31
10	Colliford Lake	29
11	Ladybower Res.	28
12	Hanningfield Res.	27
13	Abberton Res.	25
14	Draycote Water	23
15	Derwent Res.	22
16	Grimwith Res.	22
17	Wimbleball Lake	21
18	Chew Valley Lake	20
19	Balderhead Res.	20
20	Thames Valley (linked reservoirs)	
21	Lea Valley (linked reservoirs)	
22	Longendale (linked reservoirs)	

Wales
23	Elan Valley	99
24	Llyn Celyn	74
25	Llyn Brianne	62
26	Llyn Brenig	60
27	Llyn Vyrnwy	60
28	Llyn Clywedog	48
29	Llandegfedd Res.	22

Scotland
30	Loch Lomond	86
31	Loch Katrine	64
32	Megget Res.	64
33	Loch Ness	26
34	Blackwater Res.	25
35	Daer Res.	23
36	Carron Valley Res.	21

Ireland
37	Poulaphouca Res.	168
38	Inishcarra Res.	57
39	Carrigadrohid Res.	33

WATER SUPPLY IN THE UK

The pie graph represents the 16,076 million litres a day that were supplied by the public water authority and services companies in the UK in 2003.

Total water abstraction in England and Wales in 2003 was approximately 58,593 million litres a day.

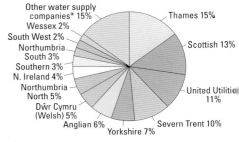

- Other water supply companies* 15%
- Wessex 2%
- South West 2%
- Northumbria South 3%
- Southern 3%
- N. Ireland 4%
- Northumbria North 5%
- Dŵr Cymru (Welsh) 5%
- Anglian 6%
- Yorkshire 7%
- Severn Trent 10%
- United Utilities 11%
- Scottish 13%
- Thames 15%

*This is a group of 12 privately-owned companies who are not connected with the other water authorities

WATER ABSTRACTIONS

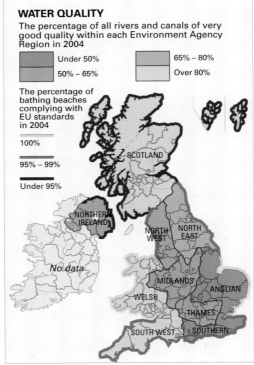

THAMES — Environment Agency Region

1883 (16%) — Water supply* in megalitres per day (with percentage of total abstraction from groundwater in brackets)

*Piped mains water, excluding water abstracted for agricultural and industrial use

- SCOTLAND 2397 (7%)
- N. IRELAND 710 (8%)
- NORTH EAST 2256 (14%)
- NORTH WEST 1602 (11%)
- No data
- MIDLANDS 2637 (36%)
- ANGLIAN 2153 (37%)
- WELSH 1505 (3%)
- THAMES 4214 (35%)
- SOUTH WEST 1249 (30%)
- SOUTHERN 1303 (74%)

WATER QUALITY

The percentage of all rivers and canals of very good quality within each Environment Agency Region in 2004

- Under 50%
- 50% – 65%
- 65% – 80%
- Over 80%

The percentage of bathing beaches complying with EU standards in 2004

- 100%
- 95% – 99%
- Under 95%

SCOTLAND

NORTHERN IRELAND

No data

NORTH WEST

NORTH EAST

MIDLANDS

WELSH

ANGLIAN

THAMES

SOUTH WEST

SOUTHERN

FLOOD RISK IN ENGLAND AND WALES

- Areas at greatest risk from flooding (as designated by the Environment Agency in 2002)
- ● Settlements with over 100 properties flooded in 2001

- Ponteland
- Skinningrove
- Malton and Norton
- York
- Stockbridge
- Barlby
- Gowdall
- Catcliffe
- Mold
- Ruthin
- Hatton
- Shrewsbury
- Bewdley
- Newport
- Waltham Abbey
- Wanstead
- Woking
- Portsmouth
- Uckfield
- Lewes

COPYRIGHT PHILIP

EU AIR QUALITY Emissions in thousand tonnes

	Sulphur dioxide			Nitrogen oxides		
	1975	1990	2002	1975	1990	2002
Austria	–	90	204	–	221	36
Belgium/Lux.	–	105	307	–	172	153
Denmark	418	183	200	182	270	25
Finland	–	260	211	–	290	85
France	3,329	1,200	1,434	1,608	1,487	596
Germany	3,325	5,633	1,479	2,532	3,033	608
Greece	–	–	318	–	338	509
Ireland	186	187	121	60	128	96
Italy	3,250	1,682	1,267	1,499	2,041	665
Netherlands	386	204	430	447	575	85
Portugal	178	286	293	104	216	295
Spain	–	2,205	1,929	–	1,247	1,968
Sweden	–	169	243	–	411	59
United Kingdom	5,310	3,754	1,587	2,365	2,731	1,003

FORESTRY

The percentage of the total area covered by woodland and forest

- Over 20%
- 15% – 20%
- 10% – 15%
- 5% – 10%
- Under 5%
- △ Over 50% coniferous
- ◇ Over 50% broadleaves

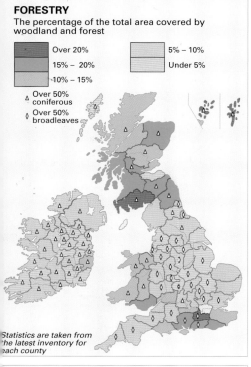

Statistics are taken from the latest inventory for each county

NATURAL VEGETATION

The plant cover associated with a particular environment if it is unaffected by human activity

- Oak
- Beech and oak
- Ash and oak
- Birch and oakwood
- Scots pine
- Heath, moorland, water meadows, fen, bog and marsh

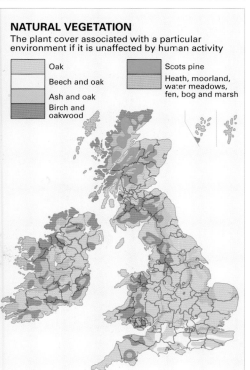

ACID RAIN

Average acidity of precipitation in the UK (pH scale)

- 4.29 and under (most acidic)
- 4.30 – 4.39
- 4.40 – 4.49
- 4.50 – 4.59
- 4.60 – 4.69
- 4.70 – 4.79
- 4.80 and over (least acidic)

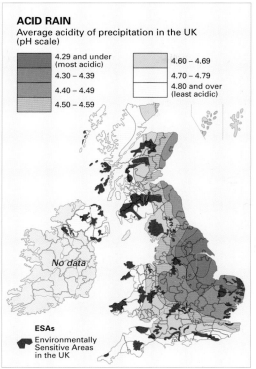

ESAs
Environmentally Sensitive Areas in the UK

GROUND LEVEL OZONE

The number of days each year with 8 hour periods with ozone levels exceeding 50 parts per billion

- More than 50
- 40 – 50
- 30 – 40
- 20 – 30
- Less than 20

Greenhouse Gas Emissions
- Carbon dioxide
- Methane
- Nitrous oxide

131 Total emissions in million tonnes of Carbon Equivalent (2003)

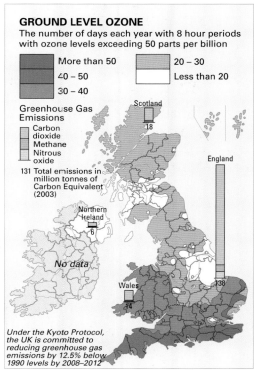

Under the Kyoto Protocol, the UK is committed to reducing greenhouse gas emissions by 12.5% below 1990 levels by 2008–2012

CONSERVATION

- National Parks
- Areas of Outstanding Natural Beauty
- National Scenic Areas
- Forest Parks, Regional Parks in Scotland and Special Protected Areas
- Green Belts (and the urban areas they surround)
- Heritage Coast (England and Wales)/Coastal Conservation Zones (Scotland)

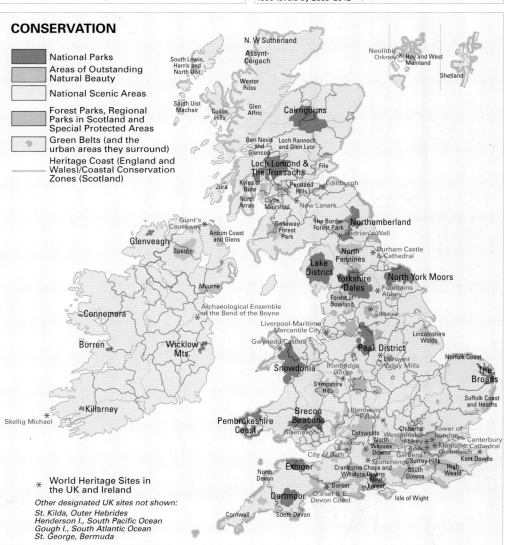

✳ World Heritage Sites in the UK and Ireland

Other designated UK sites not shown:
St. Kilda, Outer Hebrides
Henderson I., South Pacific Ocean
Gough I., South Atlantic Ocean
St. George, Bermuda

TYPES OF FARM

Dairy cattle
Beef cattle
Sheep
● Pigs and/or poultry
Mixed farming
Market gardening (fruit and vegetables)
Cereals
Other crops (mainly potatoes, sugar beet)
Northern limit of 9 month growing season
Forests
Built-up areas

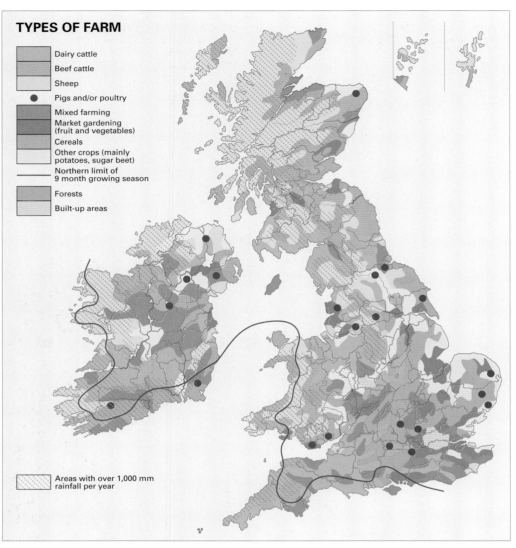

Areas with over 1,000 mm rainfall per year

CEREAL FARMING

The percentage of the total farmland used for growing cereals in 2003

Over 40%
30 – 40%
20 – 30%
10 – 20%
0 – 10%
No data

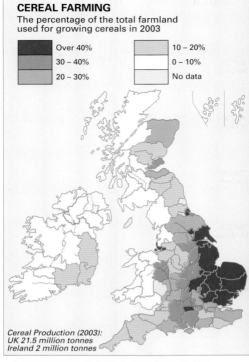

Cereal Production (2003):
UK 21.5 million tonnes
Ireland 2 million tonnes

AGRICULTURAL LAND USE IN THE UK

Other agricultural land 12.1%
Oats 0.6%
Sugar beet 0.8%
Potatoes 0.8%
Horticultural 1.0%
Rapeseed 3.2%
Barley 5.8%
Wheat 11.6%
Rough grazing 25.2%
Pasture 38.9%

Total agricultural land area (2004): 17.2 million hectares

DAIRY FARMING

The number of dairy cows per 100 hectares of farmland in 2003

Over 40
30 – 40
20 – 30
10 – 20
0 – 10
No data

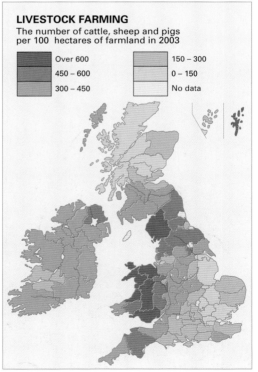

Milk Production (2003):
UK 15,056 million litres
Ireland 529 million litres

LIVESTOCK FARMING

The number of cattle, sheep and pigs per 100 hectares of farmland in 2003

Over 600
450 – 600
300 – 450
150 – 300
0 – 150
No data

FOOT-AND-MOUTH DISEASE

The number of confirmed cases of foot-and-mouth disease in 2001

Over 200
100 – 200
50 – 100
25 – 50
0 – 25
Unaffected areas

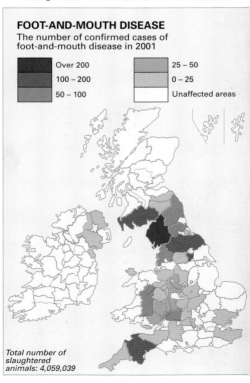

Total number of slaughtered animals: 4,059,039

NUMBER AND SIZE OF AGRICULTURAL HOLDINGS IN THE UK

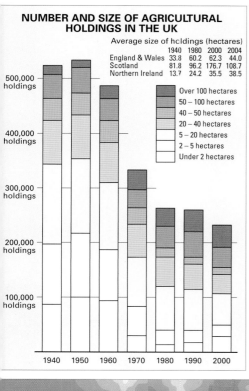

Average size of holdings (hectares)

	1940	1980	2000	2004
England & Wales	33.8	60.2	62.3	44.0
Scotland	81.8	96.2	176.7	108.7
Northern Ireland	13.7	24.2	35.5	38.5

Over 100 hectares
50 – 100 hectares
40 – 50 hectares
20 – 40 hectares
5 – 20 hectares
2 – 5 hectares
Under 2 hectares

LAND UNDER AGRICULTURE

The percentage of the total land area used for agriculture in 2003

Over 80%
60 – 80%
40 – 60%
20 – 40%
0 – 20%
No data

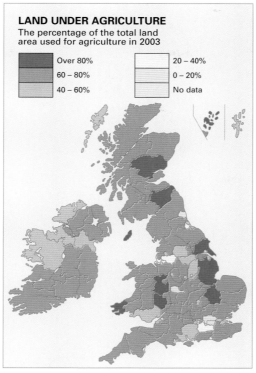

EMPLOYMENT IN AGRICULTURE

The percentage of the total workforce employed in agriculture in 2002

Over 10%
2.5 – 10%
1 – 2.5%
0 – 1%

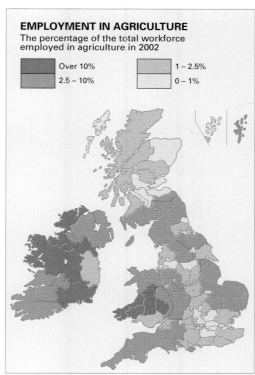

FISHING

Quantities of fish landed at major ports in 2003 (Ireland 2000)

('000 tonnes)
100
50
25
10
5

Type of fish landed

Demersal (Deep-sea fish)
Pelagic (Shallow-water fish)
Shellfish

Fishing Regions
IV   North Sea
VIa   West Scotland
VIIa   Irish Sea
VIIb/h/j W. Ireland & Sole Bank
VIId/e   English Channel
VIIf/g   Bristol Ch. & S.E. Ireland

Fish landed according to region of capture (2003)

Demersal
Pelagic
Shellfish

Each symbol represents 10,000 tonnes caught

Region boundary

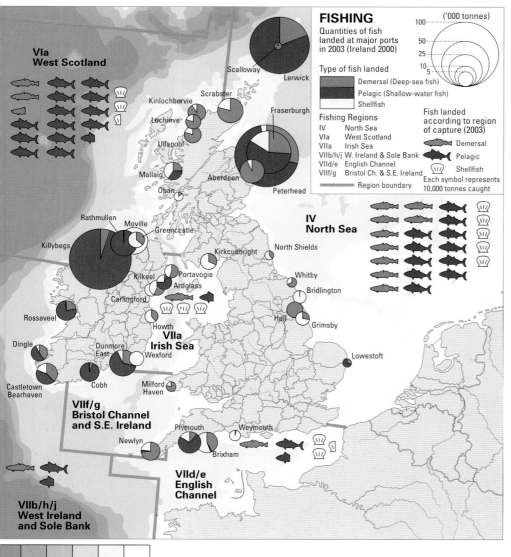

VIa West Scotland

Scalloway
Lerwick
Kinlochbervie
Scrabster
Lochinve
Fraserburgh
Ullapool
Mallaig
Aberdeen
Oban
Peterhead

IV North Sea

North Shields
Whitby
Bridlington
Hull
Grimsby
Lowestoft

Rathmullen
Moville
Greencastle
Killybegs
Kirkcudbright
Kilkeel
Portavogie
Ardglass
Carlingford
Rossaveel
Dingle
Dunmore East
Wexford
Castletown Bearhaven
Cobh
Howth
Milford Haven
VIIa Irish Sea

VIIf/g Bristol Channel and S.E. Ireland

Plymouth
Weymouth
Newlyn
Brixham

VIId/e English Channel

VIIb/h/j West Ireland and Sole Bank

1000 500 200 100 50 m

CHANGES IN THE UK FISHING INDUSTRY

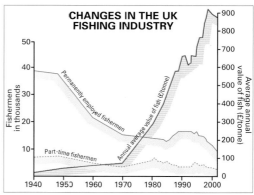

Fishermen in thousands
50
40
30
20
10

Average annual value of fish (£/tonne)
900
800
700
600
500
400
300
200
100

Permanently employed fishermen
Part-time fishermen
Annual average value of fish (£/tonne)

1940 1950 1960 1970 1980 1990 2000

FORESTRY – WOODLAND COVER

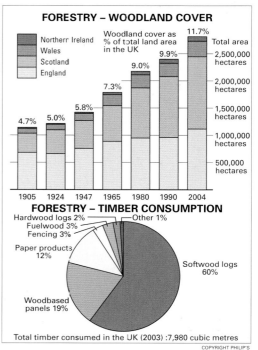

Northern Ireland
Wales
Scotland
England

Woodland cover as % of total land area in the UK

11.7%
Total area
2,500,000 hectares
2,000,000 hectares
1,500,000 hectares
1,000,000 hectares
500,000 hectares

4.7% 5.0% 5.8% 7.3% 9.0% 9.9% 11.7%

1905 1924 1947 1965 1980 1990 2004

FORESTRY – TIMBER CONSUMPTION

Hardwood logs 2%
Other 1%
Fuelwood 3%
Fencing 3%
Paper products 12%
Softwood logs 60%
Woodbased panels 19%

Total timber consumed in the UK (2003) : 7,980 cubic metres

EMPLOYMENT IN MANUFACTURING

The percentage of the workforce employed in manufacturing in 2003

- Over 25%
- 20 – 25%
- 15 – 20%
- 12.5 – 15%
- 10 – 12.5%
- Under 10%

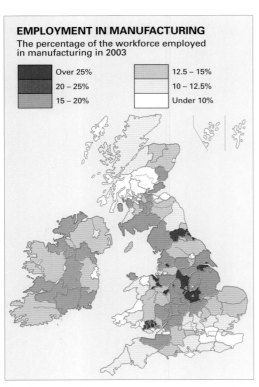

CHANGE IN MANUFACTURING EMPLOYMENT

The percentage change in the number of people employed in manufacturing by region 1991–2004*

- Over 20% gain
- 10 – 20% gain
- 0 – 10% gain
- 0 – 15% loss
- 15 – 25% loss
- Over 25% loss

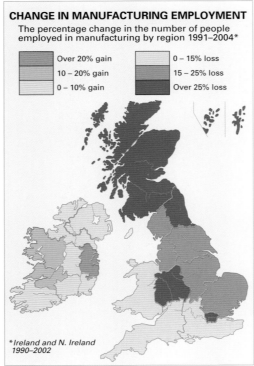

Ireland and N. Ireland 1990–2002

LOCATION OF MANUFACTURING INDUSTRY

Heavy Industry
- ▲ Chemicals
- ■ Iron and steel
- ● Motor vehicles

Light Industry
- ◆ Electrical engineering
- ○ Science parks

Grangemouth
Sunderland
Teesside
Sheffield
Halewood
Scunthorpe
Ellesmere Port
Killingholme
Crewe
Derby
Dublin
Solihull
Birmingham
Coventry
Longbridge
Luton
Llandarcy
Cowley
Port Talbot
Swindon
Llanwern
Avonmouth
Fawley
Dagenham
Southampton

EMPLOYMENT IN SERVICES

The percentage of the workforce employed in the service industry in 2003

- Over 85%
- 80 – 85%
- 75 – 80%
- 70 – 75%
- Under 70%

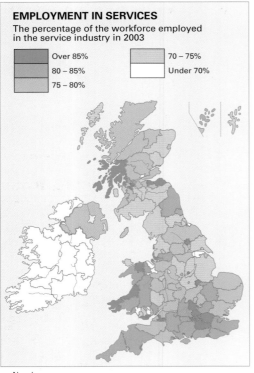

UNEMPLOYMENT

The percentage of the workforce unemployed in 2004

- Over 7%
- 6 – 7%
- 5 – 6%
- 4 – 5%
- 3 – 4%
- Under 3%

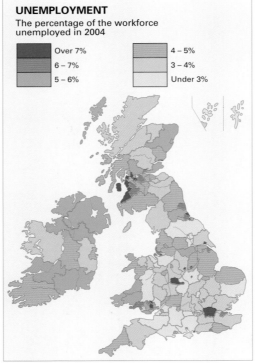

ASSISTED AREAS

The areas in which extra financial support from central government is focused to encourage economic growth

- Tier 1 with 40% aid limit
- Tier 2 with 30% aid limit

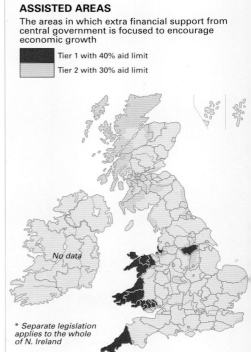

No data

Separate legislation applies to the whole of N. Ireland

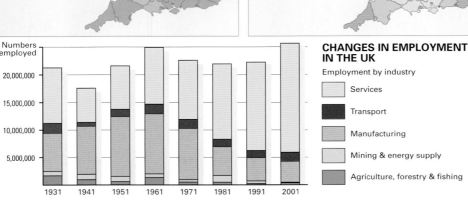

Numbers employed

20,000,000

15,000,000

10,000,000

5,000,000

1931 1941 1951 1961 1971 1981 1991 2001

CHANGES IN EMPLOYMENT IN THE UK

Employment by industry

- Services
- Transport
- Manufacturing
- Mining & energy supply
- Agriculture, forestry & fishing

MANUFACTURING OUTPUT IN THE UK

Total value 2003: £152.8 billion

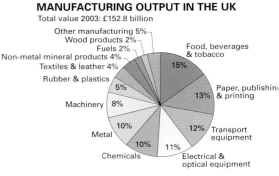

Other manufacturing 5%
Wood products 2%
Fuels 2%
Non-metal mineral products 4%
Textiles & leather 4%
Rubber & plastics 5%
Machinery 8%
Metal 10%
Chemicals 10%
Electrical & optical equipment 11%
Transport equipment 12%
Paper, publishing & printing 13%
Food, beverages & tobacco 15%

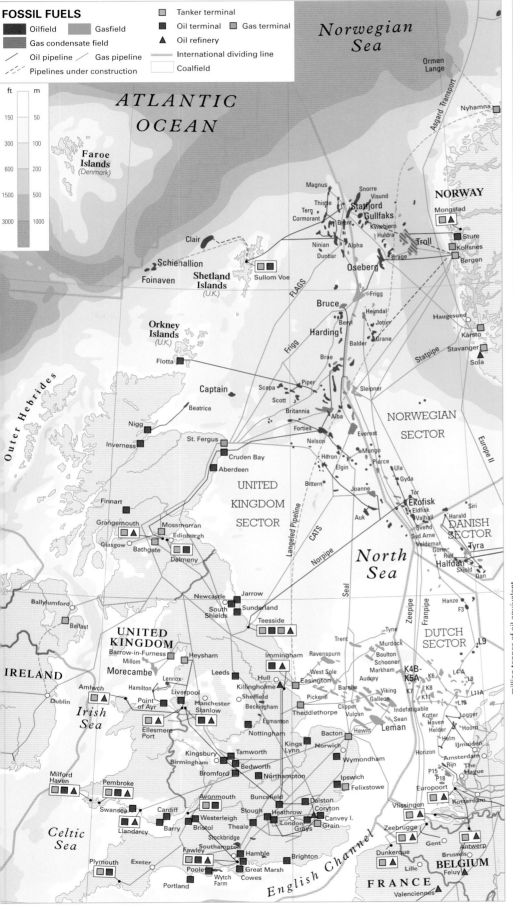

FOSSIL FUELS

- ■ Oilfield
- ■ Gas condensate field
- ■ Gasfield
- ⊡ Tanker terminal
- ■ Oil terminal
- ■ Gas terminal
- ▲ Oil refinery
- ⧸ Oil pipeline
- ⧸ Gas pipeline
- ⫶ Pipelines under construction
- ▬ International dividing line
- ▭ Coalfield

ft / m scale:
150 / 50
300 / 100
600 / 200
1500 / 500
3000 / 1000

ATLANTIC OCEAN

Norwegian Sea

Faroe Islands (Denmark)

NORWAY

Outer Hebrides

Orkney Islands (U.K.)

Shetland Islands (U.K.)

Ormen Lange

Nyhamna

Magnus, Snorre, Visund, Thistle, Terg, Cormorant, Statfjord, Gullfaks, Kvitebjorn, Brent, Alpha, Huldra, Troll, Mongstad, Sture, Kollsnes, Bergen, Oseberg

Clair, Schiehallion, Foinaven, Sullom Voe, FLAGS, Ninian, Dunbar, Bruce, Frigg, Heimdal, Jotun, Beryl, Harding, Balder, Grane, Haugesund, Karsto, Flotta, Brae, Frigg, Statpipe, Stavanger, Sola

Captain, Scapa, Piper, Scott, Britannia, Sleipner

Beatrice, Forties, Alba, Everest, NORWEGIAN SECTOR, Europe II

Nigg, Inverness, St. Fergus, Nelson, Mungo, Heron, Pierce, Ula, Gyda

UNITED KINGDOM SECTOR, Cruden Bay, Aberdeen, Elgin, Bittern, Joanne, Tor, Ekofisk, Eldfisk, Valhall, Siri, Harald, DANISH SECTOR, Auk, Svend, Syd Arne, Gorm, Rolf, Halfdan, Skjold, Dan, Tyra

Finnart, Grangemouth, Mossmorran, Edinburgh, Glasgow, Bathgate, Dalmeny, North Sea, Langeled Pipeline, CATS, Norpipe, Seal, Zeepipe, Franpipe, Hanze, F3

Newcastle, Jarrow, South Shields, Sunderland, Teesside, Trent, Murdock, Ravenspurn, Boulton, Schooner, Markham, Audrey, K4B-K5A, K6, L4-A, L8, Hanze, L9

Ballylumford, Belfast, UNITED KINGDOM, Barrow-in-Furness, Millom, Heysham, Immingham, West Sole, Easington, Barque, Viking, Galleon, K7, K8, K11, L10, L11A, DUTCH SECTOR, Tyne

IRELAND, Amlwch, Hamilton, Lennox, Liverpool, Point of Ayr, Manchester, Stanlow, Sheffield, Beckingham, Killingholme, Hull, Pickerill, Clipper, Vulcan, Indefatigable, Sean, Logger, Kotter, Haven, Helder, Hoord

Irish Sea, Ellesmere Port, Egmanton, Theddlethorpe, Leman, Hewitt, Helm, Horizon, IJmuiden

Milford Haven, Pembroke, Kingsbury, Tamworth, Birmingham, Bromford, Bedworth, Nottingham, Kings Lynn, Bacton, Norwich, Wymondham, Amsterdam, The Hague, P15, P18

Swansea, Llandarcy, Cardiff, Barry, Avonmouth, Westerleigh, Bristol, Theale, Slough, Heathrow, Northampton, Ipswich, Felixstowe, Europoort, Rotterdam, Vlissingen, Zeebrugge, Gent, Antwerp, Feluy

Celtic Sea, Plymouth, Exeter, Fawley, Poole, Wytch Farm, Portland, Stockbridge, Southampton, Hamble, Great Marsh, Cowes, Brighton, Buncefield, Dalston, Coryton, Canvey I., London, Grays, Grain, Dunkerque, Lille, BELGIUM, Brussels

English Channel, FRANCE, Valenciennes

ELECTRICITY GENERATION
Power Stations (with capacity) 2005

- □ Coal-fired (over 1,000 MW)
- ■ Peat-fired (over 50 MW)
- ■ Oil-fired (over 500 MW)
- ■ Combined Cycle Gas Turbine (over 1,000 MW)
- □ Nuclear (over 1,000 MW)
- ▲ Pumped storage scheme
- ■ Hydro-electric (over 40 MW)
- ■ Coal & gas-fired (over 1,000 MW)

Fasnakyle, Foyers, Peterhead, Rannoch, Errochty, Clunie, Cruachan, Lochay, Clachan, Sloy, Longannet, Cockenzie, Torness, Hunterston, Ballylumford, Hartlepool, Teesside, Lanesboro, Heysham, Saltend, Shannonbridge, Poolbeg, Ferrybridge, Drax, Connahs Quay, Fiddler's Ferry, Eggborough, West Burton, Turlough Hill, Dinorwig, Cottam, Tarbert, Ardnacrusha, Ffestiniog, Rugeley, Ratcliffe, Rheidol, Sizewell, Aberthaw, Didcot, Barking, Tilbury, Littlebrook, Kingsnorth, Grain, Hinkley Point, Fawley, Dungeness

ENERGY CONSUMPTION BY FUEL IN THE UK

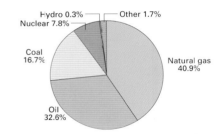

- Hydro 0.3%
- Nuclear 7.8%
- Other 1.7%
- Coal 16.7%
- Natural gas 40.9%
- Oil 32.6%

Total consumption in 2004: 234.9 million tonnes of oil equivalent

PRODUCTION OF PRIMARY FUELS IN THE UK

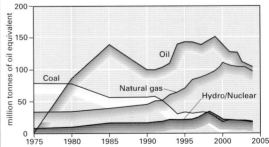

million tonnes of oil equivalent

Coal, Oil, Natural gas, Hydro/Nuclear

1975, 1980, 1985, 1990, 1995, 2000, 2005

RENEWABLE ENERGY PRODUCTION IN THE UK

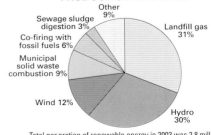

- Other 9%
- Sewage sludge digestion 3%
- Landfill gas 31%
- Co-firing with fossil fuels 6%
- Municipal solid waste combustion 9%
- Wind 12%
- Hydro 30%

Total generation of renewable energy in 2003 was 2.8 million tonnes of oil equivalent, 3.3% of total energy production in the UK

ROADS AND FERRIES

- **M6** — Motorways
- —— Main primary routes

56 Average 24 hour flow of vehicles for major sections of motorway network. Figures are given in thousands for 2004

---- Principal car ferry routes

Esbjerg Long-haul sea ferry destinations

RAILWAYS

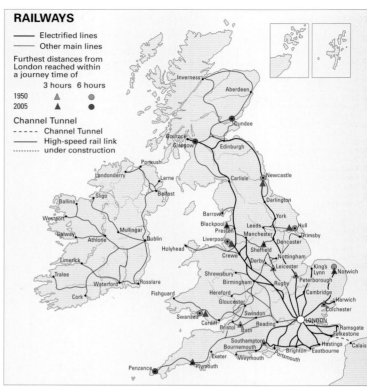

- —— Electrified lines
- —— Other main lines

Furthest distances from London reached within a journey time of
	3 hours	6 hours
1950	▲	●
2005	▲	●

Channel Tunnel
- - - - Channel Tunnel
- —— High-speed rail link
- ······ under construction

CHANNEL TUNNEL AND HIGH-SPEED LINKS IN EUROPE
Estimated journey times between London and other European cities

London – Berlin
London – Amsterdam
London – Paris
London – Brussels

Hours: 5 10 15 20

- 1990 Best time achievable using existing networks
- 2002 Since opening of Channel Tunnel in 1994 and completion of high-speed links in Europe
- 2007 Estimated journey times on completion of new link from London to Folkestone

MEANS OF TRANSPORTATION WITHIN THE UK

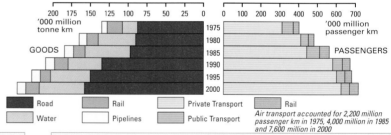

GOODS
200 175 150 125 100 75 50 25 0
'000 million tonne km

1975 1980 1985 1990 1995 2000

PASSENGERS
0 100 200 300 400 500 600 700
'000 million passenger km

- Road
- Water
- Rail
- Pipelines
- Private Transport
- Public Transport
- Rail

Air transport accounted for 2,200 million passenger km in 1975, 4,000 million in 1985 and 7,600 million in 2000

SEAPORTS

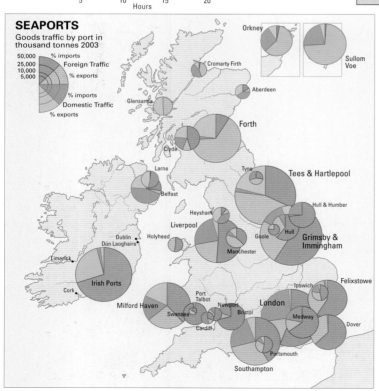

Goods traffic by port in thousand tonnes 2003

50,000 % imports
25,000 Foreign Traffic
10,000 % exports
5,000
% imports
Domestic Traffic
% exports

AIRPORTS

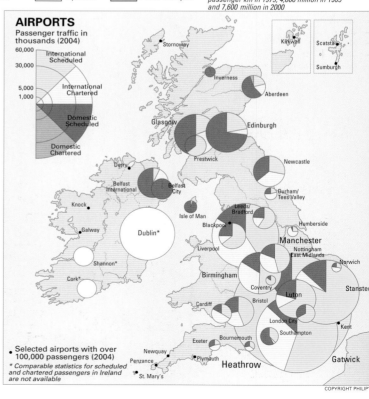

Passenger traffic in thousands (2004)

60,000 International Scheduled
30,000
International Chartered
5,000 Domestic Scheduled
1,000
Domestic Chartered

• Selected airports with over 100,000 passengers (2004)

* Comparable statistics for scheduled and chartered passengers in Ireland are not available

COPYRIGHT PHILIP'

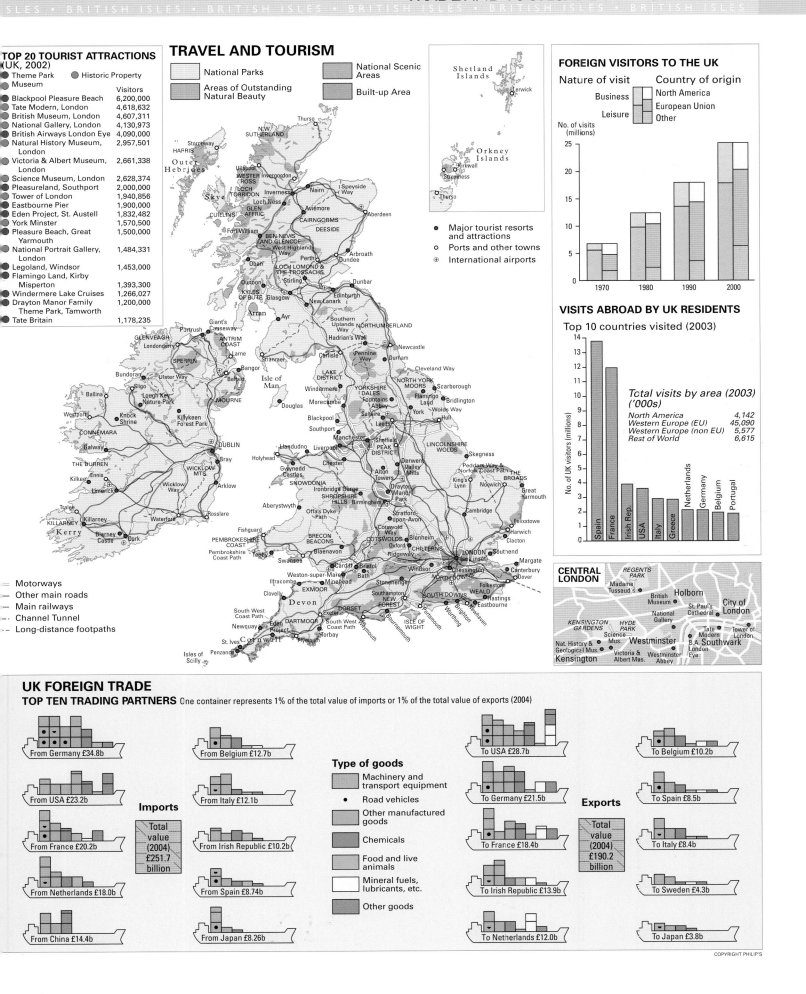

TRAVEL AND TOURISM

TOP 20 TOURIST ATTRACTIONS (UK, 2002)

- Theme Park
- Museum
- Historic Property

	Visitors
Blackpool Pleasure Beach	6,200,000
Tate Modern, London	4,618,632
British Museum, London	4,607,311
National Gallery, London	4,130,973
British Airways London Eye	4,090,000
Natural History Museum, London	2,957,501
Victoria & Albert Museum, London	2,661,338
Science Museum, London	2,628,374
Pleasureland, Southport	2,000,000
Tower of London	1,940,856
Eastbourne Pier	1,900,000
Eden Project, St. Austell	1,832,482
York Minster	1,570,500
Pleasure Beach, Great Yarmouth	1,500,000
National Portrait Gallery, London	1,484,331
Legoland, Windsor	1,453,000
Flamingo Land, Kirby Misperton	1,393,300
Windermere Lake Cruises	1,266,027
Drayton Manor Family Theme Park, Tamworth	1,200,000
Tate Britain	1,178,235

Map legend:
- National Parks
- Areas of Outstanding Natural Beauty
- National Scenic Areas
- Built-up Area

- ● Major tourist resorts and attractions
- ○ Ports and other towns
- ⊕ International airports

= Motorways
— Other main roads
— Main railways
-- Channel Tunnel
-- Long-distance footpaths

FOREIGN VISITORS TO THE UK

Nature of visit — Business, Leisure

Country of origin — North America, European Union, Other

No. of visits (millions): 0, 5, 10, 15, 20, 25
Years: 1970, 1980, 1990, 2000

VISITS ABROAD BY UK RESIDENTS

Top 10 countries visited (2003)

No. of UK visitors (millions): 0–14
Spain, France, Irish Rep., USA, Italy, Greece, Netherlands, Germany, Belgium, Portugal

Total visits by area (2003) ('000s)

North America	4,142
Western Europe (EU)	45,090
Western Europe (non EU)	5,577
Rest of World	6,615

CENTRAL LONDON

UK FOREIGN TRADE

TOP TEN TRADING PARTNERS One container represents 1% of the total value of imports or 1% of the total value of exports (2004)

Imports

- From Germany £34.8b
- From USA £23.2b
- From France £20.2b
- From Netherlands £18.0b
- From China £14.4b
- From Belgium £12.7b
- From Italy £12.1b
- From Irish Republic £10.2b
- From Spain £8.74b
- From Japan £8.26b

Total value (2004) £251.7 billion

Type of goods
- Machinery and transport equipment
- • Road vehicles
- Other manufactured goods
- Chemicals
- Food and live animals
- Mineral fuels, lubricants, etc.
- Other goods

Exports

- To USA £28.7b
- To Germany £21.5b
- To France £18.4b
- To Irish Republic £13.9b
- To Netherlands £12.0b
- To Belgium £10.2b
- To Spain £8.5b
- To Italy £8.4b
- To Sweden £4.3b
- To Japan £3.8b

Total value (2004) £190.2 billion

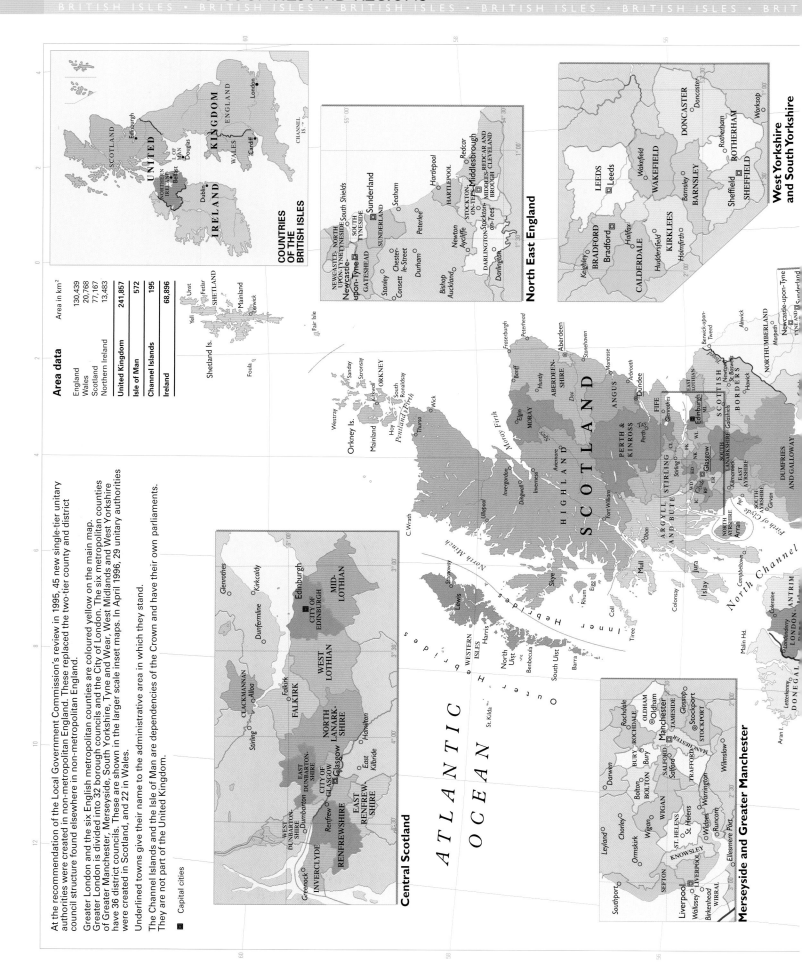

At the recommendation of the Local Government Commission's review in 1995, 45 new single-tier unitary authorities were created in non-metropolitan England. These replaced the two-tier county and district council structure found elsewhere in non-metropolitan England.

Greater London and the six English metropolitan counties are coloured yellow on the main map. Greater London is divided into 32 borough councils and the City of London. The six metropolitan counties of Greater Manchester, Merseyside, South Yorkshire, Tyne and Wear, West Midlands and West Yorkshire have 36 district councils. These are shown in the larger scale inset maps. In April 1996, 29 unitary authorities were created in Scotland, and 22 in Wales.

Underlined towns give their name to the administrative area in which they stand.

The Channel Islands and the Isle of Man are dependencies of the Crown and have their own parliaments. They are not part of the United Kingdom.

■ Capital cities

Area data

	Area in km²
England	130,439
Wales	20,768
Scotland	77,167
Northern Ireland	13,483
United Kingdom	**241,857**
Isle of Man	572
Channel Islands	195
Ireland	68,896

COUNTRIES OF THE BRITISH ISLES

North East England

West Yorkshire and South Yorkshire

Central Scotland

Merseyside and Greater Manchester

ATLANTIC OCEAN

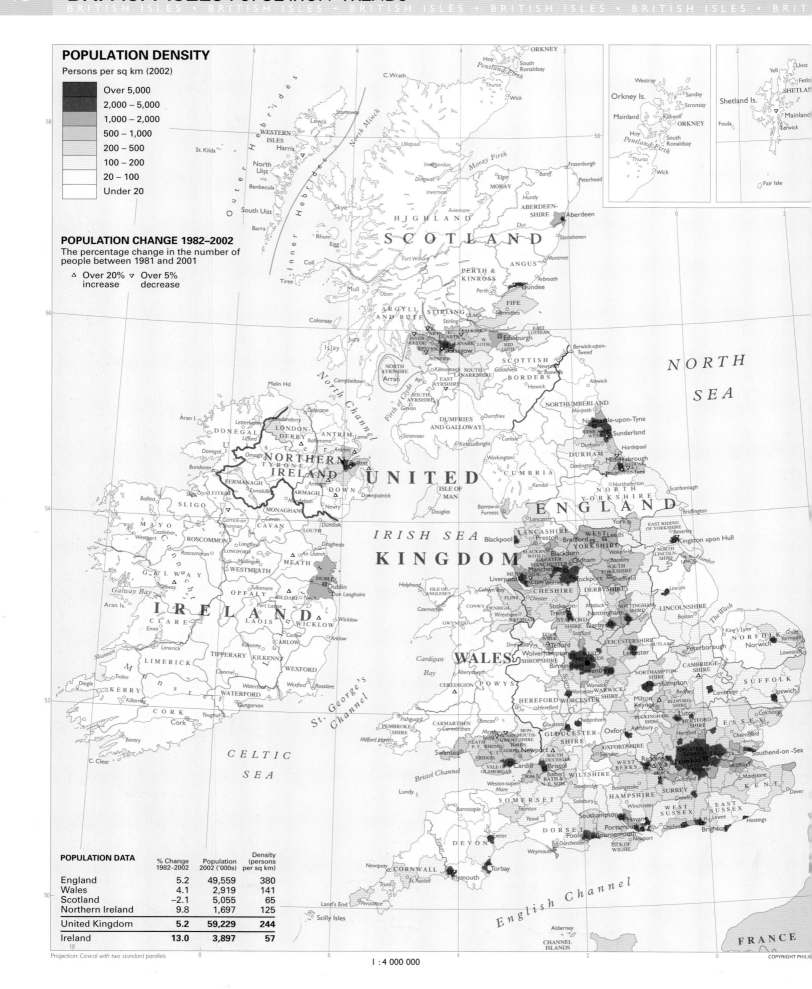

POPULATION DENSITY

Persons per sq km (2002)

- Over 5,000
- 2,000 – 5,000
- 1,000 – 2,000
- 500 – 1,000
- 200 – 500
- 100 – 200
- 20 – 100
- Under 20

POPULATION CHANGE 1982–2002

The percentage change in the number of
people between 1981 and 2001

△ Over 20%
increase

▽ Over 5%
decrease

POPULATION DATA

	% Change 1982–2002	Population 2002 ('000s)	Density (persons per sq km)
England	5.2	49,559	380
Wales	4.1	2,919	141
Scotland	–2.1	5,055	65
Northern Ireland	9.8	1,697	125
United Kingdom	5.2	59,229	244
Ireland	13.0	3,897	57

Projection: Conical with two standard parallels

1 : 4 000 000

COPYRIGHT PHILIP

POPULATION DENSITY IN 1891

Persons per sq km

Over 1,000	50 – 100
500 – 1,000	25 – 50
200 – 500	Under 25
100 – 200	

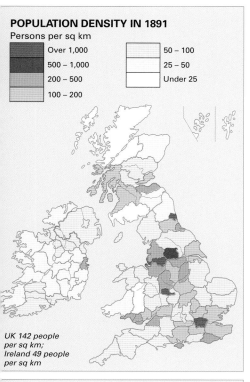

UK 142 people
per sq km;
Ireland 49 people
per sq km

ETHNIC GROUPS

Ethnic minorities as a % of total population in 2000–1

Over 6%	2 – 4%
4 – 6%	0 – 2%

Ethnic minority groups

Indian/ Pakistani/
Bangladeshi

W. Indian/
African

Other

77 000 Total number of
ethnic minority
people in each
region

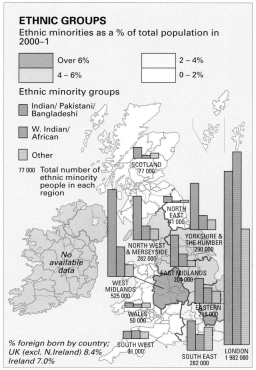

SCOTLAND
77 000

NORTH
EAST
41 000

YORKSHIRE &
THE HUMBER
290 000

NORTH WEST
& MERSEYSIDE
282 000

EAST MIDLANDS
204 000

WEST
MIDLANDS
525 000

WALES
50 000

EASTERN
216 000

SOUTH WEST
91 000

SOUTH EAST
282 000

LONDON
1 982 000

*No
available
data*

% foreign born by country;
UK (excl. N.Ireland) 8.4%
Ireland 7.0%

MIGRATION

The difference between the number moving in and
the number moving away (per 1,000 inhabitants)*

Over 10 moved in	0 – 5 moved away
5 – 10 moved in	5 – 10 moved away
0 – 5 moved in	Over 10 moved away

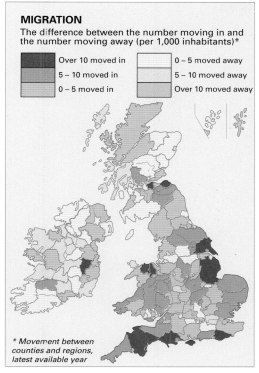

* Movement between
counties and regions,
latest available year

NATURAL POPULATION CHANGE

The difference between the number of births and the
number of deaths per thousand inhabitants in 2001

Over 7.5 more births	0 – 2.5 more births
5 – 7.5 more births	0 – 2.5 more deaths
2.5 – 5 more births	Over 2.5 more deaths

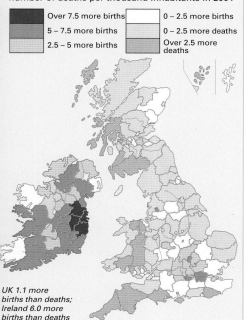

UK 1.1 more
births than deaths;
Ireland 6.0 more
births than deaths

YOUNG PEOPLE

The percentage of the population
under 15 years old in 2002

Over 22.5%	18 – 19%
20 – 22.5%	Under 18%
19 – 20%	

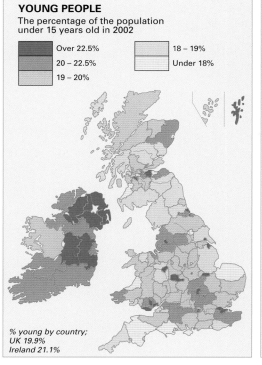

% young by country;
UK 19.9%
Ireland 21.1%

OLD PEOPLE

The percentage of the population
over pensionable age* in 2002

Over 22.5%	15 – 17.5%
20 – 22.5%	12.5 – 15%
17.5 – 20%	Under 12.5%

*Pensionable age is
65 for males, 60 for
females

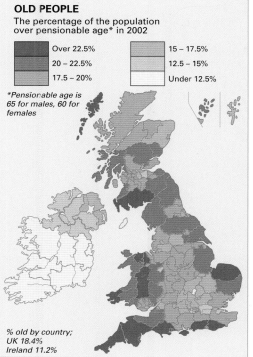

% old by country;
UK 18.4%
Ireland 11.2%

UK VITAL STATISTICS (1900–2000)

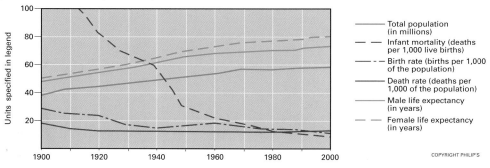

Units specified in legend

— Total population
(in millions)

– – Infant mortality (deaths
per 1,000 live births)

–·– Birth rate (births per 1,000
of the population)

— Death rate (deaths per
1,000 of the population)

— Male life expectancy
(in years)

– – Female life expectancy
(in years)

AGE STRUCTURE OF THE UK

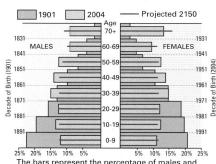

| 1901 | 2004 | — Projected 2150 |

Age

MALES   FEMALES

Decade of Birth (1901)

Decade of Birth (2004)

The bars represent the percentage of males and
females in the age group shown

HOME OWNERSHIP
The percentage of dwellings that were owner-occupied in 2003

- Over 75%
- 70 – 75%
- 65 – 70%
- Under 65%

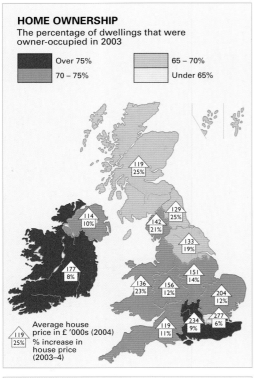

119 / 25%
114 / 10%
129 / 25%
142 / 21%
133 / 19%
177 / 8%
151 / 14%
136 / 23%
156 / 12%
204 / 12%
277 / 6%
119 / 11%
234 / 9%

119 / 25% Average house price in £ '000s (2004)
% increase in house price (2003–4)

CAR OWNERSHIP
The number of new cars per thousand people in 2001*

- Over 50
- 40 – 50
- 30 – 40
- 20 – 30
- 10 – 20

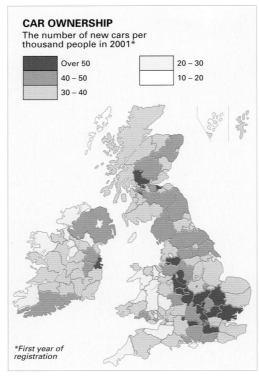

*First year of registration

INCOME
The average gross weekly earnings of males and females in full employment in 2004

- Over £450
- £425 – £450
- £400 – £425
- £375 – £400
- £350 – £375
- Under £350

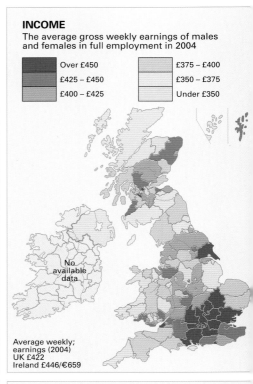

No available data

Average weekly; earnings (2004)
UK £422
Ireland £446/€659

HEALTH
The number of doctors per 100,000 people by region in 2002

- Over 70
- 65 – 70
- 60 – 65
- 55 – 60
- 50 – 55
- Under 50

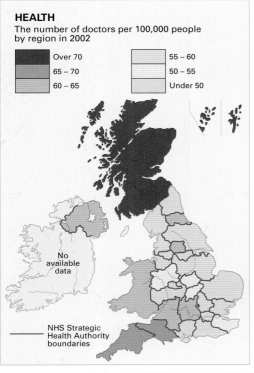

No available data

— NHS Strategic Health Authority boundaries

EDUCATION
The percentage of pupils aged 16 staying on in full-time education in 2003–2004

- Over 77.5%
- 75 – 77.5%
- 72.5 – 75%
- 70 – 72.5%
- 67.5 – 70%
- Under 67.5%

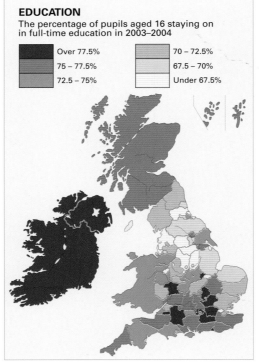

CRIME RATE
The number of recorded crimes per thousand people in 2003–4

- Over 125
- 100 – 125
- 75 – 100
- 50 – 75
- 25 – 50
- Under 25

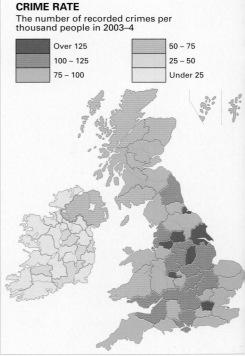

COMPARISON OF HOUSEHOLD EXPENDITURE IN THE UK

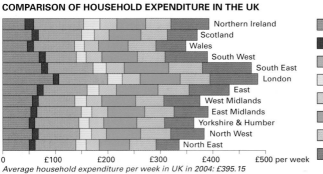

Northern Ireland
Scotland
Wales
South West
South East
London
East
West Midlands
East Midlands
Yorkshire & Humber
North West
North East

0   £100   £200   £300   £400   £500 per week
Average household expenditure per week in UK in 2004: £395.15

- Housing
- Fuel, light & power
- Food, beverages and tobacco
- Clothing and footwear
- Household goods & services
- Transport & communication
- Leisure goods & services
- Miscellaneous goods

COPYRIGHT PHILIP'S

CHANGES IN LIFESTYLE IN THE U
Percentage of household owning goods listed belov

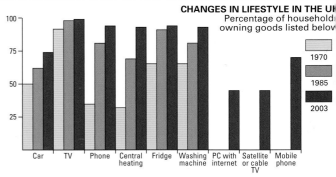

- 1970
- 1985
- 2003

Car | TV | Phone | Central heating | Fridge | Washing machine | PC with internet | Satellite or cable TV | Mobile phone

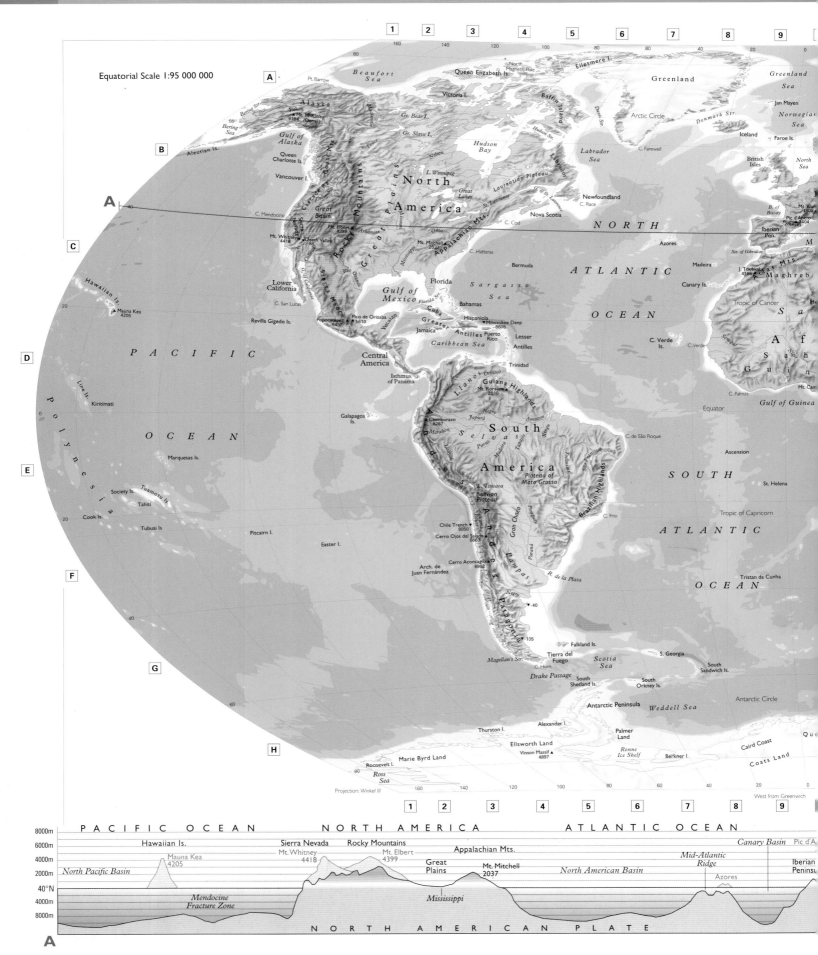

Equatorial Scale 1:95 000 000

Projection: Winkel III

West from Greenwich

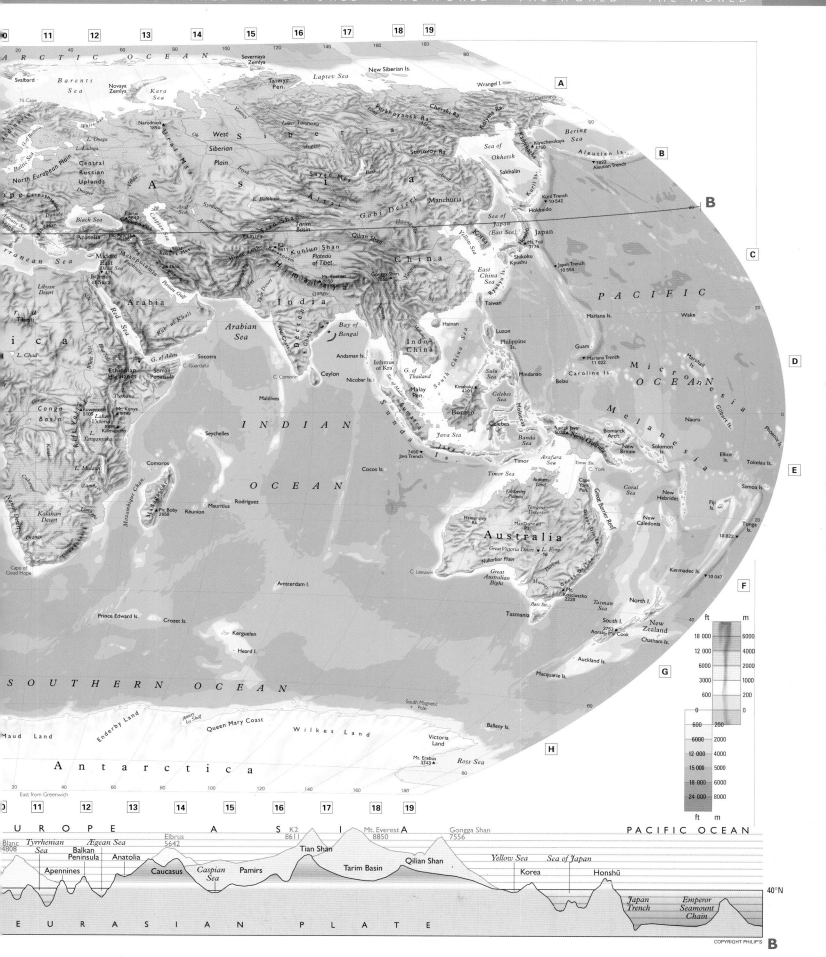

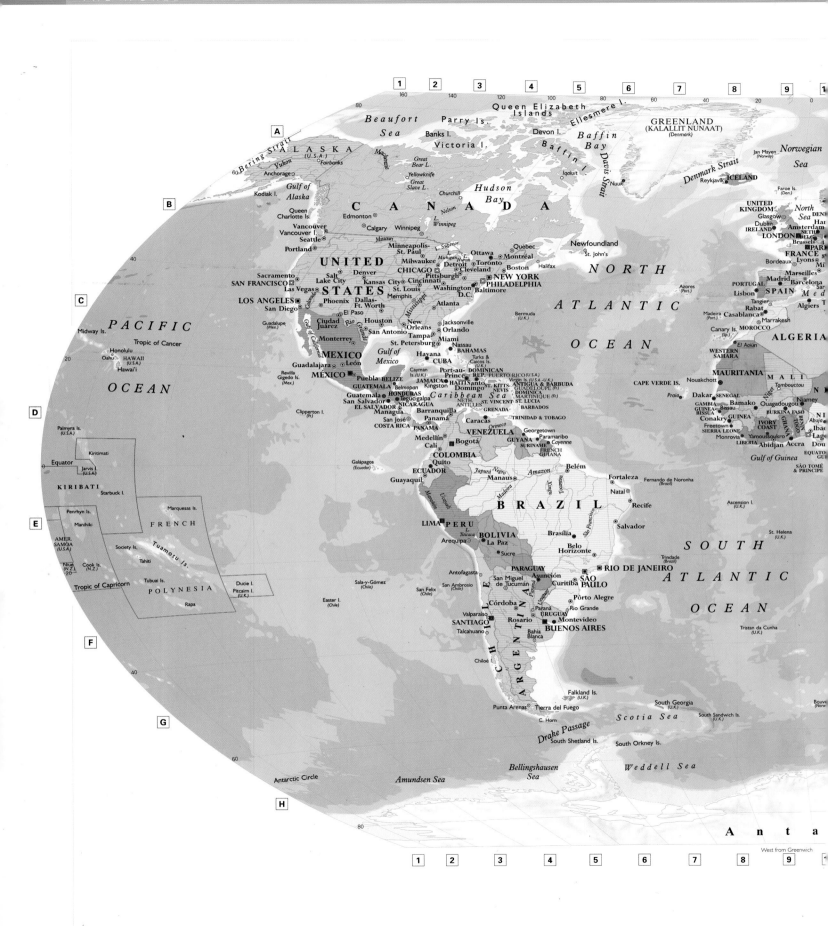

Projection: Winkel III

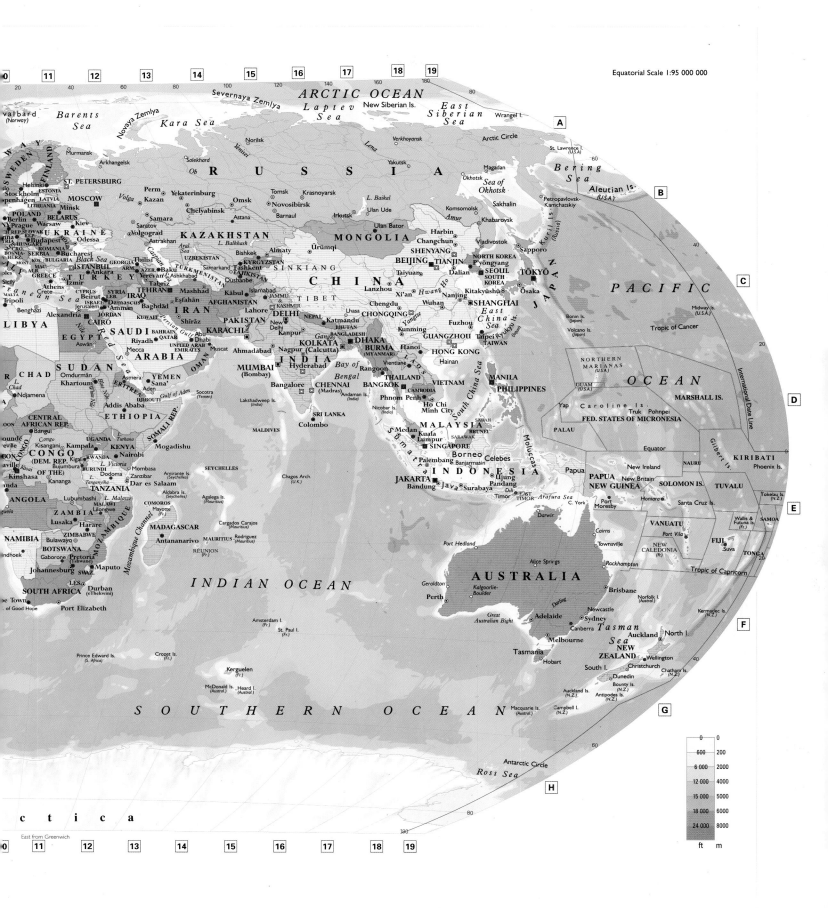

Equatorial Scale 1:95 000 000

COPYRIGHT PHILIP'S

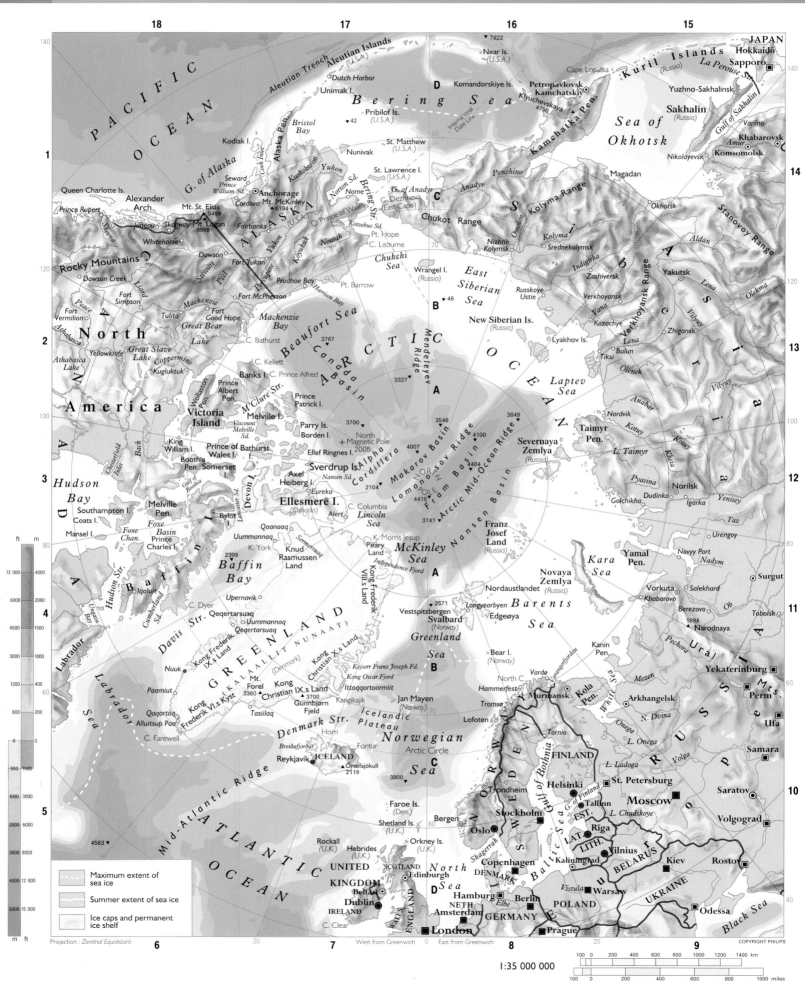

Maximum extent of sea ice

Summer extent of sea ice

Ice caps and permanent ice shelf

Projection : Zenithal Equidistant

West from Greenwich | East from Greenwich

COPYRIGHT PHILIPS

1:35 000 000

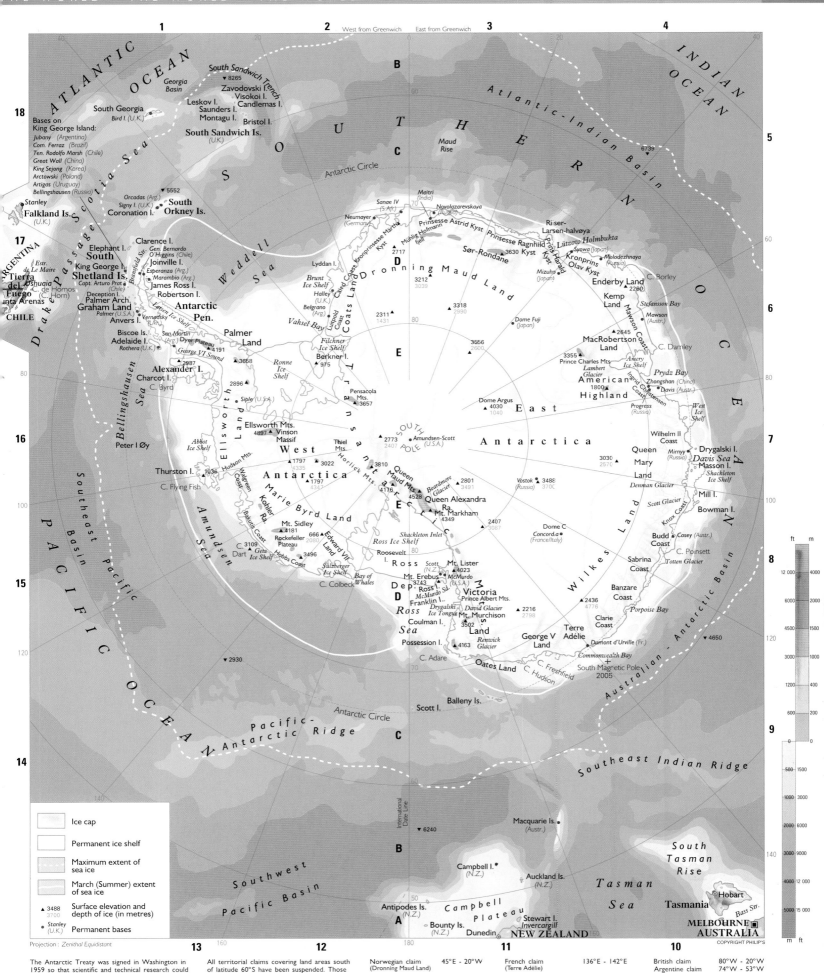

Legend:

- Ice cap
- Permanent ice shelf
- Maximum extent of sea ice
- March (Summer) extent of sea ice
- ▲ 3488 / 3700 Surface elevation and depth of ice (in metres)
- • Stanley (U.K.) Permanent bases

Bases on King George Island:
Jubany (Argentina)
Com. Ferraz (Brazil)
Ten. Rodolfo Marsh (Chile)
Great Wall (China)
King Sejong (Korea)
Arctowski (Poland)
Artigas (Uruguay)
Bellingshausen (Russia)

Projection: Zenithal Equidistant

The Antarctic Treaty was signed in Washington in 1959 so that scientific and technical research could continue unhampered by international politics.

All territorial claims covering land areas south of latitude 60°S have been suspended. Those claims were:

Norwegian claim (Dronning Maud Land)	45°E – 20°W
Australian claims	45°E – 136°E / 142°E – 160°E
French claim (Terre Adélie)	136°E – 142°E
New Zealand claim (Ross Dependency)	160°E – 150°W
British claim	80°W – 20°W
Argentine claim	74°W – 53°W
Chilean claim	90°W – 53°W

COPYRIGHT PHILIP'S

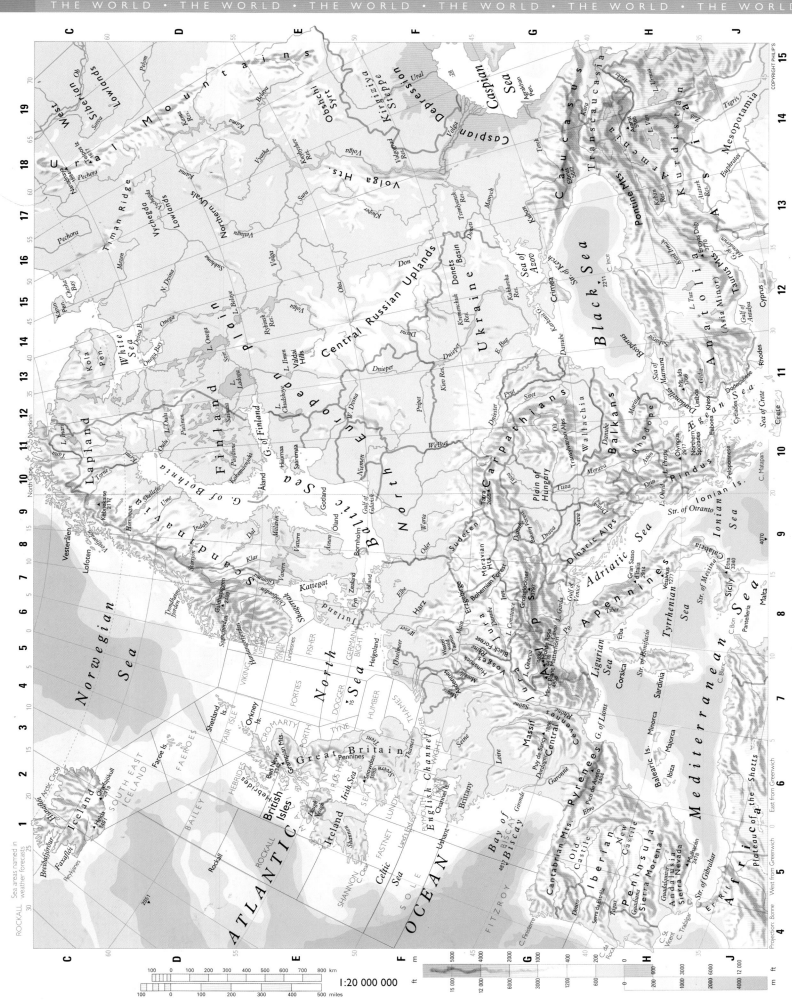

ROCKALL Sea areas named in
weather forecasts

Projection: Bonne

1:20 000 000

100 0 100 200 300 400 500 600 700 800 km

100 0 100 200 300 400 500 miles

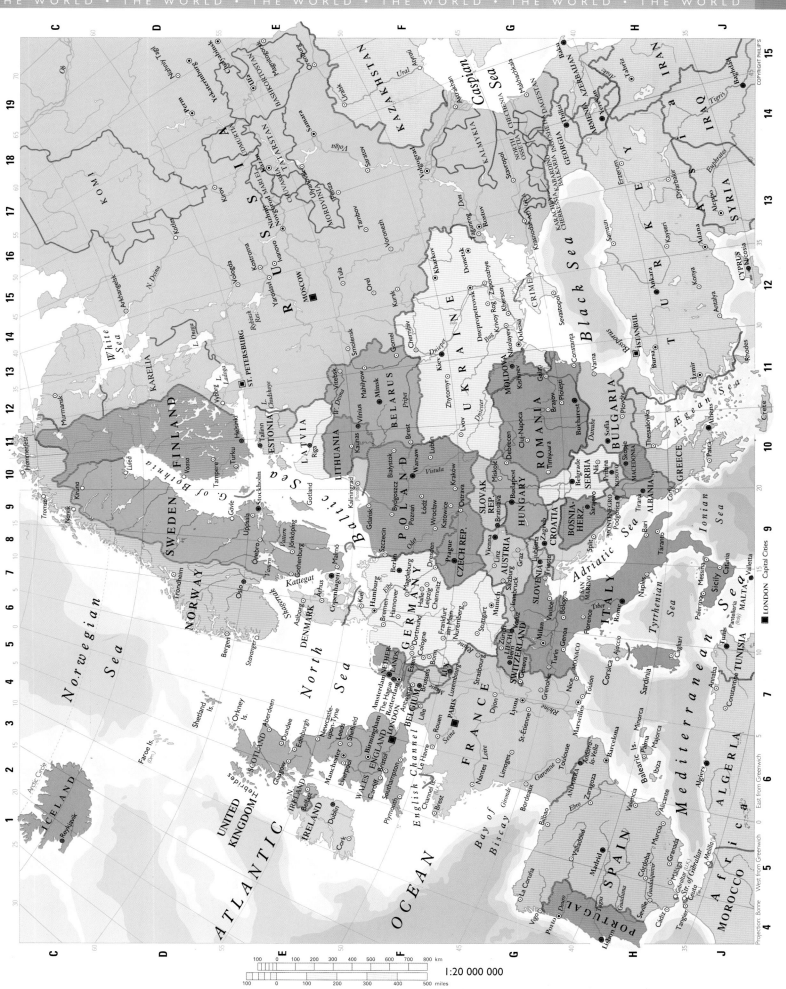

1:20 000 000

COPYRIGHT PHILIP'S

Projection: Bonne

LONDON Capital Cities

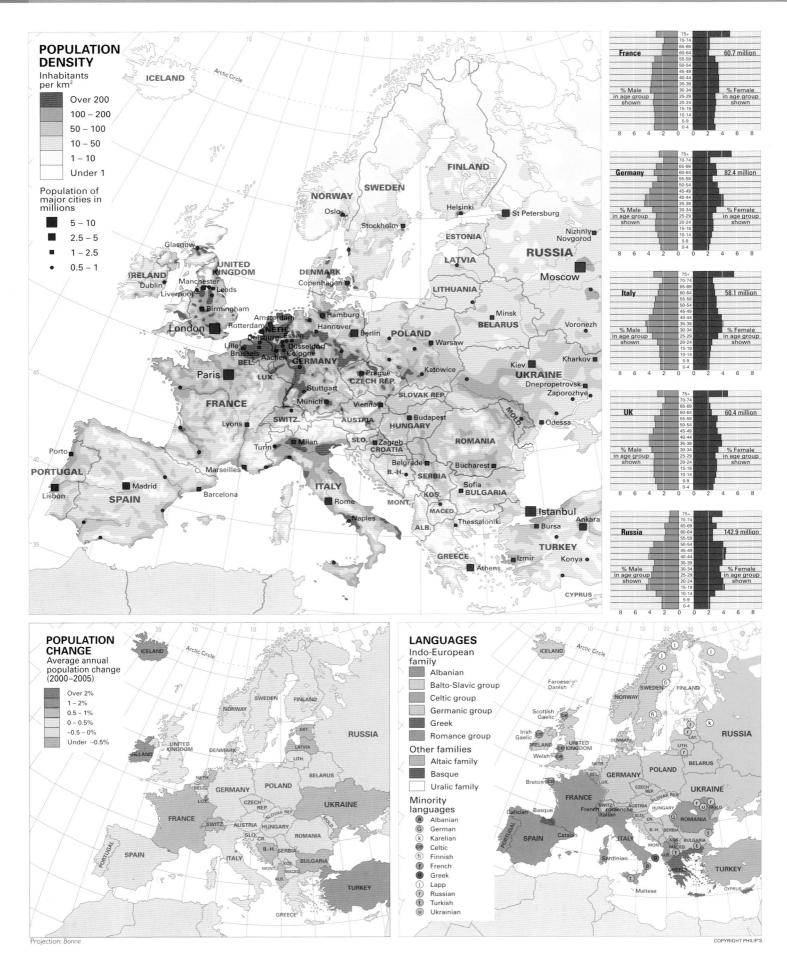

POPULATION DENSITY

Inhabitants per km²

- Over 200
- 100 – 200
- 50 – 100
- 10 – 50
- 1 – 10
- Under 1

Population of major cities in millions

- 5 – 10
- 2.5 – 5
- 1 – 2.5
- 0.5 – 1

Age pyramids

- France — 60.7 million
- Germany — 82.4 million
- Italy — 58.1 million
- UK — 60.4 million
- Russia — 142.9 million

% Male in age group shown / % Female in age group shown

POPULATION CHANGE

Average annual population change (2000–2005)

- Over 2%
- 1 – 2%
- 0.5 – 1%
- 0 – 0.5%
- -0.5 – 0%
- Under -0.5%

LANGUAGES

Indo-European family

- Albanian
- Balto-Slavic group
- Celtic group
- Germanic group
- Greek
- Romance group

Other families

- Altaic family
- Basque
- Uralic family

Minority languages

- ⓐ Albanian
- Ⓖ German
- Ⓚ Karelian
- ⓒⓔ Celtic
- ⓕⓘ Finnish
- ⓕ French
- Ⓖ Greek
- ⓘ Lapp
- ⓡ Russian
- ⓣ Turkish
- ⓤ Ukrainian

Projection: Bonne

COPYRIGHT PHILIP'S

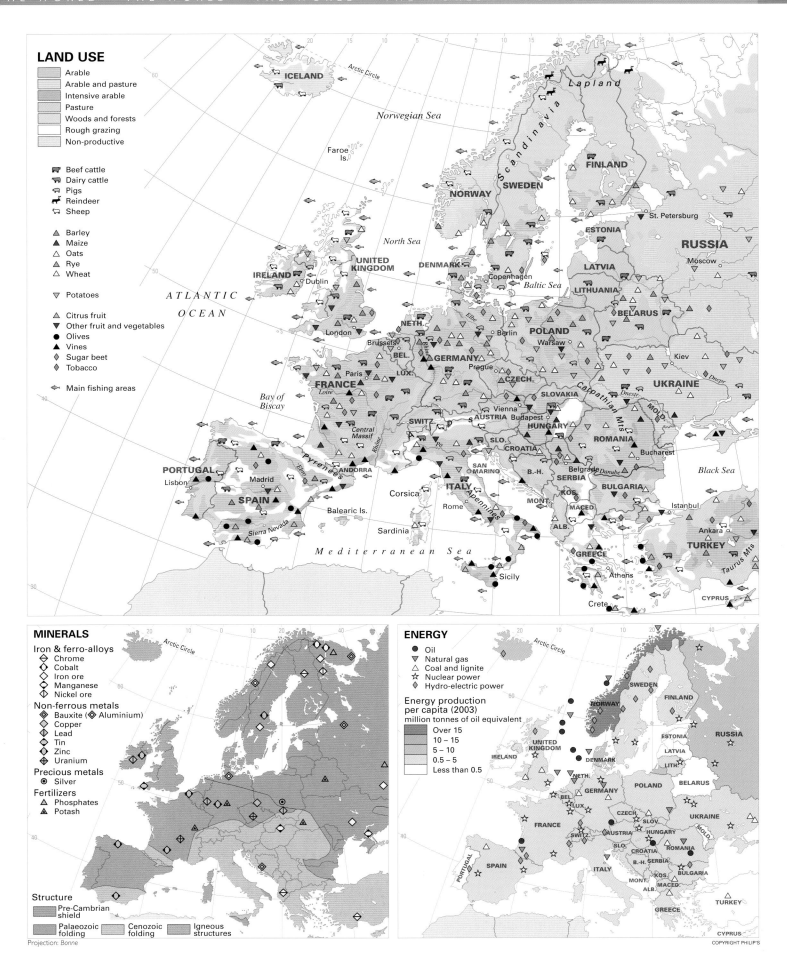

LAND USE

- Arable
- Arable and pasture
- Intensive arable
- Pasture
- Woods and forests
- Rough grazing
- Non-productive

- Beef cattle
- Dairy cattle
- Pigs
- Reindeer
- Sheep

- △ Barley
- ▲ Maize
- △ Oats
- ▲ Rye
- △ Wheat

- ▽ Potatoes

- △ Citrus fruit
- ▼ Other fruit and vegetables
- ● Olives
- ▲ Vines
- ◆ Sugar beet
- ◇ Tobacco

- Main fishing areas

MINERALS

Iron & ferro-alloys
- ◇ Chrome
- ◇ Cobalt
- ◇ Iron ore
- ◇ Manganese
- ◇ Nickel ore

Non-ferrous metals
- ◇ Bauxite (◈ Aluminium)
- ◇ Copper
- ◇ Lead
- ◇ Tin
- ◇ Zinc
- ⊕ Uranium

Precious metals
- ⊙ Silver

Fertilizers
- △ Phosphates
- ▲ Potash

Structure
- Pre-Cambrian shield
- Palaeozoic folding
- Cenozoic folding
- Igneous structures

ENERGY
- ● Oil
- ▽ Natural gas
- △ Coal and lignite
- ☆ Nuclear power
- ◆ Hydro-electric power

Energy production per capita (2003)
million tonnes of oil equivalent
- Over 15
- 10 – 15
- 5 – 10
- 0.5 – 5
- Less than 0.5

Projection: Bonne

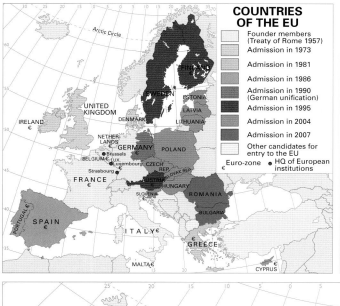

COUNTRIES OF THE EU

- Founder members (Treaty of Rome 1957)
- Admission in 1973
- Admission in 1981
- Admission in 1986
- Admission in 1990 (German unification)
- Admission in 1995
- Admission in 2004
- Admission in 2007
- Other candidates for entry to the EU

€ Euro-zone ● HQ of European institutions

EU COUNTRY COMPARISONS	Population (thousands)	Annual Income (US$ per capita)
Austria	8,185	31,300
Belgium	10,364	30,600
Cyprus	780	20,300
Czech Republic	10,241	16,800
Denmark	5,432	32,200
Estonia	1,333	14,300
Finland	5,223	29,000
France	60,656	28,700
Germany	82,431	28,700
Greece	10,668	21,300
Hungary	10,007	14,900
Ireland	4,016	31,900
Italy	58,103	27,700
Latvia	2,290	11,500
Lithuania	3,597	12,500
Luxembourg	469	58,900
Malta	399	18,200
Netherlands	16,407	29,500
Poland	38,635	12,000
Portugal	10,566	17,900
Slovakia	5,431	14,500
Slovenia	2,011	19,600
Spain	40,341	23,300
Sweden	9,002	28,400
United Kingdom	60,441	29,600
Total EU 2005 (25 countries)	**457,028**	**24,100**
Bulgaria (admitted in 2007)	7,450	9,000
Romania (admitted in 2007)	22,330	8,300

REGIONS OF THE EU

Austria *(States)* — A
1 Niederösterreich 4 Kärnten 7 Tirol
2 Oberösterreich 5 Salzburg 8 Wien
3 Burgenland 6 Steiermark 9 Vorarlberg

Belgium *(Regions)* — B
1 Bruxelles 2 Vlaanderen 3 Wallonie

Bulgaria *(member state from 2007)* — BU

Cyprus *(member state with no corresponding division)* — CY

Czech Republic *(Kraj)* — CZ
1 Jihovychod 4 Praha 7 Stredni Cechy
2 Jihozapad 5 Severovychod 8 Stredni Morava
3 Moravskoslezsko 6 Severozapad

Denmark *(member state with no corresponding division)* — DK

Estonia *(member state with no corresponding division)* — EE

Finland *(Provinces)* — FIN
1 Åland 3 Väli-Suomi 5 Uusimaa (Suuralue)
2 Itä-Suomi 4 Pohjois-Suomi 6 Etelä-Suomi

France *(Regions)* — F
1 Alsace 9 Franche-Comté 17 Normandie (Basse-)
2 Aquitaine 10 Ile-de-France 18 Normandie (Haute-)
3 Auvergne 11 Languedoc-Roussillon 19 Picardie
4 Bourgogne 12 Limousin 20 Poitou-Charentes
5 Bretagne 13 Loire (Pays de la) 21 Provence-Alpes-Côte d'Azur
6 Centre 14 Lorraine 22 Rhône-Alpes
7 Champagne-Ardenne 15 Midi-Pyrénées
8 Corse 16 Nord-Pas-de-Calais

Germany *(Länder)* — D
1 Baden-Württemberg 7 Hamburg 11 Rheinland-Pfalz
2 Niedersachsen 8 Hessen 12 Saarland
3 Bayern 9 Mecklenburg- 13 Sachsen
4 Berlin Vorpommern 14 Sachsen-Anhalt
5 Brandenburg 10 Nordrhein- 15 Schleswig-Holstein
6 Bremen Westfalen 16 Thüringen

Greece *(Regions)* — EL
1 Anatoliki Makedonia 5 Epiros 10 Dytiki Makedonia
   kai Thraki 6 Attiki 11 Kentriki Makedonia
2 Kriti 7 Sterea Ellas 12 Peloponnese
3 Voreio Aigaio 8 Dytiki Ellas 13 Thessaly
4 Notio Aigaio 9 Ionioi Nisoi

Hungary *(Megyék)* — HU
1 Del-Alfold 4 Eszak-Magyarorszag 7 Nyugat-Dunantul
2 Del-Dunantul 5 Kozep-Dunantul
3 Eszak-Alfold 6 Kozep-Magyarorszag

Ireland *(Provinces)* — IRL
1 Border, Midlands & Western
2 Southern & Eastern

Italy *(Regions)* — I
1 Abruzzo 8 Liguria 15 Sardegna
2 Basilicata 9 Lombardia 16 Sicilia
3 Celábria 10 Marche 17 Toscana
4 Campánia 11 Molise 18 Trentino-Alto Adige
5 Emília-Romagna 12 Umbria 19 Valle d'Aosta
6 Friuli-Venézia Giulia 13 Piemonte 20 Véneto
7 Lazio 14 Puglia

Latvia *(member state with no corresponding division)* — LV

Lithuania *(member state with no corresponding division)* — LT

Luxembourg *(member state with no corresponding division)* — L

Malta *(member state with no corresponding division)* — MT

Netherlands *(Regions)* — NL
1 Noord-Nederland 3 West-Nederland
2 Oost-Nederland 4 Zuid-Nederland

Poland *(Voivodships)* — PL
1 Dolnośląskie 7 Mazowieckie 13 Swietokrzyskie
2 Kujawsko-Pomorskie 8 Opolskie 14 Warmińsko-Mazurskie
3 Łódzkie 9 Podkarpackie 15 Wielkopolskie
4 Lubelskie 10 Podlaskie 16 Zachodniopomorskie
5 Lubuskie 11 Pomorskie
6 Małopolskie 12 Śląskie

Portugal *(Autonomous regions)* — P
1 Alentejo 3 Centro 5 Norte
2 Algarve 4 Lisboa-Vale do Tejo

Romania *(member state from 2007)* — RO

Slovak Republic *(Kraj)* — SK
1 Bratislavsky Kraj 3 Vychodne Slovensko
2 Stredne Slovensko 4 Zapadne Slovensko

Slovenia *(member state with no corresponding division)* — SI

Spain *(Autonomous communities)* — E
1 Andalucía 7 Cantabria 13 Madrid
2 Aragon 8 Castilla y Léon 14 Murcia
3 Asturias 9 Castilla-La Mancha 15 Navarra
4 Islas Baleares 10 Cataluña 16 Rioja (La)
5 País Vasco 11 Extremadura 17 Valencia
6 Islas Canarias 12 Galicia

Sweden *(Regions)* — S
1 Stockholm 4 Västsverige 7 Övre Norrland
2 Östra Mellansverige 5 Norra Mellansverige 8 Småland med öarna
3 Sydsverige 6 Mellersta Norrland

United Kingdom *(Government Office Regions)* — UK
1 North East 5 West Midlands 9 South West
2 North West 6 Eastern 10 Wales
3 Yorkshire & The Humber 7 London 11 Scotland
4 East Midlands 8 South East 12 Northern Ireland

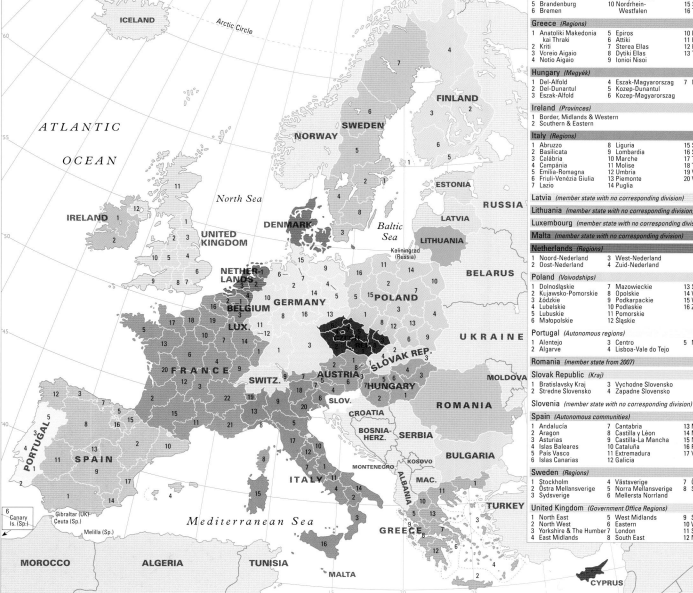

Projection: *Bonne*

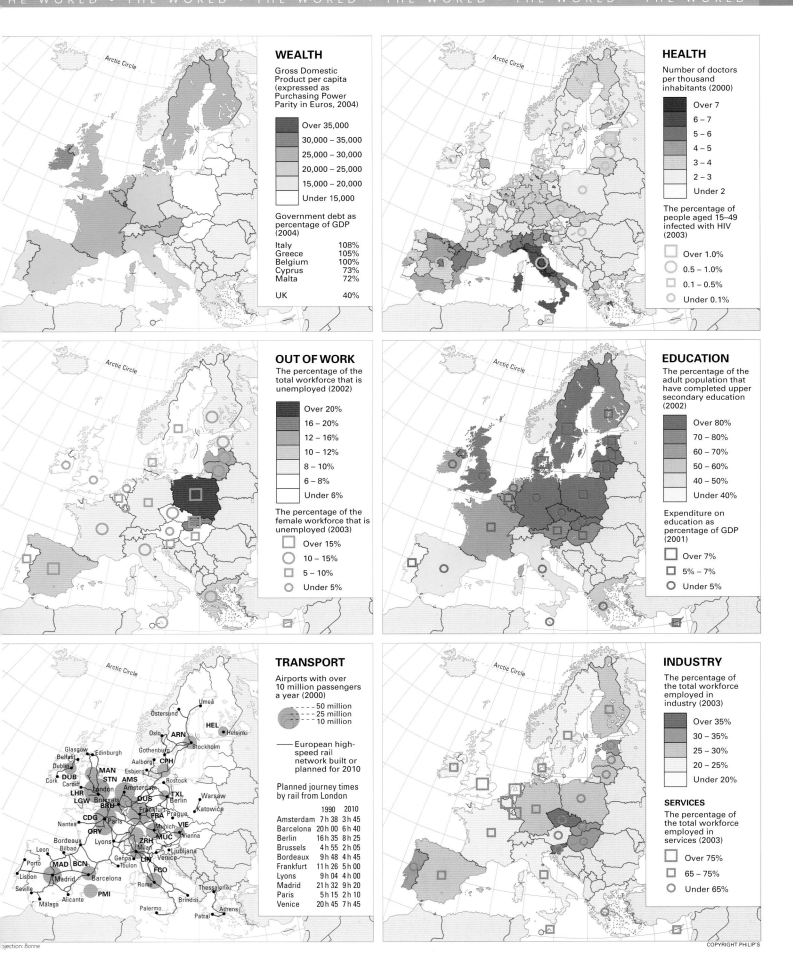

WEALTH

Gross Domestic
Product per capita
(expressed as
Purchasing Power
Parity in Euros, 2004)

- Over 35,000
- 30,000 – 35,000
- 25,000 – 30,000
- 20,000 – 25,000
- 15,000 – 20,000
- Under 15,000

Government debt as
percentage of GDP
(2004)

Italy	108%
Greece	105%
Belgium	100%
Cyprus	73%
Malta	72%
UK	40%

HEALTH

Number of doctors
per thousand
inhabitants (2000)

- Over 7
- 6 – 7
- 5 – 6
- 4 – 5
- 3 – 4
- 2 – 3
- Under 2

The percentage of
people aged 15–49
infected with HIV
(2003)

- Over 1.0%
- 0.5 – 1.0%
- 0.1 – 0.5%
- Under 0.1%

OUT OF WORK

The percentage of the
total workforce that is
unemployed (2002)

- Over 20%
- 16 – 20%
- 12 – 16%
- 10 – 12%
- 8 – 10%
- 6 – 8%
- Under 6%

The percentage of the
female workforce that is
unemployed (2003)

- Over 15%
- 10 – 15%
- 5 – 10%
- Under 5%

EDUCATION

The percentage of the
adult population that
have completed upper
secondary education
(2002)

- Over 80%
- 70 – 80%
- 60 – 70%
- 50 – 60%
- 40 – 50%
- Under 40%

Expenditure on
education as
percentage of GDP
(2001)

- Over 7%
- 5% – 7%
- Under 5%

TRANSPORT

Airports with over
10 million passengers
a year (2000)

- 50 million
- 25 million
- 10 million

— European high-
speed rail
network built or
planned for 2010

Planned journey times
by rail from London

	1990	2010
Amsterdam	7 h 38	3 h 45
Barcelona	20 h 00	6 h 40
Berlin	16 h 35	8 h 25
Brussels	4 h 55	2 h 05
Bordeaux	9 h 48	4 h 45
Frankfurt	11 h 26	5 h 00
Lyons	9 h 04	4 h 00
Madrid	21 h 32	9 h 20
Paris	5 h 15	2 h 10
Venice	20 h 45	7 h 45

INDUSTRY

The percentage of
the total workforce
employed in
industry (2003)

- Over 35%
- 30 – 35%
- 25 – 30%
- 20 – 25%
- Under 20%

SERVICES

The percentage of
the total workforce
employed in
services (2003)

- Over 75%
- 65 – 75%
- Under 65%

Projection: Bonne

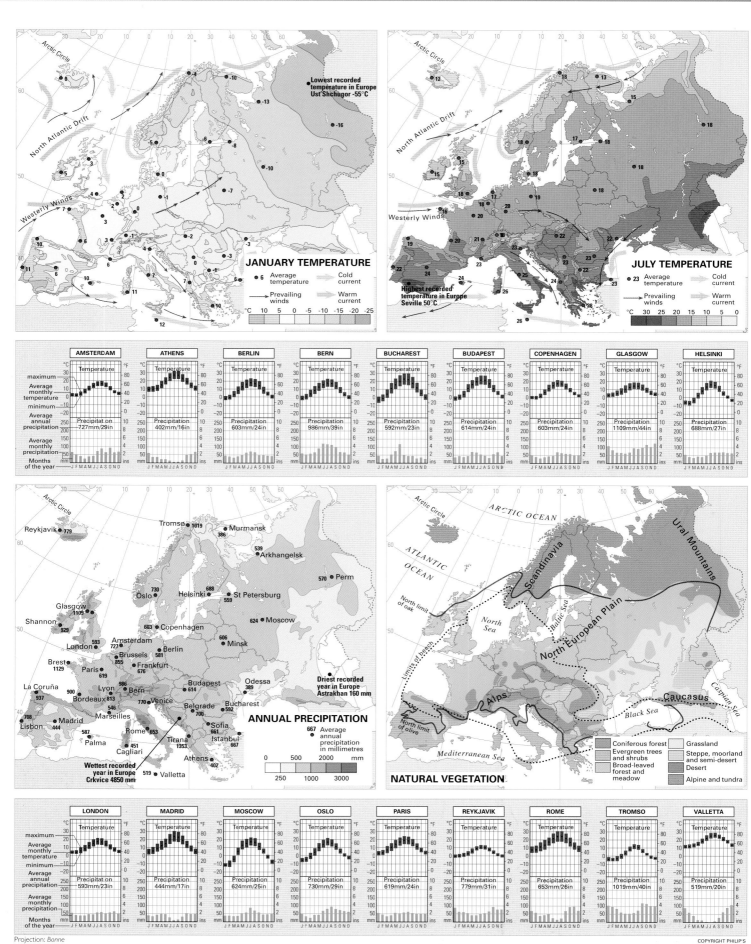

Projection: Bonne

COPYRIGHT PHILIP'S

ICELAND
ICELAND on same scale

NORWEGIAN SEA

BARENTS SEA

NORWAY

SWEDEN

FINLAND

Lapland

Kola Peninsula

WHITE SEA

KARELIA

RUSSIA

Gulf of Bothnia

STOCKHOLM

Gulf of Finland

Helsinki

Tallinn

ESTONIA

BALTIC SEA

Gulf of Riga

LATVIA

Rīga

MOSCOW

LITHUANIA

Vilnius

Kaliningrad (Russia)

MINSK

BELARUS

DENMARK

COPENHAGEN

HAMBURG

BERLIN

GERMANY

POLAND

WARSAW

Kraków

PRAGUE

CZECH REP.

UKRAINE

KIEV

Projection: Conical with two standard parallels

1:10 000 000

COPYRIGHT PHILIP'S

Projection: Conical with two standard parallels

1:5 000 000

COPYRIGHT PHILIP'S

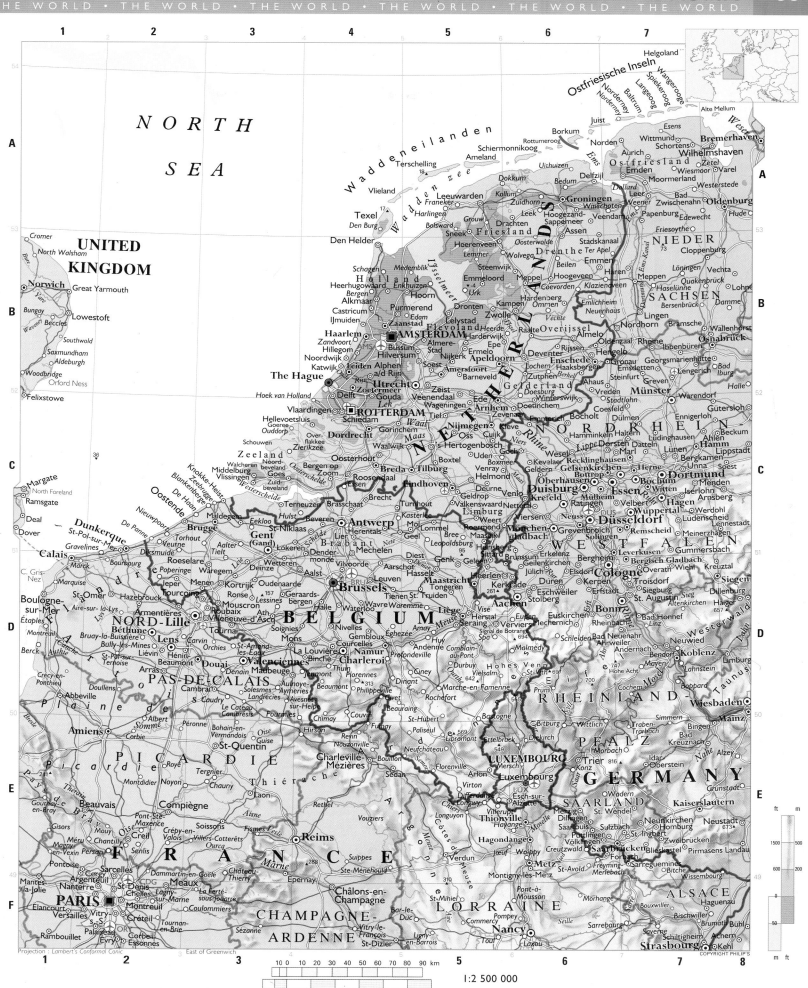

Projection : Lambert's Conformal Conic

East of Greenwich

COPYRIGHT PHILIP'S

1:2 500 000

1:5 000 000

East from Greenwich

COPYRIGHT PHILIP'S

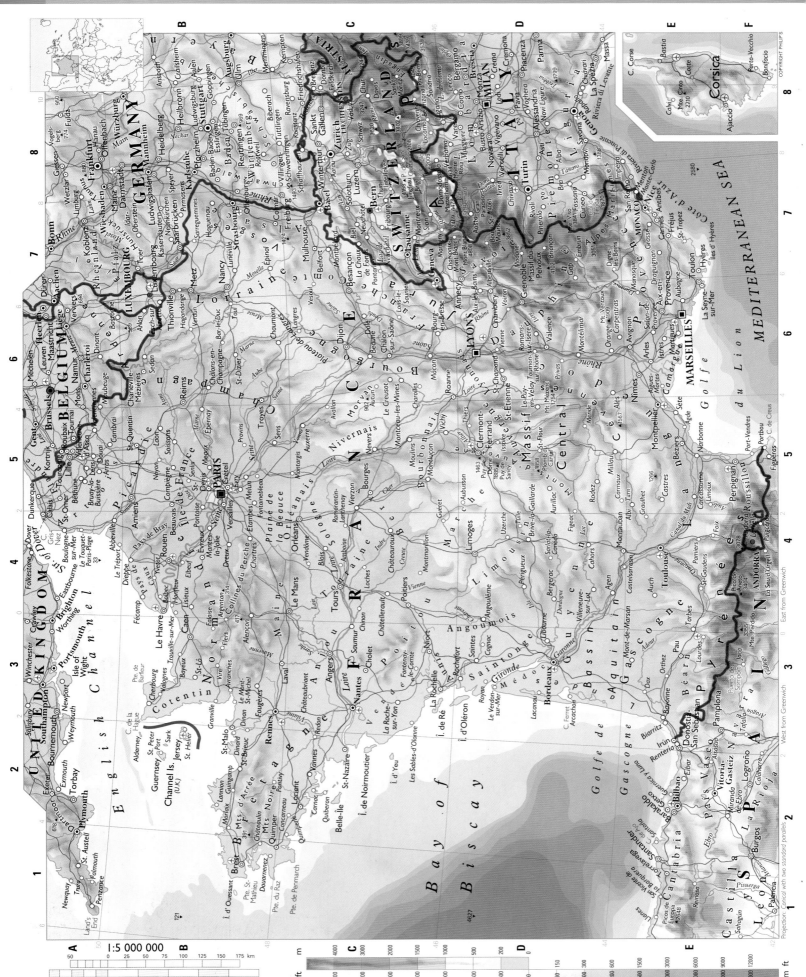

1:5 000 000

1:5 000 000

Projection: Conical with two standard parallels

Projection: Conical with two standard parallels

MALTA
1:1 000 000
Gozo
MALTA

MEDITERRANEAN SEA

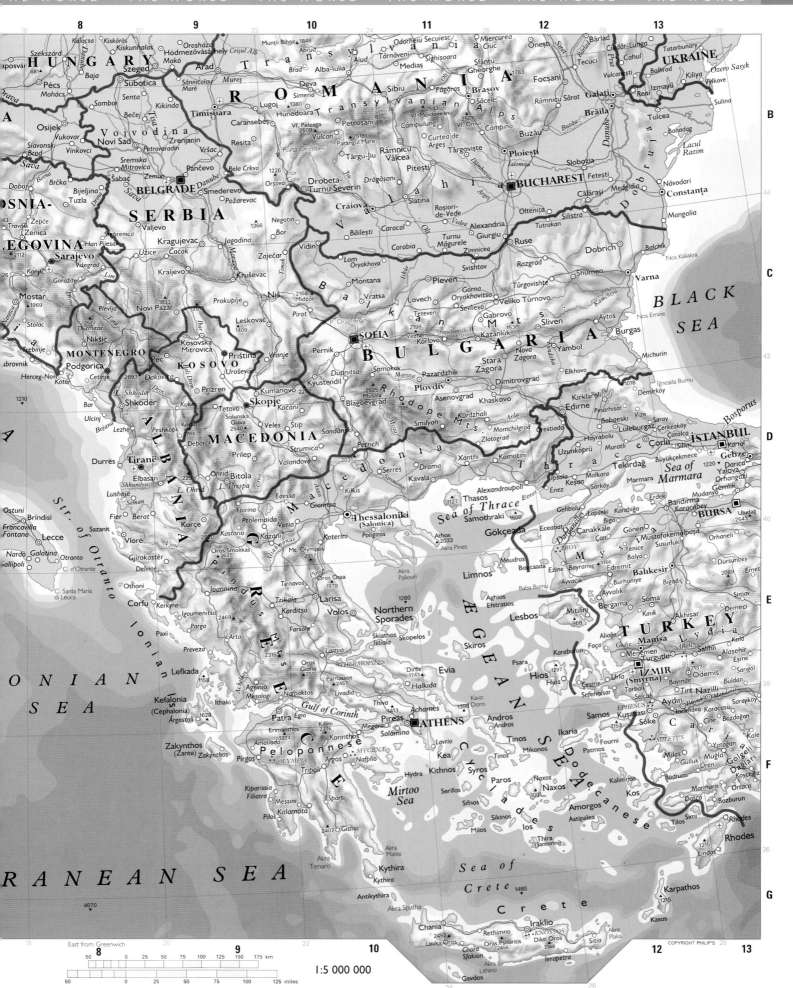

East from Greenwich

1:5 000 000

COPYRIGHT PHILIP'S

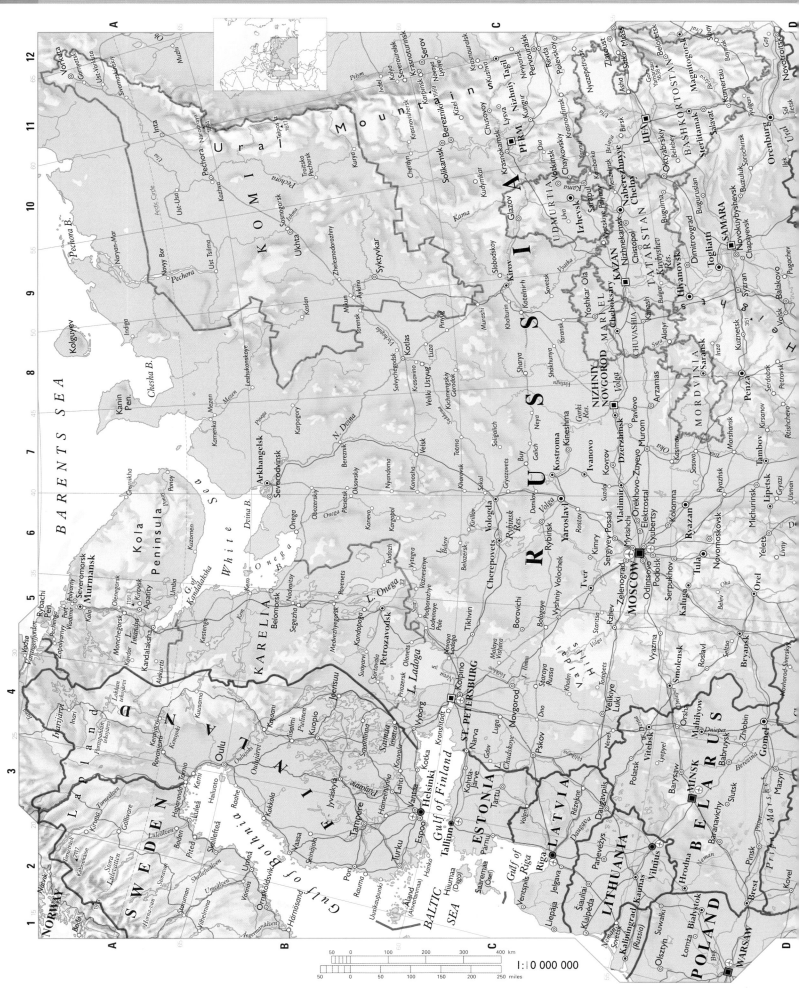

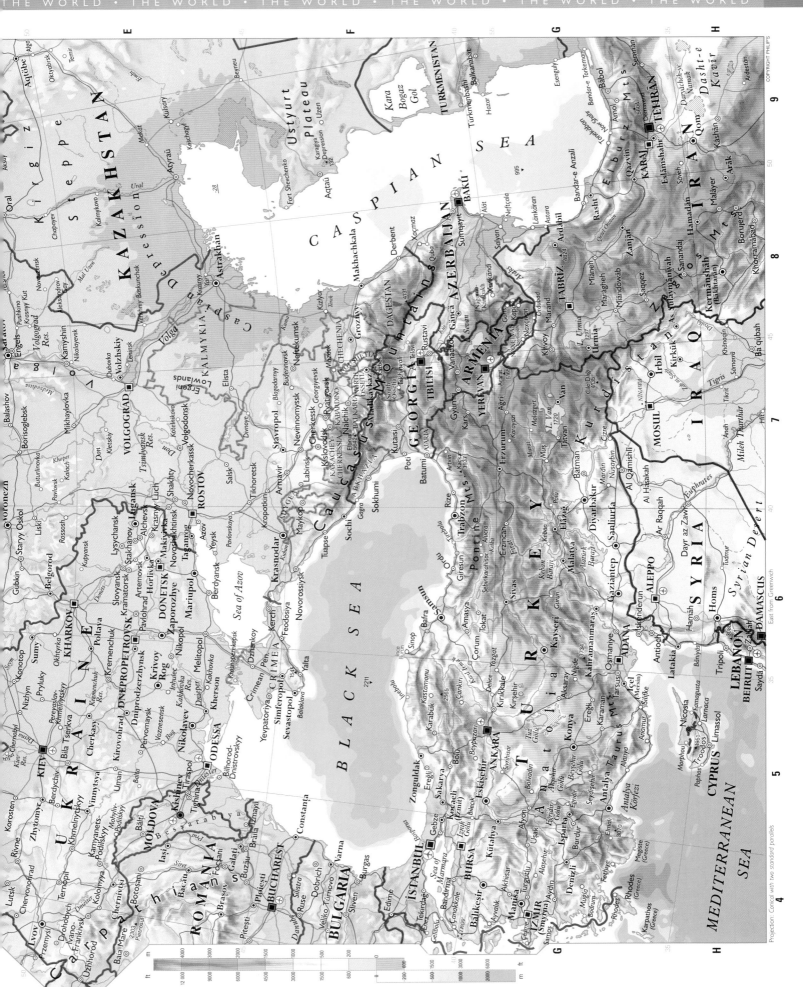

Projection: Conical with two standard parallels

East from Greenwich

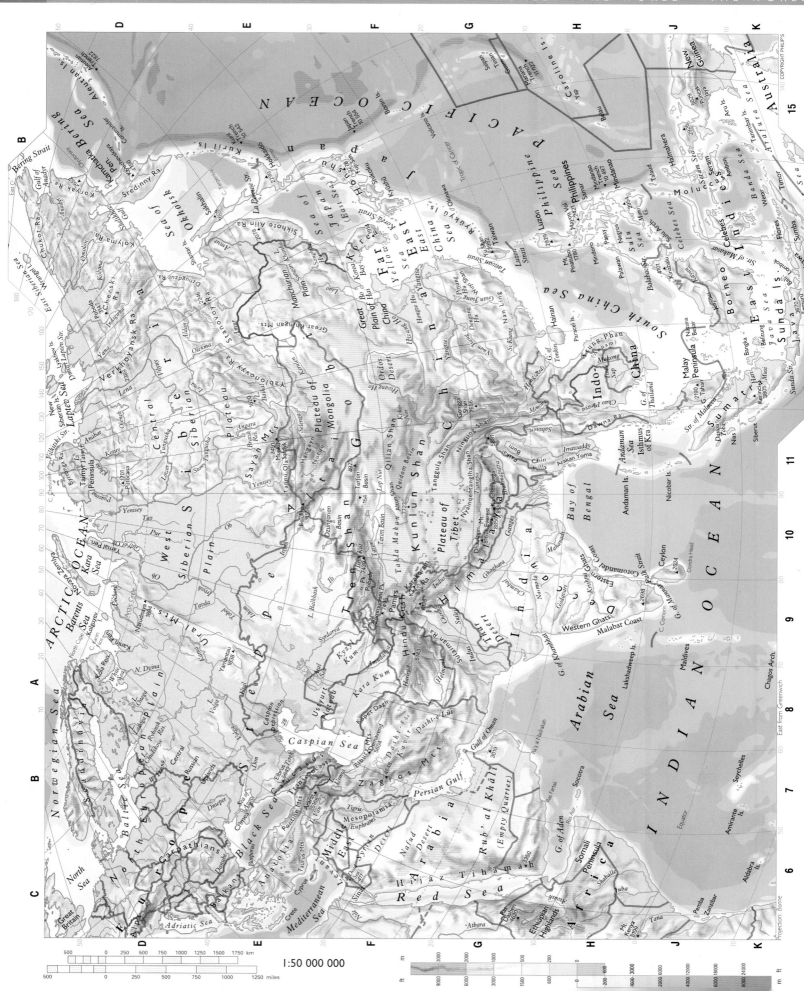

1:50 000 000

RUSSIA
1 Adygea
2 Karachev-Cherkessia
3 Kabardino-Balkaria
4 North Ossetia
5 Ingushetia
6 Chechenia
7 Dagestan
8 Mordvinia
9 Chuvashia
10 Mari El
11 Tatarstan
12 Udmurtia

AZERBAIJAN
13 Naxçivan

GEORGIA
14 Ajaria
15 Abkhazia

Projection: Borne

1:50 000 000

Hanoi ● Capital Cities

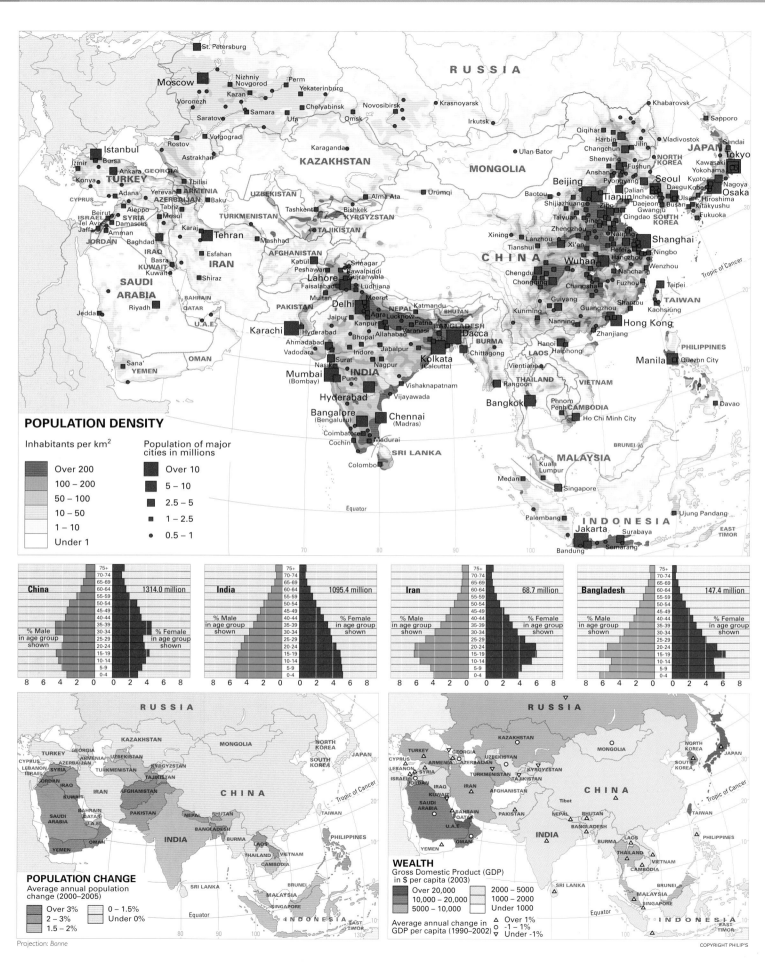

POPULATION DENSITY

Inhabitants per km²

- Over 200
- 100 – 200
- 50 – 100
- 10 – 50
- 1 – 10
- Under 1

Population of major cities in millions

- Over 10
- 5 – 10
- 2.5 – 5
- 1 – 2.5
- 0.5 – 1

China — 1314.0 million

India — 1095.4 million

Iran — 68.7 million

Bangladesh — 147.4 million

POPULATION CHANGE

Average annual population change (2000–2005)

- Over 3%
- 2 – 3%
- 1.5 – 2%
- 0 – 1.5%
- Under 0%

WEALTH

Gross Domestic Product (GDP) in $ per capita (2003)

- Over 20,000
- 10,000 – 20,000
- 5000 – 10,000
- 2000 – 5000
- 1000 – 2000
- Under 1000

Average annual change in GDP per capita (1990–2002)

- △ Over 1%
- ○ -1 – 1%
- ▽ Under -1%

Projection: Bonne

COPYRIGHT PHILIP'S

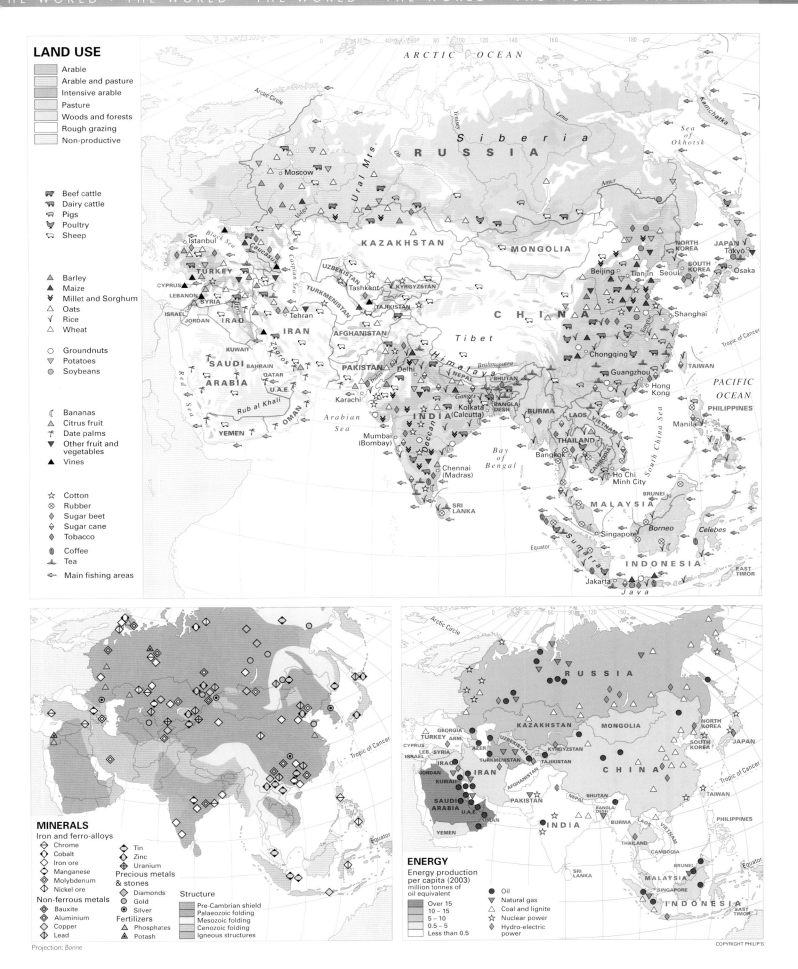

LAND USE

- Arable
- Arable and pasture
- Intensive arable
- Pasture
- Woods and forests
- Rough grazing
- Non-productive

- Beef cattle
- Dairy cattle
- Pigs
- Poultry
- Sheep

- △ Barley
- ▲ Maize
- ⩔ Millet and Sorghum
- △ Oats
- Ⅴ Rice
- △ Wheat

- ○ Groundnuts
- ▽ Potatoes
- ● Soybeans

- ☾ Bananas
- △ Citrus fruit
- ⴶ Date palms
- ▼ Other fruit and vegetables
- ▲ Vines

- ☆ Cotton
- ⊗ Rubber
- ◇ Sugar beet
- ◆ Sugar cane
- ◆ Tobacco
- ◗ Coffee
- ⚘ Tea
- ⤚ Main fishing areas

MINERALS

Iron and ferro-alloys
- ◇ Chrome
- ◆ Cobalt
- ◇ Iron ore
- ◇ Manganese
- ◇ Molybdenum
- ◇ Nickel ore

- ◇ Tin
- ◆ Zinc
- ◇ Uranium

Non-ferrous metals
- ◆ Bauxite
- ◇ Aluminium
- ◇ Copper
- ◇ Lead

Precious metals & stones
- ◇ Diamonds
- ○ Gold
- ⊙ Silver

Fertilizers
- △ Phosphates
- ▲ Potash

Structure
- Pre-Cambrian shield
- Palaeozoic folding
- Mesozoic folding
- Cenozoic folding
- Igneous structures

Projection: Bonne

ENERGY

Energy production per capita (2003)
million tonnes of oil equivalent
- Over 15
- 10 – 15
- 5 – 10
- 0.5 – 5
- Less than 0.5

- ● Oil
- ▽ Natural gas
- △ Coal and lignite
- ☆ Nuclear power
- ◇ Hydro-electric power

COPYRIGHT PHILIP'S

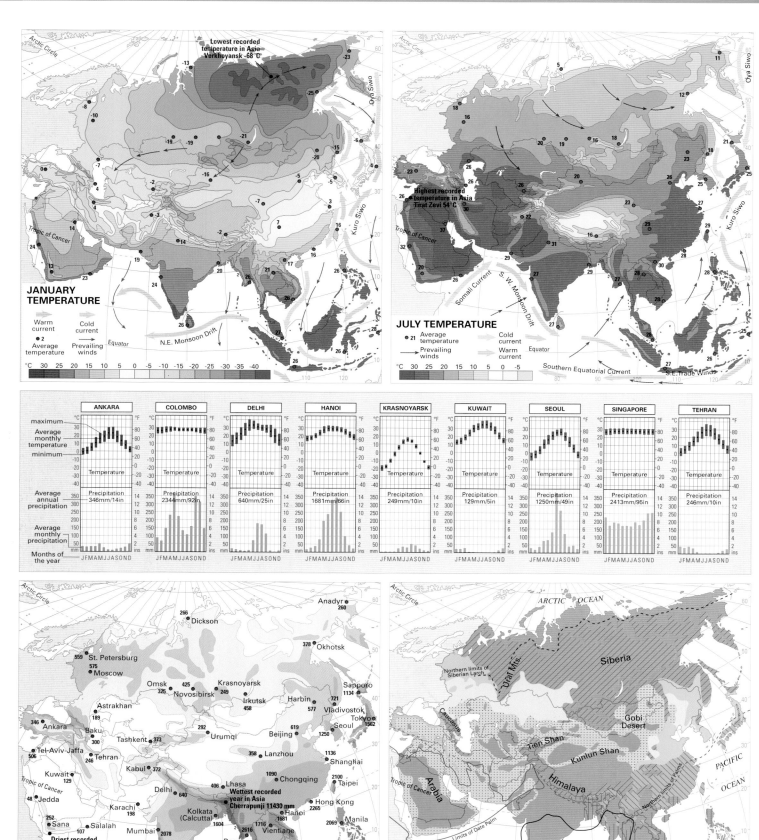

JANUARY TEMPERATURE

Lowest recorded temperature in Asia Verkhoyansk -68 °C

- → Warm current
- ⇒ Cold current
- • 2 Average temperature
- → Prevailing winds

°C 30 25 20 15 10 5 0 -5 -10 -15 -20 -25 -30 -35 -40

N.E. Monsoon Drift

Equator

JULY TEMPERATURE

Highest recorded temperature in Asia Tirat Zevi 54 °C

- • 21 Average temperature
- → Prevailing winds
- ⇒ Cold current
- ⇒ Warm current

°C 30 25 20 15 10 5 0 -5

Somali Current
S. W. Monsoon Drift
Southern Equatorial Current
S.E. Trade Winds

Climate graphs

ANKARA · COLOMBO · DELHI · HANOI · KRASNOYARSK · KUWAIT · SEOUL · SINGAPORE · TEHRAN

- maximum
- Average monthly temperature
- minimum
- Average annual precipitation
- Average monthly precipitation
- Months of the year

City	Annual precipitation
Ankara	346mm/14in
Colombo	2344mm/92in
Delhi	640mm/25in
Hanoi	1681mm/66in
Krasnoyarsk	249mm/10in
Kuwait	129mm/5in
Seoul	1250mm/49in
Singapore	2413mm/95in
Tehran	246mm/10in

ANNUAL PRECIPITATION

- Anadyr 260
- Dickson 266
- Okhotsk 378
- St. Petersburg 559
- Moscow 575
- Omsk 325
- Novosibirsk 425
- Krasnoyarsk 249
- Irkutsk 458
- Sapporo 1134
- Harbin 721
- Vladivostok 577
- Tokyo 1562
- Seoul 1250
- Astrakhan 189
- Ankara 346
- Baku 300
- Tashkent 373
- Urumqi 292
- Beijing 619
- Lanzhou 358
- Shanghai 1136
- Tel-Aviv-Jaffa 506
- Tehran 246
- Kabul 372
- Chongqing 1090
- Lhasa 406
- Delhi 640
- Taipei 2100
- Kuwait 129
- Jedda 48
- Karachi 198
- Kolkata (Calcutta) 1604
- Wettest recorded year in Asia Cherrapunji 11430 mm
- Hong Kong 2265
- Hanoi 1716
- Sana 252
- Salalah 107
- Mumbai 2078
- Vientiane 1681
- Manila 2069
- Driest recorded year in Asia Aden 46 mm
- Rangoon 2616
- Ho Chi Minh City 1984
- Colombo 2344
- Singapore 2413
- Ambon 3459
- Ujung Pandang 2851
- Jakarta 1799

- • 665 Average annual precipitation

mm 5000 4000 3000 2000 1000 500 250 0

NATURAL VEGETATION

ARCTIC OCEAN
Siberia
Northern limits of Siberian Larch
Ural Mts.
Gobi Desert
Caucasus
Tien Shan
Kunlun Shan
Himalaya
Arabia
Northern limits of Palms
PACIFIC OCEAN
Tropic of Cancer
Limits of Date Palm
INDIAN OCEAN
Borneo
Limits of Teak

- Tropical rainforest
- Monsoon woodland and jungle
- Subtropical and temperate rainforest
- Evergreen trees and shrubs
- Broad-leaved forest and meadow
- Coniferous forest
- Grassland
- Steppe and semi-desert
- Desert
- Alpine, tundra and high plateau

Projection: Bonne

1:35 000 000

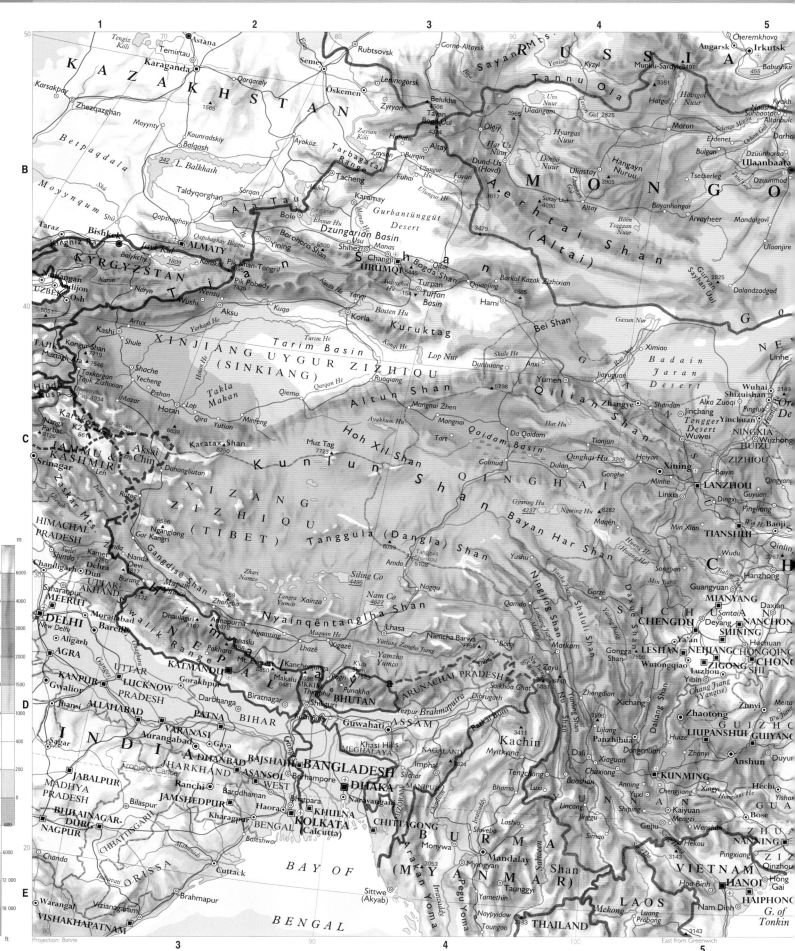

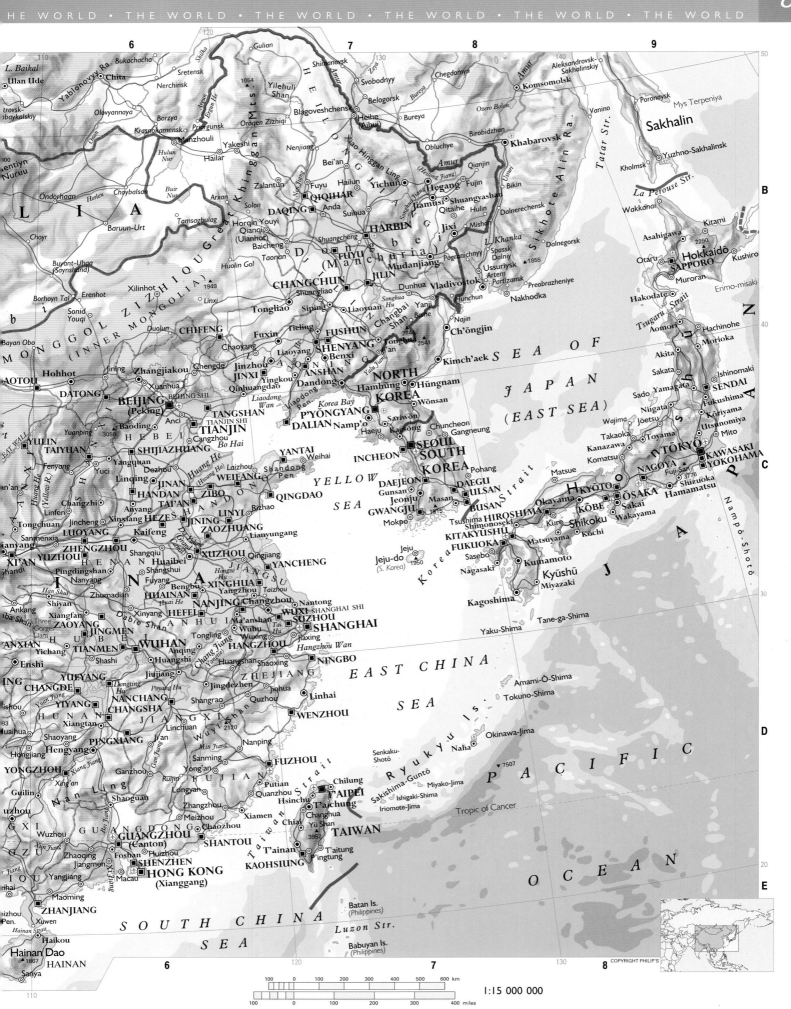

1:15 000 000

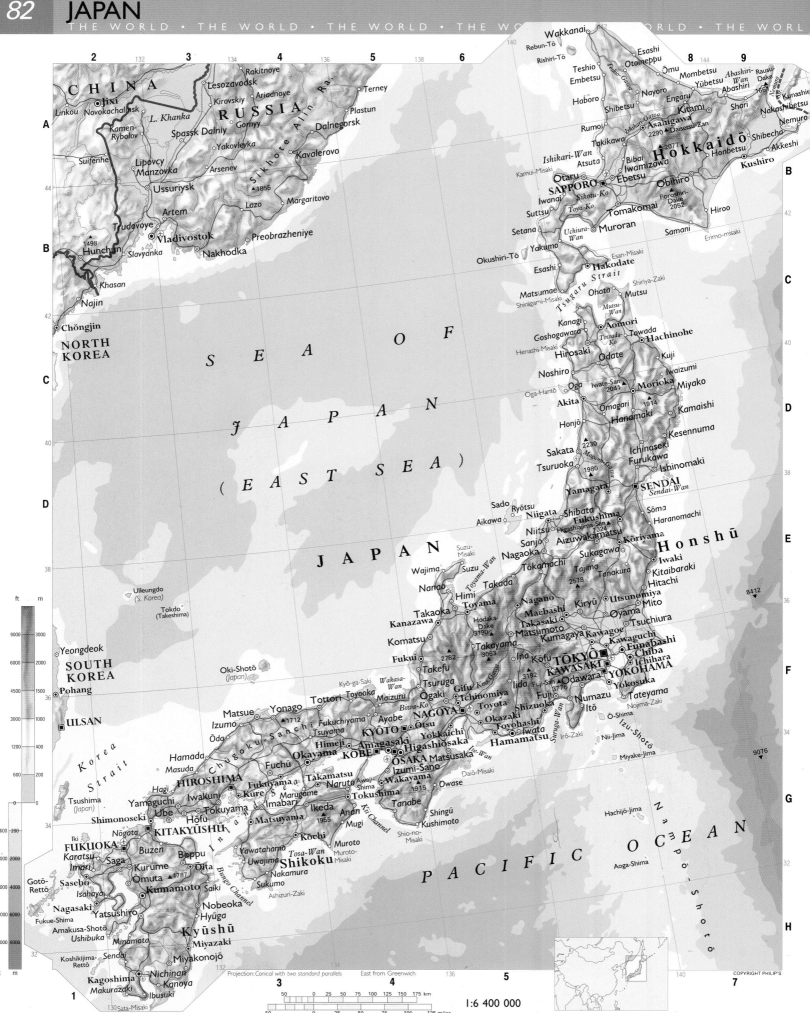

CHINA

RUSSIA

Linkou
Jixi
Novokachalinsk
Kamen-Rybolov
Suifenhe
Manzovka
Lipovcy
Ussuriysk
1498
Hunchun
Slavyanka
Vladivostok
Nakhodka
Khasan
Najin
Chŏngjin

NORTH
KOREA

L. Khanka
Kirovskiy
Spassk Dalniy
Yakovleyka
Arsenev
1855
Lazo
Artem
Preobrazheniye

Lesozavodsk
Rakitnoye
Ariadnoye
Gornyy
Kavalerovo
Margaritovo

Terney
Plastun
Dalnegorsk

Wakkanai
Rebun-Tō
Rishiri-Tō
Teshio
Embetsu
Haboro
Rumoi
Shibetsu
Otaru
SAPPORO
Iwanai
Suttsu
Setana
Okushiri-Tō
Esashi
Matsumae
Shiragami-Misaki

Esashi
Otoineppu
Ōmu
Mombetsu
Yūbetsu
Nayoro
Engaru
Kitami
Takikawa
Asahigawa
2290 Daisetsu-Zan
2077
Hokkaidō
Bibai
Ebetsu
Iwamizawa
Atsuta
Kamui-Misaki
Shikotsu-Ko
Toya-Ko
Uchiura-Wan
Muroran
Esan-Misaki
Hakodate
Tsugaru Strait
Ohata
Shiragami-Misaki

Abashiri-Wan
Shari
Nakashibetsu
Nemuro
Kunashiri
Shibecha
Akkeshi
Kushiro
Honbetsu
Obihiro
Poroshiri-Dake
2052
Hiroo
Tomakomai
Samani
Erimo-misaki
Shiriya-Zaki
Mutsu

SEA OF

JAPAN

(EAST SEA)

JAPAN

Yeongdeok

SOUTH
KOREA

Pohang

ULSAN

Ulleungdo
(S. Korea)

Tokdo
(Takeshima)

Korea
Strait

Tsushima
(Japan)

Iki
Nōgata
FUKUOKA
Karatsu
Imari
Saga
Sasebo
Nagasaki
Yatsushiro
Fukue-Shima
Amakusa-Shotō
Ushibuka
Koshikijima-Rettō
Goto-Rettō

Oki-Shotō
(Japan)

Matsue
Izumo
Ōda
Hamada
Masuda
Hagi
Iwakuni
HIROSHIMA
Yamaguchi
Ube
Tokuyama
Hōfu
Shimonoseki
KITAKYUSHU
Buzen
Beppu
Ōita
Kumamoto
Ōmuta
1787
Kurume
Isahaya
Minamata
Nagasaki
Miyazaki
Miyakonojō
Sendai
Kagoshima
Makurazaki
Ibusuki
Sata-Misaki
Kanoya
Nichinan

Tottori
Yonago
Tsuyama
Fukuchiyama
Tsuyama
Chūgoku-Sanchi
Fuchū
Fukuyama
Kure
Kitakyushu
Iwakuni

Toyooka
Maizuru
Ayabe
Himeji
Okayama
KOBE
Takamatsu
Marugame
Imabari
Matsuyama
Uwajima
Nakamura
Sukumo
Ashizuri-Zaki

Kyō-ga-Saki
Wakasa-Wan
KYŌTO
Ōtsu
Amagasaki
Higashiōsaka
ŌSAKA
Naruto
Awaji-Shima
Tokushima
Ikeda
Anan
Mugi
Kōchi
Muroto
Tosa-Wan
Muroto-misaki

Shikoku

Sado
Ryōtsu
Aikawa
Niigata
Niitsu
Sanjo
Nagaoka

Suzu-Misaki
Suzu-Wan
Wajima
Nanao
Himi
Takaoka
Toyama
Toyama-Wan
Takada

Kanazawa
Komatsu
Fukui
Takefu
Tsuruga
Ōgaki
Ichinomiya
NAGOYA
Yokkaichi
Gifu
Toyota
Okazaki
Toyohashi
Iwata
Hamamatsu
Matsusaka
Ise-Wan
Ise
Daiō-Misaki

Nanao
Takayama
2782
3063
Ina
Kōfu
Fuji-San
3776
Fuji
Shizuoka
Suruga-Wan
Irō-Zaki

Aizuwakamatsu
Kōriyama
Sukagawa
Tajima
2578

Niitsu
Higashiajima-San
2024
Fukushima
Sōma
Haranomachi

Yamagata
SENDAI
Sendai-Wan

Tsuruoka
Sakata
1980
2230
Mogami-Gawa

Akita
Honjō
Oga
Oga-Hantō
Noshiro

Iwate-San
2041
Hanamaki
1914
Morioka
Kamaishi
Kesennuma
Ichinoseki
Furukawa
Ishinomaki

Aomori
Towada-Ko
Towada
Hachinohe
Kuji
Iwaizumi
Miyako

Kanagi
Goshogawara
Hirosaki
Odate
Henashi-Misaki

Honshū

Nagano
Maebashi
Takasaki
Matsumoto
Takayama
Hodaka-Dake
3190
3192
Iida

Kiryū
Ōyama
Kumagaya
Kawagoe
Kawaguchi
Funabashi
TOKYO
KAWASAKI
YOKOHAMA
Yokosuka
Odawara
Itō
Numazu
Tateyama
Nojima-Zaki

Utsunomiya
Mito
Tsuchiura
Iwaki
Kitaibaraki
Hitachi

8412

36

9076
Miyake-Jima

Ō-Shima
Izu-Shotō
Nii-Jima

PACIFIC OCEAN

Hachijō-Jima
Aoga-Shima

Nampō-Shotō

Inland Sea

34

32

ft   m
9000 3000
6000 1500
4500 1500
3000 1000
1200 400
600   200
0   0
600   200
6000 2000
12 000 4000
18 000 6000
24 000 8000
ft   m

50 0 25 50 75 100 125 150 175 km
50 0 25 50 75 100 125 miles

COPYRIGHT PHILIP'S

East from Greenwich

Projection: Bonne

1:20 000 000

100   0   100 200 300 400 500 600 700 800 km

100   0   100   200   300   400   500 miles

Continuation Southwards on same scale

Projection: Conical with two standard parallels

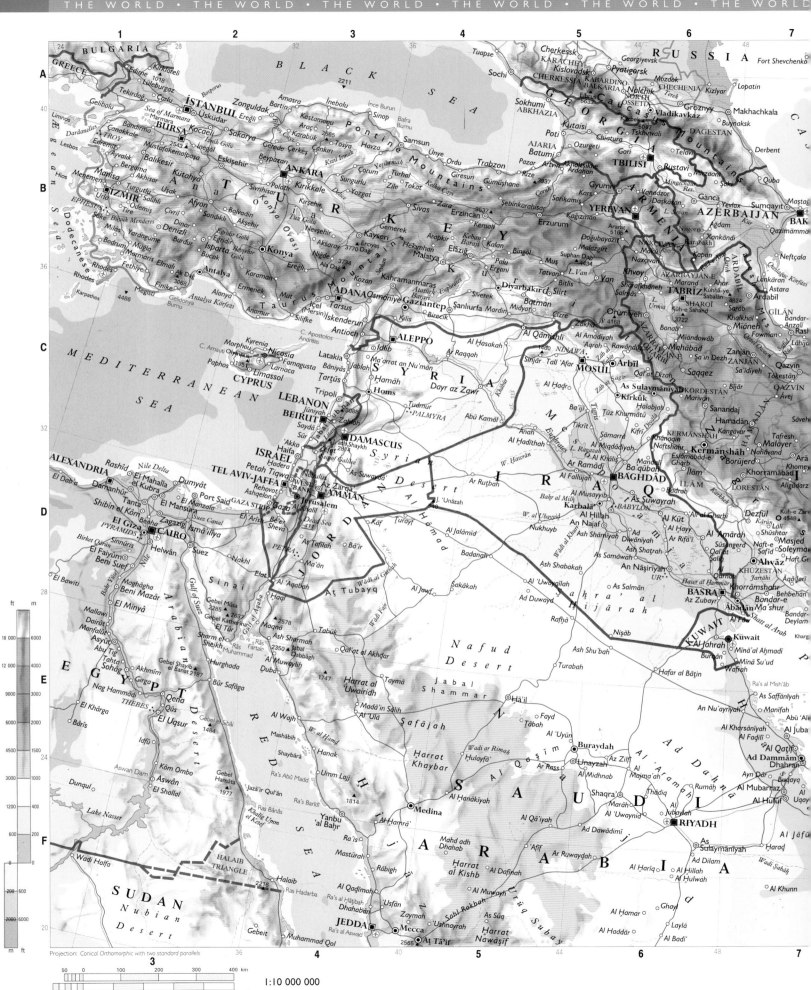

Projection: Conical Orthomorphic with two standard parallels

1:10 000 000

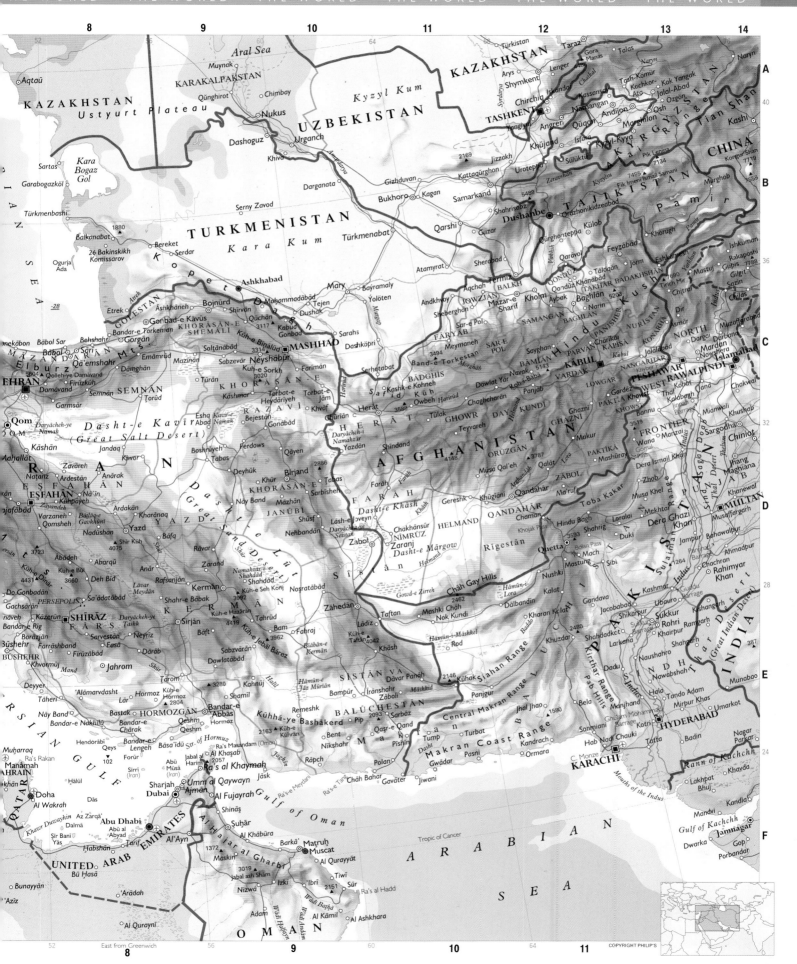

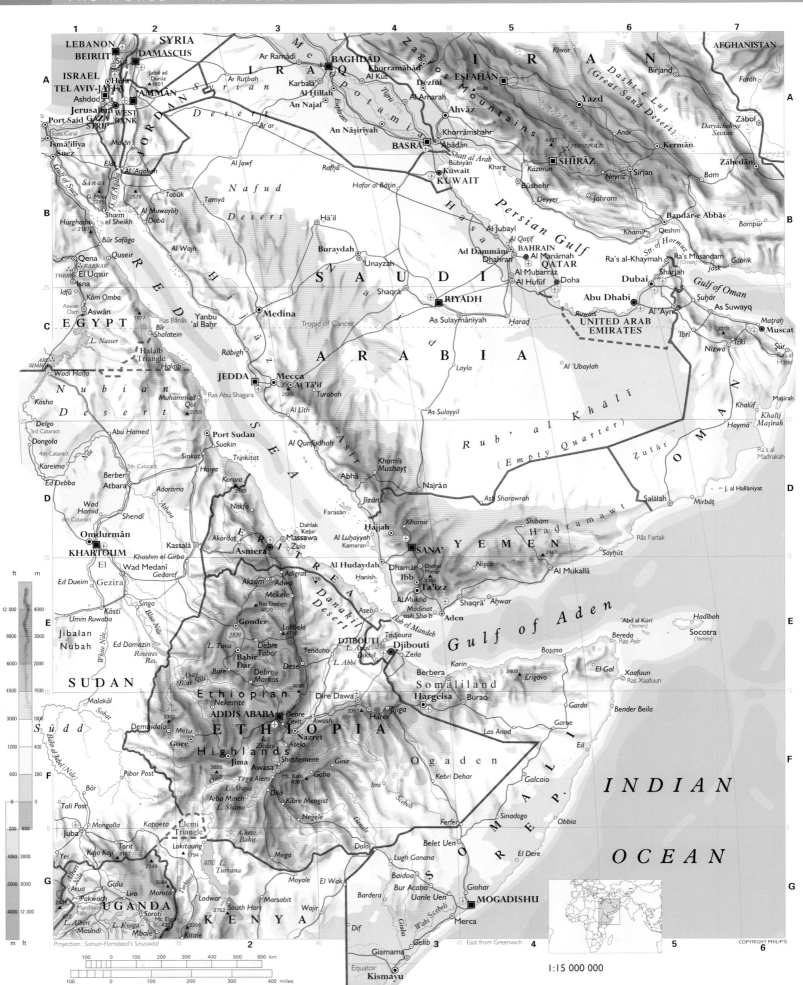

Projection : Sanson-Flamsteed's Sinusoidal

East from Greenwich

1:15 000 000

COPYRIGHT PHILIP'S

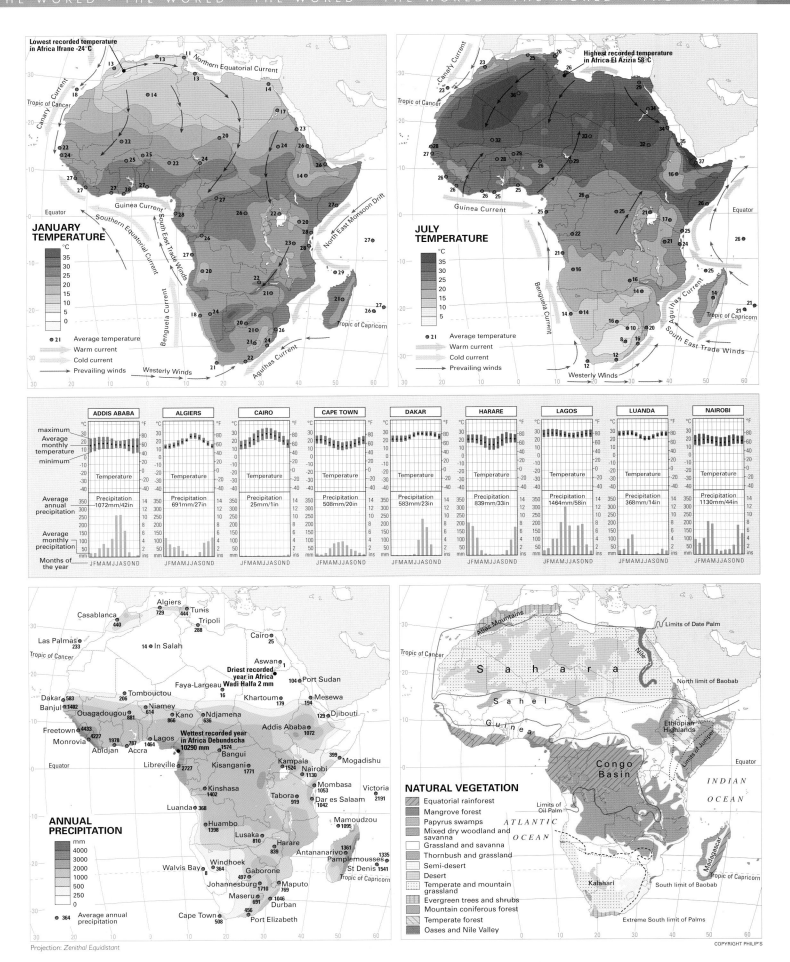

JANUARY TEMPERATURE

Lowest recorded temperature in Africa Ifrane -24°C

Northern Equatorial Current
Canary Current
Tropic of Cancer
Guinea Current
Southern Equatorial Current
South East Trade Winds
Benguela Current
North East Monsoon Drift
Equator
Tropic of Capricorn
Agulhas Current
Westerly Winds

°C
35
30
25
20
15
10
5
0

21 Average temperature
Warm current
Cold current
Prevailing winds

JULY TEMPERATURE

Highest recorded temperature in Africa El Azizia 58°C

Canary Current
Tropic of Cancer
Guinea Current
Benguela Current
Agulhas Current
South East Trade Winds
Equator
Tropic of Capricorn
Westerly Winds

°C
35
30
25
20
15
10
5

21 Average temperature
Warm current
Cold current
Prevailing winds

Climate graphs

ADDIS ABABA	ALGIERS	CAIRO	CAPE TOWN	DAKAR	HARARE	LAGOS	LUANDA	NAIROBI

maximum
Average monthly temperature
minimum
Temperature
Average annual precipitation
Average monthly precipitation
Months of the year

Precipitation 1072mm/42in (ADDIS ABABA)
Precipitation 691mm/27in (ALGIERS)
Precipitation 25mm/1in (CAIRO)
Precipitation 508mm/20in (CAPE TOWN)
Precipitation 583mm/23in (DAKAR)
Precipitation 839mm/33in (HARARE)
Precipitation 1464mm/58in (LAGOS)
Precipitation 368mm/14in (LUANDA)
Precipitation 1130mm/44in (NAIROBI)

JFMAMJJASOND

ANNUAL PRECIPITATION

Algiers 729
Tunis 444
Tripoli 288
Casablanca 440
Las Palmas 233
Cairo 25
Tropic of Cancer
In Salah 14
Aswan 1
Driest recorded year in Africa Wadi Halfa 2 mm
Faya-Largeau 16
Port Sudan 104
Tombouctou 206
Dakar 583
Banjul 1402
Niamey 614
Khartoum 179
Mesewa 194
Ouagadougou 881
Kano 866
Ndjamena 636
Djibouti 129
Freetown 4433
Monrovia 4227
1978
787
Lagos 1464
Abidjan Accra
Wettest recorded year in Africa Debundscha 10290 mm
Addis Ababa 1072
Bangui 1574
Libreville 2727
Kisangani 1771
Kampala 1524
Nairobi 1130
Mogadishu 399
Equator
Kinshasa 1402
Tabora 919
Mombasa 1053
Dar es Salaam 1042
Victoria 2191
Luanda 368
Mamoudzou 1095
Huambo 1398
Lusaka 810
Harare 839
Antananarivo 1361
Pamplemousses 1335
Walvis Bay 8
Windhoek 364
Gaborone 497
St Denis 1541
Tropic of Capricorn
Johannesburg 1710
Maputo 769
Maseru 691
Durban 1046
Cape Town 508
Port Elizabeth 456

mm
4000
3000
2000
1000
500
250
0

364 Average annual precipitation

NATURAL VEGETATION

Atlas Mountains
Limits of Date Palm
Sahara
Nile
North limit of Baobab
Sahel
Guinea
Ethiopian Highlands
Limits of Juniper
Congo Basin
Equator
Limits of Oil Palm
INDIAN OCEAN
ATLANTIC OCEAN
Kalahari
South limit of Baobab
Madagascar
Tropic of Capricorn
Extreme South limit of Palms

- Equatorial rainforest
- Mangrove forest
- Papyrus swamps
- Mixed dry woodland and savanna
- Grassland and savanna
- Thornbush and grassland
- Semi-desert
- Desert
- Temperate and mountain grassland
- Evergreen trees and shrubs
- Mountain coniferous forest
- Temperate forest
- Oases and Nile Valley

Projection: Zenithal Equidistant

COPYRIGHT PHILIP'S

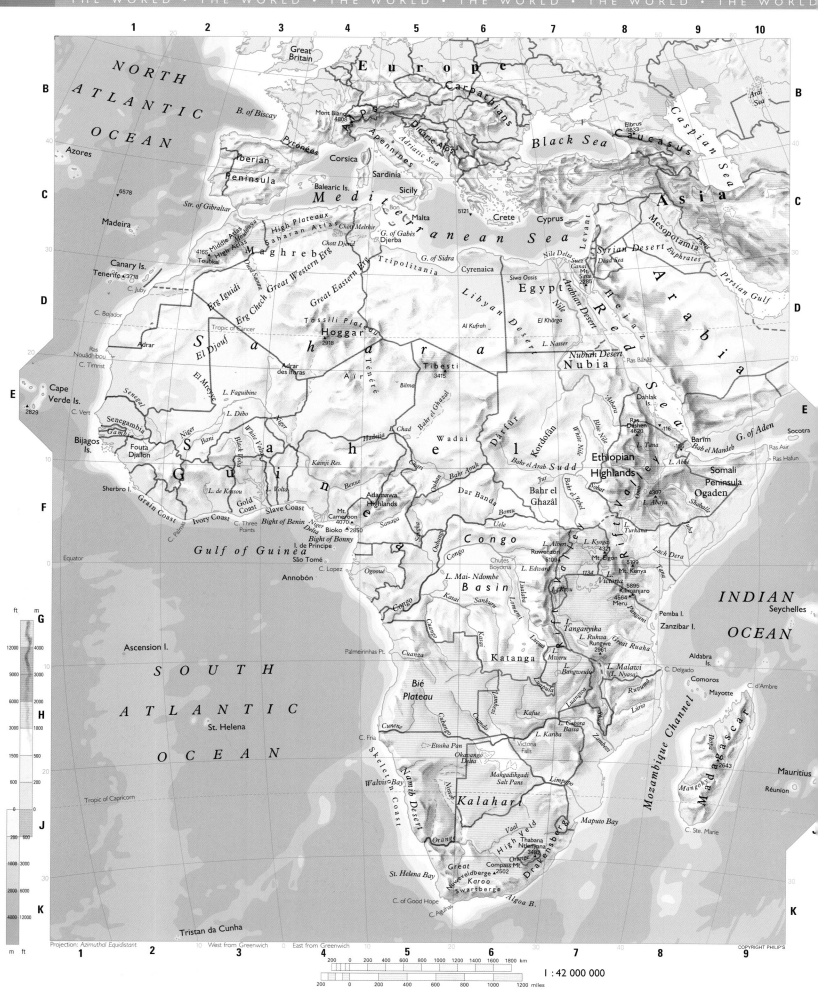

NORTH

ATLANTIC

OCEAN

Europe

Great Britain

Carpathians

B. of Biscay

Alps
Mont Blanc
4808

Apennines

Dinaric Alps

Adriatic Sea

Black Sea

Caucasus

Elbrus
5633

Aral Sea

Caspian Sea

Azores

Pyrénées

Iberian

Peninsula

Corsica

Sardinia

Balearic Is.

Sicily

Crete

Cyprus

Asia

Mesopotamia

6578

Madeira

Str. of Gibraltar

Mediterranean Sea

Malta

C. Bon

5121

Levant

Syrian Desert

Euphrates

Tigris

Persian Gulf

Middle Atlas
4165
High Atlas
Toubkal

High Plateaux

Saharan Atlas
Chott Melrhir

G. of Gabès

Djerba

Dead Sea

Canary Is.
Tenerife
3718

Maghreb

High Moulouya

Chott Djerid

Suez Canal
Mt. Sinai
2285

Hejaz

Arabia

C. Juby

Oued Saoura

Erg Iguidi

Erg Chech

Great Western Erg

Great Eastern Erg

Tripolitania

Cyrenaica

Libyan Desert

Egypt

Siwa Oasis

Nile Delta

Arabian Desert

Nile

Red Sea

C. Bojador

Tassili Plateau

Hoggar
2918

S a h a r a

Al Kufrah

El Khârga

L. Nasser

Ras Nouâdhibou

C. Timiris

Adrar

El Djouf

Adrar des Iforas

Aïr

Ténéré

Tibesti
3415

Bilma

Nubian Desert

Nubia

Ras Bânâs

El Mreyye

Senegal

L. Faguibine

Cape Verde Is.
2829

C. Vert

Senegambia

Gambia

Bijagos Is.

Bani

Niger

L. Débo

White Volta

Niger

Fouta Djallon

S a h e l

Hadejia

L. Chad

Bahr el Ghazâl

W a d a i

D a r f û r

Kordofan

White Nile

Blue Nile

Albara

Dahlak Is.

Ras Dashen
4620

116

Barim

Bab el Mandeb

G. of Aden

Socotra

Ras Asir

Sherbro I.

Grain Coast

Ivory Coast

C. Palmas

C. Three Points

Gold Coast

Slave Coast

Bight of Benin

L. de Kossou

L. Volta

G u i n e a

Kainji Res.

Benue

Niger Delta

Bioko
2850

Bight of Bonny

I. de Principe

São Tomé

Adamawa Highlands

Mt. Cameroon
4070

Sanaga

Chari

Bahr Aouk

Dar Banda

Bomu

Uele

Bahr el Arab

Jur

Bahr el Ghazâl

Bahr el Jebel

Sobat

S u d d

Ethiopian Highlands

L. Tana

L. Abbé

Turkana

Somali Peninsula

Ogaden

Shabelle

L. Abaya
4307

Juba

Gulf of Guinea

C. Lopez

Ogooué

Annobón

Congo

Oubangui

Sangha

Congo

C o n g o

Chutes Boyoma

Ruwenzori
5106

L. Albert
4321

Mt. Elgon

L. Kyoga

Mt. Kenya
5199

Great Ruaha

Pemba I.

Zanzibar I.

INDIAN

OCEAN

Seychelles

Equator

B a s i n

L. Mai-Ndombe

Kasai

Sankuru

Lomami

Lualaba

L. Edward

1134

L. Kivu

L. Victoria

Kilimanjaro
5895

Meru
4564

Pangani

Congo

Kasai

Cuango

Luilaka

Kwilu

Cuanza

L. Tanganyika

L. Rukwa

Rungwe
2961

Aldabra Is.

Comoros

C. d'Ambre

Mayotte

Palmeirinhas Pt.

Ascension I.

SOUTH

ATLANTIC

OCEAN

St. Helena

Bié Plateau

Cuanza

Katanga

L. Mweru

Luapula

L. Bangweulu

Luangwa

Kafue

Luena

L. Malawi
(L. Nyasa)

Ruvuma

Lúrio

C. Delgado

Madagascar

Palmeirinhas Pt.

Cunene

Cubango

Chando

Zambezi

L. Gabora Bassa

L. Kariba

Victoria Falls

Shire

Mangoky

2643

Mauritius

Réunion

Walvis Bay

Namib Desert

Skeleton Coast

C. Fria

Etosha Pan

Okavango Delta

Makgadikgadi Salt Pans

Limpopo

K a l a h a r i

Nossob

Maputo Bay

Mozambique Channel

Tropic of Capricorn

C. Ste. Marie

St. Helena Bay

Orange

Vaal

High Veld

Orange

Thabana Ntlenyana
3482

Drakensberg

Great Nuweveldberge

Karoo

Swartberge

Compass Mt.
2502

Algoa B.

C. of Good Hope

C. Agulhas

Tristan da Cunha

ft   m
12000   4000
9000   3000
6000   2000
3000   1000
1500   500
600   200
0   0
200   600
1000   3000
2000   6000
4000   12000
m   ft

200 0 200 400 600 800 1000 1200 1400 1600 1800 km
200 0 200 400 600 800 1000 1200 miles

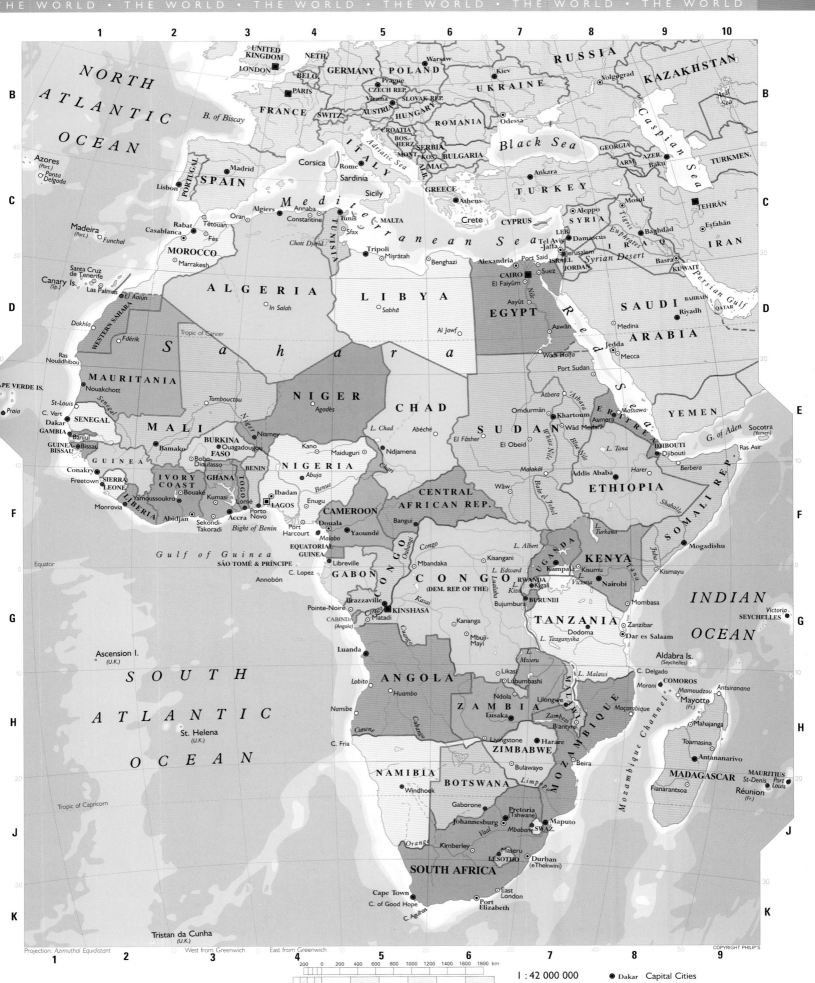

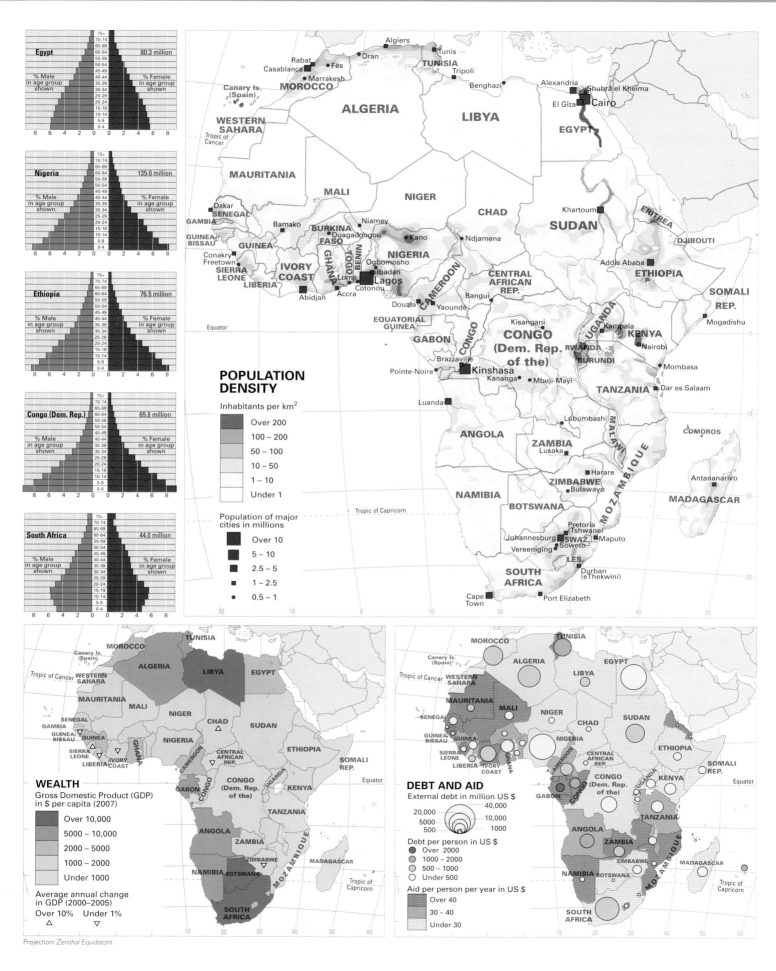

Egypt — 80.3 million
% Male in age group shown / % Female in age group shown

Nigeria — 135.0 million
% Male in age group shown / % Female in age group shown

Ethiopia — 76.5 million
% Male in age group shown / % Female in age group shown

Congo (Dem. Rep.) — 65.8 million
% Male in age group shown / % Female in age group shown

South Africa — 44.0 million
% Male in age group shown / % Female in age group shown

POPULATION DENSITY

Inhabitants per km²

- Over 200
- 100 – 200
- 50 – 100
- 10 – 50
- 1 – 10
- Under 1

Population of major cities in millions

- Over 10
- 5 – 10
- 2.5 – 5
- 1 – 2.5
- 0.5 – 1

WEALTH

Gross Domestic Product (GDP) in $ per capita (2007)

- Over 10,000
- 5000 – 10,000
- 2000 – 5000
- 1000 – 2000
- Under 1000

Average annual change in GDP (2000–2005)

Over 10% △   Under 1% ▽

DEBT AND AID

External debt in million US $

- 20,000
- 5000
- 500
- 40,000
- 10,000
- 1000

Debt per person in US $

- Over 2000
- 1000 – 2000
- 500 – 1000
- Under 500

Aid per person per year in US $

- Over 40
- 30 – 40
- Under 30

Projection: Zenithal Equidistant

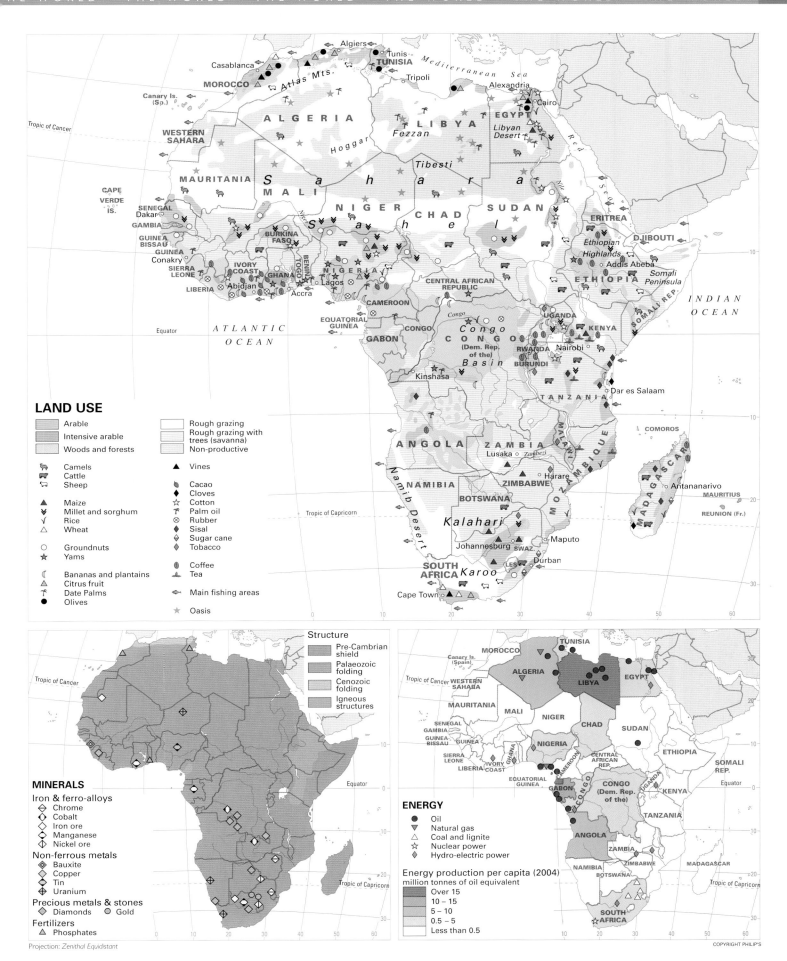

LAND USE

Arable
Intensive arable
Woods and forests
Rough grazing
Rough grazing with trees (savanna)
Non-productive

- 🐫 Camels
- 🐄 Cattle
- 🐑 Sheep

- ▲ Maize
- ⋎ Millet and sorghum
- ⋎ Rice
- △ Wheat

- ○ Groundnuts
- ★ Yams

- ☾ Bananas and plantains
- △ Citrus fruit
- ⵝ Date Palms
- ● Olives

- ▲ Vines

- ⬮ Cacao
- ◆ Cloves
- ☆ Cotton
- ⵝ Palm oil
- ⊗ Rubber
- ◆ Sisal
- ◇ Sugar cane
- ◇ Tobacco

- ◉ Coffee
- ⚘ Tea

- 🐟 Main fishing areas

- ★ Oasis

MINERALS

Iron & ferro-alloys
- ◈ Chrome
- ◇ Cobalt
- ◇ Iron ore
- ◇ Manganese
- ◈ Nickel ore

Non-ferrous metals
- ◆ Bauxite
- ◇ Copper
- ◆ Tin
- ⊕ Uranium

Precious metals & stones
- ◇ Diamonds
- ● Gold

Fertilizers
- △ Phosphates

Structure
- Pre-Cambrian shield
- Palaeozoic folding
- Cenozoic folding
- Igneous structures

ENERGY

- ● Oil
- ▽ Natural gas
- △ Coal and lignite
- ☆ Nuclear power
- ◇ Hydro-electric power

Energy production per capita (2004)
million tonnes of oil equivalent
- Over 15
- 10 – 15
- 5 – 10
- 0.5 – 5
- Less than 0.5

Projection: Zenithal Equidistant

COPYRIGHT PHILIP'S

1:15 000 000

COPYRIGHT PHILIPS

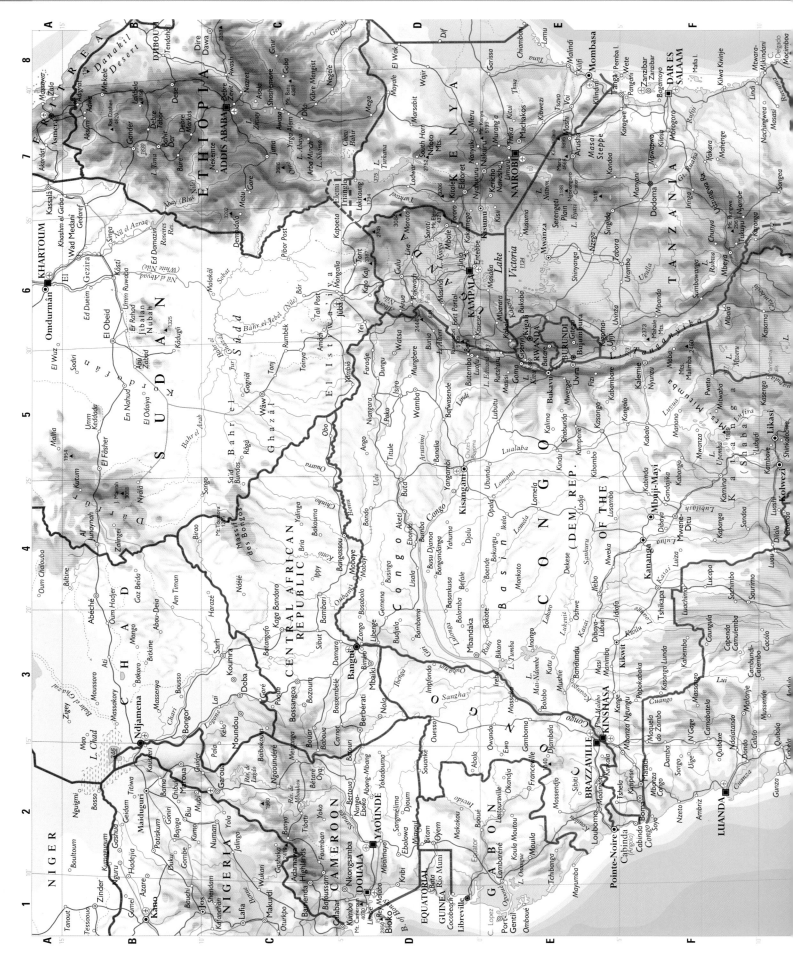

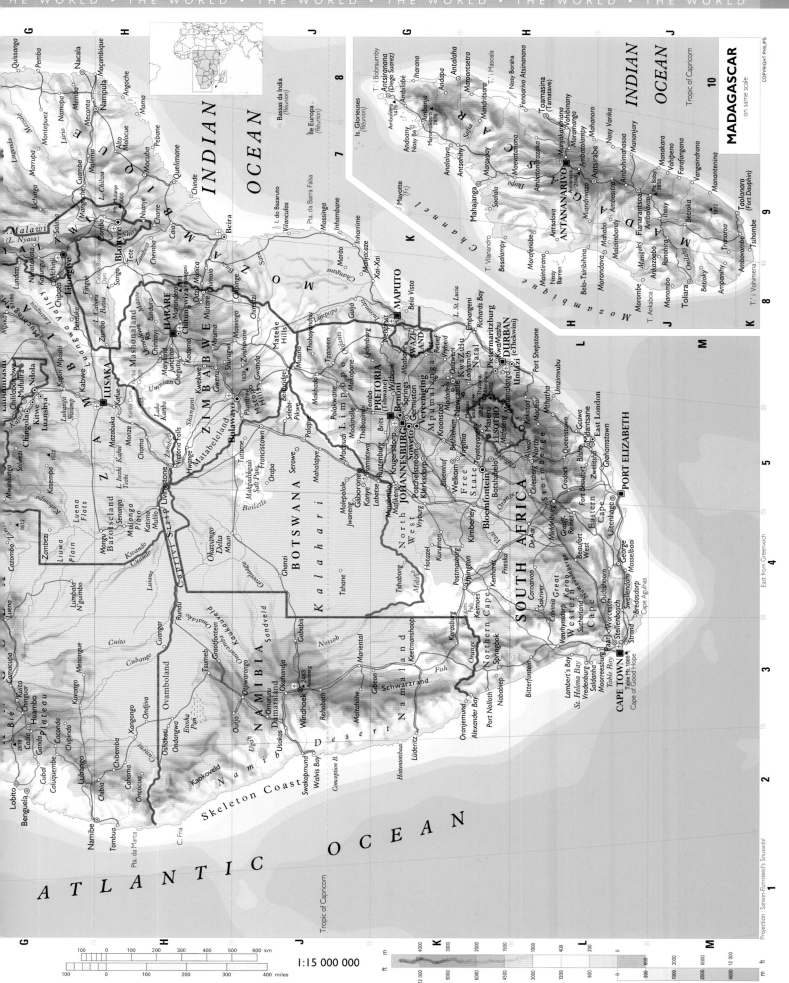

MADAGASCAR
on same scale

COPYRIGHT PHILIPS

INDIAN OCEAN

INDIAN OCEAN

ATLANTIC OCEAN

Tropic of Capricorn

Tropic of Capricorn

East from Greenwich

Projection : Sanson-Flamsteed's Sinusoidal

1:15 000 000

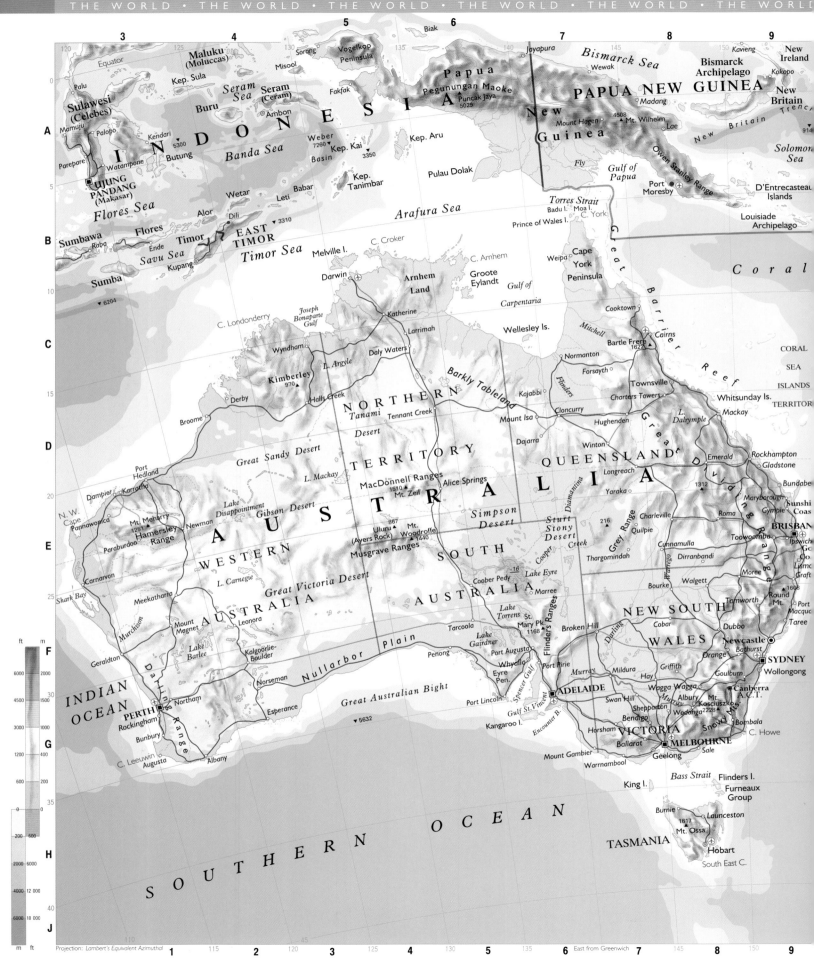

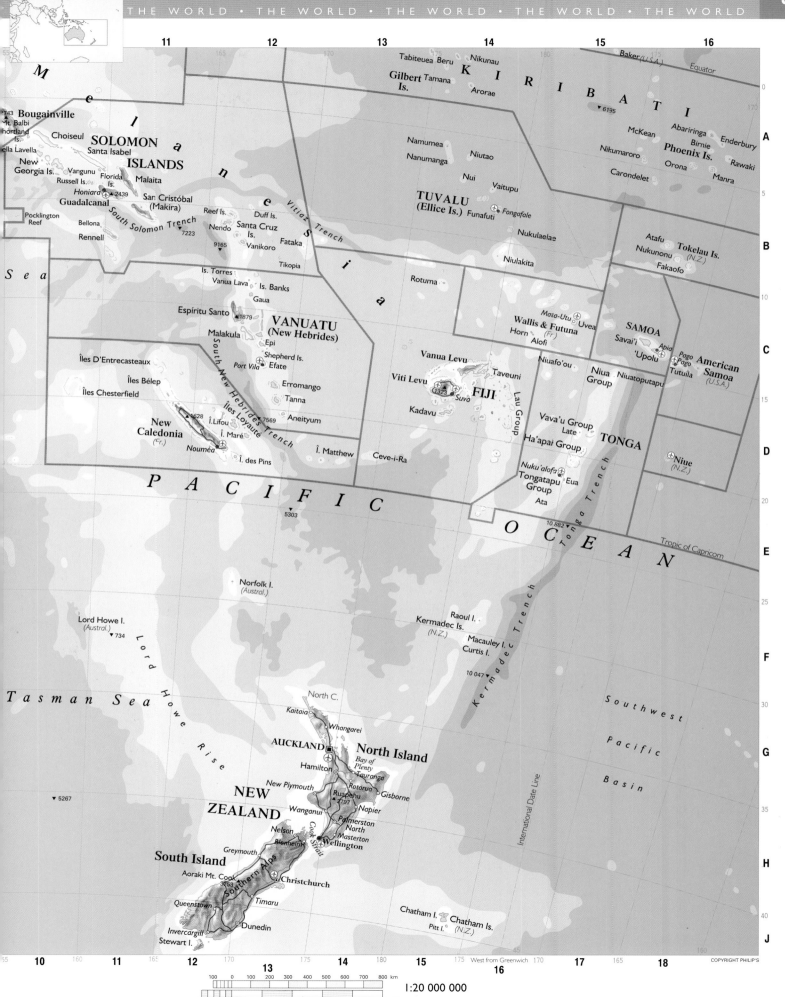

Melanesia

Bougainville
▲7743 Mt. Balbi
Shortland Is.
Choiseul
SOLOMON
Santa Isabel
ISLANDS
New Georgia Is.
Vangunu
Florida Is.
Malaita
Russell Is.
Honiara ▲2439
Guadalcanal
San Cristóbal (Makira)
Bellona
Pocklington Reef
Rennell

Sea

Reef Is.
Duff Is.
Nendo
Santa Cruz Is.
▼7223
Fataka
▼9165
Vanikoro
Tikopia

Is. Torres
Vanua Lava
Is. Banks
Gaua
Espíritu Santo ▲1879
VANUATU (New Hebrides)
Malakula
Epi
Shepherd Is.
Port Vila
Efate
Erromango
Tanna
Aneityum

Îles D'Entrecasteaux
Îles Bélep
Îles Chesterfield
New Caledonia (Fr.)
▲1628 Î. Lifou
Î. Maré
Nouméa
Î. des Pins

Tabiteuea Beru   Nikunau
Gilbert Tamana   Arorae
Is.
KIRIBATI
Baker (U.S.A.)
Equator
▼6195

Namumea
Nanumanga
Niutao
Nui
Vaitupu
TUVALU (Ellice Is.)
Fongafale
Funafuti
Nukulaelae
Niulakita

Rotuma

Mata-Utu
Uvea
Wallis & Futuna
Horn
Alofi (Fr.)
Vanua Levu
Taveuni
Viti Levu ▲1323
Suva
FIJI
Kadavu
Lau Group

Niuafo'ou
Niua Group
Niuatoputapu

Vava'u Group
Late
Ha'apai Group
TONGA

Nuku'alofa
Eua
Tongatapu Group
Ata

McKean
Abariringa
Birnie
Enderbury
Nikumaroro
Phoenix Is.
Orona
Rawaki
Carondelet
Manra

Atafu
Tokelau Is.
Nukunonu
(N.Z.)
Fakaofo

SAMOA
Savai'i
'Upolu
Apia
Pago
Pago
Tutuila
American Samoa (U.S.A.)

Niue (N.Z.)

PACIFIC
▼5303

OCEAN

Tropic of Capricorn

10 882 ▼
Tonga Trench

Norfolk I. (Austral.)

Lord Howe I. (Austral.)
▼734

Tasman Sea

Lord Howe Rise

South New Hebrides Trench
Îles Loyauté
Vitiaz Trench
South Solomon Trench

M e l a n e s i a

Raoul I.
Kermadec Is. (N.Z.)
Macauley I.
Curtis I.
10 047 ▼

Kermadec Trench

Southwest
Pacific
Basin

International Date Line

North C.
Kaitaia
Whangarei
AUCKLAND
Hamilton
Bay of Plenty
Tauranga
North Island
New Plymouth
Rotorua
Gisborne
Ruapehu ▲2797
Wanganui
Napier
NEW
ZEALAND
Palmerston North
Masterton
Nelson
Cook Strait
Wellington
Greymouth
Blenheim
South Island
Aoraki Mt. Cook
▲3753
Christchurch
Southern Alps
Queenstown
Timaru
Invercargill
Dunedin
Stewart I.

Chatham I.
Chatham Is.
Pitt I. (N.Z.)

▼5267

West from Greenwich

COPYRIGHT PHILIP'S

100 0 100 200 300 400 500 600 700 800 km
100 0 100 200 300 400 500 miles
1:20 000 000

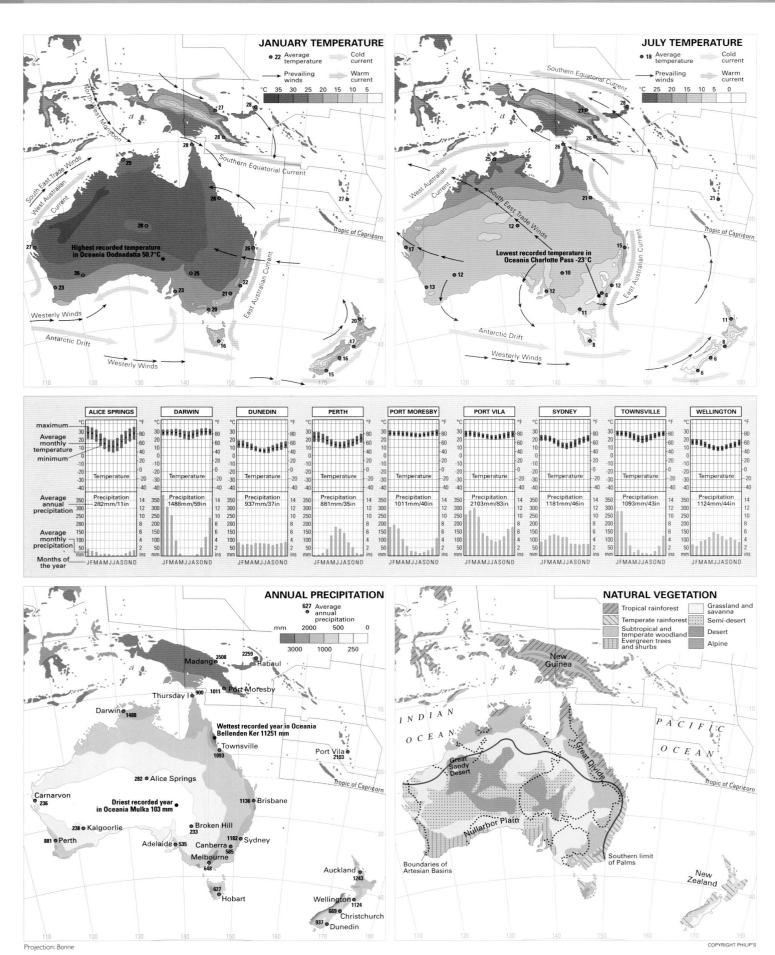

JANUARY TEMPERATURE

- 22 Average temperature
- Prevailing winds
- Cold current
- Warm current

°C 35 30 25 20 15 10 5

Highest recorded temperature in Oceania Oodnadatta 50.7°C

JULY TEMPERATURE

- 18 Average temperature
- Prevailing winds
- Cold current
- Warm current

°C 25 20 15 10 5 0

Lowest recorded temperature in Oceania Charlotte Pass -23°C

Climate graphs

ALICE SPRINGS · DARWIN · DUNEDIN · PERTH · PORT MORESBY · PORT VILA · SYDNEY · TOWNSVILLE · WELLINGTON

maximum
Average monthly temperature
minimum
Temperature
Average annual precipitation
Average monthly precipitation
Months of the year: J F M A M J J A S O N D

- Alice Springs: Precipitation 282mm/11in
- Darwin: Precipitation 1488mm/59in
- Dunedin: Precipitation 937mm/37in
- Perth: Precipitation 881mm/35in
- Port Moresby: Precipitation 1011mm/40in
- Port Vila: Precipitation 2103mm/83in
- Sydney: Precipitation 1181mm/46in
- Townsville: Precipitation 1093mm/43in
- Wellington: Precipitation 1124mm/44in

ANNUAL PRECIPITATION

- 627 Average annual precipitation

mm 3000 2000 1000 500 250 0

- Madang 3508
- Rabaul 2259
- Thursday I. 900
- Port Moresby 1011
- Darwin 1488
- Townsville 1093
- Port Vila 2103
- Alice Springs 282
- Carnarvon 236
- Brisbane 1136
- Kalgoorlie 238
- Broken Hill 233
- Perth 881
- Sydney 1182
- Adelaide 535
- Canberra 585
- Melbourne 648
- Hobart 627
- Auckland 1243
- Wellington 1124
- Christchurch 669
- Dunedin 937

Wettest recorded year in Oceania Bellenden Ker 11251 mm

Driest recorded year in Oceania Mulka 103 mm

NATURAL VEGETATION

- Tropical rainforest
- Temperate rainforest
- Subtropical and temperate woodland
- Evergreen trees and shurbs
- Grassland and savanna
- Semi-desert
- Desert
- Alpine

INDIAN OCEAN

PACIFIC OCEAN

New Guinea

Great Sandy Desert

Great Divide

Nullarbor Plain

Southern limit of Palms

Boundaries of Artesian Basins

New Zealand

Tropic of Capricorn

Projection: Bonne

COPYRIGHT PHILIP'S

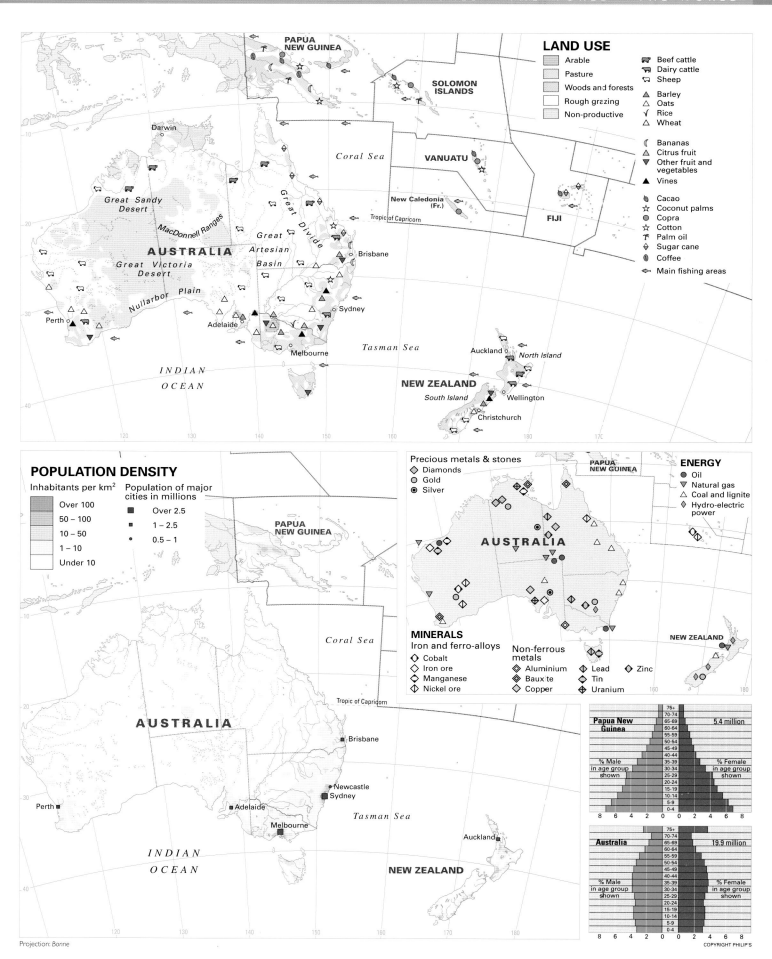

LAND USE

Arable		Beef cattle	
Pasture		Dairy cattle	
Woods and forests		Sheep	
Rough grazing		Barley	
Non-productive		Oats	

- Rice
- Wheat

- Bananas
- Citrus fruit
- Other fruit and vegetables
- Vines

- Cacao
- Coconut palms
- Copra
- Cotton
- Palm oil
- Sugar cane
- Coffee

- Main fishing areas

POPULATION DENSITY

Inhabitants per km²

- Over 100
- 50 – 100
- 10 – 50
- 1 – 10
- Under 10

Population of major cities in millions

- Over 2.5
- 1 – 2.5
- 0.5 – 1

Precious metals & stones

- Diamonds
- Gold
- Silver

ENERGY

- Oil
- Natural gas
- Coal and lignite
- Hydro-electric power

MINERALS

Iron and ferro-alloys

- Cobalt
- Iron ore
- Manganese
- Nickel ore

Non-ferrous metals

- Aluminium
- Bauxite
- Copper
- Lead
- Tin
- Uranium
- Zinc

Papua New Guinea — 5.4 million

	% Male in age group shown	75+ 70-74 65-69 60-64 55-59 50-54 45-49 40-44 35-39 30-34 25-29 20-24 15-19 10-14 5-9 0-4	% Female in age group shown

8 6 4 2 0 0 2 4 6 8

Australia — 19.9 million

	% Male in age group shown	75+ 70-74 65-69 60-64 55-59 50-54 45-49 40-44 35-39 30-34 25-29 20-24 15-19 10-14 5-9 0-4	% Female in age group shown

8 6 4 2 0 0 2 4 6 8

Projection: Bonne

COPYRIGHT PHILIP'S

RUSSIA

Yekaterinburg
MOSCOW
Volga
Novosibirsk
Tomsk
Ob
Lena
Irkutsk
L. Baikal
Chita
Astana
Semey
Alma Ata
KAZAKHSTAN
L. Balkhash
Aral Sea
Tashkent
KYRGYZSTAN
TAJIKISTAN
Ürümqi
Altai
MONGOLIA
Ulan Bator
Changchun
SHENYANG
Harbin
Blagoveshchensk
Amur
Khabarovsk
Okhotsk
Sea of Okhotsk
Sakhalin
Kamchatka
Petropavlovsk-Kamchatskiy
Komandorskiye Islands (Russia)
Near Is. (U.S.A.)
Andreanof (U.S.A.)
Bering Sea
Aleutia
7822
Aleutian Trench

Kabul
Srinagar
AFGHANISTAN
PAKISTAN
Lahore
DELHI
Kanpur
Himalaya
Mt. Everest 8850
NEPAL
TIBET
Kunlun Shan
CHINA
Lanzhou
Xi'an
Lhasa
CHONGQING
Yangtse
Changsha
WUHAN
Nanjing
Hwang Ho
BEIJING
TIANJIN
Taiyuan
Dalian
Qingdao
SHANGHAI
HANGZHOU
East China Sea
NORTH KOREA
SOUTH KOREA
SEOUL
Vladivostok
Hakodate
Sapporo
Sea of Japan
La Pérouse Str.
Kuril Is. (Russia)
Kuril-Kamchatka Trench
10,542
Emperor Seamount Chain

Sendai
Nagoya
Kyōto
Osaka
TOKYŌ
Yokohama
JAPAN
Fuji-San 3776
Shikoku
Kyūshū
Kitakyūshū
Yellow Sea
10,554
Japan Trench
Japan Trench

Hawaii
Midway Is. (U.S.A.)
Lisianski I. (U.S.A.)

INDIA
KOLKATA (Calcutta)
DHAKA
BANGLADESH
Mandalay
BURMA
Ganges
Brahmaputra
Irrawaddy
Salween
Hyderabad
Bay of Bengal
Rangoon
CHENNAI (Madras)
Andaman Is. (India)
THAILAND
BANGKOK
Mekong
CAMBODIA
Phnom Penh
VIETNAM
Ho Chi Minh City
G. of Thailand
South China Sea
Hainan
C. Engano
Luzon
Paracel Is.
Mindoro
Samar
MANILA
PHILIPPINES
Palawan
10,497
Sulu Sea
Mindanao
Davao
Mindanao Trench

Kunming
Fuzhou
Taipei
GUANGZHOU
HONG KONG
TAIWAN
Ryukyu Is. (Japan)
Hanoi
LAOS
Kazan-Rettō (Japan)
South Honshu Ridge
Ogasawara Gunto (Japan)
Minami-Tori-Shima (Japan)
Mid-Pacific Seamount
Wake I. (U.S.A.)
International Dateline
PA

NORTHERN MARIANAS (U.S.A.)
Saipan
GUAM (U.S.A.)
Challenger Deep 11,022
Mariana Trench
Yap
Caroline Is.
Micronesia
MARSHALL IS.
Enewetak Atoll
Bikini Atoll
Majuro
Jaluit I.
Truk
Pohnpei
Palikir
FEDERATED STATES OF MICRONESIA
PALAU
Melekeok
Butaritari
Tarawa
Gilbert Is.
Banaba
NAURU
Howland I. (U.S.)
Baker I. (U.S.)
Phoenix Is.
Abariringa
Enderbury
O
KI

SRI LANKA
Colombo
Nicobar Is. (India)
MALAYSIA
Celebes Sea
BRUNEI
SABAH
Kuala Lumpur
SINGAPORE
Sumatra
Borneo
SARAWAK
PEN. MALAYSIA
INDONESIA
Sulawesi
Buru
Seram
Halmahera
Moluccas
Banda Sea
7440
EAST TIMOR
Timor
Flores Sea
Flores
Bali
Sumbawa
Sumba
Java Sea
JAKARTA
Surabaya
Java
Ujung Pandang
Palembang
Selat Sunda
Sunda Islands
Java Trench

PAPUA NEW GUINEA
Admiralty Is.
Bismarck Arch.
New Ireland
Kokopo
New Britain
New Guinea
PAPUA
Puncak Jaya 5029
Lae
Port Moresby
Torres Strait
C. York
Louisiade Arch.
SOLOMON IS.
Bougainville
Honiara
Guadalcanal
Santa Cruz Is.
9165
Melanesia
TUVALU
Fongafale
Rotuma
Îs. Wallis & Futuna (Fr.)
SAMOA
Apia
Tokelau Is. (N.Z.)

INDIAN OCEAN

Cocos Is. (Austral.)
Christmas I. (Austral.)
C. Arnhem
Darwin
Gulf of Carpentaria
Broome
North West C.
Geraldton
Perth
AUSTRALIA
Alice Springs
L. Eyre
Mount Isa
Cairns
Townsville
Great Dividing Ra.
Rockhampton
Brisbane
Coral Sea
Espíritu Santo
VANUATU
Port Vila
Îs. Chesterfield
7570
NEW CALEDONIA (Fr.)
Nouméa
Îs. Loyauté
Vanua Levu
Viti Levu
Suva
FIJI
Nuku'alofa
TONGA
10,822
Tonga Trench
Lord Howe Rise

Albany
Great Australian Bight
Adelaide
Murray
Darling
Canberra
Sydney
Melbourne
Bass Str.
Tasmania
Hobart
Mt. Kosciuszko 2228
Norfolk I. (Austral.)
Lord Howe I. (Austral.)
Tasman Sea
NEW ZEALAND
Auckland
Cook Strait
Wellington
Christchurch
Chatham (N.Z.)
Aoraki Mt. Cook 3753
Dunedin
Invercargill
Bounty Is. (N.Z.)
Antipodes Is. (N.Z.)
Kermadec Is. (N.Z.)
Kermadec Trench 10,047

Mid-Indian Ridge
Nouvelle Amsterdam (Fr.)
I. St. Paul (Fr.)
Is. Crozet (Fr.)
Kerguelen (Fr.)
Heard I. (Austral.)
SOUTHERN OCEAN
Macquarie Is. (Austral.)
Auckland Is. (N.Z.)
Campbell I. (N.Z.)

ft	m
12 000	4000
9000	3000
6000	2000
3000	1000
1500	500
600	200
0	0
600	200
3000	1000
6000	2000
12 000	4000
18 000	6000
24 000	8000

m ft

ALASKA
(U.S.A.)
Anchorage
Bristol Bay
Is. (U.S.A.)
Gulf of Alaska
Juneau
5959
Prince of Wales I.
(U.S.A.) Prince Rupert
Queen Charlotte Is.
(Canada)
CANADA
NORTH
Edmonton
L. Winnipeg
Newfoundland
Calgary
Regina
Winnipeg
St. Lawrence
Vancouver
Vancouver I.
Victoria
L. Superior
Québec
St. John's
Seattle
L. Michigan
L. Huron
Montréal
Ottawa
Portland
Boise
Snake
Missouri
Minneapolis
Toronto
Detroit
L. Ontario
Buffalo
Boston
C. Mendocino
Salt Lake
City
Denver
CHICAGO
Pittsburgh
L. Erie
NEW YORK
PHILADELPHIA
Sacramento
Kansas City
St. Louis
Cincinnati
Baltimore
Washington D.C.
ATLANTIC
SAN FRANCISCO
4418
UNITED STATES
Appalachian Mts.
6741
Oklahoma City
Memphis
Atlanta
C. Hatteras
LOS ANGELES
Phoenix
Dallas
Bermuda
(U.K.)
San Diego
Colorado
Houston
Jacksonville
Ciudad
Juárez
San Antonio
New
Orleans
Sargasso Sea
Guadalupe
(Mex.)
Baja California
Gulf of Mexico
Miami
BAHAMAS
OCEAN
Tropic of Cancer
Monterrey
Havana
West Indies
C. San Lucas
Gulfo de California
CUBA
Florida Str.
Honolulu
C. San Lucas
Guadalajara
MEXICO
Mérida
JAMAICA
HAITI
8605
DOMINICAN REP.
O'ahu
HAWAI'I
4205
Puebla
7680
Leeward
Is.
Hawai'i
Is. de Revillagigedo
(Mex.)
Acapulco
BELIZE
Canal de Yucatán
Kingston
PUERTO
RICO
(U.S.A.)
CIFIC
5610
GUATEMALA
HONDURAS
Caribbean Sea
BARBADOS
North West Christmas I. Ridge
Guatemala
San Salvador
EL SALVADOR
Managua
NICARAGUA
Barranquilla
Windward Is.
Maracaibo
Palmyra Is.
(U.S.A.)
I. Clipperton
(Fr.)
COSTA
RICA
Colón
Panamá
PANAMA
Caracas
Orinoco
VENEZUELA
Teraina
Tabuaeran
Kiritimati
OCEAN
I. del Coco
(Costa Rica)
Medellín
Bogotá
Jarvis I.
(U.S.A.)
Equator
I. de Malpelo
(Colombia)
Cali
COLOMBIA
Malden I.
Galápagos
(Ecuador)
Quito
ECUADOR
IBATI
Starbuck I.
Guayaquil
Iquitos
Amazonas
Tongareva
Îs. Marquises
C. Paliñas
BRAZIL
Pukapuka
Manihiki
Vostok I.
Caroline I.
(Millennium I.)
Flint I.
Trujillo
Suwarrow Is.
Îs. de la
Société
6369
PERU
AMER.
SAMOA
(U.S.A.)
Îs. Tuamotu
LIMA
Cuzco
Nevada Ancohuma
6550
Papeete
Tahiti
Arequipa
L. Titicaca
La Paz
Niue
(N.Z.)
Cook Is.
(N.Z.)
FRENCH POLYNESIA
6866
Peru-
Arica
BOLIVIA
Rarotonga
Îs. Tubuaï
Mururoa
Tropic of Capricorn
Iquique
Chile
Antofagasta
PARAGUAY
Henderson I.
8050
Trench
Asunción
Pitcairn I.
(U.K.)
Sala-y-Gómez
(Chile)
San Félix
(Chile)
San Ambrosio
(Chile)
San Miguel
de Tucumán
Rapa
I. de Pascua
(Chile)
Pôrto
Alegre
Arch. de
Juan Fernández
(Chile)
Córdoba
Aconcagua
6962
Valparaíso
Rosario
URUGUAY
Montevideo
SANTIAGO
BUENOS
AIRES
Río de la Plata
Concepción
ARGENTINA
SOUTH
Chile Rise
ATLANTIC
Pacific-Antarctic Ridge
OCEAN
6212
Punta Arenas
Falkland Is.
(U.K.)
Est. de Magallanes
South Georgia
(U.K.)
Tierra del Fuego
C. de Hornos

Equatorial Scale 1:54 000 000

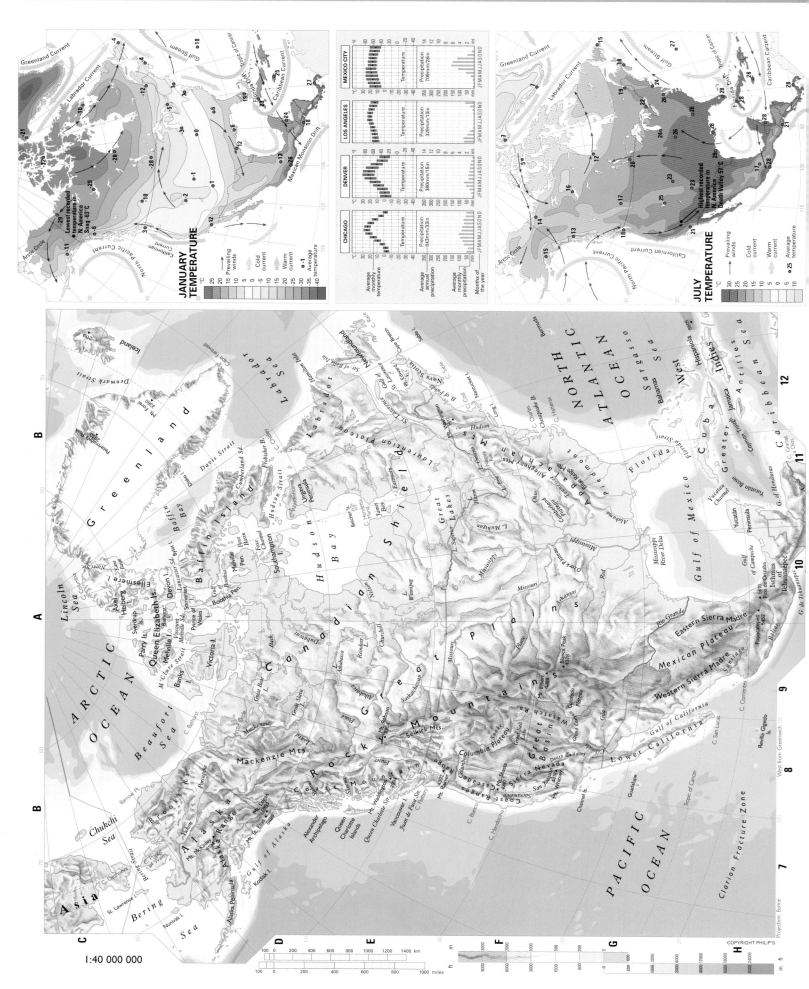

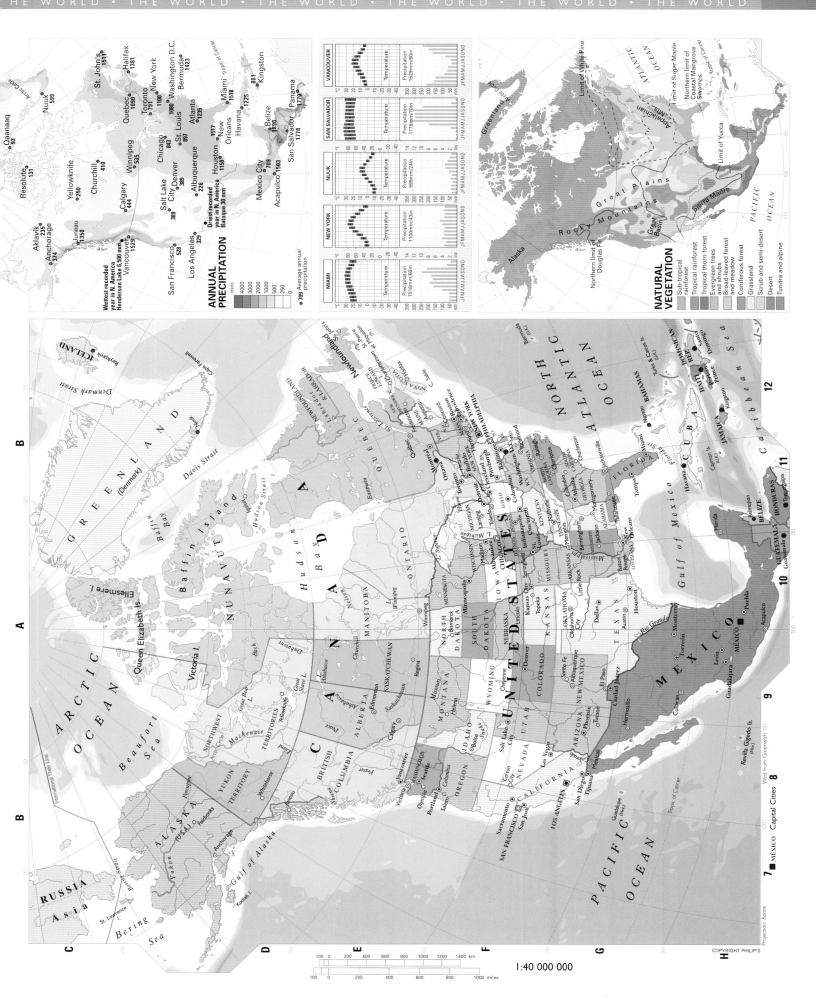

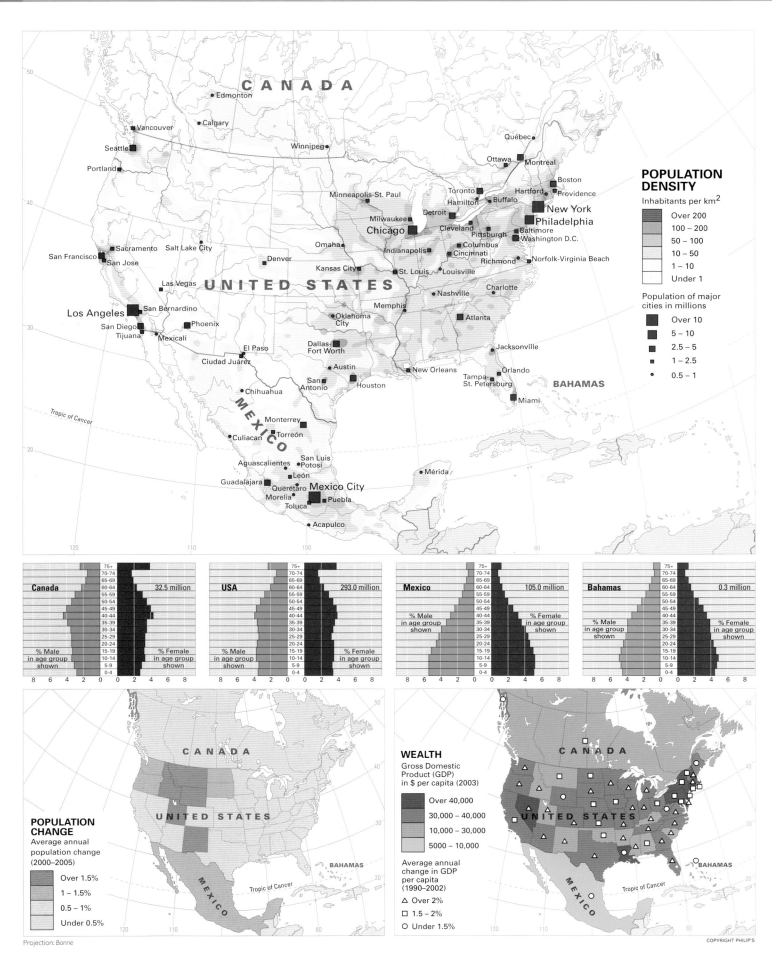

POPULATION DENSITY

Inhabitants per km²

- Over 200
- 100 – 200
- 50 – 100
- 10 – 50
- 1 – 10
- Under 1

Population of major cities in millions

- Over 10
- 5 – 10
- 2.5 – 5
- 1 – 2.5
- 0.5 – 1

Canada — 32.5 million

USA — 293.0 million

Mexico — 105.0 million

Bahamas — 0.3 million

% Male in age group shown / % Female in age group shown

POPULATION CHANGE

Average annual population change (2000–2005)

- Over 1.5%
- 1 – 1.5%
- 0.5 – 1%
- Under 0.5%

WEALTH

Gross Domestic Product (GDP) in $ per capita (2003)

- Over 40,000
- 30,000 – 40,000
- 10,000 – 30,000
- 5000 – 10,000

Average annual change in GDP per capita (1990–2002)

- △ Over 2%
- ▢ 1.5 – 2%
- ○ Under 1.5%

Projection: *Bonne*

COPYRIGHT PHILIP'S

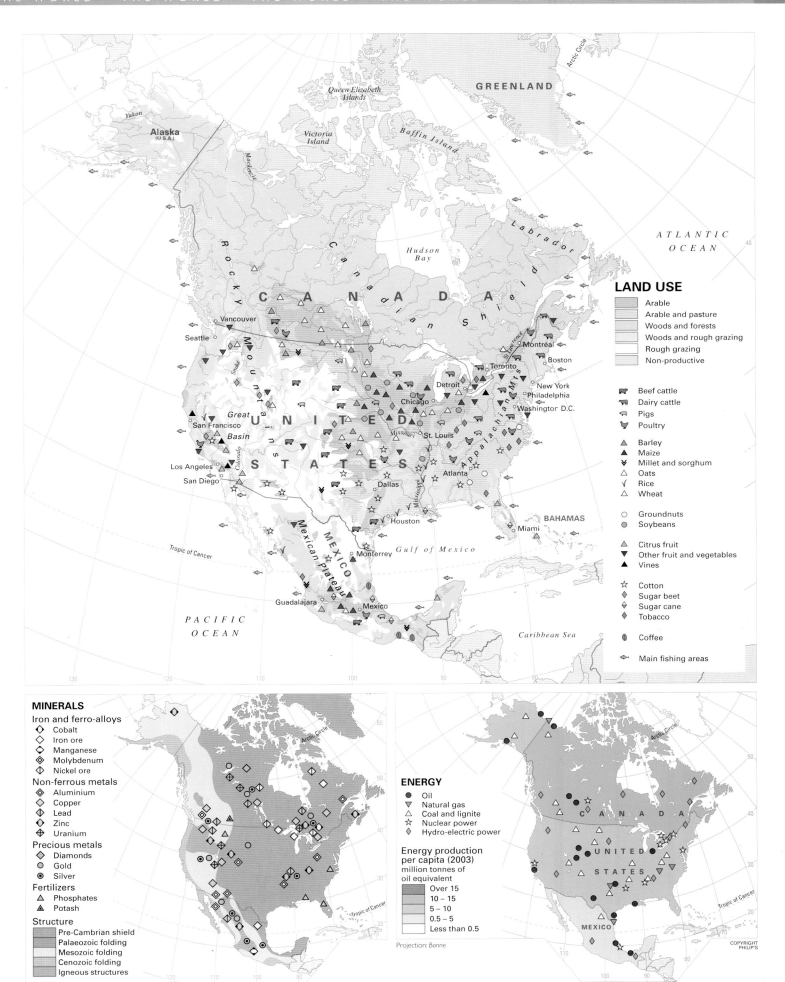

GREENLAND

Queen Elizabeth
Islands

Yukon
Alaska
(U.S.A.)

Victoria
Island

Baffin Island

Mackenzie

ATLANTIC
OCEAN

R o c k y

C A N A D A

Hudson
Bay

Labrador

C a n a d i a n   S h i e l d

Vancouver

Seattle

M o u n t a i n s

St. Lawrence

Montréal

Boston

Snake

Toronto

Detroit

New York

Philadelphia

Washington D.C.

Great
Basin

U N I T E D

San Francisco

Chicago

Appalachian Mts

Missouri

St. Louis

Colorado

S T A T E S

Los Angeles

San Diego

Atlanta

Dallas

Mississippi

BAHAMAS

Houston

Miami

M E X I C O

Monterrey

Gulf of Mexico

Tropic of Cancer

Mexican Plateau

Caribbean Sea

Guadalajara

Mexico

PACIFIC
OCEAN

LAND USE

Arable
Arable and pasture
Woods and forests
Woods and rough grazing
Rough grazing
Non-productive

Beef cattle
Dairy cattle
Pigs
Poultry

△ Barley
▲ Maize
⋎ Millet and sorghum
△ Oats
√ Rice
△ Wheat

○ Groundnuts
◉ Soybeans

△ Citrus fruit
▼ Other fruit and vegetables
▲ Vines

☆ Cotton
◇ Sugar beet
◇ Sugar cane
◆ Tobacco

◉ Coffee

⬳ Main fishing areas

MINERALS

Iron and ferro-alloys
◇ Cobalt
◇ Iron ore
◇ Manganese
◈ Molybdenum
◇ Nickel ore

Non-ferrous metals
◇ Aluminium
◇ Copper
◇ Lead
◇ Zinc
⊕ Uranium

Precious metals
◇ Diamonds
○ Gold
◉ Silver

Fertilizers
△ Phosphates
▲ Potash

Structure
Pre-Cambrian shield
Palaeozoic folding
Mesozoic folding
Cenozoic folding
Igneous structures

Arctic Circle

ENERGY

● Oil
▽ Natural gas
△ Coal and lignite
☆ Nuclear power
◇ Hydro-electric power

Energy production
per capita (2003)
million tonnes of
oil equivalent
Over 15
10 – 15
5 – 10
0.5 – 5
Less than 0.5

C A N A D A

U N I T E D

S T A T E S

MEXICO

Tropic of Cancer

Projection: Bonne

COPYRIGHT
PHILIP'S

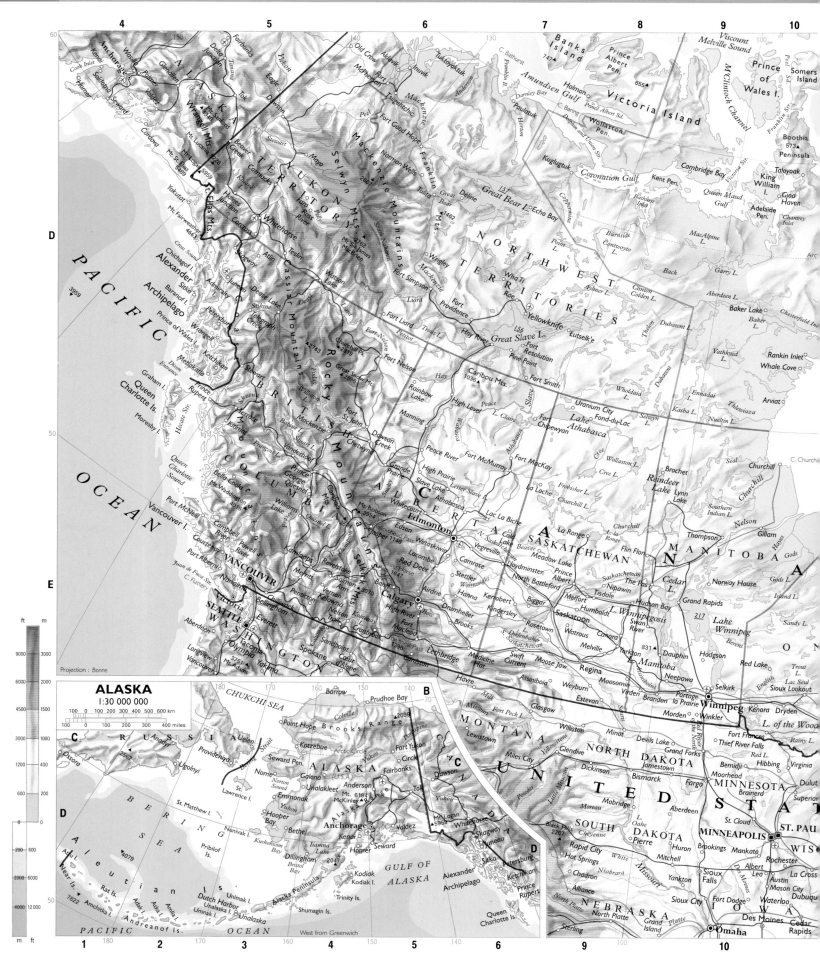

ALASKA
1:30 000 000

Projection : Bonne

West from Greenwich

NORTHERN CANADA
Continuation northwards on same scale as main map

West from Greenwich

1:15 000 000

COPYRIGHT PHILIP'S

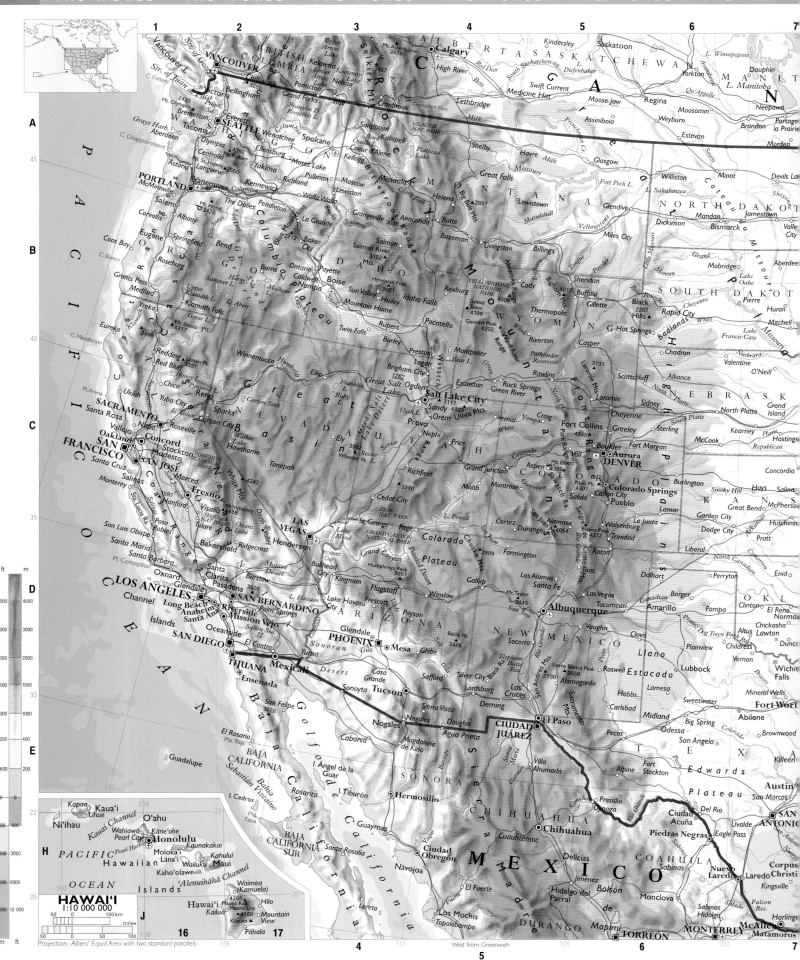

Projection: Albers' Equal Area with two standard parallels

West from Greenwich

1:12 000 000

COPYRIGHT PHILIP'S

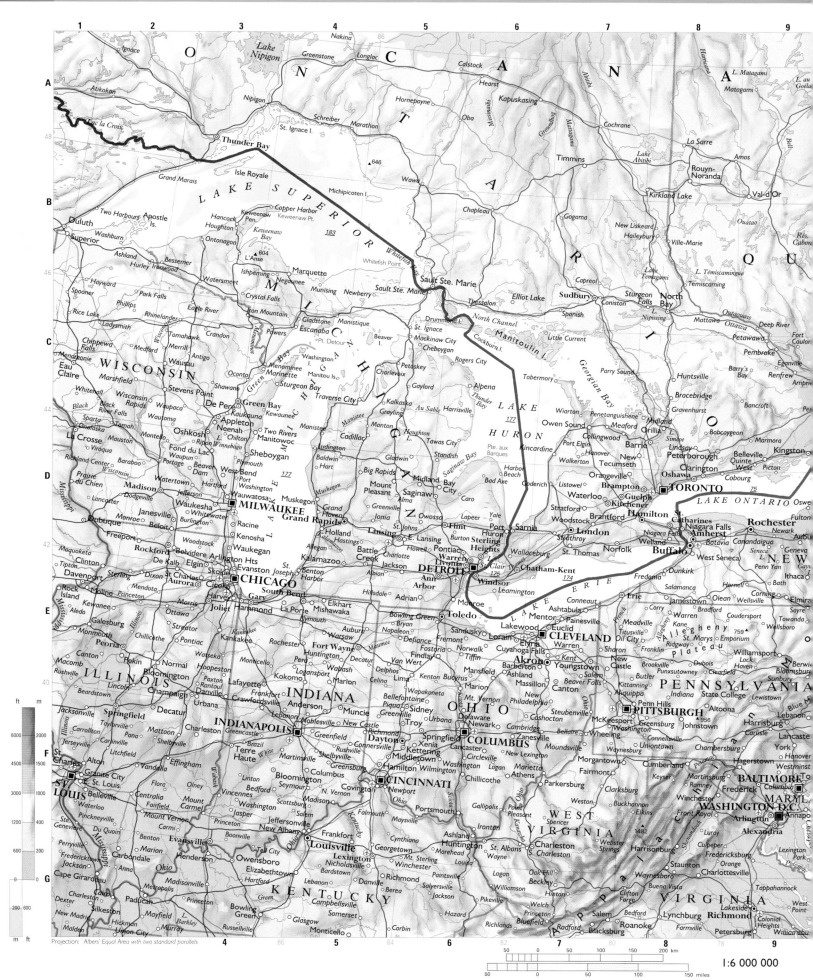

Projection: Albers' Equal Area with two standard parallels

1:6 000 000

UNITED STATES

San Diego, Tijuana, Ensenada, Mexicali, Yuma, Phoenix, Tucson, Casa Grande, Nogales, Douglas, Agua Prieta, Cananea, Deming, Las Cruces, El Paso, Ciudad Juárez, Roswell, Lubbock, Wichita Falls, Little Rock, Huntsville

Carlsbad, Pecos, Odessa, San Angelo, Abilene, Fort Worth, Dallas, Tyler, Shreveport, Monroe, Greenville, Birmingham, Tuscaloosa

Pta. Baja, San Felipe, I. Ángel de la Guarda, Sonoyta, Nacozari de García, Nuevo Casas Grandes, Villa Ahumada, Fort Stockton, Del Rio, San Antonio, Houston, Austin, Bryan, Waco, Brazos, Beaumont, Port Arthur, Lake Charles, Lafayette, Baton Rouge, Mobile, Pensacola, Natchez, Alexandria, Hattiesburg, Jackson, Meridian, Montgomery, Dothan

Bahía Sebastián Vizcaíno, Rosarito, Santa Rosalía, Pta. Falsa, Hermosillo, Caborca, Magdalena de Kino, Madera, Chihuahua, Cuauhtémoc, Ciudad Camargo, Jiménez, Hidalgo del Parral, Ojinaga, Piedras Negras, Eagle Pass, Nueva Rosita, Sabinas, Ciudad Acuña, Victoria, Corpus Christi, Padre I., Matagorda I., Mississippi River Delta, C. San Blas

Ciudad Obregón, Navojoa, Huatabampo, Guaymas, Empalme, El Fuerte, Sierra Madre, Gómez Palacio, San Pedro de las Colonias, Monclova, Sabinas Hidalgo, Nuevo Laredo, Laredo, McAllen, Reynosa, Brownsville, Matamoros

Loreto, Los Mochis, Guasave, Guamúchil, Tepehuanes, Durango, Concepción del Oro, Saltillo, Monterrey, Montemorelos, Linares, San Fernando, **GULF OF MEXICO**

B. de La Paz, La Paz, C. San Lázaro, Culiacán, El Salto, Sombrerete, Matehuala, Ciudad Victoria, Ciudad Mante

Cabo San Lucas, C. San Lucas, Mazatlán, Rosario, Escuinapa de Hidalgo, Jerez, Zacatecas, Fresnillo, Charcas, San Luis Potosí, Ciudad Madero, Tampico, Ciudad Valles, Tropic of Cancer

Islas Marías, Tuxpan, Acaponeta, Tepic, Rio Grande de Santiago, Aguascalientes, León, Guanajuato, Irapuato, Celaya, Querétaro, Pachuca, Tulancingo, Magozal, Tuxpan, Poza Rica, Papantla, C. Rojo

Is. de Revillagigedo (Mex.), Puerto Vallarta, C. Corrientes, Guadalajara, Ameca, L. de Chapala, Zamora, Morelia, Uruapan, Toluca, México, Cuernavaca, Popocatépetl, Pico de Orizaba, Xalapa, Veracruz

Progreso, Mérida, Motul, Tizimín, Cancún, Ticul, Peto, Valladolid, Cozumel I., Cozumel, Campeche, **Yucatán**, Felipe Carrillo Puerto, Chetumal, C. Catoche, C. S. Antón

Nevado de Colima, Colima, Manzanillo, Tecomán, Lázaro Cárdenas, Balsas, Iguala, Puebla, Córdoba, Orizaba, San Andrés Tuxtla, Coatzacoalcos, Ciudad del Carmen, Laguna de Términos, Golfo de Campeche, Champotón, Escárcega

Chilpancingo, Chilapa, Tlapa, Oaxaca, Tlaxiaco, Minatitlán, Villahermosa, Palenque, Corozal, Ambergris Cay, Belize City, Turneffe Is., Belmopan, **BELIZE**

Acapulco, Ometepec, Istmo de Tehuantepec, Tuxtla Gutiérrez, San Cristóbal de las Casas, Juchitán de Zaragoza, Comitán, Dangriga, Puerto Barrios, Gulf of Honduras, Puerto Cortés, Tela, La Ceiba, Trujillo

Tehuantepec, Salina Cruz, Tonalá, G. de Tehuantepec, Huixtla, Tapachula, Quezaltenango, **GUATEMALA**, Cobán, Escuintla, Santa Ana, Sonsonate, Comayagua, **HONDURAS**, San Pedro Sula, Juticalpa, Tegucigalpa, Ocotal, Matagalpa

EL SALVADOR, SAN SALVADOR, San Vincente, San Miguel, La Unión, G. de Fonseca, Choluteca, Chinandega, León, **NICARAGUA**, MANAGUA, Masaya, Granada, Lago de Nicaragua, Rivas, Pen. de Nicoya, Puntarenas

PACIFIC OCEAN

JAMAICA
1:3 000 000

CARIBBEAN SEA

Montego Bay, Lucea, Negril, South Negril Pt., Falmouth, Runaway Bay, St. Ann's Bay, Wakefield, The Cockpit Country, Ocho Rios, Dry Harbour Mountains, Galina Point, Port Maria, Port Antonio, Cambridge, Mount Denham 985, Moneague, Annotto Bay

Savanna-la-Mar, Maggotty, Black River, Don Figuero Mts., Santa Cruz Mts., Mandeville, Linstead, Spanish Town, Portmore, Blue Mountains 2256, Blue Mt. Pk., John Crow Mts., Port Antonio, Morant Point

Great Pedro Bluff, May Pen, Alligator Pond, Kingston, Portland Bight, Portland Point, Morant Bay, Port Morant

JAMAICA

GUADELOUPE
(Fr.)

Pte. de la Grande Vigie, Port-Louis, Grande-Terre, Petit-Canal, Le Moule, La Désirade, Pointe Allègre, Ste-Rose, Pointe-à-Pitre, Le Gosier, Ste-Anne, Pointe des Châteaux, Pointe-Noire, Basse-Terre, Bouillante, Soufrière 1467, Capesterre-Belle-Eau, St-Louis, Trois-Rivières, Basse-Terre, Îles des Saintes, Marie-Galante, Capesterre-de-Marie-Galante, Grand Bourg 204, Pte. des Basses, Îles de la Petite Terre

---

MARTINIQUE
(Fr.)

Cap St-Martin, Le Prêcheur, St-Pierre, Basse-Pointe, Montagne Pelée 1397, Ste-Marie, Presqu'île de la Caravelle, La Trinité, Le Robert, Schoelcher, Fort-de-France, Le François, Le Lamentin, Rivière-Salée, Le St-Esprit, Rivière-Pilote, Le Marin, Ste-Anne, Pte. d'Enfer, St-Joseph

---

GUADELOUPE AND MARTINIQUE
1:2 000 000

Projection : Bonne

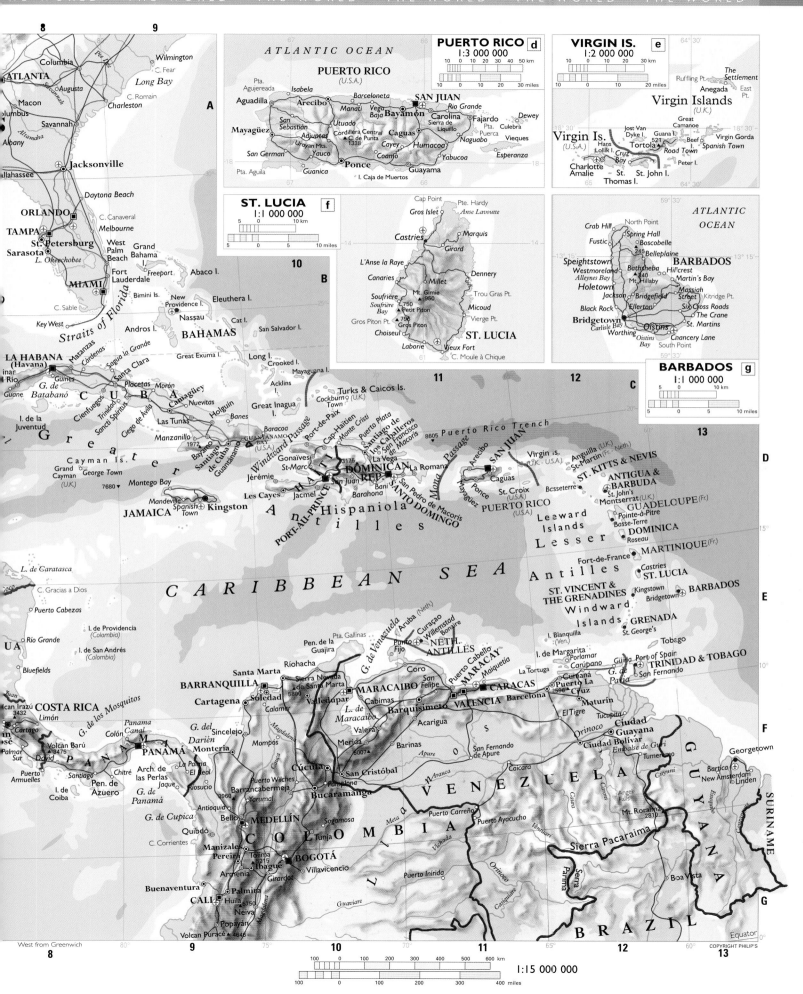

PUERTO RICO d
1:3 000 000

ATLANTIC OCEAN
PUERTO RICO
(U.S.A.)

Pta. Aguijereada
Isabela
Aguadilla
Arecibo
Manati
Vega Baja
Barceloneta
Rio Grande
SAN JUAN
Bayamón
Carolina
Mayagüez
San Sebastián
Adjuntas
Utuado
Cordillera Central
1338
C. de Punta
Caguas
Cayey
Humacoa
Fajardo
Pta. Puerca
Culebra
Vieques
Dewey
San German
Uroyan Mts.
Yauco
Coamo
Yabucoa
Ponce
Guayama
Esperanza
Naguabo
Pta. Aguila
Guanica
Guanica
I. Caja de Muertos

VIRGIN IS. e
1:2 000 000

Ruffling Pt.
Anegada
The Settlement
East Pt.
Virgin Islands
(U.K.)
Virgin Is.
(U.S.A.)
Jost Van Dyke I.
Guana I.
Great Camanoe
521
Tortola
Road Town
Beef
Spanish Town
Virgin Gorda
Hans Lollik I.
Cruz Bay
Charlotte Amalie
St. Thomas I.
St. John I.
Peter I.

ST. LUCIA f
1:1 000 000

Cap Point
Pte. Hardy
Gros Islet
Anse Lavoutte
Castries
Marquis
Girard
L'Anse la Raye
Canaries
Millet
Dennery
Soufrière
Mt. Gimie
950
Trou Gras Pt.
Soufrière Bay
Petit Piton
750
Micoud
796
Vierge Pt.
Gros Piton Pt.
Gros Piton
ST. LUCIA
Choiseul
Laborie
Vieux Fort
C. Moule à Chique

BARBADOS g
1:1 000 000

ATLANTIC OCEAN
Crab Hill
North Point
Spring Hall
Fustic
Boscobelle
Belleplaine
Speightstown
245
BARBADOS
Westmoreland
Bathsheba
340
Hil'crest
Alleynes Bay
Mt. Hillaby
Martin's Bay
Holetown
Jackson
Bridgefield
Messiah Street
Kitridge Pt.
Black Rock
Ellerton
Six Cross Roads
The Crane
Bridgetown
Oistins
St. Martins
Carlisle Bay
Worthing
Oistins Bay
South Point
Chancery Lane

ATLANTA
Columbia
Wilmington
Long Bay
Macon
Augusta
C. Fear
Columbus
Charleston
Albany
Savannah
C. Romain
Altamaha
Jacksonville
Tallahassee
ORLANDO
Daytona Beach
TAMPA
C. Canaveral
Melbourne
St. Petersburg
Sarasota
L. Okeechobee
West Palm Beach
Grand Bahama I.
MIAMI
Fort Lauderdale
Freeport
Abaco I.
C. Sable
Bimini Is.
New Providence I.
Key West
Nassau
Eleuthera I.
Straits of Florida
Andros I.
Cat I.
BAHAMAS
San Salvador I.
LA HABANA (Havana)
Matanzas
Cárdenas
Sagua la Grande
Santa Clara
Great Exuma I.
Pinar del Río
Güines
Placetas
Morón
Long I.
Crooked I.
Guane
G. de Batabanó
CUBA
Cienfuegos
Trinidad
Sancti Spíritus
Ciego de Avila
Camagüey
Nuevitas
Mayaguana I.
Acklins I.
I. de la Juventud
Greater
Manzanillo
Las Tunas
Holguín
Banes
Great Inagua I.
1972
Bayamo
Santiago de Cuba
Baracoa
Turks & Caicos Is.
Cockburn Town (U.K.)
Cayman Is.
Guantánamo
GUANTANAMO BAY (U.S.A.)
Cap-Haitien
Monte Cristi
Puerto Plata
Grand Cayman (U.K.)
George Town
Gonaïves
Port-de-Paix
Santiago de los Caballeros
8605
Puerto Rico Trench
7680
St-Marc
La Vega
San Francisco de Macoris
Montego Bay
Jérémie
HAITI
DOMINICAN REP.
La Romana
Mandeville
JAMAICA
Spanish Town
Kingston
PORT-AU-PRINCE
Jacmel
Les Cayes
San Juan
SANTO DOMINGO
Bani
San Pedro de Macoris
Barahona
Hispaniola
Mona Passage
Arecibo
SAN JUAN
Virgin Is. (U.K. - U.S.A.)
Anguilla (U.K.)
St-Martin (Fr.-Neth.)
Caguas
Mayagüez
Ponce
St. Croix (U.S.A.)
PUERTO RICO (U.S.A.)
St. KITTS & NEVIS
Basseterre
ANTIGUA & BARBUDA
St. John's
Montserrat (U.K.)
GUADELOUPE (Fr.)
Pointe-à-Pitre
Basse-Terre
Leeward Islands
DOMINICA
Roseau
Lesser
Antilles
MARTINIQUE (Fr.)
Fort-de-France
Castries
ST. LUCIA
CARIBBEAN SEA
Antilles
ST. VINCENT & THE GRENADINES
Kingstown
BARBADOS
Bridgetown
Windward
Islands
GRENADA
St. George's
L. de Caratasca
C. Gracias a Dios
Puerto Cabezas
I. de Providencia (Colombia)
I. Blanquilla (Ven.)
Tobago
Río Grande
I. de San Andrés (Colombia)
I. de Margarita
Port of Spain
Bluefields
Porlamar
TRINIDAD & TOBAGO
Pen. de la Guajira
Pta. Gallinas
Aruba (Neth.)
Curaçao
Bonaire
NETH. ANTILLES
Willemstad
Punto Fijo
La Tortuga
San Fernando
Güiria
G. de Paria
Santa Marta
Riohacha
Coro
Puerto Cabello
Cumaná
Carúpano
COSTA RICA
Cartagena
Soledad
BARRANQUILLA
Calamar
Sierra Nevada de Santa Marta
5800
MARACAIBO
San Felipe
MARACAY
Maiquetia
CARACAS
Barcelona
Maturín
G. de los Mosquitos
Valledupar
Cabimas
BARQUISIMETO
VALENCIA
Volcán Irazú
3432
Limón
Panama Canal
G. del Darién
Sincelejo
L. de Maracaibo
Acarigua
El Tigre
Tucupita
Ciudad Guayana
Colón
Montería
Valera
Barinas
PANAMÁ
Mompós
San Fernando de Apure
Orinoco
Ciudad Bolívar
Embalse de Guri
Georgetown
Volcán Barú
3475
Mérida
5007
Apure
David
Chitré
La Palma
Barrancabermeja
Cúcuta
Caicara
Tumeremo
Bartica
Puerto Armuelles
Santiago
El Real
San Cristóbal
Arauca
Angel Falls
New Amsterdam
Linden
Pen. de Azuero
Arch. de las Perlas
Yarumal
Pamplona
Puerto Carreño
Mt. Roraima
2810
I. de Coiba
G. de Panamá
Jaqué
Riosucio
Bucaramanga
Puerto Ayacucho
Sierra Pacaraima
Meta
SURINAME
3960
Antioquia
Sogamoso
VENEZUELA
G. de Cupica
Bello
MEDELLÍN
Tunja
Puerto Inírida
GUYANA
Quibdó
COLOMBIA
Vichada
Boa Vista
C. Corrientes
Manizales
Pereira
Tolima
5215
Villavicencio
Guaviare
Armenia
Ibagué
BOGOTÁ
Girardot
Buenaventura
Palmira
Huila
5750
BRAZIL
CALI
Neiva
Volcán Puracé
4646
Equator

1:15 000 000

Projection: Lambert's Azimuthal Equal Area

1:35 000 000

COPYRIGHT PHILIP'S

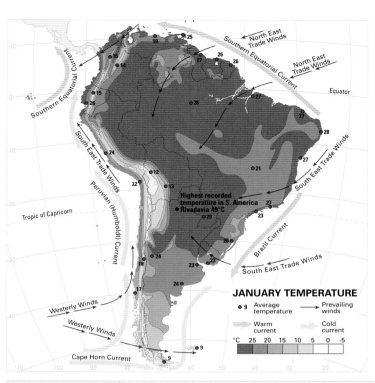

JANUARY TEMPERATURE

Highest recorded temperature in S. America Rivadavia 49°C

- 9 Average temperature
- → Prevailing winds
- Warm current
- Cold current

°C 25 20 15 10 5 0 -5

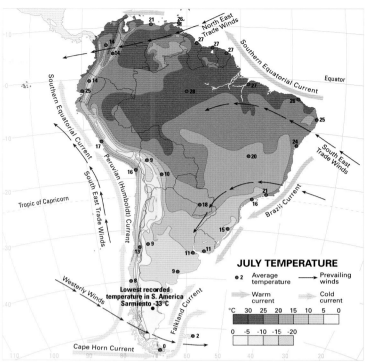

JULY TEMPERATURE

Lowest recorded temperature in S. America Sarmiento -33°C

- 2 Average temperature
- → Prevailing winds
- Warm current
- Cold current

°C 30 25 20 15 10 5 0
0 -5 -10 -15 -20

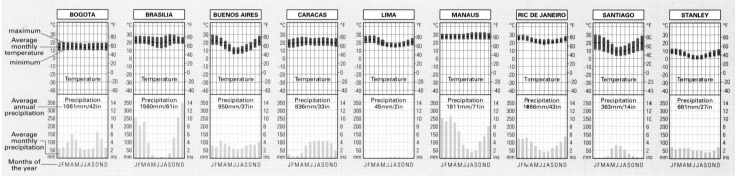

Climate graphs for: BOGOTA, BRASILIA, BUENOS AIRES, CARACAS, LIMA, MANAUS, RIO DE JANEIRO, SANTIAGO, STANLEY

City	Precipitation
Bogota	1061mm/42in
Brasilia	1560mm/61in
Buenos Aires	950mm/37in
Caracas	836mm/33in
Lima	45mm/2in
Manaus	1811mm/71in
Rio de Janeiro	1086mm/43in
Santiago	363mm/14in
Stanley	681mm/27in

maximum, Average monthly temperature, minimum

Average annual precipitation

Average monthly precipitation

Months of the year: JFMAMJJASOND

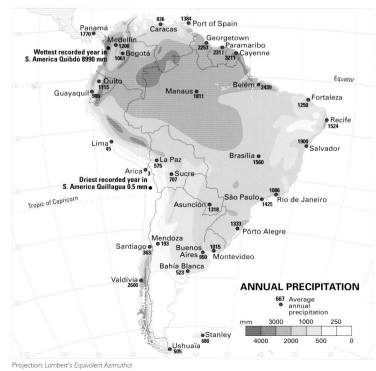

ANNUAL PRECIPITATION

Wettest recorded year in S. America Quibdó 8990 mm

Driest recorded year in S. America Quillagua 0.5 mm

- Panamá 1770
- Caracas 836
- Port of Spain 1384
- Medellín 1200
- Bogotá 1061
- Georgetown 2253
- Paramaribo 2311
- Cayenne 3211
- Quito 1115
- Guayaquil 986
- Manaus 1811
- Belém 2439
- Fortaleza 1250
- Recife 1524
- Lima 45
- La Paz 575
- Salvador 1900
- Brasília 1560
- Arica 3
- Sucre 707
- São Paulo 1086
- Rio de Janeiro 1425
- Asunción 1318
- Pôrto Alegre 1333
- Mendoza 193
- Santiago 363
- Buenos Aires 950
- Montevideo 1015
- Bahía Blanca 523
- Valdivia 2600
- Stanley 680
- Ushuaïa 505

667 Average annual precipitation

mm 3000 1000 250
4000 2000 500 0

NATURAL VEGETATION

- Guiana Highlands
- Amazon Basin
- Andes
- Atacama Desert
- Brazilian Highlands
- Pampas
- Patagonia
- PACIFIC OCEAN
- ATLANTIC OCEAN
- South limit of wild rubber
- South limit of Quebracho

Legend:
- Tropical rainforest
- Tropical thorn forest
- Temperate rainforest
- Evergreen trees and shrubs
- Grassland and savanna
- Semi-desert
- Desert
- Alpine and high plateau

Projection: Lambert's Equivalent Azimuthal

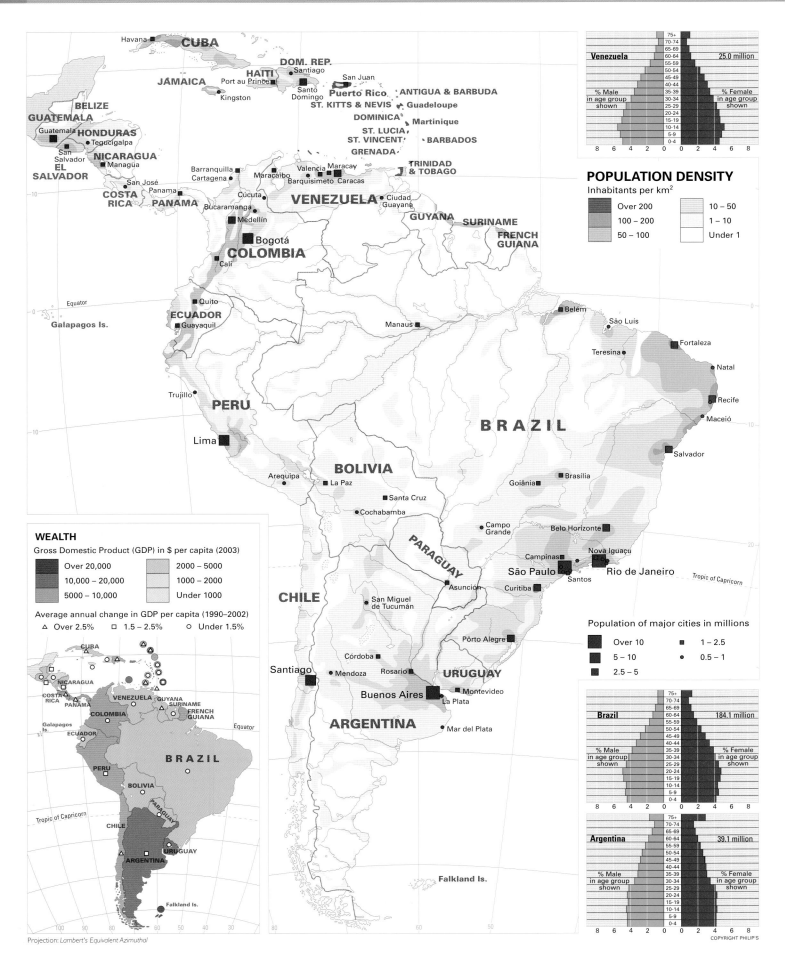

POPULATION DENSITY

Inhabitants per km²

Over 200	10 – 50
100 – 200	1 – 10
50 – 100	Under 1

WEALTH

Gross Domestic Product (GDP) in $ per capita (2003)

Over 20,000	2000 – 5000
10,000 – 20,000	1000 – 2000
5000 – 10,000	Under 1000

Average annual change in GDP per capita (1990–2002)

△ Over 2.5%   □ 1.5 – 2.5%   ○ Under 1.5%

Population of major cities in millions

■ Over 10		■ 1 – 2.5	
■ 5 – 10		• 0.5 – 1	
■ 2.5 – 5			

Venezuela — 25.0 million

Brazil — 184.1 million

Argentina — 39.1 million

Projection: Lambert's Equivalent Azimuthal

COPYRIGHT PHILIP'S

LAND USE

- Arable
- Intensive arable
- Pasture
- Woods and forests
- Rough grazing
- Non-productive
- Main fishing areas

- Beef cattle
- Dairy cattle
- Pigs
- Poultry
- Sheep

- Maize
- Millet and sorghum
- Rice
- Wheat

- Groundnuts
- Potatoes
- Soybeans

- Bananas
- Citrus fruit
- Other fruit and vegetables
- Vines

- Cacao
- Coconut palms
- Cotton
- Sugar cane
- Tobacco

- Coffee
- Tea

MINERALS

Iron and ferro-alloys
- Chrome
- Cobalt
- Iron ore
- Manganese
- Molybdenum
- Nickel ore

Non-ferrous metals
- Aluminium
- Bauxite
- Copper
- Lead
- Tin

Precious metals & stones
- Diamonds
- Gold
- Silver

Fertilizers
- Phosphates

Structure
- Pre-Cambrian shield
- Palaeozoic folding
- Mesozoic folding
- Cenozoic folding
- Igneous structures

ENERGY
- Oil
- Natural gas
- Coal and lignite
- Nuclear power
- Hydro-electric power

Energy production per capita (2003)
million tonnes of oil equivalent
- Over 15
- 10 – 15
- 5 – 10
- 0.5 – 5
- Less than 0.5

Projection: *Lambert's Equivalent Azimuthal*

COPYRIGHT PHILIP'S

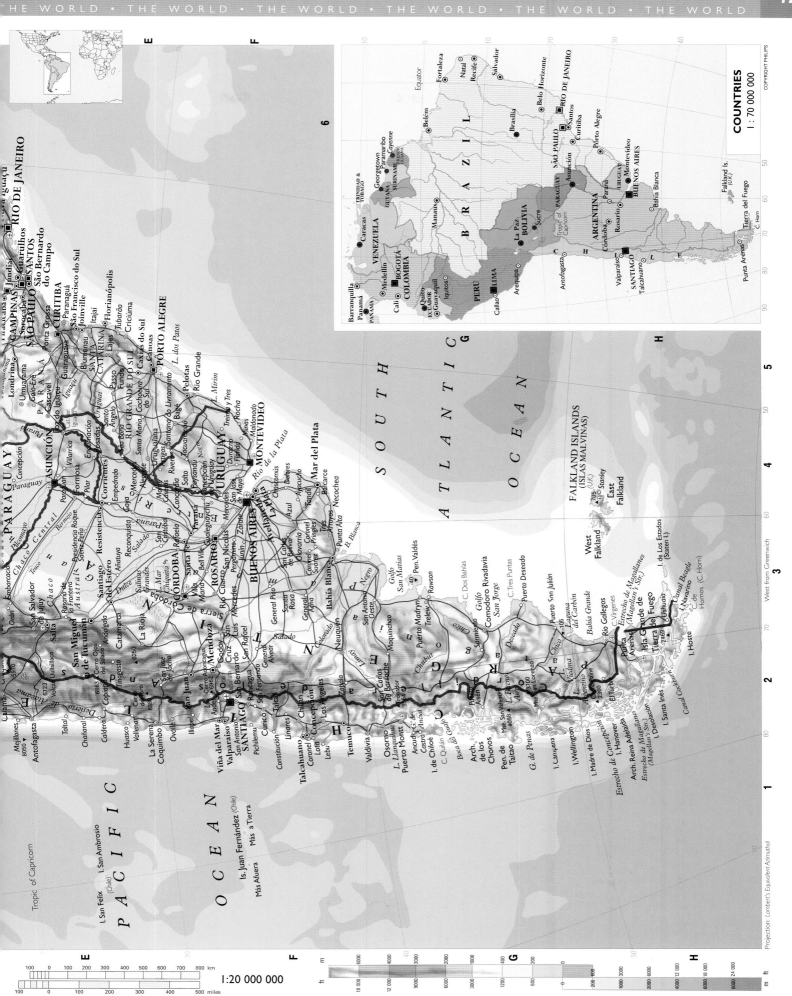

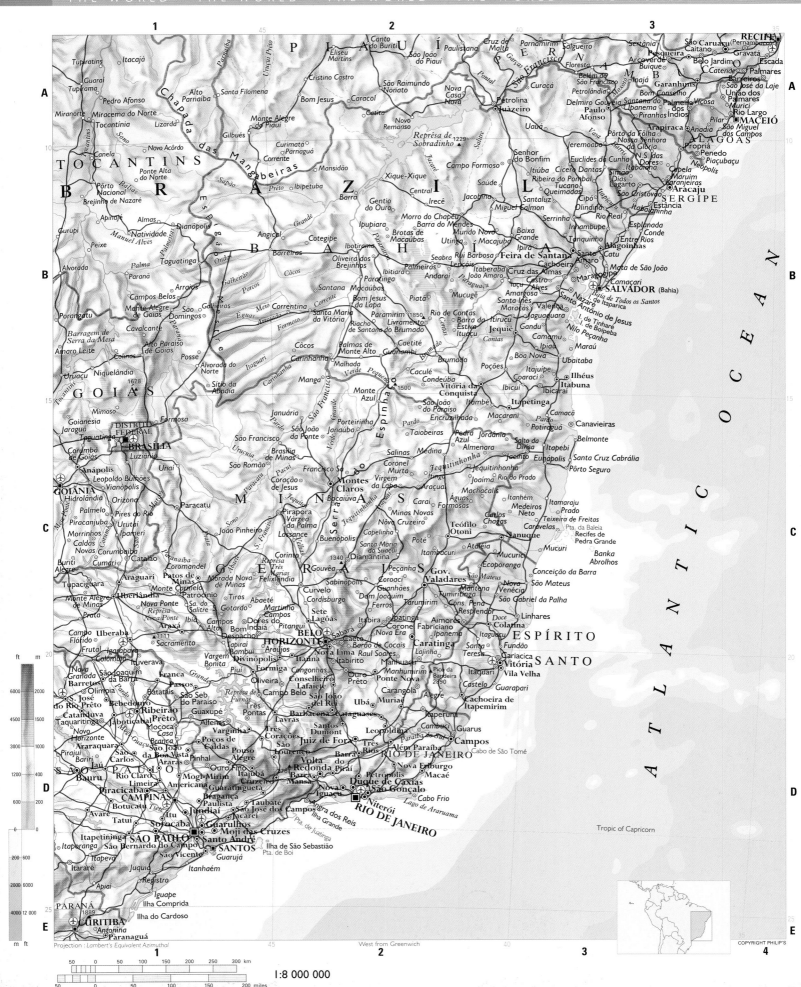

Projection : Lambert's Equivalent Azimuthal

West from Greenwich

COPYRIGHT PHILIP'S

1:8 000 000

50   100   150   200   250   300 km

50   100   150   200 miles

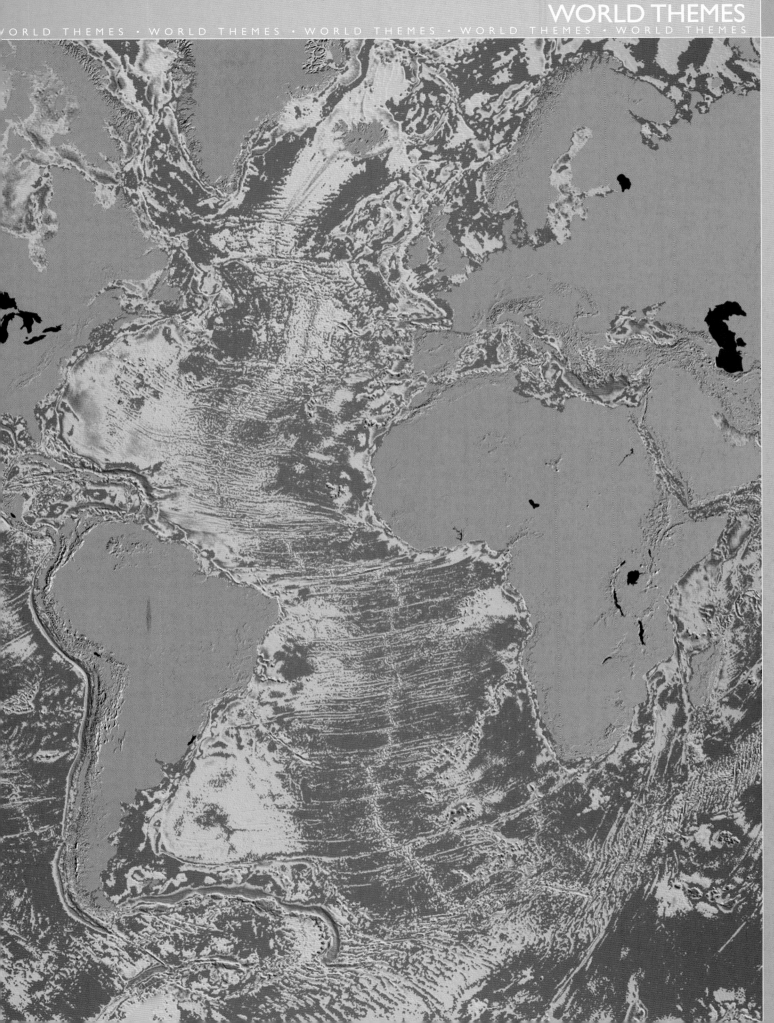

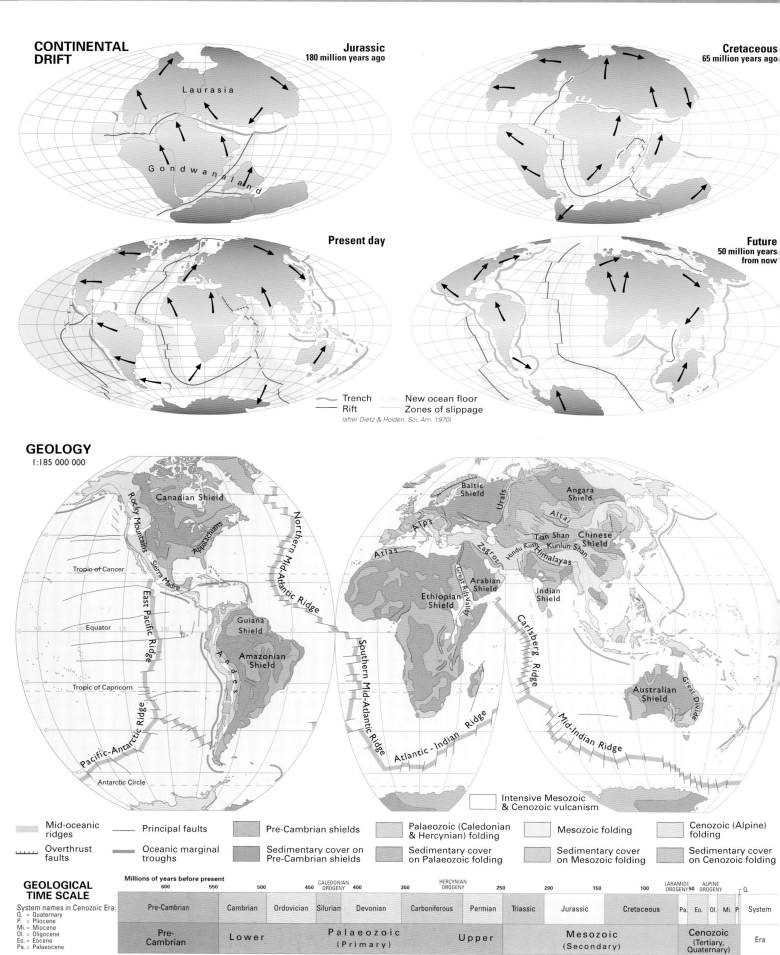

CONTINENTAL DRIFT

Jurassic
180 million years ago

Laurasia
Gondwanaland

Cretaceous
65 million years ago

Present day

Future
50 million years from now

Trench   New ocean floor
Rift   Zones of slippage
(after Dietz & Holden, Sci. Am. 1970)

GEOLOGY
1:185 000 000

Rocky Mountains
Canadian Shield
Appalachians
Northern Mid-Atlantic Ridge
Sierra Madre
Tropic of Cancer
East Pacific Ridge
Equator
Guiana Shield
Andes
Amazonian Shield
Tropic of Capricorn
Southern Mid-Atlantic Ridge
Pacific-Antarctic Ridge
Antarctic Circle

Baltic Shield
Urals
Angara Shield
Alps
Altai
Atlas
Tian Shan
Chinese Shield
Zagros
Hindu Kush
Kunlun Shan
Himalayas
Ethiopian Shield
Great Rift Valley
Arabian Shield
Indian Shield
Carlsberg Ridge
Atlantic - Indian Ridge
Mid-Indian Ridge
Australian Shield
Great Divide

Intensive Mesozoic & Cenozoic vulcanism

Mid-oceanic ridges   Principal faults   Pre-Cambrian shields   Palaeozoic (Caledonian & Hercynian) folding   Mesozoic folding   Cenozoic (Alpine) folding

Overthrust faults   Oceanic marginal troughs   Sedimentary cover on Pre-Cambrian shields   Sedimentary cover on Palaeozoic folding   Sedimentary cover on Mesozoic folding   Sedimentary cover on Cenozoic folding

GEOLOGICAL TIME SCALE

System names in Cenozoic Era:
Q. = Quaternary
P. = Pliocene
Mi. = Miocene
Ol. = Oligocene
Eo. = Eocene
Pa. = Palaeocene

Millions of years before present

					CALEDONIAN OROGENY				HERCYNIAN OROGENY							LARAMIDE OROGENY	ALPINE OROGENY		
600	550	500	450	400		350			250	200	150		100		50		Q.		
Pre-Cambrian		Cambrian	Ordovician	Silurian	Devonian		Carboniferous	Permian		Triassic	Jurassic		Cretaceous		Pa.	Eo.	Ol.	Mi.	P.	Q.	System
Pre-Cambrian		Lower		Palaeozoic (Primary)			Upper			Mesozoic (Secondary)					Cenozoic (Tertiary, Quaternary)					Era

VOLCANOES AND PLATE TECTONICS

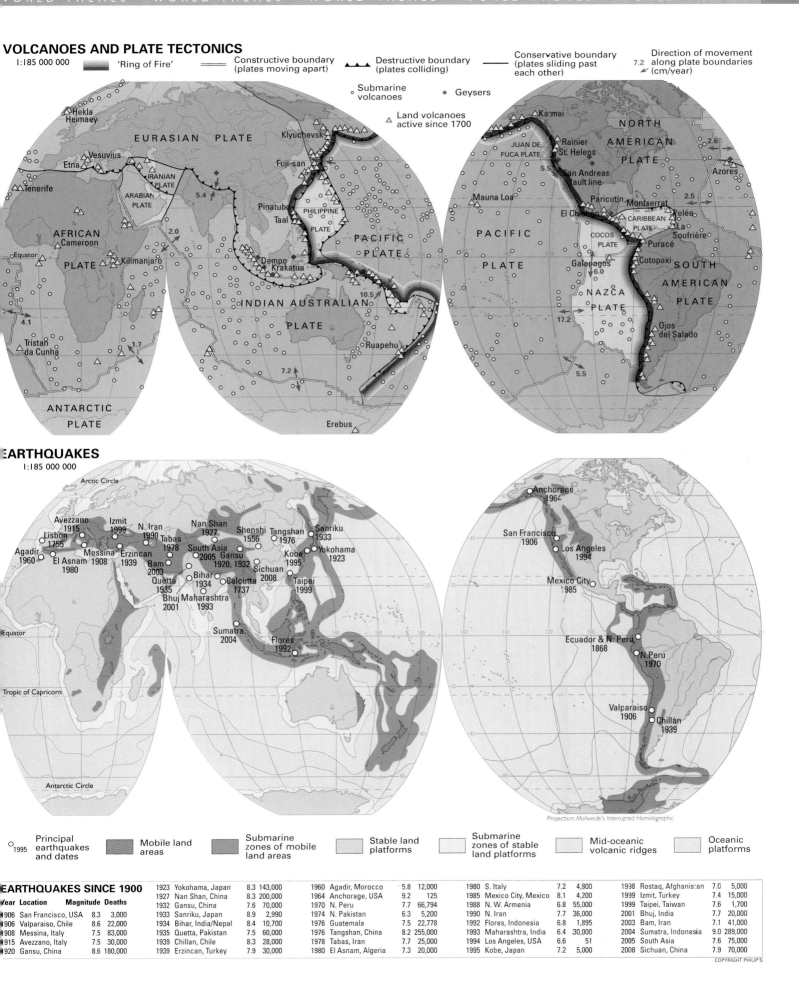

EARTHQUAKES SINCE 1900

Year	Location	Magnitude	Deaths	Year	Location	Magnitude	Deaths	Year	Location	Magnitude	Deaths	Year	Location	Magnitude	Deaths	Year	Location	Magnitude	Deaths
1906	San Francisco, USA	8.3	3,000	1923	Yokohama, Japan	8.3	143,000	1960	Agadir, Morocco	5.8	12,000	1980	S. Italy	7.2	4,800	1938	Rostaq, Afghanistan	7.0	5,000
1906	Valparaiso, Chile	8.6	22,000	1927	Nan Shan, China	8.3	200,000	1964	Anchorage, USA	9.2	125	1985	Mexico City, Mexico	8.1	4,200	1999	Izmit, Turkey	7.4	15,000
1908	Messina, Italy	7.5	83,000	1932	Gansu, China	7.6	70,000	1970	N. Peru	7.7	66,794	1988	N. W. Armenia	6.8	55,000	1999	Taipei, Taiwan	7.6	1,700
1915	Avezzano, Italy	7.5	30,000	1933	Sanriku, Japan	8.9	2,990	1974	N. Pakistan	6.3	5,200	1990	N. Iran	7.7	36,000	2001	Bhuj, India	7.7	20,000
1920	Gansu, China	8.6	180,000	1934	Bihar, India/Nepal	8.4	10,700	1976	Guatemala	7.5	22,778	1992	Flores, Indonesia	6.8	1,895	2003	Bam, Iran	7.1	41,000
				1935	Quetta, Pakistan	7.5	60,000	1976	Tangshan, China	8.2	255,000	1993	Maharashtra, India	6.4	30,000	2004	Sumatra, Indonesia	9.0	289,000
				1939	Chillan, Chile	8.3	28,000	1978	Tabas, Iran	7.7	25,000	1994	Los Angeles, USA	6.6	51	2005	South Asia	7.6	75,000
				1939	Erzincan, Turkey	7.9	30,000	1980	El Asnam, Algeria	7.3	20,000	1995	Kobe, Japan	7.2	5,000	2008	Sichuan, China	7.9	70,000

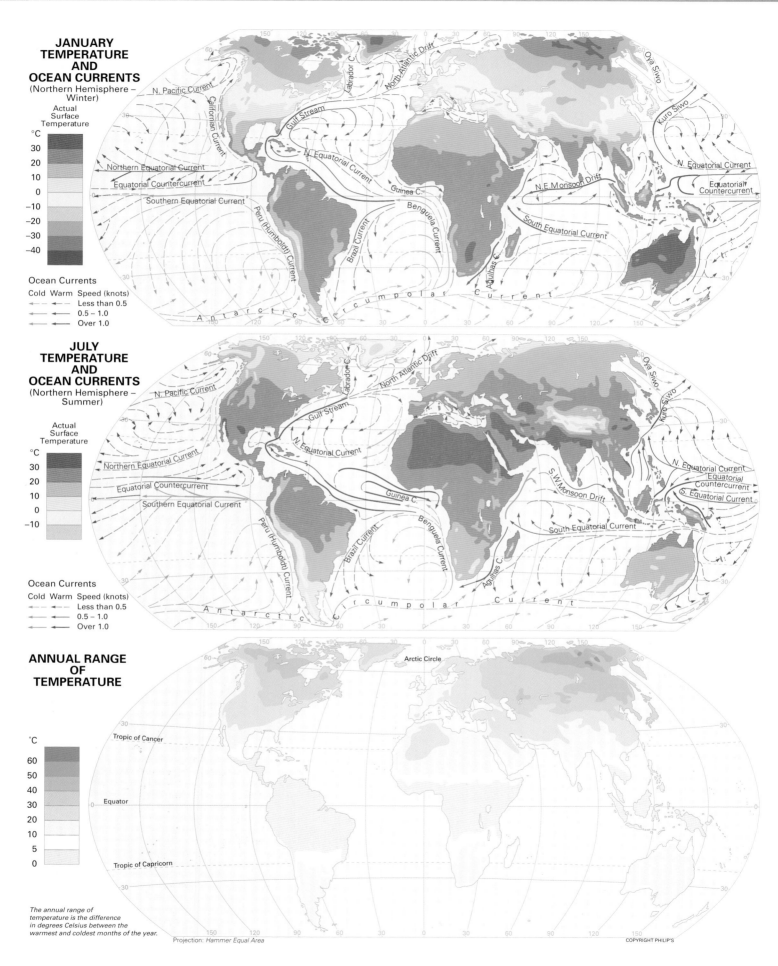

JANUARY TEMPERATURE AND OCEAN CURRENTS
(Northern Hemisphere – Winter)

Actual Surface Temperature

°C
30
20
10
0
–10
–20
–30
–40

Ocean Currents

Cold Warm Speed (knots)
Less than 0.5
0.5 – 1.0
Over 1.0

JULY TEMPERATURE AND OCEAN CURRENTS
(Northern Hemisphere – Summer)

Actual Surface Temperature

°C
30
20
10
0
–10

Ocean Currents

Cold Warm Speed (knots)
Less than 0.5
0.5 – 1.0
Over 1.0

ANNUAL RANGE OF TEMPERATURE

°C
60
50
40
30
20
10
5
0

The annual range of temperature is the difference in degrees Celsius between the warmest and coldest months of the year.

Projection: *Hammer Equal Area*

COPYRIGHT PHILIP'S

1 : 190 000 000

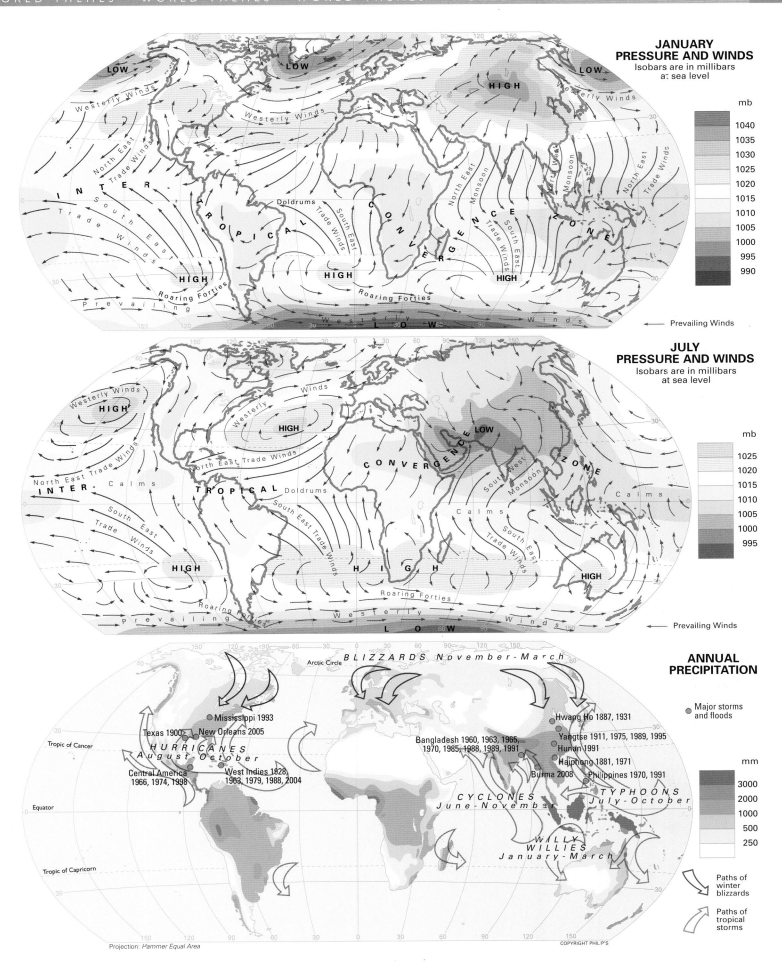

JANUARY PRESSURE AND WINDS
Isobars are in millibars at sea level

mb
1040
1035
1030
1025
1020
1015
1010
1005
1000
995
990

⟵ Prevailing Winds

JULY PRESSURE AND WINDS
Isobars are in millibars at sea level

mb
1025
1020
1015
1010
1005
1000
995

⟵ Prevailing Winds

ANNUAL PRECIPITATION

⬤ Major storms and floods

mm
3000
2000
1000
500
250

Paths of winter blizzards

Paths of tropical storms

Projection: Hammer Equal Area

COPYRIGHT PHILIP'S

CLIMATE REGIONS (after Köppen)

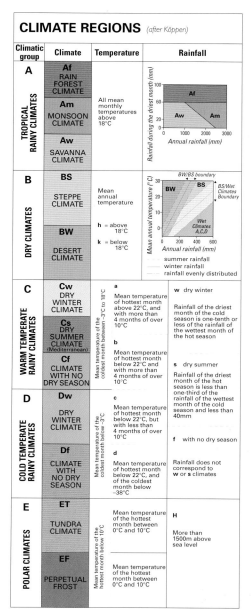

Climatic group	Climate	Temperature	Rainfall
A TROPICAL RAINY CLIMATES	**Af** RAIN FOREST CLIMATE / **Am** MONSOON CLIMATE / **Aw** SAVANNA CLIMATE	All mean monthly temperatures above 18°C	*(rainfall graph: Rainfall during the driest month vs Annual rainfall; Af, Aw, Am)*
B DRY CLIMATES	**BS** STEPPE CLIMATE / **BW** DESERT CLIMATE	Mean annual temperature; h = above 18°C; k = below 18°C	*(graph: Mean annual temperature vs Annual rainfall; BW, BS, Wet Climates A,C,D; summer rainfall; winter rainfall; rainfall evenly distributed)*
C WARM TEMPERATE RAINY CLIMATES	**Cw** DRY WINTER CLIMATE / **Cs** DRY SUMMER CLIMATE (Mediterranean) / **Cf** CLIMATE WITH NO DRY SEASON	Mean temperature of the coldest month between −3°C to 18°C	**a** Mean temperature of hottest month above 22°C, and with more than 4 months of over 10°C **b** Mean temperature of hottest month below 22°C and with more than 4 months of over 10°C **w** dry winter — Rainfall of the driest month of the cold season is one-tenth or less of the rainfall of the wettest month of the hot season **s** dry summer — Rainfall of the driest month of the hot season is less than one-third of the rainfall of the wettest month of the cold season and less than 40mm
D COLD TEMPERATE RAINY CLIMATES	**Dw** DRY WINTER CLIMATE / **Df** CLIMATE WITH NO DRY SEASON	Mean temperature of the coldest month below −3°C	**c** Mean temperature of hottest month below 22°C, but with less than 4 months of over 10°C **d** Mean temperature of hottest month below 22°C, and of the coldest month below −38°C **f** with no dry season — Rainfall does not correspond to **w** or **s** climates
E POLAR CLIMATES	**ET** TUNDRA CLIMATE / **EF** PERPETUAL FROST	Mean temperature of the hottest month below 10°C / Mean temperature of the hottest month between 0°C and 10°C / Mean temperature of the hottest month between 0°C and 10°C	**H** More than 1500m above sea level

CLIMATE RECORDS

Highest recorded temperature: Al Aziziyah, Libya, 58°C, 13 September 1922.

Lowest recorded temperature (outside poles): Verkhoyansk, Siberia, −68°C, 6 February 1933. Verkhoyansk also registered the greatest annual range of temperature: −70°C to 37°C.

Highest barometric pressure: Agata, Siberia, 1,083.8 mb at altitude 262 m, 31 December 1968.

Lowest barometric pressure: Typhoon Tip, 480 km west of Guam, Pacific Ocean, 870 mb, 12 October 1979.

Driest place: Quillagua, N. Chile, 0.5 mm, 1964–2001.

Wettest place (12 months): Cherrapunji, Meghalaya, N.E. India, August 1860 to August 1861. Cherrapunji also holds the record for rainfall in one month: 2930 mm, July 1861.

Highest recorded wind speed: Mt Washington, New Hampshire, USA, 371 km/h, 12 April 1934. This is three times as strong as hurricane force on the Beaufort Scale.

Windiest place: Commonwealth Bay, George V Coast, Antarctica, where gales frequently reach over 320 km/h.

Projection: Interrupted Mollweide's Homolographic

THE MONSOON

In early March, which normally marks the end of the subcontinent's cool season and the start of the hot season, winds blow outwards from the mainland. But as the overhead sun and the ITCZ move northwards, the land is intensely heated, and a low-pressure system develops. The south-east trade winds, which are drawn across the Equator, change direction and are sucked into the interior to become south-westerly winds, bringing heavy rain. By November, the overhead sun and the ITCZ have again moved southwards and the wind directions are again reversed. Cool winds blow from the Asian interior to the sea, losing any moisture on the Himalayas before descending to the coast.

Monthly rainfall
mm
400
200
100
50
25

→ wind direction

▬ ITCZ (intertropical convergence zone)

March – Start of the hot, dry season, the ITCZ is over the southern Indian Ocean.

July – The rainy season, the ITCZ has migrated northwards; winds blow onshore.

November – The ITCZ has returned south, the offshore winds are cool and dry.

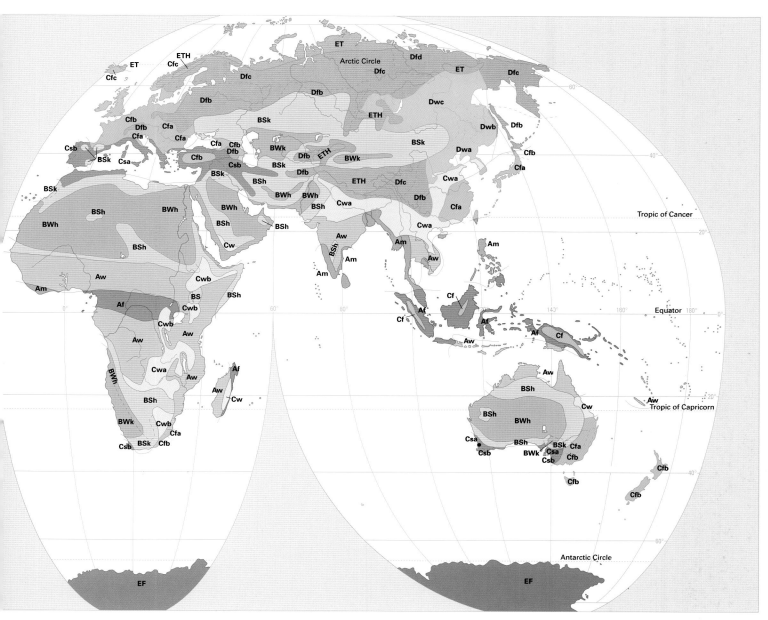

EL NIÑO

In a normal year, south-easterly trade winds drive surface waters westwards off the coast of South America, drawing cold, nutrient-rich water up from below. In an El Niño year (which occurs every 2–7 years), warm water from the west Pacific suppresses up-welling in the east, depriving the region of nutrients. The water is warmed by as much as 7°C, disturbing the tropical atmospheric circulation. During an intense El Niño, the south-east trade winds change direction and become equatorial westerlies, resulting in climatic extremes in many regions of the world, such as drought in parts of Australia and India, and heavy rainfall in south-eastern USA. An intense El Niño occurred in 1997–8, with resultant freak weather conditions across the entire Pacific region.

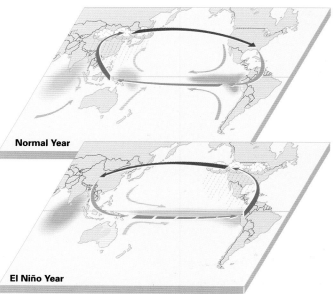

Normal Year

El Niño Year

WINDCHILL FACTOR

In sub-zero weather, even moderate winds significantly reduce effective temperatures. The chart below shows the windchill effect across a range of speeds.

	Wind speed (km/h)				
	16	32	48	64	80
0°C	−8	−14	−17	−19	−20
−5°C	−14	−21	−25	−27	−28
−10°C	−20	−28	−33	−35	−36
−15°C	−26	−36	−40	−43	−44
−20°C	−32	−42	−48	−51	−52
−25°C	−38	−49	−56	−59	−60
−30°C	−44	−57	−63	−66	−68
−35°C	−51	−64	−72	−74	−76
−40°C	−57	−71	−78	−82	−84
−45°C	−63	−78	−86	−90	−92
−50°C	−69	−85	−94	−98	−100

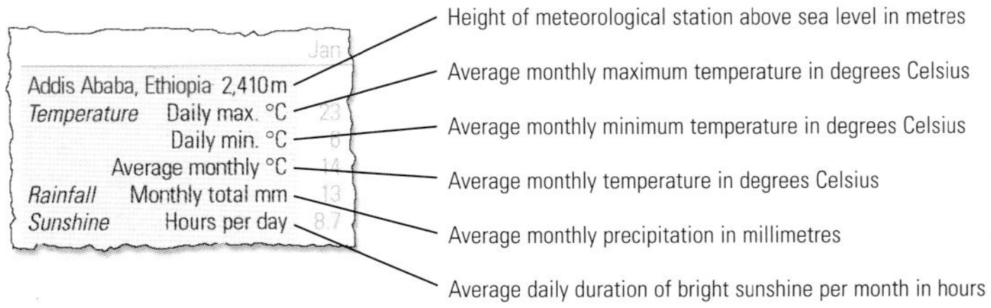
Jan
Addis Ababa, Ethiopia 2,410 m
Temperature Daily max. °C 23
Daily min. °C 6
Average monthly °C 14
Rainfall Monthly total mm 13
Sunshine Hours per day 8.7
Height of meteorological station above sea level in metres
Average monthly maximum temperature in degrees Celsius
Average monthly minimum temperature in degrees Celsius
Average monthly temperature in degrees Celsius
Average monthly precipitation in millimetres
Average daily duration of bright sunshine per month in hours

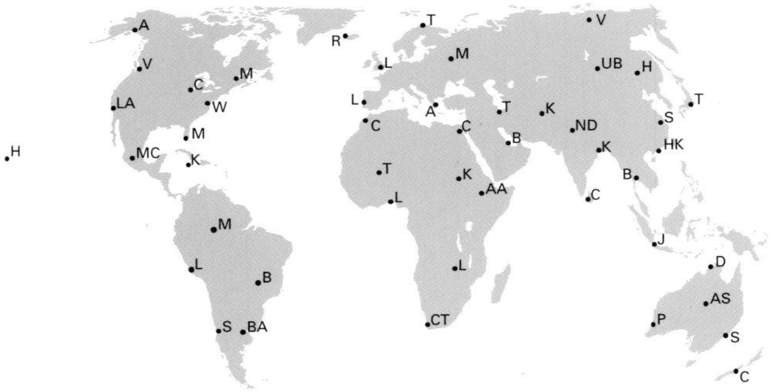

Addis Ababa, Ethiopia 2,410 m	Jan	Feb	Mar	Apr	May	June	July	Aug	Sept	Oct	Nov	Dec	Year
Temperature Daily max. °C	23	24	25	24	25	23	20	20	21	22	23	22	23
Daily min. °C	6	7	9	10	9	10	11	11	10	7	5	5	8
Average monthly °C	14	15	17	17	17	16	16	15	15	15	14	14	15
Rainfall Monthly total mm	13	35	67	91	81	117	247	255	167	29	8	5	1,115
Sunshine Hours per day	8.7	8.2	7.6	8.1	6.5	4.8	2.8	3.2	5.2	7.6	6.7	7	6.4

Alice Springs, Australia 580 m	Jan	Feb	Mar	Apr	May	June	July	Aug	Sept	Oct	Nov	Dec	Year
Temperature Daily max. °C	35	35	32	27	23	19	19	23	27	31	33	35	28
Daily min. °C	21	20	17	12	8	5	4	6	10	15	18	20	13
Average monthly °C	28	27	25	20	15	12	12	14	18	23	25	27	21
Rainfall Monthly total mm	44	33	27	10	15	13	7	8	7	18	29	38	249
Sunshine Hours per day	10.3	10.4	9.3	9.2	8	8	8.9	9.8	10	9.7	10.1	10	9.5

Anchorage, USA 183 m	Jan	Feb	Mar	Apr	May	June	July	Aug	Sept	Oct	Nov	Dec	Year
Temperature Daily max. °C	–7	–3	0	7	13	18	19	17	13	6	–2	–6	–6
Daily min. °C	–15	–12	–9	–2	4	8	10	9	5	–2	–9	–14	–2
Average monthly °C	–11	–7	–4	3	9	13	15	13	9	2	–5	–10	–4
Rainfall Monthly total mm	20	18	13	11	13	25	47	64	64	47	28	24	374
Sunshine Hours per day	2.4	4.1	6.6	8.3	8.3	9.2	8.5	6	4.4	3.1	2.6	1.6	5.4

Athens, Greece 107 m	Jan	Feb	Mar	Apr	May	June	July	Aug	Sept	Oct	Nov	Dec	Year
Temperature Daily max. °C	13	14	16	20	25	30	33	33	29	24	19	15	23
Daily min. °C	6	7	8	11	16	20	23	23	19	15	12	8	14
Average monthly °C	10	10	12	16	20	25	28	28	24	20	15	11	18
Rainfall Monthly total mm	62	37	37	23	23	14	6	7	15	51	56	71	402
Sunshine Hours per day	3.9	5.2	5.8	7.7	8.9	10.7	11.9	11.5	9.4	6.8	4.8	3.8	7.3

Bahrain City, Bahrain 2 m	Jan	Feb	Mar	Apr	May	June	July	Aug	Sept	Oct	Nov	Dec	Year
Temperature Daily max. °C	20	21	25	29	33	36	37	38	36	32	27	22	30
Daily min. °C	14	15	18	22	25	29	31	32	29	25	22	16	23
Average monthly °C	17	18	21	25	29	32	34	35	32	29	25	19	26
Rainfall Monthly total mm	18	12	10	9	2	0	0	0	0	0.4	3	16	70
Sunshine Hours per day	5.9	6.9	7.9	8.8	10.6	13.2	12.1	12	12	10.3	7.7	6.4	9.5

Bangkok, Thailand 10 m	Jan	Feb	Mar	Apr	May	June	July	Aug	Sept	Oct	Nov	Dec	Year
Temperature Daily max. °C	32	33	34	35	34	33	32	32	32	31	31	31	33
Daily min. °C	20	23	24	26	25	25	25	24	24	24	23	20	24
Average monthly °C	26	28	29	30	30	29	28	28	28	28	27	26	28
Rainfall Monthly total mm	9	30	36	82	165	153	168	183	310	239	55	8	1,438
Sunshine Hours per day	8.2	8	8	10	7.5	6.1	4.7	5.2	5.2	6.1	7.3	7.8	7

Brasilia, Brazil 910 m	Jan	Feb	Mar	Apr	May	June	July	Aug	Sept	Oct	Nov	Dec	Year
Temperature Daily max. °C	28	28	28	28	27	27	27	29	30	29	28	27	28
Daily min. °C	18	18	18	17	15	13	13	14	16	18	18	18	16
Average monthly °C	23	23	23	22	21	20	20	21	23	24	23	22	22
Rainfall Monthly total mm	252	204	227	93	17	3	6	3	30	127	255	343	1,560
Sunshine Hours per day	5.8	5.7	6	7.4	8.7	9.3	9.6	9.8	7.9	6.5	4.8	4.4	7.2

Buenos Aires, Argentina 25 m	Jan	Feb	Mar	Apr	May	June	July	Aug	Sept	Oct	Nov	Dec	Year
Temperature Daily max. °C	30	29	26	22	18	14	14	16	18	21	25	28	22
Daily min. °C	17	17	16	12	9	5	6	6	8	10	14	16	11
Average monthly °C	23	23	21	17	13	10	10	11	13	15	19	22	16
Rainfall Monthly total mm	79	71	109	89	76	61	56	61	79	86	84	99	950
Sunshine Hours per day	9.2	8.5	7.5	6.8	4.9	3.5	3.8	5.2	6	6.8	8.1	8.5	6.6

Cairo, Egypt 75 m	Jan	Feb	Mar	Apr	May	June	July	Aug	Sept	Oct	Nov	Dec	Year
Temperature Daily max. °C	19	21	24	28	32	35	35	35	33	30	26	21	28
Daily min. °C	9	9	12	14	18	20	22	22	20	18	14	10	16
Average monthly °C	14	15	18	21	25	28	29	28	26	24	20	16	22
Rainfall Monthly total mm	4	4	3	1	2	1	0	0	1	1	3	7	27
Sunshine Hours per day	6.9	8.4	8.7	9.7	10.5	11.9	11.7	11.3	10.4	9.4	8.3	6.4	9.5

Cape Town, South Africa 44 m	Jan	Feb	Mar	Apr	May	June	July	Aug	Sept	Oct	Nov	Dec	Year
Temperature Daily max. °C	26	26	25	23	20	18	17	18	19	21	24	25	22
Daily min. °C	15	15	14	11	9	7	7	7	8	10	13	15	11
Average monthly °C	21	20	20	17	14	13	12	12	14	16	18	20	16
Rainfall Monthly total mm	12	19	17	42	67	98	68	76	36	45	12	13	505
Sunshine Hours per day	11.4	10.2	9.4	7.7	6.1	5.7	6.4	6.6	7.6	8.6	10.2	10.9	8.4

Casablanca, Morocco 59 m	Jan	Feb	Mar	Apr	May	June	July	Aug	Sept	Oct	Nov	Dec	Year
Temperature Daily max. °C	17	18	20	21	22	24	26	26	26	24	21	18	22
Daily min. °C	8	9	11	12	15	18	19	20	18	15	12	10	14
Average monthly °C	13	13	15	16	18	21	23	23	22	20	17	14	18
Rainfall Monthly total mm	78	61	54	37	20	3	0	1	6	28	58	94	440
Sunshine Hours per day	5.2	6.3	7.3	9	9.4	9.7	10.2	9.7	9.1	7.4	5.9	5.3	7.9

Chicago, USA 186 m	Jan	Feb	Mar	Apr	May	June	July	Aug	Sept	Oct	Nov	Dec	Year
Temperature Daily max. °C	1	2	6	14	21	26	29	28	24	17	8	2	15
Daily min. °C	–7	–6	–2	5	11	16	20	19	14	8	0	–5	–6
Average monthly °C	–3	–2	2	9	16	21	24	23	19	13	4	–2	4
Rainfall Monthly total mm	47	41	70	77	96	103	86	80	69	71	56	48	844
Sunshine Hours per day	4	5	6.6	6.9	8.9	10.2	10	9.2	8.2	6.9	4.5	3.7	7

Christchurch, New Zealand 5 m	Jan	Feb	Mar	Apr	May	June	July	Aug	Sept	Oct	Nov	Dec	Year
Temperature Daily max. °C	21	21	19	17	13	11	10	11	14	17	19	21	16
Daily min. °C	12	12	10	7	4	2	1	3	5	7	8	11	7
Average monthly °C	16	16	15	12	9	6	6	7	9	12	13	16	11
Rainfall Monthly total mm	56	46	43	46	76	69	61	58	51	51	51	61	669
Sunshine Hours per day	7	6.5	5.6	4.7	4.3	3.9	4.1	4.7	5.6	6.1	6.9	6.3	5.5

Colombo, Sri Lanka 10 m	Jan	Feb	Mar	Apr	May	June	July	Aug	Sept	Oct	Nov	Dec	Year
Temperature Daily max. °C	30	31	31	31	30	30	29	29	30	29	29	30	30
Daily min. °C	22	22	23	24	25	25	25	25	25	24	23	22	24
Average monthly °C	26	26	27	28	28	27	27	27	27	27	26	26	27
Rainfall Monthly total mm	101	66	118	230	394	220	140	102	174	348	333	142	2,368
Sunshine Hours per day	7.9	9	8.1	7.2	6.4	5.4	6.1	6.3	6.2	6.5	6.4	7.8	6.9

Darwin, Australia 30 m	Jan	Feb	Mar	Apr	May	June	July	Aug	Sept	Oct	Nov	Dec	Year
Temperature Daily max. °C	32	32	33	33	33	31	31	32	33	34	34	33	33
Daily min. °C	25	25	25	24	23	21	19	21	23	25	26	26	24
Average monthly °C	29	29	29	29	28	26	25	26	28	29	30	29	28
Rainfall Monthly total mm	405	309	279	77	8	2	0	1	15	48	108	214	1,466
Sunshine Hours per day	5.8	5.8	6.6	9.8	9.3	10	9.9	10.4	10.1	9.4	9.6	6.8	8.6

Harbin, China 175 m	Jan	Feb	Mar	Apr	May	June	July	Aug	Sept	Oct	Nov	Dec	Year
Temperature Daily max. °C	–14	–9	0	12	21	26	29	27	20	12	–1	–11	9
Daily min. °C	–26	–23	–12	–1	7	14	18	16	8	0	–12	–22	–3
Average monthly °C	–20	–16	–6	6	14	20	23	22	14	6	–7	–17	3
Rainfall Monthly total mm	4	6	17	23	44	92	167	119	52	36	12	5	577
Sunshine Hours per day	6.4	7.8	8	7.8	8.3	8.6	8.6	8.2	7.2	6.9	6.1	5.7	7.5

Hong Kong, China 35 m	Jan	Feb	Mar	Apr	May	June	July	Aug	Sept	Oct	Nov	Dec	Year
Temperature Daily max. °C	18	18	20	24	28	30	31	31	30	27	24	20	25
Daily min. °C	13	13	16	19	23	26	26	26	25	23	19	15	20
Average monthly °C	16	15	18	22	25	28	28	28	27	25	21	17	23
Rainfall Monthly total mm	30	60	70	133	332	479	286	415	364	33	46	17	2,265
Sunshine Hours per day	4.7	3.5	3.1	3.8	5	5.4	6.8	6.5	6.6	7	6.2	5.5	5.3

Honolulu, Hawaii 5 m	Jan	Feb	Mar	Apr	May	June	July	Aug	Sept	Oct	Nov	Dec	Year
Temperature Daily max. °C	26	26	26	27	28	29	29	29	30	29	28	26	28
Daily min. °C	19	19	19	20	21	22	23	23	23	22	21	20	21
Average monthly °C	23	22	23	23	24	26	26	26	26	26	24	23	24
Rainfall Monthly total mm	96	84	73	33	25	8	11	23	25	47	55	76	556
Sunshine Hours per day	7.3	7.7	8.3	8.6	8.8	9.1	9.4	9.3	9.2	8.3	7.5	6.2	8.3

Jakarta, Indonesia 10 m	Jan	Feb	Mar	Apr	May	June	July	Aug	Sept	Oct	Nov	Dec	Year
Temperature Daily max. °C	29	29	30	31	31	31	31	31	31	31	30	29	30
Daily min. °C	23	23	23	24	24	23	23	23	23	23	23	23	23
Average monthly °C	26	26	27	27	27	27	27	27	27	27	27	26	27
Rainfall Monthly total mm	300	300	211	147	114	97	64	43	66	112	142	203	1,799
Sunshine Hours per day	6.1	6.5	7.7	8.5	8.4	8.5	9.1	9.5	9.6	9	7.7	7.1	8.1

Kabul, Afghanistan 1,791 m	Jan	Feb	Mar	Apr	May	June	July	Aug	Sept	Oct	Nov	Dec	Year
Temperature Daily max. °C	2	4	12	19	26	31	33	33	30	22	17	8	20
Daily min. °C	–8	–6	1	6	11	13	16	15	11	6	1	–3	5
Average monthly °C	–3	–1	6	13	18	22	25	24	20	14	9	3	12
Rainfall Monthly total mm	28	61	72	117	33	1	7	1	0	1	37	14	372
Sunshine Hours per day	5.9	6	5.7	6.8	10.1	11.5	11.4	11.2	9.8	9.4	7.8	6.1	8.5

Khartoum, Sudan 380 m	Jan	Feb	Mar	Apr	May	June	July	Aug	Sept	Oct	Nov	Dec	Year
Temperature Daily max. °C	32	33	37	40	42	41	38	36	38	39	35	32	37
Daily min. °C	16	17	20	23	26	27	26	25	25	25	21	17	22
Average monthly °C	24	25	28	32	34	34	32	30	32	32	28	25	30
Rainfall Monthly total mm	0	0	0	1	7	5	56	80	28	2	0	0	179
Sunshine Hours per day	10.6	11.2	10.4	10.8	10.4	10.1	8.6	8.6	9.6	10.3	10.8	10.6	10.2

Kingston, Jamaica 35 m	Jan	Feb	Mar	Apr	May	June	July	Aug	Sept	Oct	Nov	Dec	Year
Temperature Daily max. °C	30	30	30	31	31	32	32	32	32	31	31	31	31
Daily min. °C	20	20	20	21	22	24	23	23	23	23	22	21	22
Average monthly °C	25	25	25	26	26	28	28	28	27	27	26	26	26
Rainfall Monthly total mm	23	15	23	31	102	89	38	91	99	180	74	36	801
Sunshine Hours per day	8.3	8.8	8.7	8.7	8.3	7.8	8.5	8.5	7.6	7.3	8.3	7.7	8.2

	Jan	Feb	Mar	Apr	May	June	July	Aug	Sept	Oct	Nov	Dec	Year
Kolkata (Calcutta), India 5 m													
Temperature Daily max. °C	27	29	34	36	35	34	32	32	32	32	29	26	31
Daily min. °C	13	15	21	24	25	26	26	26	26	23	18	13	21
Average monthly °C	20	22	27	30	30	30	29	29	29	28	23	20	26
Rainfall Monthly total mm	10	30	34	44	140	297	325	332	253	114	20	5	1,604
Sunshine Hours per day	8.6	8.7	8.9	9	8.7	5.4	4.1	4.1	5.1	6.5	8.3	8.4	7.1
Lagos, Nigeria 40 m													
Temperature Daily max. °C	32	33	33	32	31	29	28	28	29	30	31	32	31
Daily min. °C	22	23	23	23	23	22	22	21	22	22	23	22	22
Average monthly °C	27	28	28	28	27	26	25	24	25	26	27	27	26
Rainfall Monthly total mm	28	41	99	99	203	300	180	56	180	190	63	25	1,464
Sunshine Hours per day	5.9	6.8	6.3	6.1	5.6	3.8	2.8	3.3	3	5.1	6.6	6.5	5.2
Lima, Peru 120 m													
Temperature Daily max. °C	28	29	29	27	24	20	20	19	20	22	24	26	24
Daily min. °C	19	20	19	17	16	15	14	14	14	15	16	17	16
Average monthly °C	24	24	24	22	20	17	17	16	17	18	20	21	20
Rainfall Monthly total mm	1	1	1	1	5	5	8	8	8	3	3	1	45
Sunshine Hours per day	6.3	6.8	6.9	6.7	4	1.4	1.1	1	1.1	2.5	4.1	5	3.9
Lisbon, Portugal 77 m													
Temperature Daily max. °C	14	15	17	20	21	25	27	28	26	22	17	15	21
Daily min. °C	8	8	10	12	13	15	17	17	17	14	11	9	13
Average monthly °C	11	12	14	16	17	20	22	23	21	18	14	12	17
Rainfall Monthly total mm	111	76	109	54	44	16	3	4	33	62	93	103	708
Sunshine Hours per day	4.7	5.9	6	8.3	9.1	10.6	11.4	10.7	8.4	6.7	5.2	4.6	7.7
London (Kew), UK 5 m													
Temperature Daily max. °C	6	7	10	13	17	20	22	21	19	14	10	7	14
Daily min. °C	2	2	3	6	8	12	14	13	11	8	5	4	7
Average monthly °C	4	5	7	9	12	16	18	17	15	11	8	5	11
Rainfall Monthly total mm	54	40	37	37	46	45	57	59	49	57	64	48	593
Sunshine Hours per day	1.7	2.3	3.5	5.7	6.7	7	6.6	6	5	3.3	1.9	1.4	4.3
Los Angeles, USA 30 m													
Temperature Daily max. °C	18	18	18	19	20	22	24	24	24	23	22	19	21
Daily min. °C	7	8	9	11	13	15	17	17	16	14	11	9	12
Average monthly °C	12	13	14	15	17	18	21	21	20	18	16	14	17
Rainfall Monthly total mm	69	74	46	28	3	3	0	0	5	10	28	61	327
Sunshine Hours per day	6.9	8.2	8.9	8.8	9.5	10.3	11.7	11	10.1	8.6	8.2	7.6	9.2
Lusaka, Zambia 1,154 m													
Temperature Daily max. °C	26	26	26	27	25	23	23	26	29	31	29	27	27
Daily min. °C	17	17	16	15	12	10	9	11	15	18	18	17	15
Average monthly °C	22	22	21	21	18	17	16	19	22	25	23	22	21
Rainfall Monthly total mm	224	173	90	19	3	1	0	1	1	17	85	196	810
Sunshine Hours per day	5.1	5.4	6.9	8.9	9	9	9.1	9.6	9.5	9	7	5.5	7.8
Manaus, Brazil 45 m													
Temperature Daily max. °C	31	31	31	31	31	31	32	33	34	34	33	32	32
Daily min. °C	24	24	24	24	24	24	24	24	24	25	25	24	24
Average monthly °C	28	28	28	27	28	28	28	29	29	29	29	28	28
Rainfall Monthly total mm	278	278	300	287	193	99	61	41	62	112	165	220	2,096
Sunshine Hours per day	3.9	4	3.6	3.9	5.4	6.9	7.9	8.2	7.5	6.6	5.9	4.9	5.7
Mexico City, Mexico 2,309 m													
Temperature Daily max. °C	21	23	26	27	26	25	23	24	23	22	21	21	24
Daily min. °C	5	6	7	9	10	11	11	11	11	9	6	5	8
Average monthly °C	13	15	16	18	18	18	17	17	17	16	14	13	16
Rainfall Monthly total mm	8	4	9	23	57	111	160	149	119	46	16	7	709
Sunshine Hours per day	7.3	8.1	8.5	8.1	7.8	7	6.2	6.4	5.6	6.3	7	7.3	7.1
Miami, USA 2 m													
Temperature Daily max. °C	24	25	27	28	30	31	32	32	31	29	27	25	28
Daily min. °C	14	15	16	19	21	23	24	24	24	22	18	15	20
Average monthly °C	19	20	21	23	25	27	28	28	27	25	22	20	24
Rainfall Monthly total mm	51	43	58	99	163	188	170	178	241	208	71	43	1,518
Sunshine Hours per day	7.7	8.3	8.7	9.4	8.9	8.5	8.7	8.4	7.1	6.5	7.5	7.1	8.1
Montreal, Canada 57 m													
Temperature Daily max. °C	−6	−4	2	11	18	23	26	25	20	14	5	−3	11
Daily min. °C	−13	−11	−5	2	9	14	17	16	11	6	0	−9	3
Average monthly °C	−9	−3	−2	6	13	19	22	20	16	10	3	−6	7
Rainfall Monthly total mm	87	73	86	83	81	91	98	87	96	84	89	89	1,047
Sunshine Hours per day	2.8	3.4	4.5	5.2	6.7	7.7	8.2	7.7	5.6	4.3	2.4	2.2	5.1
Moscow, Russia 156 m													
Temperature Daily max. °C	−6	−4	1	9	18	22	24	22	17	10	1	−5	9
Daily min. °C	−14	−16	−11	−1	5	9	12	9	4	−2	−6	−12	−2
Average monthly °C	−10	−10	−5	4	12	15	18	16	10	4	−2	−8	4
Rainfall Monthly total mm	31	28	33	35	52	67	74	74	58	51	36	36	575
Sunshine Hours per day	1	1.9	3.7	5.2	7.8	8.3	8.4	7.1	4.4	2.4	1	0.6	4.4
New Delhi, India 220 m													
Temperature Daily max. °C	21	24	29	36	41	39	35	34	34	34	28	23	32
Daily min. °C	6	10	14	20	26	28	27	26	24	17	11	7	18
Average monthly °C	14	17	22	28	33	34	31	30	29	26	20	15	25
Rainfall Monthly total mm	25	21	13	8	13	77	178	184	123	10	2	11	665
Sunshine Hours per day	7.7	8.2	8.2	8.7	9.2	7.9	6	6.3	6.9	9.4	8.7	8.3	8

	Jan	Feb	Mar	Apr	May	June	July	Aug	Sept	Oct	Nov	Dec	Year
Perth, Australia 60 m													
Temperature Daily max. °C	29	30	27	25	21	18	17	18	19	21	25	27	23
Daily min. °C	17	18	13	14	12	10	9	9	10	11	14	16	13
Average monthly °C	23	24	22	19	16	14	13	13	15	16	19	22	18
Rainfall Monthly total mm	8	13	22	44	128	189	177	145	84	58	19	13	900
Sunshine Hours per day	10.4	9.8	8.3	7.5	5.7	4.8	5.4	6	7.2	8.1	9.6	10.4	7.8
Reykjavik, Iceland 18 m													
Temperature Daily max. °C	2	3	5	6	10	13	15	14	12	8	5	4	8
Daily min. °C	−3	−3	−1	1	4	7	9	8	6	3	0	−2	3
Average monthly °C	0	0	2	4	7	10	12	11	9	5	3	1	5
Rainfall Monthly total mm	89	64	62	56	42	42	50	56	67	94	78	79	779
Sunshine Hours per day	0.8	2	3.6	4.5	5.9	6.1	5.8	5.4	3.5	2.3	1.1	0.3	3.7
Santiago, Chile 520 m													
Temperature Daily max. °C	30	29	27	24	19	15	15	17	19	22	26	29	23
Daily min. °C	12	11	10	7	5	3	3	4	6	7	9	11	7
Average monthly °C	21	20	18	15	12	9	9	10	12	15	17	20	15
Rainfall Monthly total mm	3	3	5	13	64	84	76	56	31	15	8	5	363
Sunshine Hours per day	10.8	8.9	8.5	5.5	3.6	3.3	3.3	3.6	4.8	6.1	8.7	10.1	6.4
Shanghai, China 5 m													
Temperature Daily max. °C	8	8	13	19	24	28	32	32	27	23	17	10	20
Daily min. °C	−1	0	4	9	14	19	23	23	19	13	7	2	11
Average monthly °C	3	4	8	14	19	23	27	27	23	18	12	6	15
Rainfall Monthly total mm	48	59	84	94	94	180	147	142	130	71	51	36	1,136
Sunshine Hours per day	4	3.7	4.4	4.8	5.4	4.7	6.9	7.5	5.3	5.6	4.7	4.5	5.1
Sydney, Australia 40 m													
Temperature Daily max. °C	26	26	25	22	19	17	17	18	20	22	24	25	22
Daily min. °C	18	19	17	14	11	9	8	9	11	13	16	17	14
Average monthly °C	22	22	21	18	15	13	12	13	16	18	20	21	18
Rainfall Monthly total mm	89	101	127	135	127	117	117	76	74	71	74	74	1,182
Sunshine Hours per day	7.5	7	6.4	6.1	5.7	5.3	6.1	7	7.3	7.5	7.5	7.5	6.8
Tehran, Iran 1,191 m													
Temperature Daily max. °C	9	11	16	21	29	30	37	36	29	24	16	11	22
Daily min. °C	−1	1	4	10	16	20	23	23	18	12	6	1	11
Average monthly °C	4	6	10	15	22	25	30	29	23	18	11	6	17
Rainfall Monthly total mm	37	23	36	31	14	2	1	1	1	5	29	27	207
Sunshine Hours per day	5.9	6.7	7.5	7.4	8.6	11.6	11.2	11	10.1	7.6	6.9	6.3	8.4
Timbuktu, Mali 269 m													
Temperature Daily max. °C	31	35	38	41	43	42	38	35	38	40	37	31	37
Daily min. °C	13	16	18	22	26	27	25	24	24	23	18	14	21
Average monthly °C	22	25	28	31	34	34	32	30	31	31	28	23	29
Rainfall Monthly total mm	0	0	0	1	4	20	54	93	31	3	0	0	206
Sunshine Hours per day	9.1	9.6	9.6	9.7	9.8	9.4	9.6	9	9.3	9.5	9.5	8.9	9.4
Tokyo, Japan 5 m													
Temperature Daily max. °C	9	9	12	18	22	25	29	30	27	20	16	11	19
Daily min. °C	−1	−1	3	4	13	17	22	23	19	13	7	1	10
Average monthly °C	4	4	8	11	18	21	25	26	23	17	11	6	14
Rainfall Monthly total mm	48	73	101	135	131	182	146	147	217	220	101	61	1,562
Sunshine Hours per day	6	5.9	5.7	6	6.2	5	5.8	6.6	4.5	4.4	4.8	5.4	5.5
Tromsø, Norway 100 m													
Temperature Daily max. °C	−2	−2	0	3	7	12	16	14	10	5	2	0	5
Daily min. °C	−6	−6	−5	−2	1	6	9	8	5	1	−2	−4	0
Average monthly °C	−4	−4	−3	0	4	9	13	11	7	3	0	−2	3
Rainfall Monthly total mm	96	79	91	65	61	59	56	80	109	115	88	95	994
Sunshine Hours per day	0.1	1.6	2.9	6.1	5.7	6.9	7.9	4.8	3.5	1.7	0.3	0	3.5
Ulan Bator, Mongolia 1,305 m													
Temperature Daily max. °C	−19	−13	−4	7	13	21	22	21	14	6	−6	−16	4
Daily min. °C	−32	−29	−22	−8	−2	7	11	8	2	−8	−20	−28	−11
Average monthly °C	−26	−21	−13	−1	6	14	16	14	8	−1	−13	−22	−4
Rainfall Monthly total mm	1	1	2	5	10	28	76	51	23	5	5	2	209
Sunshine Hours per day	6.4	7.8	8	7.8	8.3	8.6	8.6	8.2	7.2	6.9	6.1	5.7	7.5
Vancouver, Canada 5 m													
Temperature Daily max. °C	6	7	10	14	17	20	23	22	19	14	9	7	14
Daily min. °C	0	1	3	5	8	11	13	12	10	7	3	2	6
Average monthly °C	3	4	6	9	13	16	18	17	14	10	6	4	10
Rainfall Monthly total mm	214	161	151	90	69	65	39	44	83	172	198	243	1,529
Sunshine Hours per day	1.6	3	3.8	5.9	7.5	7.4	9.5	8.2	6	3.7	2	1.4	5
Verkhoyansk, Russia 137 m													
Temperature Daily max. °C	−47	−40	−20	−1	11	21	24	21	12	−8	−33	−42	−8
Daily min. °C	−51	−48	−40	−25	−7	4	6	1	−6	−20	−39	−50	−23
Average monthly °C	−49	−44	−30	−13	2	12	15	11	3	−14	−36	−46	−16
Rainfall Monthly total mm	7	5	5	4	5	25	33	30	13	11	10	7	155
Sunshine Hours per day	0	2.6	6.9	9.6	9.7	10	9.7	7.5	4.1	2.4	0.6	0	5.4
Washington, USA 22 m													
Temperature Daily max. °C	7	8	12	19	25	29	31	30	26	20	14	8	19
Daily min. °C	−1	−1	2	8	13	18	21	20	16	10	4	−1	9
Average monthly °C	3	3	7	13	19	24	26	25	21	15	9	4	14
Rainfall Monthly total mm	84	68	96	85	103	88	108	120	100	78	75	75	1,080
Sunshine Hours per day	4.4	5.7	6.7	7.4	8.2	8.8	8.6	8.2	7.5	6.5	5.3	4.5	6.8

Tropical Rain Forest
Tall broadleaved evergreen forest, trees 30–50m high with climbers and epiphytes forming continuous canopies. Associated with wet climate 2–3000mm precipitation per year and high temperatures 24–28°C. High diversity of species, typically 100 per ha including lianas, bamboo, palms, rubber, mahogany. Mangrove swamps form in coastal areas.

Diagram shows the highly stratified nature of the tropical rain forest. Crowns of trees form numerous layers at different heights and the dense shade limits undergrowth.

Temperate Deciduous and Coniferous Forest
A transition zone between broadleaves and conifers. Broadleaves are better suited to the warmer, damper and flatter locations.

Northern Coniferous Forest (Taiga)
Forming a large continuous belt across Northern America and Eurasia with a uniformity in tree species. Characteristically trees are tall, conical with short branches and wax-covered needle-shaped leaves to retain moisture. Cold climate with prolonged harsh winters and cool summers where average temperatures for more than six months of the year are under 0°C. Undergrowth is sparse with mosses and lichens. Tree species include pine, fir, spruce, larch, tamarisk.

Mountainous Forest, mainly Coniferous
Mild winters, high humidity and high levels of rainfall throughout the year provide habitat for dense needle-leaf evergreen forests and the largest trees in the world, up to 100m, including the Douglas fir, redwood and giant sequoia.

High Plateau Steppe and Tundra
Similar to arctic tundra with frozen ground for the majority of the year. Very sparse ground coverage of low, shallow-rooted herbs, small shrubs, mosses, lichens and heather interspersed with bare soil.

Arctic Tundra
Average temperatures are 0°C, precipitation is mainly snowfall and the ground remains frozen for 10 months of the year. Vegetation flourishes when the shallow surface layer melts in the long summer days. Underlying permafrost remains frozen and surface water cannot drain away, making conditions marshy. Consisting of sedges, snow lichen, arctic meadow grass, cotton grasses and dwarf willow.

Polar and Mountainous Ice Desert
Areas of bare rock and ice with patches of rock-strewn lithosols, low in organic matter and low water content. In sheltered patches only a few mosses, lichens and low shrubs can grow, including woolly moss and purple saxifrage.

Subtropical and Temperate Rain Forest
Precipitation which is less than in the Tropical Rain Forest falls in the long wet season interspersed with a season of reduced rainfall and lower temperatures. As a result there are fewer species, a thinner canopy, fewer lianas and denser ground level foliage. Vegetation consists of evergreen oak, laurel, bamboo, magnolia and tree ferns.

Monsoon Woodland and Open Jungle
Mostly deciduous trees because of the long dry season and lower temperatures. Trees can reach 30m but are sparser than in the rain forests; there is less competition for light and thick jungle vegetation grows at lower levels. High species diversity including lianas, bamboo, teak, sandalwood, sal and banyan.

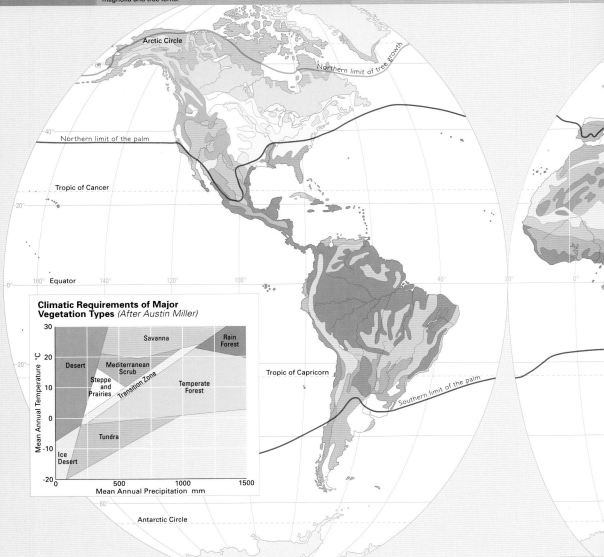

Climatic Requirements of Major Vegetation Types *(After Austin Miller)*

SOIL REGIONS
1:220 000 000

- Tundra soil
- Podzols
- Brown forest soil
- Lightly leached dry forest soil
- Red and yellow subtropical forest soil
- Reddish savanna soil and tropical red earths
- Laterites
- Chernozem
- Degraded chernozem
- Black savanna soil
- Chestnut steppe soil
- Desertic (arid) soil
- Alluvium
- Mountain and high plateau soils
- Oases soil
- Tropical and mangrove swamp

(after Glinka, Stremme, Marbut, and others)

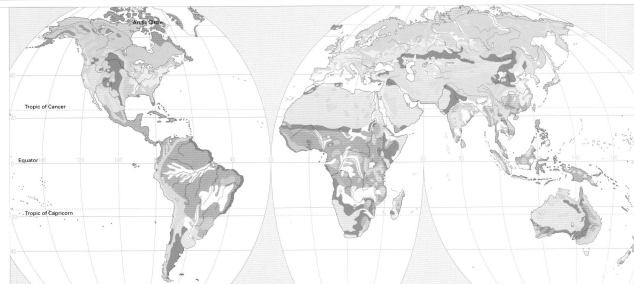

Projection: *Interrupted Mollweide's Homolographic*

Subtropical and Temperate Woodland, Scrub and Bush

Vast clearings with woody shrubs and tall grasses. Trees are fire-resistant and either deciduous or xerophytic because of long dry periods. Species include eucalyptus, acacia, mimosa and euphorbia.

Tropical Savanna with Low Trees and Bush

Tall, coarse grass with enough precipitation to support a scattering of short deciduous trees and thorn scrub. Vegetation consisting of elephant grass, acacia, palms and baobob is limited by aridity, grazing animals and periodic fires; trees have developed thick, woody bark, small leaves or thorns.

Tropical Savanna and Grassland

Areas with a hot climate and long dry season. Extensive areas of tall grasses often reach ng 3.5m with scattered fire and drought resistant bushes, low trees and thickets of elephant grass. Shrubs include acacia, baobab and palms.

NATURAL VEGETATION
(after Austin Miller)

1:116 000 000

Dry Semi-desert with Shrub and Grass

Xerophytic shrubs with thin grass cover and few trees, limited by a long dry season and short, hot, rainy period. Sagebrush, bunch grass and acacia shrubs are common.

Desert Shrub

Scattered xerophytic plants able to withstand daytime extremes in temperature and long periods of drought. There is a large diversity of desert flora such as cacti, yucca, tamarisk, hard grass and artemisia.

Desert

Precipitation less than 250mm per year; vegetation is very sparse, mainly bare rock, sand dunes and salt flats. Vegetation comprises a few xerophytic shrubs and ephemeral flowers.

Dry Steppe and Shrub

Semi-arid with cold, dry winters and hot summers. Bare soil with sparsely distributed short grasses and scattered shrubs and short trees. Species include acacia, artemisia, saksaul and tamarisk.

Temperate Grasslands, Prairie and Steppe

Continuous, tall, dense and deep-rooted swards of ancient grasslands, considered to be natural climax vegetation as determined by soil and climate. Average precipitation 250–750mm with a long dry season, limiting growth of trees and shrubs. Includes Stipa grass, buffalo grass, blue stems and loco weed.

Mediterranean Hardwood Forest and Scrub

Areas with hot and arid summers. Sparse evergreen trees are short and twisted with thick bark, interspersed with areas of scrub land. Trees have waxy leaves or thorns and deep root systems to resist drought. Many of the hardwood forests have been cleared by man, resulting in extensive scrub formation – maquis and chaparral. Species found are evergreen oak, stone pine, cork, olive and myrtle.

Temperate Deciduous Forest and Meadow

Areas of relatively high, well-distributed rainfall and temperatures favourable for forest growth. The tall broadleaved trees form a canopy in the summer, but shed their leaves in the winter. The undergrowth is sparse and poorly developed, but in the spring, herbs and flowers develop quickly. Diverse species with up to 20 per ha, including oak, beech, birch, maple, ash, elm, chestnut and hornbeam. Many of these forests have been cleared for urbanization and farming.

SOIL DEGRADATION

1:220 000 000

Areas of Concern

- Areas of serious concern
- Areas of some concern
- Stable terrain
- Non-vegetated land

Causes of soil degradation (by region)

- Grazing practices
- Other agricultural practices
- Industrialization
- Deforestation
- Fuelwood collection

(after Wageningen 1990)

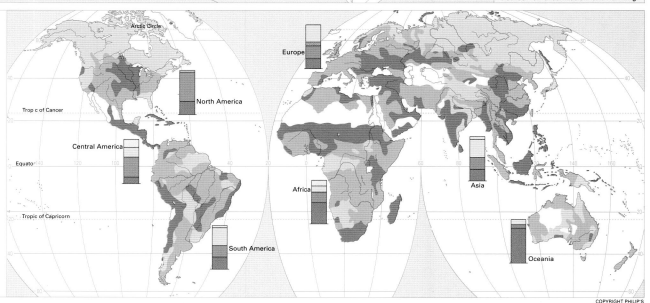

COPYRIGHT PHILIP'S

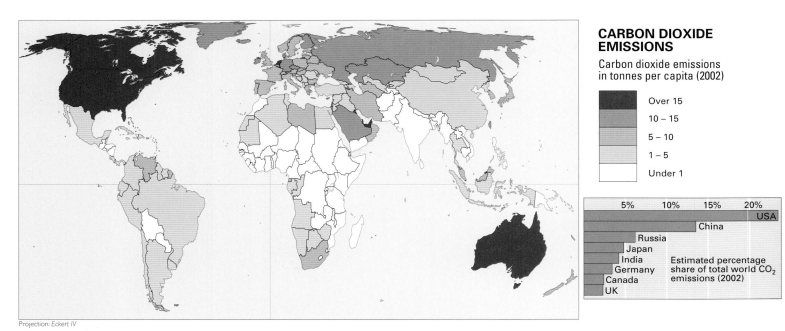

CARBON DIOXIDE EMISSIONS

Carbon dioxide emissions in tonnes per capita (2002)

- Over 15
- 10 – 15
- 5 – 10
- 1 – 5
- Under 1

	5%	10%	15%	20%
USA				
China				
Russia				
Japan				
India				
Germany				
Canada				
UK				

Estimated percentage share of total world CO₂ emissions (2002)

Projection: Eckert IV

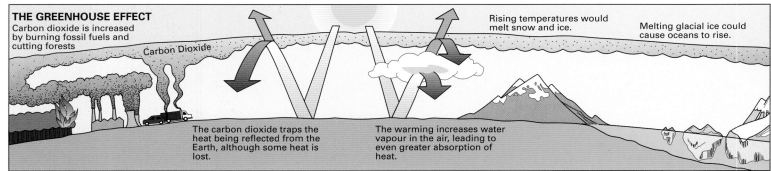

THE GREENHOUSE EFFECT

Carbon dioxide is increased by burning fossil fuels and cutting forests

Carbon Dioxide

The carbon dioxide traps the heat being reflected from the Earth, although some heat is lost.

The warming increases water vapour in the air, leading to even greater absorption of heat.

Rising temperatures would melt snow and ice.

Melting glacial ice could cause oceans to rise.

Northern Hemisphere   Southern Hemisphere

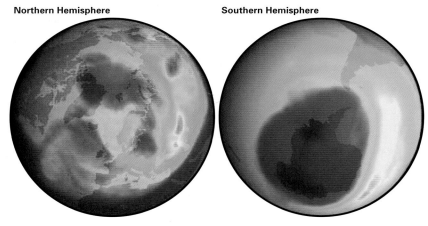

THINNING OZONE LAYER

Total atmospheric ozone concentration in the southern and northern hemispheres (Dobson Units, 2000)

In 1985, scientists working in Antarctica discovered a thinning of the ozone layer, commonly known as an 'ozone hole'. This caused immediate alarm because the ozone layer absorbs most of the Sun's dangerous ultraviolet radiation, which is believed to cause an increase in skin cancer, cataracts and damage to the immune system. Since 1985, ozone depletion has increased and, by 2003, the ozone hole over the South Pole was estimated to be larger than North America. The false-colour images, left, show the total atmospheric ozone concentration in the southern hemisphere (in September 2000) and the northern hemisphere (in March 2000) with the ozone hole clearly identifiable at the centre. The data is from the Tiros Ozone Vertical Sounder, an instrument on the American TIROS weather satellite. The colours represent the ozone concentration in Dobson Units (DU). Scientists agree that ozone depletion is caused by CFCs, a group of manufactured chemicals used in air-conditioning systems and refrigerators. In a 1987 treaty most industrial nations agreed to phase out CFCs and a complete ban on most CFCs was agreed after the end of 1995. However, scientists believe that the chemicals will remain in the atmosphere for 50 to 100 years. As a result, ozone depletion will continue for many years.

PROJECTED CHANGE IN GLOBAL WARMING

C°
+3.0
+2.0
+1.0
0
–0.5

1950   1970   1990   2010   2030   2050

COPYRIGHT PHILIP'S

Rise in average temperatures assuming present trends in CO₂ emissions continue

Assuming some cuts are made in emissions

Assuming drastic cuts are made in emissions

POSSIBLE EFFECT OF SEA LEVEL RISE IN FLORIDA

Sea levels have risen worldwide by about 2 cm since 1900. If CO₂ emissions continue at the same rate, the sea level is expected to rise by 7.4 m by 2200. The map shows the dramatic effects that such a rise could have on the southern part of Florida in the USA.

Submerged land area if sea level rises 7.4 m

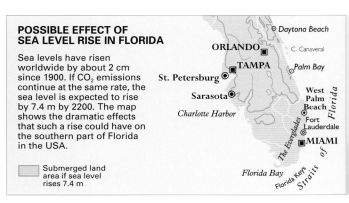

Daytona Beach
ORLANDO
C. Canaveral
TAMPA
Palm Bay
St. Petersburg
Sarasota
West Palm Beach
Charlotte Harbor
Fort Lauderdale
The Everglades
MIAMI
Florida Bay
Florida Keys
Straits of Florida

PREDICTED CHANGE IN TEMPERATURE

The difference between actual annual average surface air temperature, 1960–90, and predicted annual average surface air temperature, 2070–2100. This map shows the predicted increase, assuming a 'medium growth' of the global economy and assuming that no measures to combat the emission of greenhouse gases are taken.

5 – 10°C warmer	
3 – 5°C warmer	
2 – 3°C warmer	
1 – 2°C warmer	
0 – 1°C warmer	

Source: The Hadley Centre of Climate Prediction and Research, The Met. Office.

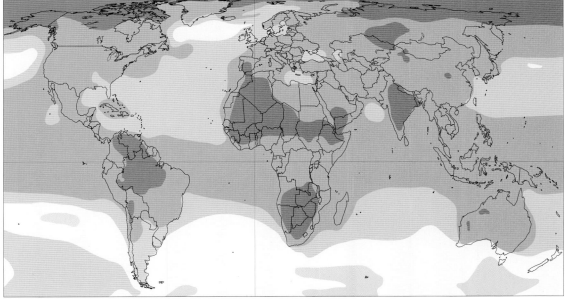

PREDICTED CHANGE IN PRECIPITATION

The difference between actual annual average precipitation, 1960–90, and predicted annual average precipitation, 2070–2100. It should be noted that these predicted annual mean changes mask quite significant seasonal detail.

Over 2 mm more rain per day	
1 – 2 mm more rain per day	
0.5 – 1 mm more rain per day	
0.2 – 0.5 mm more rain per day	
no change	
0.2 – 0.5 mm less rain per day	
0.5 – 1 mm less rain per day	
1 – 2 mm less rain per day	
Over 2 mm less rain per day	

DESERTIFICATION AND DEFORESTATION

Existing deserts and dry areas	
Areas with a very high risk of desertification	
Areas with a high risk of desertification	
Former extent of rainforest	
Existing rainforest	
Degraded rainforest	

Major famines since 1900 (with dates) ■

Deforestation 1990–2000

	Annual deforestation (thous. hectares)	Annual deforestation rate (%)
Brazil	2,309	0.4
Indonesia	1,312	1.2
Mexico	631	1.1
Congo (Dem. Rep.)	532	0.4
Burma (Myanmar)	517	1.4
Nigeria	398	2.6
Peru	269	1.4

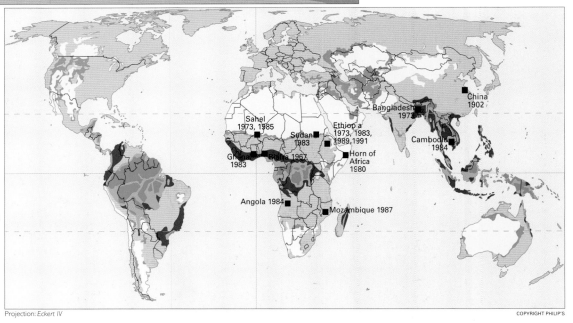

Projection: *Eckert IV*

AGRICULTURAL PRODUCTION

Staple Crops

Wheat
China 15.5% | India 11.7% | USA 11.4% | Russia 6.1% | France 5.5%

World total (2003): 556,349,000 tonnes

Rice
China 28.2% | India 22.4% | Indonesia 8.8% | Bangladesh 6.5% | Vietnam 5.9%

World total (2003): 589,126,000 tonnes

Cassava
Nigeria 17.7% | Brazil 11.7% | Indonesia 9.8% | Thailand 9.7% | D. R. Congo 7.9%

World total (2003): 189,100,000 tonnes

Barley
Russia 12.7% | Canada 8.7% | Germany 7.6% | France 6.9% | Spain 6.1% | Australia 6.0%

World total (2003): 141,503,000 tonnes

Maize
USA 40.3% | China 17.9% | Brazil 7.5% | Mexico 3.1%

World total (2003): 638,043,000 tonnes

Potatoes
China 21.5% | Russia 11.8% | India 7.5% | USA 4.6% | Ukraine 6.0%

World total (2003): 310,810,000 tonnes

Soybeans
USA 34.8% | Brazil 27.2% | Argentina 18.4% | China 8.7%

World total (2003): 189,234,000 tonnes

Millet
India 35.9% | Nigeria 20.5% | Niger 8.4% | China 6.5% | Burkina F. 4.1%

World total (2003): 29,806,000 tonnes

Animal Products

Milk
USA 14.9% | India 7.4% | Russia 6.3% | Germany 5.4% | France 4.9%

World total (2003): 526,915,000 tonnes

Eggs
China 43.2% | USA 8.5% | India 3.6% | Russia 3.4%

World total (2003): 60,469,000 tonnes

Chicken
USA 22.8% | China 14.6% | Brazil 11.9% | Mexico 3.3%

World total (2003): 65,015,000 tonnes

Beef and Veal
USA 20.2% | Brazil 12.8% | China 10.6% | Argentina 4.8% | Australia 3.5%

World total (2003): 58,922,000 tonnes

Pigmeat
China 46.7% | USA 9.2% | Germany 4.3%

World total (2003): 98,507,000 tonnes

Sugars

Sugar Cane
Brazil 28.9% | India 21.7% | China 6.9% | Thailand 4.8% | Pakistan 3.9%

World total (2003): 1,333,253,000 tonnes

Sugar Beet
France 12.5% | USA 11.9% | Germany 11.3% | Russia 8.3% | Ukraine 5.7% | Turkey 5.6% | Poland 4.7%

World total (2003): 233,487,000 tonnes

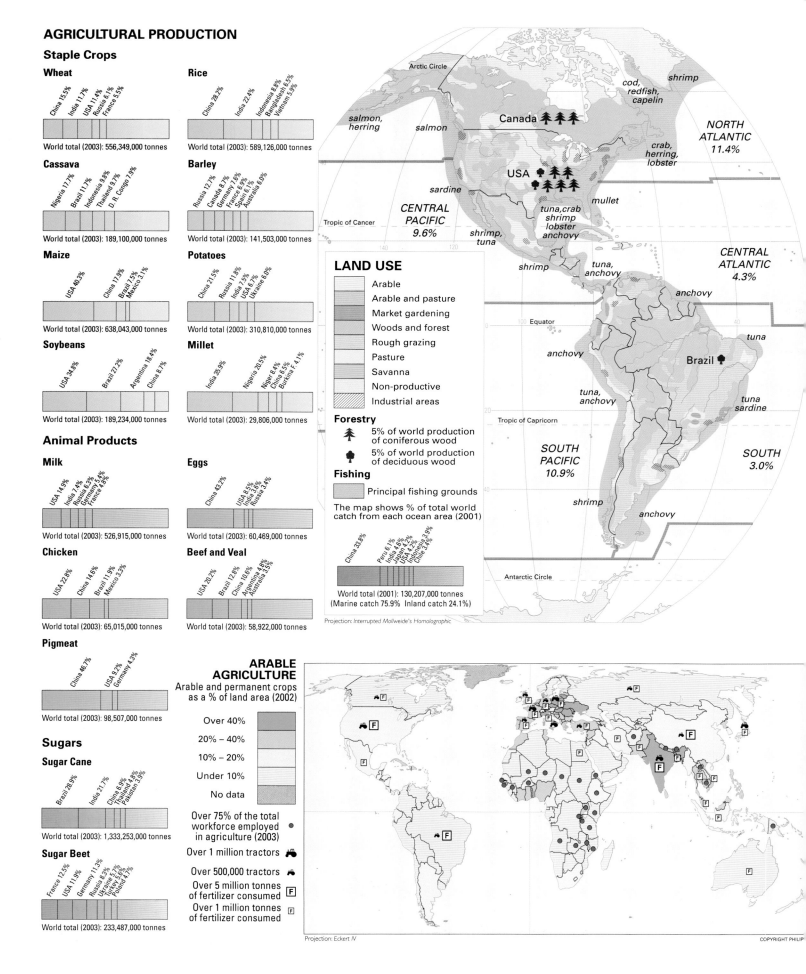

LAND USE

- Arable
- Arable and pasture
- Market gardening
- Woods and forest
- Rough grazing
- Pasture
- Savanna
- Non-productive
- Industrial areas

Forestry

🌲 5% of world production of coniferous wood

🌳 5% of world production of deciduous wood

Fishing

Principal fishing grounds

The map shows % of total world catch from each ocean area (2001)

China 33.8% | Peru 6.1% | India 4.6% | Japan 4.2% | USA 4.2% | Indonesia 3.9% | Chile 3.4%

World total (2001): 130,207,000 tonnes
(Marine catch 75.9% Inland catch 24.1%)

Projection: Interrupted Mollweide's Homolographic

NORTH ATLANTIC 11.4%

CENTRAL PACIFIC 9.6%

CENTRAL ATLANTIC 4.3%

SOUTH PACIFIC 10.9%

SOUTH 3.0%

ARABLE AGRICULTURE
Arable and permanent crops as a % of land area (2002)

- Over 40%
- 20% – 40%
- 10% – 20%
- Under 10%
- No data

● Over 75% of the total workforce employed in agriculture (2003)

🚜 Over 1 million tractors

🚜 Over 500,000 tractors

F Over 5 million tonnes of fertilizer consumed

F Over 1 million tonnes of fertilizer consumed

Projection: Eckert IV

COPYRIGHT PHILIP

LAND USE, FORESTRY AND FISHING

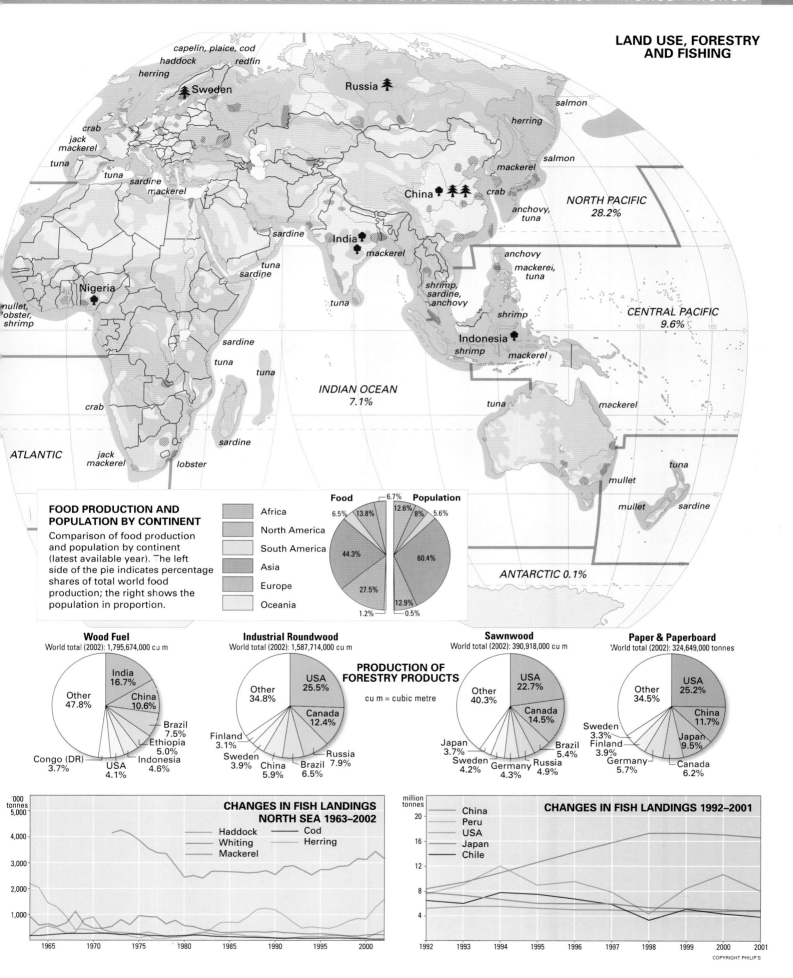

capelin, plaice, cod
haddock   redfin
herring

Sweden

Russia

crab
jack
mackerel

tuna

tuna

sardine
mackerel

salmon

herring

salmon

mackerel

China

crab

NORTH PACIFIC
28.2%

anchovy,
tuna

sardine

India

mackerel

anchovy
mackerel,
tuna

CENTRAL PACIFIC
9.6%

tuna
sardine

shrimp,
sardine,
anchovy

shrimp

Nigeria

tuna

mullet,
lobster,
shrimp

sardine

tuna

Indonesia
shrimp

mackerel

tuna

tuna

INDIAN OCEAN
7.1%

tuna

mackerel

crab

sardine

jack
mackerel

ATLANTIC

lobster

tuna

mullet

mullet   sardine

ANTARCTIC 0.1%

FOOD PRODUCTION AND POPULATION BY CONTINENT

Comparison of food production and population by continent (latest available year). The left side of the pie indicates percentage shares of total world food production; the right shows the population in proportion.

Africa
North America
South America
Asia
Europe
Oceania

Food — 6.7% **Population**
6.5% 13.8%   12.6% 8% 5.6%
44.3%   60.4%
27.5%   12.9%
1.2%   0.5%

PRODUCTION OF FORESTRY PRODUCTS

cu m = cubic metre

Wood Fuel
World total (2002): 1,795,674,000 cu m

India 16.7%
Other 47.8%
China 10.6%
Brazil 7.5%
Ethiopia 5.0%
Congo (DR) 3.7%
USA 4.1%
Indonesia 4.6%

Industrial Roundwood
World total (2002): 1,587,714,000 cu m

Other 34.8%
USA 25.5%
Canada 12.4%
Finland 3.1%
Sweden 3.9%
China 5.9%
Brazil 6.5%
Russia 7.9%

Sawnwood
World total (2002): 390,918,000 cu m

Other 40.3%
USA 22.7%
Canada 14.5%
Japan 3.7%
Sweden 4.2%
Germany 4.3%
Russia 4.9%
Brazil 5.4%

Paper & Paperboard
World total (2002): 324,649,000 tonnes

Other 34.5%
USA 25.2%
China 11.7%
Sweden 3.3%
Finland 3.9%
Germany 5.7%
Japan 9.5%
Canada 6.2%

CHANGES IN FISH LANDINGS NORTH SEA 1963–2002

'000 tonnes

Haddock   Cod
Whiting   Herring
Mackerel

5,000
4,000
3,000
2,000
1,000

1965 1970 1975 1980 1985 1990 1995 2000

CHANGES IN FISH LANDINGS 1992–2001

million tonnes

China
Peru
USA
Japan
Chile

20
16
12
8
4

1992 1993 1994 1995 1996 1997 1998 1999 2000 2001

COPYRIGHT PHILIP'S

ENERGY PRODUCTION BY REGION
Each square represents 1% of world energy production (2002)

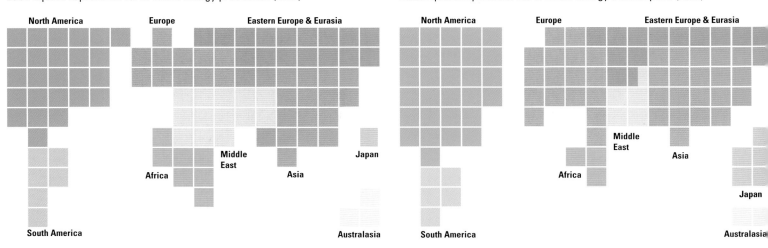

North America · Europe · Eastern Europe & Eurasia · Middle East · Japan · Asia · Africa · South America · Australasia

ENERGY CONSUMPTION BY REGION
Each square represents 1% of world energy consumption (2002)

North America · Europe · Eastern Europe & Eurasia · Middle East · Asia · Africa · Japan · South America · Australasia

ENERGY BALANCE
Difference between energy production and consumption in millions of tonnes of oil equivalent (MtOe) 2004

↑ Energy surplus in MtOe

- Over 35 surplus
- 1 – 35 surplus
- 1 deficit – 1 surplus (approx. balance)
- 1 – 35 deficit
- Over 35 deficit

↓ Energy deficit in MtOe

Fossil fuel production

	Principal	Secondary
Oilfields	●	●
Gasfields	▽	▽
Coalfields	△	△

Projection: Eckert

OIL RESERVES
World oil reserves by region and country, thousand million tonnes (2003)

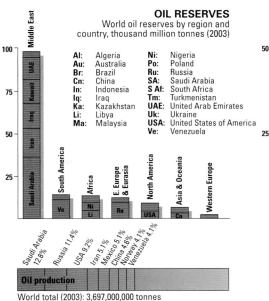

Al:	Algeria	Ni:	Nigeria
Au:	Australia	Po:	Poland
Br:	Brazil	Ru:	Russia
Cn:	China	SA:	Saudi Arabia
In:	Indonesia	S Af:	South Africa
Iq:	Iraq	Tm:	Turkmenistan
Ka:	Kazakhstan	UAE:	United Arab Emirates
Li:	Libya	Uk:	Ukraine
Ma:	Malaysia	USA:	United States of America
		Ve:	Venezuela

Oil production

Saudi Arabia 12.8% · Russia 11.4% · USA 9.2% · Iran 5.1% · Mexico 5.1% · China 4.6% · Norway 4.1% · Venezuela 4.1%

World total (2003): 3,697,000,000 tonnes

GAS RESERVES
World natural gas reserves by region and country, thousand million tonnes of oil equivalent (2003)

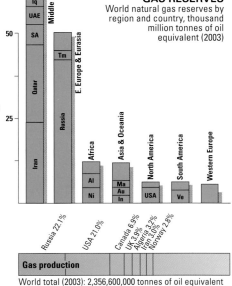

Gas production

Russia 22.1% · USA 21.0% · Canada 6.6% · UK 3.9% · Algeria 3.2% · Iran 3.0% · Norway 2.8%

World total (2003): 2,356,600,000 tonnes of oil equivalent

COAL RESERVES
World coal reserves by region and country, thousand million tonnes (2003, including lignite)

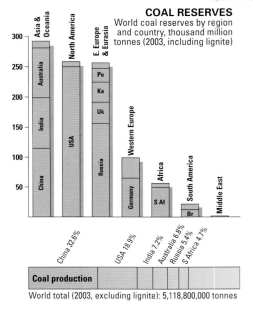

Coal production

China 32.6% · USA 18.9% · India 7.2% · Australia 6.8% · Russia 5.4% · S Africa 4.7%

World total (2003, excluding lignite): 5,118,800,000 tonnes

ELECTRICITY GENERATION

Percentage of electricity generated by source (2004)

Over 75% from thermal

50 – 75% from thermal

Over 75% from hydro

50 – 75% from hydro

Over 50% from nuclear

No dominant source

No data

Selected geothermal plants ⊙

Selected hydroelectric plants ◇

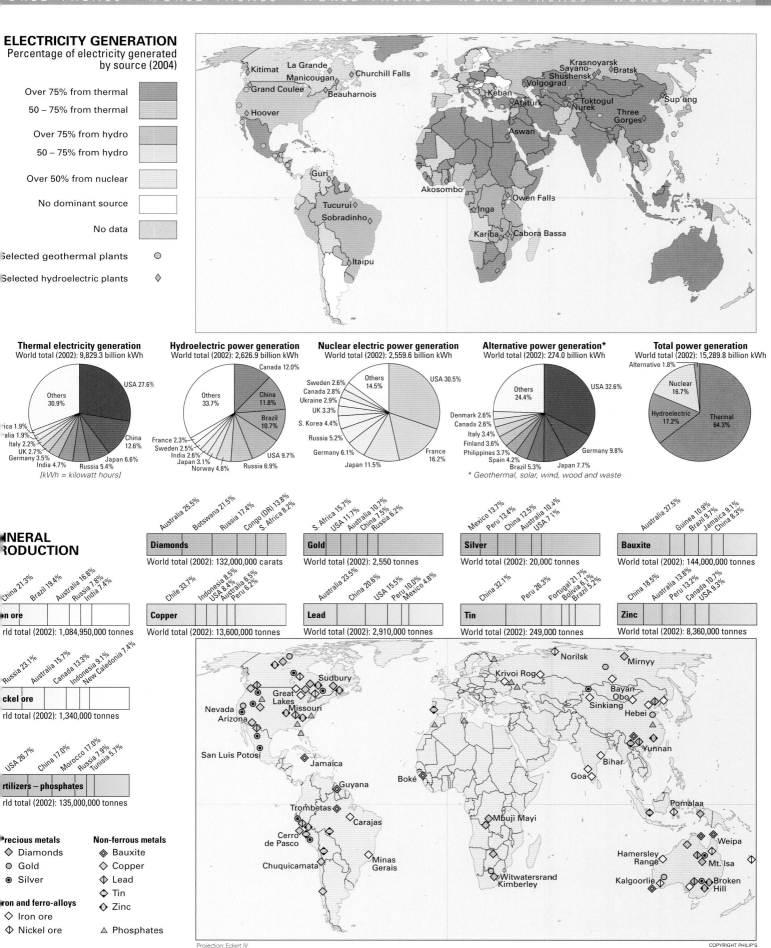

Thermal electricity generation
World total (2002): 9,829.3 billion kWh

USA 27.6%
Others 30.9%
China 12.6%
Japan 6.6%
Russia 5.4%
India 4.7%
Germany 3.5%
UK 2.7%
Italy 2.2%
...alia 1.9%
...rica 1.9%

[kWh = kilowatt hours]

Hydroelectric power generation
World total (2002): 2,626.9 billion kWh

Canada 12.0%
China 11.8%
Brazil 10.7%
Others 33.7%
USA 9.7%
Russia 6.9%
Norway 4.8%
Japan 3.1%
India 2.6%
Sweden 2.5%
France 2.3%

Nuclear electric power generation
World total (2002): 2,559.6 billion kWh

USA 30.5%
France 16.2%
Japan 11.5%
Germany 6.1%
Russia 5.2%
S. Korea 4.4%
UK 3.3%
Ukraine 2.9%
Canada 2.8%
Sweden 2.6%
Others 14.5%

Alternative power generation*
World total (2002): 274.0 billion kWh

USA 32.6%
Germany 9.8%
Japan 7.7%
Brazil 5.3%
Spain 4.2%
Philippines 3.7%
Finland 3.6%
Italy 3.4%
Canada 2.6%
Denmark 2.6%
Others 24.4%

* Geothermal, solar, wind, wood and waste

Total power generation
World total (2002): 15,289.8 billion kWh

Alternative 1.8%
Nuclear 16.7%
Hydroelectric 17.2%
Thermal 64.3%

MINERAL PRODUCTION

...China 21.3% | Brazil 19.4% | Australia 16.8% | Russia 7.8% | India 7.4%

Iron ore
World total (2002): 1,084,950,000 tonnes

Russia 23.1% | Australia 15.7% | Canada 13.3% | Indonesia 9.1% | New Caledonia 7.4%

Nickel ore
World total (2002): 1,340,000 tonnes

USA 26.7% | China 17.0% | Morocco 17.0% | Russia 7.9% | Tunisia 5.7%

Fertilizers – phosphates
World total (2002): 135,000,000 tonnes

Australia 25.5% | Botswana 21.5% | Russia 17.4% | Congo (DR) 13.8% | S. Africa 8.2%

Diamonds
World total (2002): 132,000,000 carats

S. Africa 15.7% | USA 11.7% | Australia 10.7% | China 7.5% | Russia 6.2%

Gold
World total (2002): 2,550 tonnes

Mexico 13.7% | Peru 13.4% | China 12.5% | Australia 10.4% | USA 7.1%

Silver
World total (2002): 20,000 tonnes

Australia 37.5% | Guinea 10.9% | Brazil 9.7% | Jamaica 9.1% | China 8.3%

Bauxite
World total (2002): 144,000,000 tonnes

Chile 33.7% | Indonesia 8.5% | USA 8.4% | Australia 6.5% | Peru 6.2%

Copper
World total (2002): 13,600,000 tonnes

Australia 23.5% | China 20.6% | USA 15.5% | Peru 10.0% | Mexico 4.8%

Lead
World total (2002): 2,910,000 tonnes

China 32.1% | Peru 26.3% | Portugal 21.7% | Bolivia 6.1% | Brazil 5.2%

Tin
World total (2002): 249,000 tonnes

China 18.5% | Australia 13.8% | Peru 13.2% | Canada 10.7% | USA 9.3%

Zinc
World total (2002): 8,360,000 tonnes

Precious metals
◇ Diamonds
⊙ Gold
◉ Silver

Iron and ferro-alloys
◇ Iron ore
◇ Nickel ore

Non-ferrous metals
◇ Bauxite
◇ Copper
◇ Lead
◇ Tin
◇ Zinc
△ Phosphates

Projection: Eckert IV

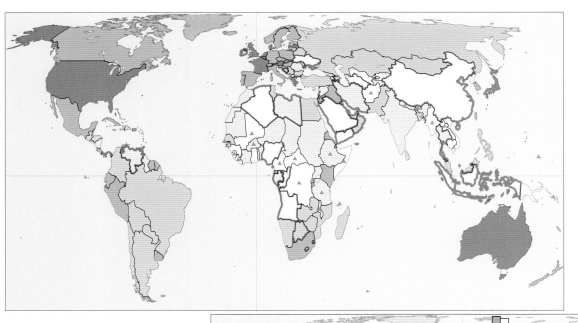

IMPORTANCE OF SERVICE INDUSTRY
Percentage of total GDP from service sector (2003)

- Over 70%
- 60 – 70%
- 50 – 60%
- 40 – 50%
- Under 40%
- No data

Over 40% of total GDP from industrial sector (2003)

▲ Over 40% of total GDP from agricultural sector (200...

LOCATION OF MANUFACTURING

- **Industrial regions**
- **Steel**
World total (2000): 845 million tonnes
- **Cement**
World total (2000): 1,600 million tonnes
- **Motor vehicles**
World total (2000): 40.3 million cars/trucks
- **Paper**
World total (2002): 324.6 million tonnes
- **Textiles***
World total (2000): 21.0 million tonnes
*cotton, silk & wool

40% / 30% / 20% / 10% Production of manufactured goods as a percentage of world total (for selected goods and countries)

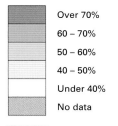

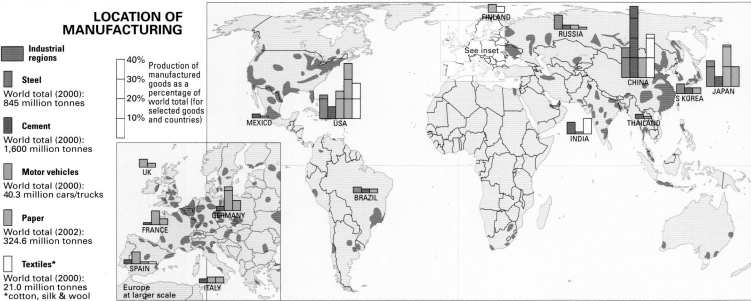

Europe at larger scale

EMPLOYMENT BY ECONOMIC ACTIVITY Selected countries (2002)

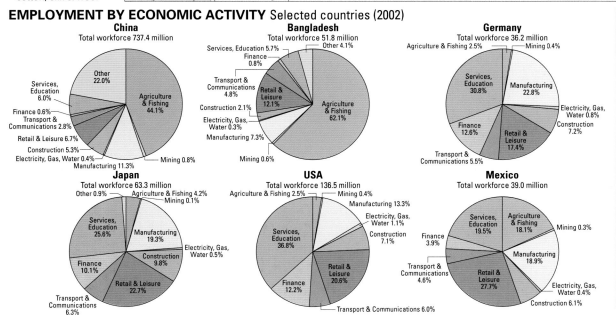

China
Total workforce 737.4 million
- Other 22.0%
- Agriculture & Fishing 44.1%
- Services, Education 6.0%
- Finance 0.6%
- Transport & Communications 2.8%
- Retail & Leisure 6.7%
- Construction 5.3%
- Electricity, Gas, Water 0.4%
- Manufacturing 11.3%
- Mining 0.8%

Bangladesh
Total workforce 51.8 million
- Services, Education 5.7%
- Finance 0.8%
- Other 4.1%
- Transport & Communications 4.8%
- Retail & Leisure 12.1%
- Construction 2.1%
- Electricity, Gas, Water 0.3%
- Manufacturing 7.3%
- Mining 0.6%
- Agriculture & Fishing 62.1%

Germany
Total workforce 36.2 million
- Agriculture & Fishing 2.5%
- Mining 0.4%
- Services, Education 30.8%
- Manufacturing 22.8%
- Electricity, Gas, Water 0.8%
- Construction 7.2%
- Finance 12.6%
- Retail & Leisure 17.4%
- Transport & Communications 5.5%

Japan
Total workforce 63.3 million
- Other 0.9%
- Agriculture & Fishing 4.2%
- Mining 0.1%
- Services, Education 25.6%
- Manufacturing 19.3%
- Electricity, Gas, Water 0.5%
- Construction 9.8%
- Finance 10.1%
- Retail & Leisure 22.7%
- Transport & Communications 6.3%

USA
Total workforce 136.5 million
- Agriculture & Fishing 2.5%
- Mining 0.4%
- Manufacturing 13.3%
- Electricity, Gas, Water 1.1%
- Construction 7.1%
- Services, Education 36.8%
- Retail & Leisure 20.6%
- Finance 12.2%
- Transport & Communications 6.0%

Mexico
Total workforce 39.0 million
- Services, Education 19.5%
- Agriculture & Fishing 18.1%
- Mining 0.3%
- Finance 3.9%
- Manufacturing 18.9%
- Transport & Communications 4.6%
- Retail & Leisure 27.7%
- Electricity, Gas, Water 0.4%
- Construction 6.1%

RESEARCH & DEVELOPMEN...

Scientists and engineers in R&D (per million people) 1990–2003

Country	Total
Finland	7,431
Iceland	6,592
Sweden	5,171
Japan	5,085
Denmark	4,822
USA	4,526
Norway	4,442
Singapore	4,352
Luxembourg	3,757
Switzerland	3,594
Canada	3,487
Australia	3,446
Russia	3,415
Germany	3,222
Belgium	3,180
France	3,134
South Korea	2,979
Netherlands	2,826
UK	2,691
New Zealand	2,593

WORLD TRADE
Percentage share of total
world exports by value (2003)

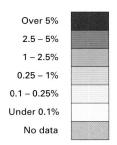

- Over 5%
- 2.5 – 5%
- 1 – 2.5%
- 0.25 – 1%
- 0.1 – 0.25%
- Under 0.1%
- No data

The members of 'G8', the inner circle
of OECD, account for more than half
the total. The majority of nations
contribute less than one quarter of 1%
to the worldwide total of exports;
EU countries account for 35%; the
Pacific Rim nations over 50%.

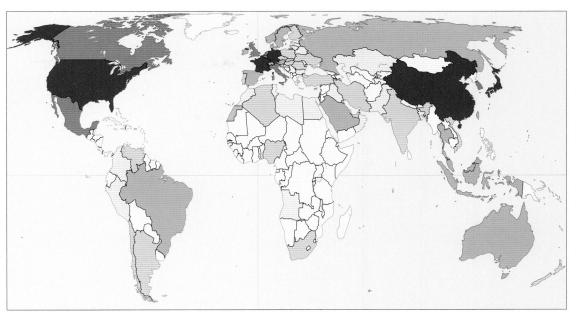

AJOR EXPORTS Leading manufactured items and their exporters

Motor Vehicles
World total (2004): US$ 265,898 million

Germany 19%, Japan 15%, USA 9%, Canada 8%, France 7%, Spain 5%, Belgium 5%, UK 4%, exico 4%, Korea 3%, Italy 3%, China 2%, Sweden 2%, Other 13%

Telecommunications Gear
World total (2004): US$ 405,989 million

China 26%, S. Korea 9%, Japan 9%, USA 7%, Germany 7%, Mexico 5%, UK 3%, Malaysia 3%, France 3%, Singapore 3%, Sweden 3%, Hungary 3%, Other 17%

Petrol Products
World total (2004): US$ 496,092 million

Russia 15%, Norway 8%, Venezuela 6%, UK 6%, Canada 5%, Mexico 5%, Algeria 4%, Netherlands 4%, Singapore 3%, USA 3%, Other 41%

Computers
World total (2004): US$ 236,396 million

China 26%, USA 10%, Neth. 8%, Germany 7%, Singapore 7%, Malaysia 5%, Mexico 5%, Korea 4%, eland 4%, UK 4%, Japan 4%, Other 15%

Electrical Components
World total (2004): US$ 838,552 million

China 13%, USA 11%, Japan 10%, Germany 9%, Singapore 7%, S. Korea 4%, Malaysia 4%, France 3%, Mexico 3%, Other 36%

Pharmaceuticals
World total (2004): US$ 311,399 million

Germany 11%, Belgium 10%, USA 8%, Switzerland 7%, UK 7%, France 7%, Ireland 6%, Italy 4%, Neth. 3%, Sweden 2%, Other 37%

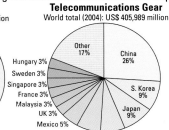

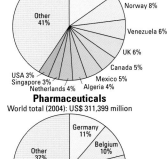
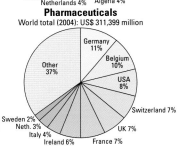
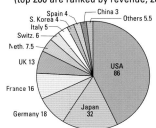

MULTINATIONAL CORPORATIONS (MNCs)
Country of origin of world's top 200 MNCs
(top 200 are ranked by revenue, 2002)

USA 86, Japan 32, Germany 18, France 16, UK 13, Neth. 7.5, Switz. 6, Italy 5, S. Korea 4, Spain 4, China 3, Others 5.5

Top ten MNCs by revenue (million US$), 2002

Wal-Mart	Supermarket chain	219,812	USA
Exxon Mobil	Petroleum	191,581	USA
General Motors	Motor vehicles	177,260	USA
BP	Petroleum	174,218	UK
Ford Motor	Motor vehicles	162,412	USA
Enron*	Energy	138,718	USA
DaimlerChrysler	Motor vehicles	136,897	Germany
Royal Dutch/Shell	Petroleum	135,211	Neth/UK
General Electric	Energy and finance	125,913	USA
Toyota Motor	Motor vehicles	120,814	Japan

* Enron ceased trading in 2002

INTERNET AND TELECOMMUNICATIONS
Percentage of total population
using the Internet (2003)

World total 604.1 million Internet users

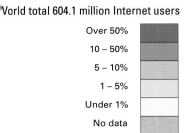

- Over 50%
- 10 – 50%
- 5 – 10%
- 1 – 5%
- Under 1%
- No data

Telecommunications

Trade in office machines and
telecom equipment,
percentage of world total
(2002)

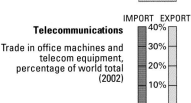

IMPORT   EXPORT
40%
30%
20%
10%

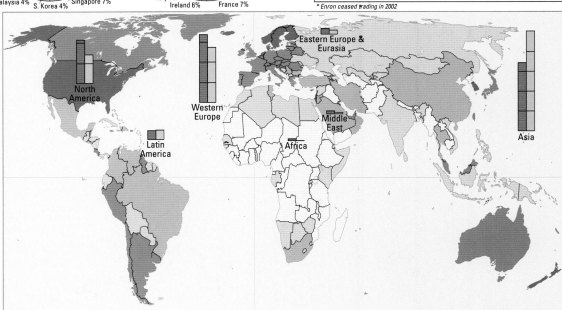

Projection: Eckert IV

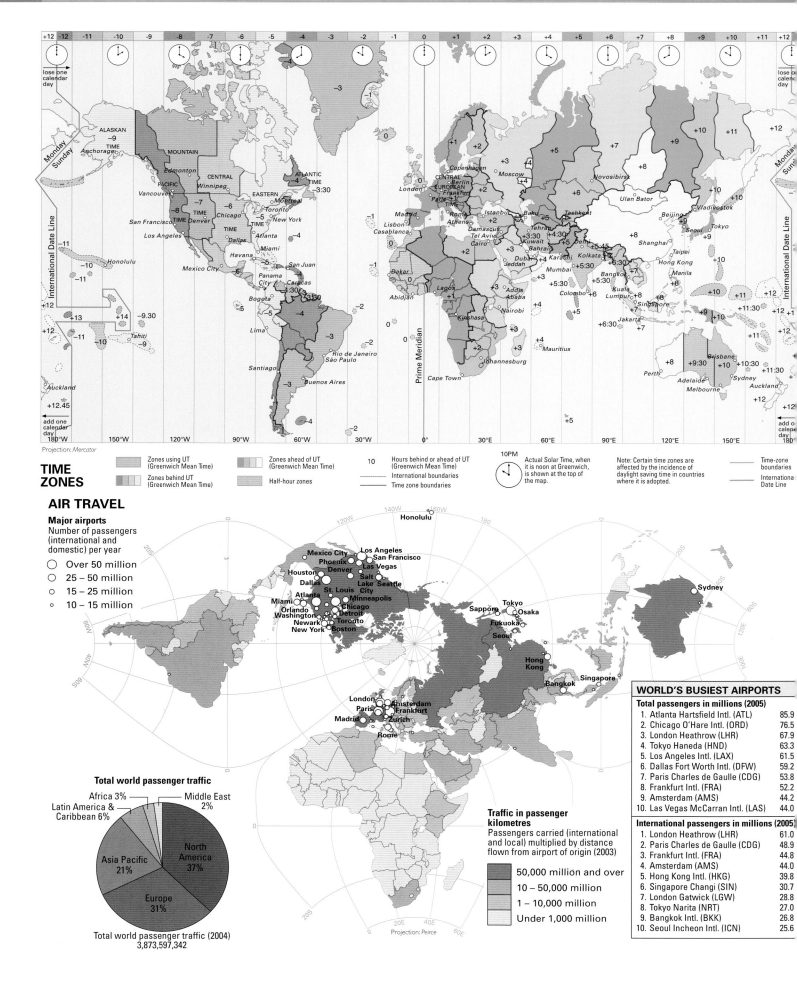

Projection: Mercator

TIME ZONES

Zones using UT (Greenwich Mean Time)	Zones ahead of UT (Greenwich Mean Time)	10 Hours behind or ahead of UT (Greenwich Mean Time)
Zones behind UT (Greenwich Mean Time)	Half-hour zones	International boundaries
		Time zone boundaries

10PM Actual Solar Time, when it is noon at Greenwich, is shown at the top of the map.

Note: Certain time zones are affected by the incidence of daylight saving time in countries where it is adopted.

Time-zone boundaries

International Date Line

AIR TRAVEL

Major airports
Number of passengers (international and domestic) per year

- ○ Over 50 million
- ○ 25 – 50 million
- ○ 15 – 25 million
- ○ 10 – 15 million

Total world passenger traffic

- Africa 3%
- Latin America & Caribbean 6%
- Middle East 2%
- North America 37%
- Asia Pacific 21%
- Europe 31%

Total world passenger traffic (2004)
3,873,597,342

Traffic in passenger kilometres
Passengers carried (international and local) multiplied by distance flown from airport of origin (2003)

- 50,000 million and over
- 10 – 50,000 million
- 1 – 10,000 million
- Under 1,000 million

Projection: Peirce

WORLD'S BUSIEST AIRPORTS

Total passengers in millions (2005)

1. Atlanta Hartsfield Intl. (ATL)	85.9
2. Chicago O'Hare Intl. (ORD)	76.5
3. London Heathrow (LHR)	67.9
4. Tokyo Haneda (HND)	63.3
5. Los Angeles Intl. (LAX)	61.5
6. Dallas Fort Worth Intl. (DFW)	59.2
7. Paris Charles de Gaulle (CDG)	53.8
8. Frankfurt Intl. (FRA)	52.2
9. Amsterdam (AMS)	44.2
10. Las Vegas McCarran Intl. (LAS)	44.0

International passengers in millions (2005)

1. London Heathrow (LHR)	61.0
2. Paris Charles de Gaulle (CDG)	48.9
3. Frankfurt Intl. (FRA)	44.8
4. Amsterdam (AMS)	44.0
5. Hong Kong Intl. (HKG)	39.8
6. Singapore Changi (SIN)	30.7
7. London Gatwick (LGW)	28.8
8. Tokyo Narita (NRT)	27.0
9. Bangkok Intl. (BKK)	26.8
10. Seoul Incheon Intl. (ICN)	25.6

UNESCO WORLD HERITAGE SITES 2005

Total sites = 812 (628 cultural, 160 natural and 24 mixed)

Region	Cultural sites	Natural sites	Mixed sites
Africa	31	32	2
Arab States	56	4	1
Asia & Pacific	112	43	9
Europe & North America	352	48	9
Latin America & Caribbean	77	33	3

Europe at larger scale

Destinations

- ■ Cultural & historical centres
- □ Coastal resorts
- □ Ski resorts
- Centres of entertainment
- Places of pilgrimage
- Places of great natural beauty

Other tourist destinations

TOURIST DESTINATIONS

Projection: Peirce

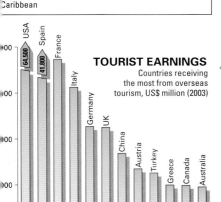

TOURIST EARNINGS

Countries receiving the most from overseas tourism, US$ million (2003)

Movement of tourists

- More than 10 million
- 5 – 10 million
- 3 – 5 million
- Less than 3 million

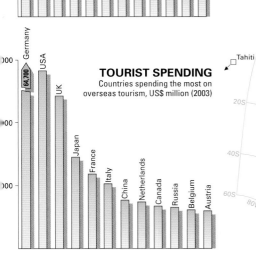

TOURIST SPENDING

Countries spending the most on overseas tourism, US$ million (2003)

IMPORTANCE OF TOURISM

Tourism receipts as a percentage of Gross National Income (2002)

- 10% and over
- 5 – 10%
- 2.5 – 5%
- 1 – 2.5%
- Under 1%
- No data

Arrivals from abroad in millions (2001)

France	75.6
Spain	49.5
USA	45.5
Italy	39.0
China	33.2

(UK = 23.4 million)

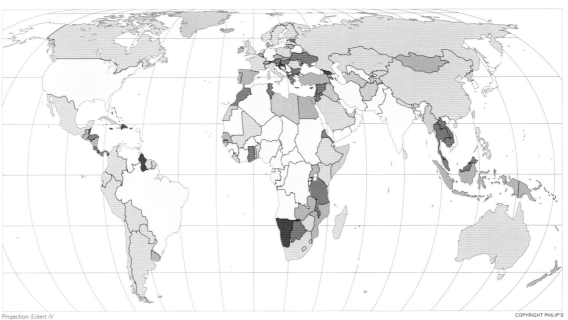

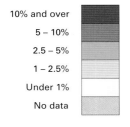

Projection: Eckert IV

WEALTH
Gross Domestic Product per capita PPP (2003)

Annual value of goods and services divided by the population, using purchasing power parity (PPP) which gives real prices instead of variable exchange rates.

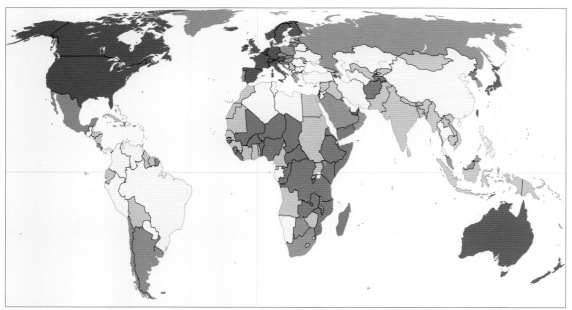

	Over 250% world average
	100 – 250% world average

World average: US$ 8,200

	50 – 100% world average
	15 – 50% world average
	Under 15% world average
	No data

Highest GDP (US$)		Lowest GDP (US$)	
Lux'bourg	55,100	East Timor	500
USA	37,800	Sierra Leone	500
Norway	37,700	Somalia	500
San Marino	34,600	Burundi	600
Switzerland	32,800	Congo (D.Rep.)	600

(UK = US$ 27,700)

WATER SUPPLY

Percentage of total population with access to safe drinking water (2000)

Over 90%	
75 – 90%	
60 – 75%	
45 – 60%	
30 – 45%	
Under 30%	

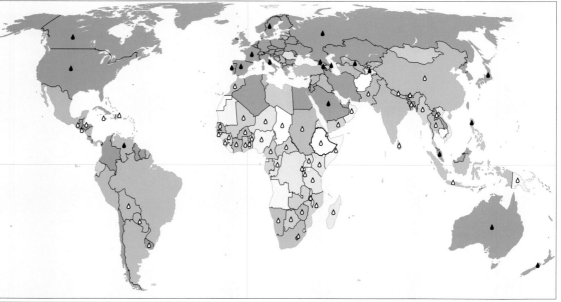

Least amount of safe drinking water

Afghanistan	13%	Cambodia	30%
Ethiopia	24%	Mauritania	37%
Chad	27%	Angola	38%
Sierra Leone	28%	Oman	39%

Daily consumption per capita
◊ Under 80 litres   ◆ Over 320 litres

80 litres a day is considered necessary for a reasonable quality of life

HUMAN DEVELOPMENT INDEX (HDI)

HDI (calculated by the UNDP) gives a value to countries using indicators of life expectancy, education and standards of living in 2002. Higher values show more developed countries.

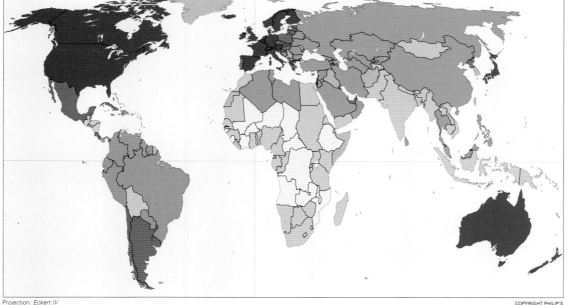

	Over 0.9
	0.8 – 0.9
	0.7 – 0.8
	0.4 – 0.7
	Under 0.4
	No data

Highest values		Lowest values	
Norway	0.952	Sierra Leone	0.273
Australia	0.946	Niger	0.292
Sweden	0.946	Burkina Faso	0.302
Canada	0.943	Mali	0.326
Netherlands	0.942	Burundi	0.339

(UK = 0.936)

Projection: *Eckert IV*

HEALTH CARE

Number of qualified doctors
per 100,000 people (2003)

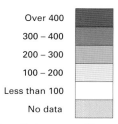

Over 400

300 – 400

200 – 300

100 – 200

Less than 100

No data

Countries with the most and least
doctors per 100,000 people

Most doctors		Least doctors	
Italy	607	Burundi	1
Cuba	596	Mozambique	2
Georgia	463	Rwanda	2
Belarus	450	Chad	3
Greece	438	Ethiopia	3

(UK = 164 doctors)

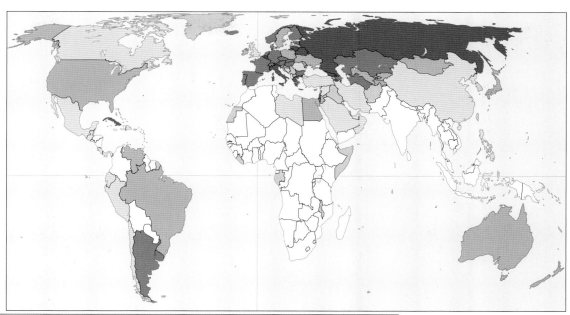

ILLITERACY AND EDUCATION

Percentage of adult population
unable to read or write (2003)

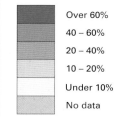

Over 60%

40 – 60%

20 – 40%

10 – 20%

Under 10%

No data

Countries with the highest
and lowest illiteracy rates

Highest (%)		Lowest (%)	
Niger	82	Australia	0
Burkina Faso	73	Denmark	0
Sierra Leone	69	Finland	0
Guinea	64	Liechtenstein	0
Afghanistan	44	Luxembourg	0

(UK = 1%)

GENDER DEVELOPMENT INDEX (GDI)

GDI shows economic and social differences
between men and women by using
various UNDP indicators (2002). Countries
with higher values of GDI have more
equality between men and women.

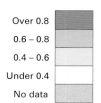

Over 0.8

0.6 – 0.8

0.4 – 0.6

Under 0.4

No data

Highest values		Lowest values	
Norway	0.955	Niger	0.278
Sweden	0.946	Burkina Faso	0.291
Australia	0.945	Mali	0.309
Canada	0.941	Guinea-Bissau	0.329
Netherlands	0.938	Burundi	0.337

(UK = 0.934)

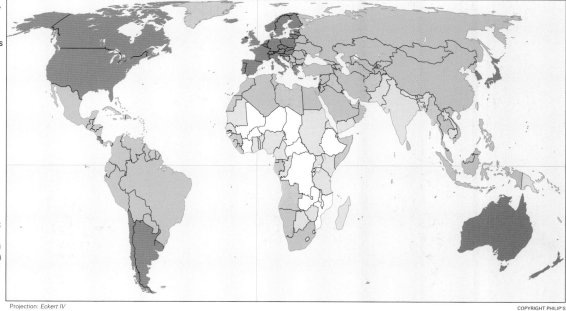

Projection: *Eckert IV*

COPYRIGHT PHILIP'S

AGE DISTRIBUTION PYRAMIDS (2005)

The bars represent the percentage of the total population (males plus females) in each age group. Developed countries such as New Zealand have populations spread evenly across age groups and usually a growing percentage of elderly people. Developing countries such as Kenya have the great majority of their people in the younger age groups, about to enter their most fertile years.

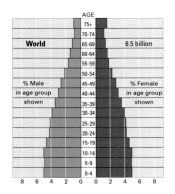

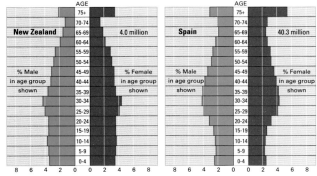

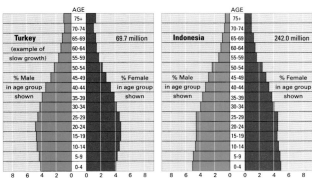

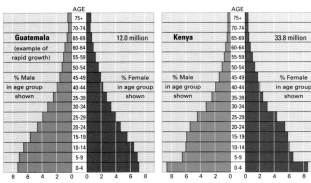

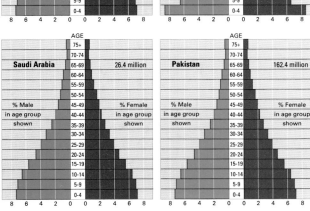

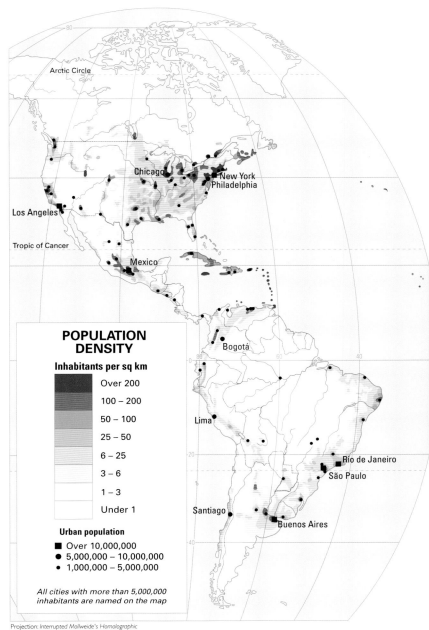

POPULATION DENSITY

Inhabitants per sq km

- Over 200
- 100 – 200
- 50 – 100
- 25 – 50
- 6 – 25
- 3 – 6
- 1 – 3
- Under 1

Urban population

- ■ Over 10,000,000
- ● 5,000,000 – 10,000,000
- • 1,000,000 – 5,000,000

All cities with more than 5,000,000 inhabitants are named on the map

Projection: Interrupted Mollweide's Homolographic

POPULATION CHANGE 1930–2020   Population totals are in millions

Figures in italics represent the percentage average annual increase for the period shown

	1930	1930–1960	1960	1960–1990	1990	1990–2020	2020
World	2,013	*1.4%*	3,019	*1.9%*	5,292	*1.4%*	8,062
Africa	155	*2.0%*	281	*2.9%*	648	*2.7%*	1,441
North America	135	*1.3%*	199	*1.1%*	276	*0.6%*	327
Latin America*	129	*1.8%*	218	*2.4%*	448	*1.6%*	719
Asia	1,073	*1.5%*	1,669	*2.1%*	3,108	*1.4%*	4,680
Europe	355	*0.6%*	425	*0.6%*	498	*0.1%*	514
Oceania	10	*1.4%*	16	*1.8%*	27	*1.1%*	37
CIS	176	*0.7%*	214	*1.0%*	288	*0.6%*	343

* South America plus Central America, Mexico and the West Indies
Commonwealth of Independent States, formerly the USSR

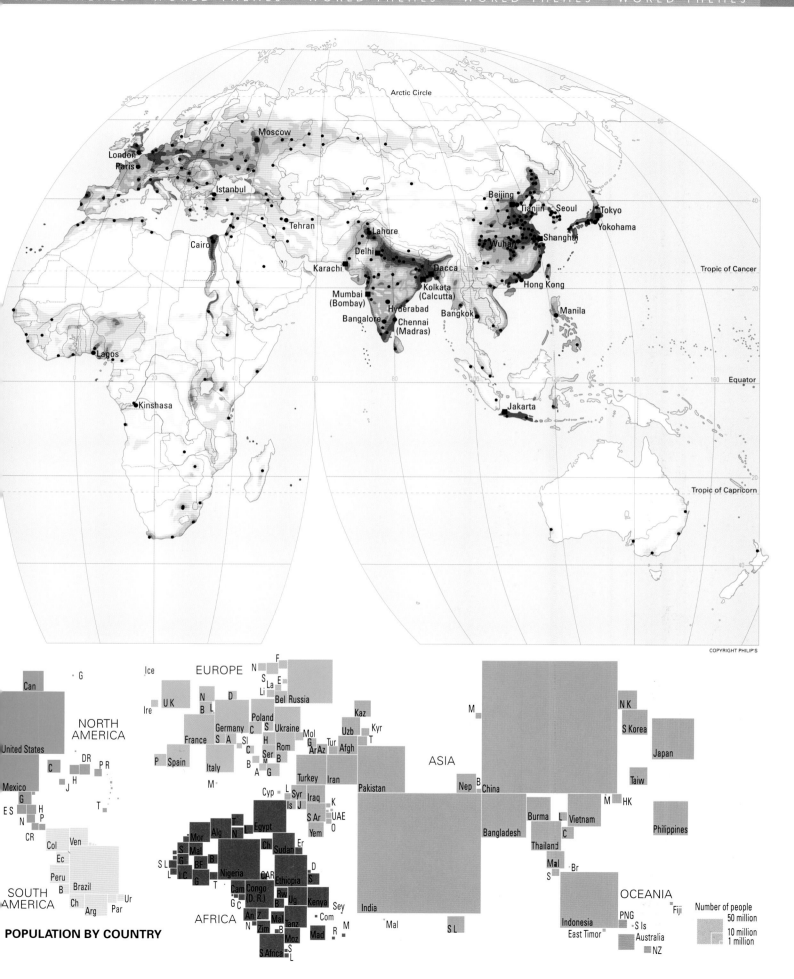

Arctic Circle

Moscow

London
Paris

Istanbul

Tehran

Cairo

Lahore

Delhi

Karachi

Beijing

Tianjin Seoul Tokyo

Wuhan Shanghai Yokohama

Dacca

Mumbai
(Bombay)

Kolkata
(Calcutta)

Hyderabad

Bangalore Chennai
(Madras)

Hong Kong

Bangkok

Manila

Tropic of Cancer

Lagos

Kinshasa

Jakarta

Equator

Tropic of Capricorn

COPYRIGHT PHILIP'S

POPULATION BY COUNTRY

EUROPE

Ice

Can

G

NORTH
AMERICA

United States

UK

Ire

N B L

D

Poland

Germany

France

P Spain

Italy

M

N

F

S E
Li La

Bel Russia

Kaz

Ukraine

S
A SI

C

H
Ser

B
A G

Rom

Mol

Kyr
Uzb
Ar Az Tur Afgh
G T

M

DR

C
J H

P R

T

Mexico

G
E S
N
CR

H
P

Turkey

Iran

Pakistan

M

Nep
B China

ASIA

N K

S Korea

Japan

Taiw

M HK

Col Ven

Ec

Peru

Cyp

Syr
Is

L
J

Iraq

S Ar

Yem

K
UAE
O

Burma

L

Bangladesh

Thailand

Vietnam

C

Mal
S

Br

Philippines

Ur

SOUTH
AMERICA

B Brazil

Ch Arg

Par

Mor

S Mal
L I C
S L
T BF B

Cam

N Z
Zim

S Africa

Alg

Nigeria

G C

Mad

T N

Ch

CAR

An

Mal
Tanz

Moz

L

B

Congo
(D. R.)

Rw
B

Mal

Egypt

Sudan

Ethiopia

Ug
Kenya

R M

AFRICA

Er

D

Sey

Com

Mal

S L

OCEANIA

Indonesia

East Timor

PNG
S Is

Fiji

Australia

NZ

Number of people
50 million
10 million
1 million

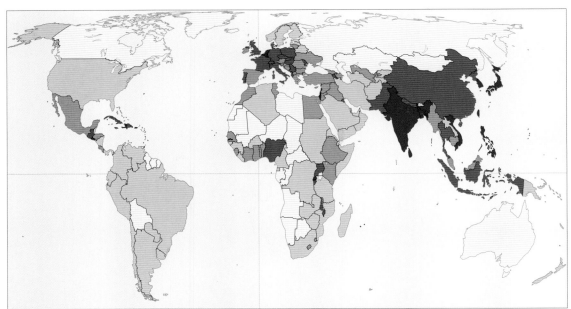

POPULATION DENSITY

Density of people per
square kilometre (2004)

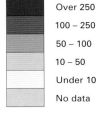

Over 250

100 – 250

50 – 100

10 – 50

Under 10

No data

Most and least densely
populated countries

Most		Least	
Singapore	6,283	W. Sahara	1.0
Malta	1,256	Mongolia	1.8
Maldives	1,131	Namibia	2.4
Bahrain	1,019	Australia	2.6
Bangladesh	982	Botswana	2.6

(UK = 246.2 people per square km)

POPULATION CHANGE

Expected change in total
population (2000–2010)

Over 40% gain

20 – 40% gain

10 – 20% gain

0 – 10% gain

Loss or no change

No data

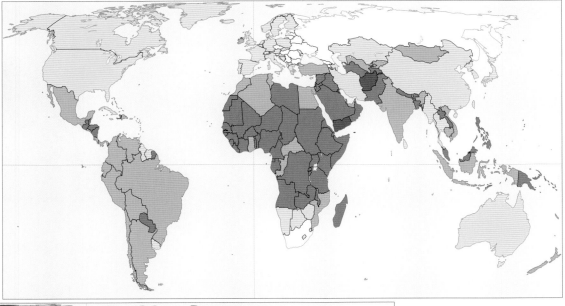

Greatest population gains
and losses

Greatest gains (%)		Greatest losses (%)	
Afghanistan	44.4	Bulgaria	– 8.6
Kuwait	41.2	Trinidad & Tob.	– 7.4
Yemen	41.0	Latvia	– 6.7
Uganda	39.8	Estonia	– 6.4
Oman	39.1	Ukraine	– 6.1

(UK = 3% gain)

URBAN POPULATION

People living in urban areas
as a percentage of total
population (2002)

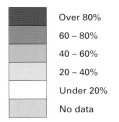

Over 80%

60 – 80%

40 – 60%

20 – 40%

Under 20%

No data

Countries that are the most
and least urbanized (%)

Most urbanized		Least urbanized	
Singapore	100	Bhutan	8.2
Belgium	97.2	Burundi	9.6
Kuwait	96.2	Uganda	12.2
Iceland	92.7	Papua N. G.	13.2
Uruguay	92.4	Nepal	14.6

(UK = 89.0%)

Projection: *Eckert IV*

CHILD MORTALITY

Deaths of children under 1 year old per 1,000 live births (2004)

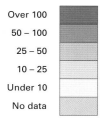

Over 100	
50 – 100	
25 – 50	
10 – 25	
Under 10	
No data	

Countries with the highest and lowest child mortality

Highest		Lowest	
Angola	193	Singapore	2
Afghanistan	166	Sweden	3
Sierra Leone	145	Japan	3
Mozambique	137	Iceland	3
Liberia	131	Finland	4

(UK = 5 deaths)

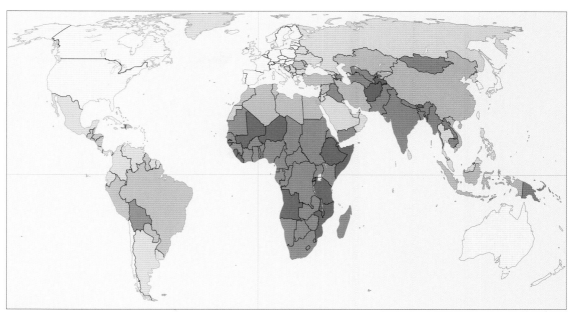

LIFE EXPECTANCY

Life expectancy at birth in years (2004)

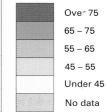

Over 75	
65 – 75	
55 – 65	
45 – 55	
Under 45	
No data	

Countries with the longest and shortest life expectancy at birth in years

Longest		Shortest	
Andorra	83.5	Botswana	30.8
San Marino	81.5	Zambia	35.2
Singapore	81.5	Angola	36.8
Japan	81.0	Lesotho	36.8
Switzerland	80.3	Mozambique	37.1

(UK = 78.3 years)

FAMILY SIZE

Children born per woman (2004)

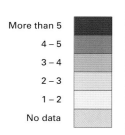

More than 5	
4 – 5	
3 – 4	
2 – 3	
1 – 2	
No data	

Countries with the largest and smallest family size

Largest		Smallest	
Somalia	6.9	Singapore	1.0
Niger	6.8	Lithuania	1.2
Afghanistan	6.8	Czech Rep.	1.2
Yemen	6.8	Slovenia	1.2
Uganda	6.6	Latvia	1.3

(UK = 1.7 children)

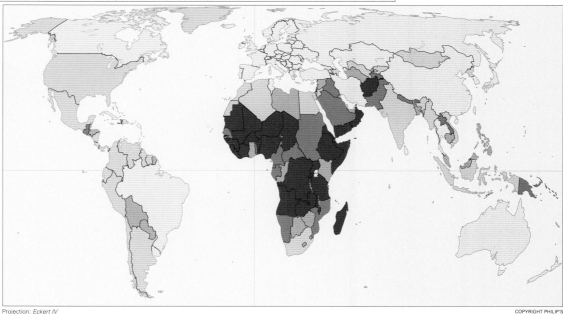

Projection: *Eckert IV*

COPYRIGHT PHILIP'S

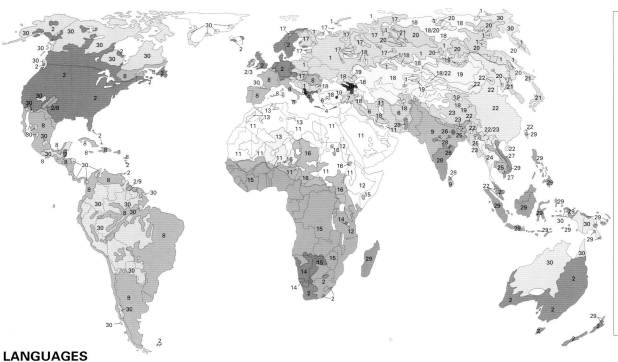

Language can be classified by ancestry and structure. For example, the Romance and Germanic groups are both derived from an Indo-European language believed to have been spoken 5,000 years ago.

First-Language Speakers, in millions (2000)
Mandarin Chinese 874, Hindi 366, English 341, Spanish 336, Bengali 207, Portuguese 176, Russian 167, Japanese 125, German 100, Korean 78, Wu Chinese 77, French 77, Javanese 75, Yue Chinese 71, Telugu 69, Vietnamese 68, Marathi 68, Tamil 66, Italian 62.

Official Languages (% of total world population)
English 27%, Chinese 19%, Hindi 13.5%, Spanish 5.4%, Russian 5.2%, French 4.2%, Arabic 3.3%, Portuguese 3%, Malay 3%, Bengali 2.9%, Japanese 2.3%.

LANGUAGES

INDO-EUROPEAN FAMILY
- 1 Balto-Slavic group (incl. Russian, Ukrainian)
- 2 Germanic group (incl. English, German)
- 3 Celtic group
- 4 Greek
- 5 Albanian
- 6 Iranian group
- 7 Armenian
- 8 Romance group (incl. Spanish, Portuguese, French, Italian)
- 9 Indo-Aryan group (incl. Hindi, Bengali, Urdu, Punjabi, Marathi)
- 10 CAUCASIAN FAMILY

AFRO-ASIATIC FAMILY
- 11 Semitic group (incl. Arabic)
- 12 Kushitic group
- 13 Berber group
- 14 KHOISAN FAMILY
- 15 NIGER-CONGO FAMILY
- 16 NILO-SAHARAN FAMILY
- 17 URALIC FAMILY

ALTAIC FAMILY
- 18 Turkic group (incl. Turkish)
- 19 Mongolian group
- 20 Tungus-Manchu group
- 21 Japanese and Korean

SINO-TIBETAN FAMILY
- 22 Sinitic (Chinese) languages (incl. Mandarin, Wu, Yue)
- 23 Tibetic-Burmic languages
- 24 TAI FAMILY

AUSTRO-ASIATIC FAMILY
- 25 Mon-Khmer group
- 26 Munda group
- 27 Vietnamese
- 28 DRAVIDIAN FAMILY (incl. Telugu, Tamil)
- 29 AUSTRONESIAN FAMILY (incl. Malay-Indonesian, Javanese)
- 30 OTHER LANGUAGES

RELIGIONS

- Roman Catholicism
- Orthodox and other Eastern Churches
- Protestantism
- Sunni Islam
- Shiite Islam
- Buddhism
- Hinduism
- Confucianism
- Judaism
- Shintoism
- Tribal Religions

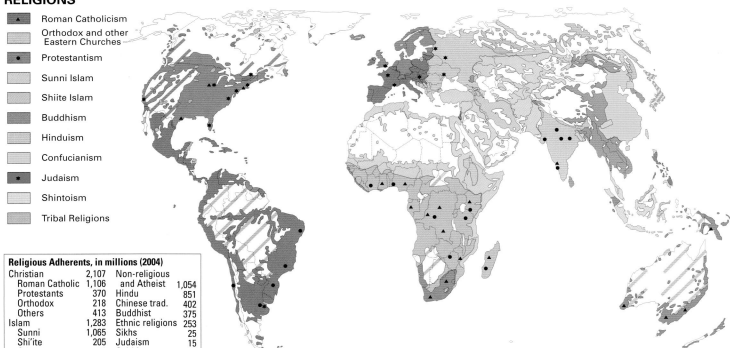

Religious Adherents, in millions (2004)			
Christian	2,107	Non-religious and Atheist	1,054
Roman Catholic	1,106	Hindu	851
Protestants	370	Chinese trad.	402
Orthodox	218	Buddhist	375
Others	413	Ethnic religions	253
Islam	1,283	Sikhs	25
Sunni	1,065	Judaism	15
Shi'ite	205	Spiritism	13
Others	13		

UNITED NATIONS

Created in 1945 to promote peace and co-operation and based in New York, the United Nations is the world's largest international organization, with an annual budget of US$1.3 billion (2002). Each member of the General Assembly has one vote, while the five permanent members of the 15-nation Security Council – China, France, Russia, UK and USA – hold a veto. The Secretariat is the UN's principal administrative arm. The 54 members of the Economic and Social Council are responsible for economic, social, cultural, educational, health and related matters. The UN has 16 specialized agencies – based in Canada, France, Switzerland and Italy, as well as the USA – which help members in fields such as education (UNESCO), agriculture (FAO), medicine (WHO) and finance (IFC). By the end of 1994, all the original 11 trust territories of the Trusteeship Council had become independent.

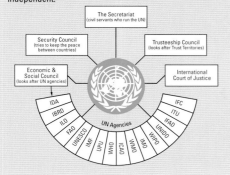

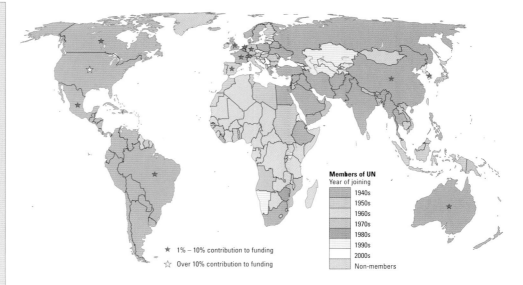

Members of UN
Year of joining
- 1940s
- 1950s
- 1960s
- 1970s
- 1980s
- 1990s
- 2000s
- Non-members

★ 1% – 10% contribution to funding
☆ Over 10% contribution to funding

MEMBERSHIP OF THE UN In 1945 there were 51 members; by the end of 2006 membership had increased to 192 following the admission of East Timor, Switzerland and Montenegro. There are 2 independent states which are not members of the UN – Taiwan and the Vatican City. All the successor states of the former USSR had joined by the end of 1992. The official languages of the UN are Chinese, English, French, Russian, Spanish and Arabic.

FUNDING The UN regular budget for 2005 was US$1.8 billion. Contributions are assessed by the members' ability to pay, with the maximum 22% of the total (USA's share), the minimum 0.01%. The European Union pays over 37% of the budget.

PEACEKEEPING The UN has been involved in 54 peacekeeping operations worldwide since 1948.

INTERNATIONAL ORGANIZATIONS

ACP African-Caribbean-Pacific (formed in 1963). Members have economic ties with the EU.

APEC Asia-Pacific Economic Co-operation (formed in 1989). It aims to enhance economic growth and prosperity for the region and to strengthen the Asia-Pacific community. APEC is the only intergovernmental grouping in the world operating on the basis of non-binding commitments, open dialogue, and equal respect for the views of all participants. There are 21 member economies.

ARAB LEAGUE (formed in 1945). The League's aim is to promote economic, social, political and military co-operation. There are 22 member nations.

ASEAN Association of South-east Asian Nations (formed in 1967). Cambodia joined in 1999.

AU The African Union replaced the Organization of African Unity (formed in 1963) in 2002. Its 53 members represent over 94% of Africa's population. Arabic, French, Portuguese and English are recognized as working languages.

COLOMBO PLAN (formed in 1951). Its 25 members aim to promote economic and social development in Asia and the Pacific.

COMMONWEALTH The Commonwealth of Nations evolved from the British Empire. Pakistan was suspended in 1999, and Zimbabwe in 2002. In response to its continued suspension, Zimbabwe left the Commonwealth in December 2003. It now comprises 16 Queen's realms, 31 republics and 6 indigenous monarchies, giving a total of 53 member states.

EU European Union (evolved from the European Community in 1993). Cyprus, the Czech Republic, Estonia, Hungary, Latvia, Lithuania, Malta, Poland, the Slovak Republic and Slovenia joined the EU in May 2004. Bulgaria and Romania joined in January 2007. The other 15 members of the EU are Austria, Belgium, Denmark, Finland, France, Germany, Greece, Ireland, Italy, Luxembourg, Netherlands, Portugal, Spain, Sweden and the UK – together they aim to integrate economies, co-ordinate social developments and bring about political union.

LAIA Latin American Integration Association (1980). Its aim is to promote freer regional trade.

NATO North Atlantic Treaty Organization (formed in 1949). It continues after 1991 despite the winding up of the Warsaw Pact. Bulgaria, Estonia, Latvia, Lithuania, Romania, the Slovak Republic and Slovenia became members in 2004.

OAS Organization of American States (formed in 1948). It aims to promote social and economic co-operation between developed countries of North America and developing nations of Latin America.

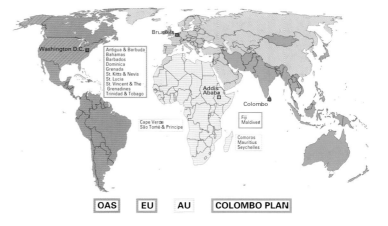

| OAS | EU | AU | COLOMBO PLAN |

OECD Organization for Economic Co-operation and Development (formed in 1961). It comprises 30 major free-market economies. Poland, Hungary and South Korea joined in 1996, and the Slovak Republic in 2000. 'G8' is its 'inner group' of leading industrial nations, comprising Canada, France, Germany, Italy, Japan, Russia, UK and USA.

OPEC Organization of Petroleum Exporting Countries (formed in 1960). It controls about three-quarters of the world's oil supply. Gabon left the organization in 1996.

| ★ G8 | OECD | ACP | OPEC | APEC |

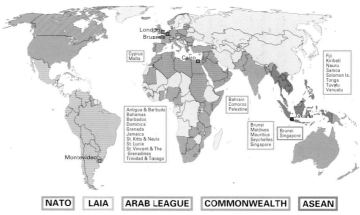

| NATO | LAIA | ARAB LEAGUE | COMMONWEALTH | ASEAN |

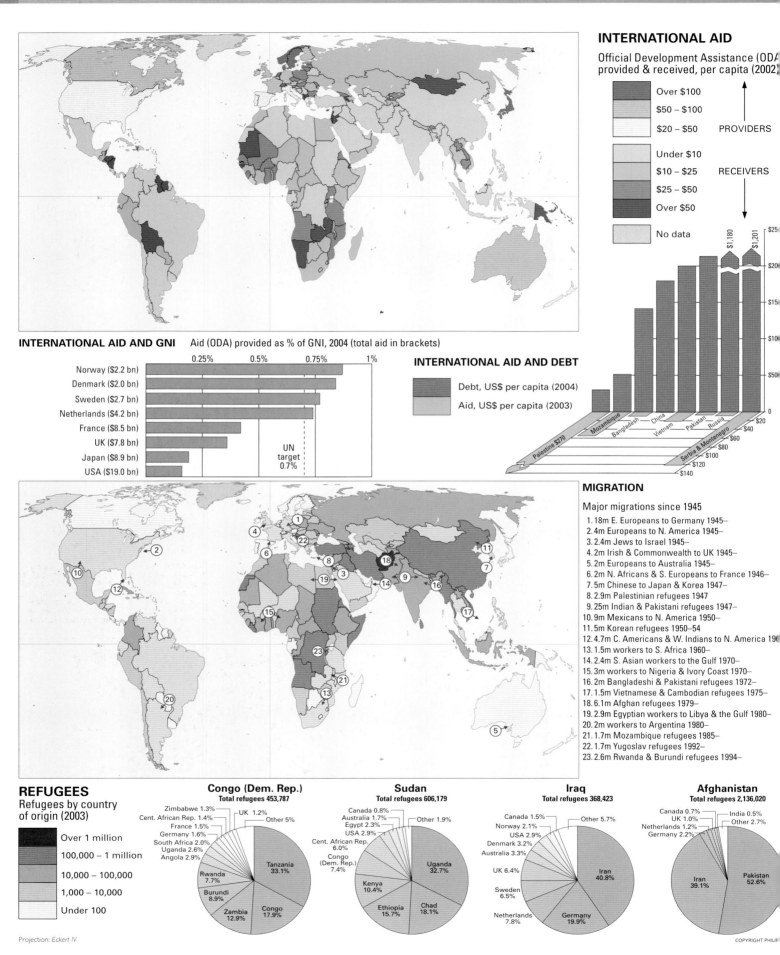

INTERNATIONAL AID

Official Development Assistance (ODA)
provided & received, per capita (2002)

- Over $100
- $50 – $100
- $20 – $50 — PROVIDERS
- Under $10
- $10 – $25 — RECEIVERS
- $25 – $50
- Over $50
- No data

$1,180 $1,201

$25
$20
$15
$10
$50
$0

Palestine $270   Mozambique   Bangladesh   China   Vietnam   Pakistan   Russia   Serbia & Montenegro

$20 $40 $60 $80 $100 $120 $140

INTERNATIONAL AID AND GNI

Aid (ODA) provided as % of GNI, 2004 (total aid in brackets)

0.25%   0.5%   0.75%   1%

- Norway ($2.2 bn)
- Denmark ($2.0 bn)
- Sweden ($2.7 bn)
- Netherlands ($4.2 bn)
- France ($8.5 bn)
- UK ($7.8 bn)
- Japan ($8.9 bn)
- USA ($19.0 bn)

UN target 0.7%

INTERNATIONAL AID AND DEBT

- Debt, US$ per capita (2004)
- Aid, US$ per capita (2003)

MIGRATION

Major migrations since 1945

1. 18m E. Europeans to Germany 1945–
2. 4m Europeans to N. America 1945–
3. 2.4m Jews to Israel 1945–
4. 2m Irish & Commonwealth to UK 1945–
5. 2m Europeans to Australia 1945–
6. 2m N. Africans & S. Europeans to France 1946–
7. 5m Chinese to Japan & Korea 1947–
8. 2.9m Palestinian refugees 1947
9. 25m Indian & Pakistani refugees 1947–
10. 9m Mexicans to N. America 1950–
11. 5m Korean refugees 1950–54
12. 4.7m C. Americans & W. Indians to N. America 196
13. 1.5m workers to S. Africa 1960–
14. 2.4m S. Asian workers to the Gulf 1970–
15. 3m workers to Nigeria & Ivory Coast 1970–
16. 2m Bangladeshi & Pakistani refugees 1972–
17. 1.5m Vietnamese & Cambodian refugees 1975–
18. 6.1m Afghan refugees 1979–
19. 2.9m Egyptian workers to Libya & the Gulf 1980–
20. 2m workers to Argentina 1980–
21. 1.7m Mozambique refugees 1985–
22. 1.7m Yugoslav refugees 1992–
23. 2.6m Rwanda & Burundi refugees 1994–

REFUGEES

Refugees by country of origin (2003)

- Over 1 million
- 100,000 – 1 million
- 10,000 – 100,000
- 1,000 – 10,000
- Under 100

Congo (Dem. Rep.)
Total refugees 453,787

- Zimbabwe 1.3%
- Cent. African Rep. 1.4%
- France 1.5%
- Germany 1.6%
- South Africa 2.0%
- Uganda 2.6%
- Angola 2.9%
- UK 1.2%
- Other 5%
- Tanzania 33.1%
- Rwanda 7.7%
- Burundi 8.9%
- Zambia 12.9%
- Congo 17.9%

Sudan
Total refugees 606,179

- Canada 0.8%
- Australia 1.7%
- Egypt 2.3%
- USA 2.9%
- Cent. African Rep. 6.0%
- Congo (Dem. Rep.) 7.4%
- Other 1.9%
- Uganda 32.7%
- Kenya 10.4%
- Ethiopia 15.7%
- Chad 18.1%

Iraq
Total refugees 368,423

- Canada 1.5%
- Norway 2.1%
- USA 2.9%
- Denmark 3.2%
- Australia 3.3%
- Other 5.7%
- UK 6.4%
- Sweden 6.5%
- Netherlands 7.8%
- Germany 19.9%
- Iran 40.8%

Afghanistan
Total refugees 2,136,020

- Canada 0.7%
- UK 1.0%
- Netherlands 1.2%
- Germany 2.2%
- India 0.5%
- Other 2.7%
- Iran 39.1%
- Pakistan 52.6%

Projection: Eckert IV

COPYRIGHT PHILIP

CONFLICTS

Armed conflict since 1994

Countries in the top half of the Human Developement Index (HDI)

Countries in the bottom half of the HDI

No data

 Countries with at least one armed conflict between 1994 and mid-2005

MAJOR WARS SINCE 1900

War	Total deaths
Second World War (1939–45)	55,000,000
First World War (1914–18)	8,500,000
Korean War (1950–53)	4,000,000
Congolese Civil War (1998–)	3,800,000
Vietnam War (1965–73)	3,000,000
Sudanese Civil War (1983–2000)	2,000,000

HIV/AIDS

Percentage of adults (15 – 49 years) living with HIV/AIDS (2003)

15 – 40%

5 – 15%

0.5 – 5%

0.1 – 0.5%

Under 0.1%

No data

Total number of adults and children living with HIV/AIDS by region (2004)

Human Immunodeficiency Virus (HIV) is passed from one person to another and attacks the body's defence against illness. It develops into the Acquired Immunodeficiency Syndrome (AIDS) when a particularly severe illness, such as cancer, takes hold. The pandemic started just over 20 years ago and, by 2005, 40.3 millon people were living with HIV or AIDS.

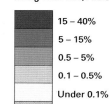

DRUGS

Countries producing illegal drugs

Cannabis

Poppy

Coca leaves

Cocaine

Amphetamines

Major routes of drug trafficking

Opium

Coca leaves

Cocaine

Heroin

Hashish and marijuana

Amphetamines (usually used within producing countries)

 Conflicts relating to drug trafficking

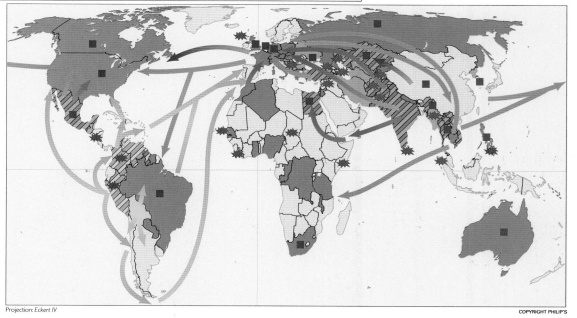

Projection: Eckert IV

COPYRIGHT PHILIP'S

COUNTRY	POPULATION							LAND & AGRICULTURE				TRADE, TOURISM & ENERGY					
	Total population (millions)	Population density (persons per km²)	Life expectancy (years)	Average annual population change (%)	Birth rate (births per thousand people)	Death rate (deaths per thousand people)	Urban population (% of total)	Land area (thousand km²)	Arable & permanent crops (% of land area)	Permanent pasture (% of land area)	Forest (% of land area)	Imports (US$ per capita)	Exports (US$ per capita)	Tourism receipts (US$ per capita)	Energy produced (tonnes of oil equiv. per capita)	Energy consumed (tonnes of oil equiv. per capita)	CO_2 emission per capita (metric tonnes)
	2005	2005	2005	2005	2005	2005	2005		2002	2002	2000	2004	2004	2003	2002	2002	2003
Afghanistan	29.9	46	43	4.8	47	21	24	652	12	46	2	126	15	–	0.01	0.02	0.03
Albania	3.6	124	77	0.5	15	5	45	29	26	19	36	577	153	145	0.39	0.69	1.16
Algeria	32.5	14	73	1.2	17	5	60	2,382	3	13	1	469	990	5	4.91	1.00	2.65
Angola	11.8	9	37	-0.1	45	26	37	1,247	3	43	56	415	1,081	6	4.41	0.29	1.17
Argentina	39.5	14	76	1.0	17	8	91	2,780	13	52	13	558	855	53	2.23	1.58	3.37
Armenia	3.0	100	72	-0.3	12	8	64	30	20	30	12	433	283	24	0.35	1.34	2.94
Australia	20.1	3	80	0.9	12	7	93	7,741	6	52	21	4,881	4,323	513	13.32	7.03	19.1
Austria	8.2	98	79	0.1	9	10	66	84	18	23	47	12,341	12,524	1,716	1.57	4.25	8.92
Azerbaijan	7.9	91	63	0.6	20	10	50	87	23	31	13	458	401	7.3	2.78	1.92	4.36
Bahamas	0.3	21	66	0.7	18	9	90	14	1	0.2	84	5,433	2,120	2,840	0	3.88	11.26
Bahrain	0.7	700	74	1.5	18	4	90	0.7	9	6	0	8,386	11,721	–	15.29	14.88	30.89
Bangladesh	144.3	1,002	62	2.1	30	8	25	144	65	5	10	70	52	0.4	0.07	0.10	0.24
Barbados	0.3	696	72	0.3	13	9	53	0.4	40	5	5	3,463	687	2,527	0.27	1.88	5.86
Belarus	10.3	50	69	-0.1	11	14	72	208	28	15	45	1,317	1,114	26	0.21	2.80	7.44
Belgium	10.4	335	79	0.2	10	10	97	31	25	21	22	22,596	24,587	782	1.20	6.63	13.66
Belize	0.3	13	67	2.3	29	6	49	23	4	2	59	1,933	1,338	520	0.07	1.14	3.08
Benin	7.6	67	51	2.8	42	14	46	113	25	5	24	123	95	11	0.01	0.09	0.25
Bhutan	2.2	47	54	2.1	34	13	9	47	4	9	64	89	70	3.6	0.24	0.21	0.15
Bolivia	8.9	8	66	1.5	24	8	64	1,099	3	31	49	179	223	13	0.92	0.44	1.23
Bosnia-Herzegovina	4.4	86	73	0.4	12	8	45	51	21	20	45	1,182	386	53	1.37	1.64	3.51
Botswana	1.6	3	34	0.0	23	29	52	582	1	45	22	1,409	1,838	223	0.38	0.81	2.13
Brazil	186.1	22	72	1.1	17	6	84	8,514	8	23	63	328	510	13	0.91	1.17	1.97
Brunei	0.4	67	75	1.9	19	3	78	6	3	1	84	13,000	19,250	–	52.12	5.75	14.97
Bulgaria	7.5	68	72	-0.9	10	14	71	111	32	16	33	1,631	1,218	221	1.42	2.84	6.5
Burkina Faso	13.5	49	44	2.5	44	19	19	274	16	22	26	64	31	1.5	0	0.03	0.09
Burma (Myanmar)	47.0	69	56	0.4	18	12	31	677	16	1	52	37	45	1.2	0.21	0.10	0.2
Burundi	7.8	279	43	2.2	40	17	11	28	52	38	4	18	4,082	0.1	0.01	0.03	0.06
Cambodia	13.6	75	59	1.8	27	9	20	181	22	8	53	230	170	29	0	0.02	0.04
Cameroon	17.0	36	48	1.9	35	15	53	475	15	4	51	116	144	2.1	0.29	0.13	0.39
Canada	32.8	3	80	0.9	11	7	81	9,971	5	3	27	7,808	9,622	323	14.00	10.05	19.05
Cape Verde Is.	0.4	100	71	0.7	25	7	58	4	1	1	21	968	153	213	0	0.15	0.33
Central African Rep.	4.2	7	41	1.5	35	20	44	623	3	5	37	32	41	0.7	0.01	0.04	0.09
Chad	9.7	8	48	3.0	46	16	26	1,284	3	36	10	52	38	2.6	0	0.01	0.02
Chile	16.0	21	77	1.0	16	6	88	757	3	17	21	1,408	1,825	54	0.49	1.67	3.4
China	1,306.3	136	72	0.6	13	7	41	9,597	17	43	18	423	446	13	0.81	0.83	2.72
Colombia	43.0	38	72	1.5	21	6	77	1,139	4	40	48	357	360	19	1.79	0.72	1.18
Comoros	0.7	350	62	2.9	38	8	36	2	66	8	4	126	40	30	0	0.05	0.13
Congo	3.0	9	49	1.3	28	15	54	342	1	29	65	12	37	0.3	4.41	0.14	0.82
Congo (Dem. Rep.)	60.1	25	49	3.0	44	14	33	2,345	3	7	60	259	394	1.9	0.05	0.04	0.03
Costa Rica	4.0	78	77	1.5	19	4	62	51	10	46	39	1,961	1,546	323	0.48	0.96	1.3
Croatia	4.5	79	74	0.0	10	11	60	57	28	28	32	3,711	1,743	1,417	1.01	2.09	5.01
Cuba	11.3	103	77	0.3	12	7	76	111	34	26	21	469	186	163	0.30	1.05	3.05
Cyprus	0.8	89	78	0.5	13	8	70	9	13	0.4	13	7,091	1,429	2,519	0	3.59	10.26
Czech Republic	10.2	129	76	-0.1	9	11	75	79	43	13	34	6,685	6,521	349	2.65	3.87	10.94
Denmark	5.4	126	78	0.3	11	11	86	43	54	9	11	11,750	13,530	975	5.44	3.85	10.94
Djibouti	0.5	22	43	2.1	40	19	85	23	0	57	0	1,330	310	8	0	1.27	2.8
Dominican Republic	9.0	184	67	1.3	23	7	60	49	33	44	28	899	605	346	0.02	0.75	2.21
East Timor	1.0	67	66	2.1	27	6	8	15	–	–	–	167	8	–	–	–	–
Ecuador	13.4	47	76	1.2	23	4	63	284	11	18	38	571	564	30	1.80	0.69	1.82
Egypt	77.5	77	71	1.8	23	5	42	1,001	3	0.0	0	248	142	59	0.89	0.77	1.88
El Salvador	6.7	319	71	1.8	27	6	60	21	43	38	6	891	485	34	0.14	0.45	0.9
Equatorial Guinea	0.5	18	56	2.4	36	12	50	28	8	4	62	2,334	5,542	28	23.55	2.51	8.02
Eritrea	4.7	39	52	2.5	39	14	21	118	4	58	16	132	1,371	16	0	0.05	0.16
Estonia	1.3	29	72	-0.7	10	13	70	45	15	2	49	5,629	4,385	519	0	3.33	13.89
Ethiopia	73.1	65	49	2.4	39	15	16	1,104	10	18	5	29	8	1	0.01	0.26	0.06
Fiji	0.9	50	70	1.4	23	6	53	18	16	10	45	928	677	388	0.17	0.53	1.71
Finland	5.2	15	78	0.2	11	10	61	338	7	0	72	8,687	11,738	364	2.04	5.91	10.41
France	60.7	111	77	0.4	12	9	77	552	36	18	28	6,914	6,903	610	2.12	4.55	6.8
Gabon	1.4	5	56	2.5	36	12	85	268	2	18	85	875	2,650	12	9.86	0.68	3.56
Gambia, The	1.6	145	55	2.9	40	12	26	11	26	46	48	113	72	18	0	0.07	0.2
Gaza Strip (OPT)*	1.4	4,667	72	3.8	40	4	–	0.4	–	–	–	1,357	146	2.9	–	–	–
Georgia	4.7	67	76	-0.4	10	9	52	70	15	28	43	384	193	31	0.32	1.01	0.73
Germany	82.4	231	79	0.0	8	11	89	357	34	14	31	8,698	10,841	279	1.60	4.33	10.21
Ghana	21.9	92	56	1.3	24	11	46	239	28	37	28	169	137	19	0.10	0.17	0.26
Greece	10.7	81	79	0.2	10	10	61	132	30	36	28	5,073	1,449	1,000	0.96	3.25	9.5

WEALTH						SOCIAL INDICATORS										COUNTRY
GNI (million US$)	GNI per capita (PPP US$)	Average annual growth in GDP per capita (%)	Agriculture (% of GDP)	Industry (% of GDP)	Services (% of GDP)	Human Develop. Index (HDI) value	Food intake (calories per capita per day)	Population per doctor	Adults living with HIV/AIDS (% 15–49 year olds)	Gender Develop. Index (GDI) value	Illiteracy rate (% adults)	Motor vehicles per thousand people	Internet usage per thousand people	Aid donated (–)/received (US$ per capita)	Military spending (% of GDP)	
2004	2004	1990–2002	2004	2004	2004	2002	2003	2003	2003	2002	2003	2002	2003	2002	2004	
5,543	–	–	60	20	20	–	1,539.0	–	0.1	–	64	0.6	1	63	2.6	Afghanistan
6,641	5,070	6.0	46.2	25.4	28.4	0.781	2,847.8	730	0.1	0.778	13	70.5	10	90	1.5	Albania
73,676	6,260	0.3	10.3	57.4	32.3	0.704	3,021.5	1,176	0.1	0.688	30	88.2	16	6	3.2	Algeria
14,441	2,030	–0.1	8	67	25	0.381	2,082.7	20,000	3.9	–	58	18.4	3	35	10.6	Angola
142,338	12,460	1.7	10.6	35.9	53.5	0.853	2,992.1	329	0.7	0.841	3	197.7	112	256	1.3	Argentina
3,424	4,270	1.7	22.9	36.1	41.1	0.754	2,267.7	348	0.1	0.752	1		37	57	6.5	Armenia
541,173	29,200	2.6	3.4	28.2	68.4	0.946	3,053.6	405	0.1	0.945	0	623.8	567	–45	2.7	Australia
262,147	31,790	1.9	2.3	30.8	66.9	0.934	3,673.3	310	0.3	0.924	2	586	462	–63	0.9	Austria
7,828	3,830	0.2	14.1	45.7	40.2	0.746	2,574.8	279	0.1	–	3	57.9	37	18	2.6	Azerbaijan
4,684	16,140	0.1	3	7	90	0.815	2,754.9	613	3.0	0.825	4	342	192	33	–	Bahamas
8,834	18,070	1.5	0.7	41	58.4	0.843	–	592	0.3	0.832	11	325.3	246	214	6.3	Bahrain
61,230	1,980	3.1	21.2	27.1	51.7	0.509	2,205.0	4,348	0.1	0.499	57	1.5	2	11	1.8	Bangladesh
2,507	15,060	1.6	6	16	78	0.888	3,091.1	730	1.5	–	3	268.2	112	30	–	Barbados
20,856	6,900	0.2	11	36.4	52.6	0.790	3,000.3	222	0.3	0.789	1	155.8	141	19	1.4	Belarus
322,837	31,360	1.8	1.3	25.7	73	0.942	3,583.8	239	0.2	0.938	2	523.1	386	–104	1.3	Belgium
1,115	6,510	1.7	17.7	15	67.3	0.737	2,868.6	980	2.4	0.718	6	161	109	230	2.0	Belize
3,667	1,120	2.1	36.3	14.3	49.4	0.421	2,547.9	10,000	1.9	0.406	59	2.3	10	47	2.4	Benin
677	660	3.6	45	10	45	0.536	–	20,000	0.1	–	58	–	15	33	1.8	Bhutan
8,656	2,590	1.1	13	28	59	0.681	2,235.2	1,316	0.1	0.674	13	55.6	32	68	1.6	Bolivia
7,841	7,430	18.0	14.2	30.8	55	0.781	2,893.6	690	0.1	–	–	–	26	163	4.5	Bosnia-Herzegovina
7,490	8,920	2.5	4	44	52	0.589	2,151.4	3,448	37.3	0.581	20	73.7	35	46	3.9	Botswana
552,096	8,020	1.3	10.1	38.6	51.3	0.775	3,049.5	485	0.7	0.768	14	111.9	82	163	1.8	Brazil
–	–	–0.5	5	45	50	0.867	2,855.3	1,010	0.1	0.768	8	629.7	102	11	5.1	Brunei
21,326	7,870	–2.1	11.5	30.1	58.4	0.796	2,847.9	291	0.1	0.795	1	313.5	206	40	2.6	Bulgaria
4,436	1,220	1.6	39.5	19.3	41.3	0.302	2,461.9	25,000	4.2	0.291	73	4	4	36	1.3	Burkina Faso
–		5.7	56.6	8.8	34.5	0.551	2,937.1	3,333	1.2	–	17	5.7	1	3	2.1	Burma (Myanmar)
669	660	–3.9	48.1	19	32.9	0.339	1,648.6	100,000	6.0	0.337	48	2.5	2	15	6.0	Burundi
4,430	2,180	4.1	35	30	35	0.568	2,045.8	6,250	2.6	0.557	30	0.9	2	41	3.0	Cambodia
13,138	2,090	–0.1	43.7	20.1	36.2	0.501	2,273.2	14,286	6.9	0.491	21	11	4	78	1.6	Cameroon
905,629	30,660	2.2	2.3	26.4	71.3	0.943	3,589.3	535	0.3	0.941	3	581.6	513	–4	1.1	Canada
852	5,650	3.4	12.1	21.9	66	0.717	3,243.2	5,882	0.1	0.709	23	39.8	36	340	1.5	Cape Verde Is.
1,226	1,110	–0.2	55	20	25	0.361	1,980.4	25,000	13.5	0.345	49	3.1	1	20	1.0	Central African Rep.
2,277	1,420	–0.5	22.6	35.6	41.7	0.379	2,113.5	33,333	4.8	0.368	52	0.9	2	25	2.1	Chad
78,407	10,500	4.4	6.3	38.2	55.5	0.839	2,863.2	870	0.3	0.830	4	135	272	3	3.8	Chile
676,846	5,530	8.6	13.8	52.9	33.3	0.745	2,951.0	610	0.1	0.741	14	10.2	63	2	4.3	China
90,626	6,820	0.4	13.4	32.1	54.5	0.773	2,584.6	1,064	0.7	0.770	7	28.4	53	7	3.4	Colombia
328	1,840	–1.4	40	4	56	0.530	1,753.9	14,286	0.1	0.510	43	–	4	14	3.0	Comoros
2,974	750	–1.6	7.4	52	40.6	0.494	2,161.7	4,000	4.9	0.488	16	14.9	4	53	2.8	Congo
6,416	680	–8.1	55	11	34	0.365	1,599.1	14,286	4.2	0.355	34	–	1	3	1.5	Congo (Dem. Rep.)
18,969	9,530	2.7	8.5	29.7	61.8	0.834	2,875.5	625	0.6	0.823	4	136.6	193	3	0.4	Costa Rica
29,700	11,670	2.1	8.2	30.1	61.7	0.830	2,779.0	420	0.1	0.827	1	312.6	232	15	2.4	Croatia
–	–	3.5	6.6	25.5	67.9	0.809	3,151.8	168	0.1	–	3	0.9	11	6	1.8	Cuba
13,633	22,330	3.2	7.35	20.2	72.45	0.883	3,254.6	372	0.1	0.875	2	516.2	294	62	3.8	Cyprus
93,155	18,400	1.4	3.4	39.3	57.3	0.868	3,171.3	292	0.1	0.865	0	394.8	308	11	2.0	Czech Republic
219,422	31,550	2.1	2.2	25.5	72.3	0.932	3,439.3	273	0.2	0.931	0	430.6	513	–302	1.5	Denmark
739	2,270	–3.8	3.5	15.8	80.7	0.454	2,219.7	7,692	2.9	–	32	2.7	7	72	4.4	Djibouti
18,443	6,750	4.2	18	24	58	0.738	2,347.1	526	1.7	0.728	15	99.7	64	27	1.1	Dominican Republic
506	430	–	25.4	17.2	57.4	–	2,805.8	–	–	–	52	–	–	2200	–	East Timor
28,783	3,690	0.0	8.7	30.5	60.9	0.735	2,754.0	690	0.3	0.721	7	47.1	46	9	2.2	Ecuador
90,129	4,120	2.5	17.2	33	49.8	0.653	3,338.0	459	0.1	0.634	42	35.4	39	6	3.4	Egypt
15,613	4,980	2.3	9.2	31.1	59.7	0.720	2,583.8	794	0.7	0.709	20	63.5	84	38	1.1	El Salvador
437	7,400	20.8	3	95.7	1.3	0.703	–	4,000	3.4	0.691	14	–	4	68	2.5	Equatorial Guinea
806	1,050	1.5	12.4	25.9	61.7	0.439	1,512.8	20,000	2.7	0.431	41	–	7	8	13.4	Eritrea
9,435	13,190	2.3	4.1	28.9	67	0.853	3,002.2	319	1.0	0.852	1	359.4	444	83	2.0	Estonia
7,747	810	2.3	47	12.4	40.6	0.359	1,857.3	33,333	4.4	0.346	27	1.7	1	5	4.6	Ethiopia
2,281	5,770	1.8	16.6	22.4	61	0.758	2,893.6	2,941	0.1	0.747	7	126.1	61	45	2.2	Fiji
171,024	29,560	2.5	3.3	30.2	66.5	0.935	3,100.4	322	0.1	0.933	0	485.7	534	–73	2.0	Finland
858,731	29,320	1.6	2.7	24.3	73	0.932	3,653.9	303	0.4	0.929	1	590.4	366	–89	2.6	France
5,415	5,600	–0.2	7.4	46.7	45.9	0.648	2,636.8	–	8.1	–	37	16.4	26	236	2.0	Gabon
414	1,900	0.0	26.8	14.5	58.7	0.452	2,272.7	25,000	1.2	0.446	60	4	19	30	0.3	Gambia, The
3,771	1,110	–4.9	9	28	63	–	2,179.8	–	–	–	–	–	40	615	–	Gaza Strip (OPT)*
4,683	2,930	–3.9	20.5	22.6	56.9	0.739	2,354.3	216	0.1	–	1	62.1	31	32	0.6	Georgia
488,974	27,950	1.3	1	31	68	0.925	3,495.6	275	0.1	0.921	1	580.5	473	–68	1.5	Germany
8,090	2,280	1.8	34.3	24.2	41.4	0.568	2,667.2	11,111	3.1	0.564	25	10.5	8	332	0.6	Ghana
183,917	22,000	2.2	7	22	71	0.902	3,721.1	228	0.2	0.894	2	414.4	150	509	4.3	Greece

COUNTRY	POPULATION							LAND & AGRICULTURE				TRADE, TOURISM & ENERGY					
	Total population (millions)	Population density (persons per km²)	Life expectancy (years)	Average annual population change (%)	Birth rate (births per thousand people)	Death rate (deaths per thousand people)	Urban population (% of total)	Land area (thousand km²)	Arable & permanent crops (% of land area)	Permanent pasture (% of land area)	Forest (% of land area)	Imports (US$ per capita)	Exports (US$ per capita)	Tourism receipts (US$ per capita)	Energy produced (tonnes of oil equiv. per capita)	Energy consumed (tonnes of oil equiv. per capita)	CO₂ emission per capita (metric tonnes)
	2005	2005	2005	2005	2005	2005	2005		2002	2002	2000	2004	2004	2003	2002	2002	2003
Guatemala	12.0	110	65	2.6	34	7	47	109	18	24	26	648	243	52	0.12	0.30	0.84
Guinea	9.5	39	50	2.4	42	15	37	246	6	43	28	68	75	0	0.01	0.06	0.16
Guinea-Bissau	1.4	39	47	2.0	38	17	36	36	20	39	78	74	39	1.4	0	0.09	0.25
Guyana	0.8	4	66	0.3	19	8	39	215	3	6	86	813	713	49	0	0.83	2.27
Haiti	8.1	289	53	2.3	37	12	39	28	39	18	3	134	42	12	0.01	0.09	0.21
Honduras	7.2	64	66	2.2	31	7	46	112	13	13	48	463	202	47	0.08	0.37	0.87
Hungary	10.0	108	72	−0.3	10	13	66	93	52	12	20	5,868	5,462	344	1.02	2.63	5.91
Iceland	0.3	3	80	0.9	14	7	93	103	0	23	0	11,023	9,673	1,063	8.20	11.59	10.41
India	1,080.3	329	64	1.4	22	8	29	3,287	57	4	22	83	64	3.3	0.24	0.33	0.96
Indonesia	242.0	126	70	1.5	21	6	48	1,905	19	6	58	186	289	17	0.86	0.47	1.45
Iran	68.0	41	70	0.9	17	6	68	1,648	10	27	5	460	570	26	3.79	2.12	5.4
Iraq	26.1	60	69	2.7	33	5	67	438	14	9	2	379	387	–	4.35	1.14	2.71
Ireland	4.0	57	78	1.2	15	8	60	70	16	48	10	15,163	25,950	969	0.27	3.92	10.26
Israel	6.3	300	79	1.2	18	6	92	21	20	7	6	5,848	5,462	324	0	3.20	10.56
Italy	58.1	193	80	0.1	9	10	68	301	38	15	34	5,668	5,790	537	0.54	3.29	8.11
Ivory Coast	17.3	54	49	2.1	36	15	46	322	22	41	–	194	296	4.9	0.16	0.15	0.32
Jamaica	2.7	245	76	0.7	17	5	52	11	26	21	30	1,342	622	502	0.02	1.39	4.25
Japan	127.4	337	81	0.1	9	9	66	378	13	1	64	3,154	4,229	70	0.84	4.31	9.44
Jordan	5.8	63	78	2.3	22	3	79	89	4	8	1	1,310	552	141	0.05	1.00	2.98
Kazakhstan	15.2	6	67	0.3	16	9	56	2,725	8	69	5	860	1,215	37	6.39	3.46	9.72
Kenya	33.8	58	48	2.6	40	15	42	580	9	37	30	124	77	10	0.03	0.12	0.25
Korea, North	22.9	189	71	0.9	16	7	62	121	23	0.4	68	92	52	–	1.14	1.20	3.13
Korea, South	48.6	496	76	0.4	10	6	80	99	19	1	63	4,407	5,156	108	0.64	4.32	9.84
Kuwait	2.3	128	77	3.4	22	3	96	18	1	8	0	4,835	11,922	51	49.91	10.35	23.17
Kyrgyzstan	5.1	26	68	1.3	22	7	34	200	7	49	5	152	127	9.4	0.59	1.13	0.97
Laos	6.2	26	55	2.4	36	12	22	237	4	4	54	93	59	14	0.14	0.16	0.18
Latvia	2.3	35	71	−0.7	9	13	66	65	30	10	47	2,596	1,552	97	0.34	2.08	3.3
Lebanon	3.8	380	73	1.3	19	6	88	10	31	2	4	2,148	469	267	0.02	1.49	4.33
Lesotho	2.0	67	37	0.1	27	25	18	30	11	67	0	365	242	10	0.04	0.08	0.11
Liberia	2.9	26	48	2.7	44	18	48	111	6	21	36	1,742	372	–	0	0.04	0.15
Libya	5.8	3	77	2.3	27	3	87	1,760	1	8	0	1,246	3,216	14	13.89	2.98	8.96
Lithuania	3.6	55	74	−0.3	9	11	67	65	46	8	31	3,061	2,467	177	1.24	3.12	5.53
Luxembourg	0.5	167	79	1.3	12	8	92	3	–	–	–	32,600	26,800	5,586	0.09	8.48	24.28
Macedonia (FYROM)	2.0	80	74	0.3	12	9	60	26	24	25	36	1,339	815	29	0.82	1.31	4.11
Madagascar	18.0	31	57	3.0	42	11	27	587	6	41	20	64	48	4.2	0.01	0.04	0.13
Malawi	12.7	108	37	2.1	44	23	17	118	26	20	28	41	40	2.6	0.02	0.05	0.07
Malaysia	24.0	73	72	1.8	23	5	65	330	23	1	59	4,138	5,146	246	3.69	2.48	5.81
Mali	11.4	9	45	2.8	47	19	34	1,240	4	25	11	81	80	9.1	0.01	0.03	0.05
Malta	0.4	127	79	0.4	10	8	92	0.3	31	0	0	8,518	6,563	1,740	0	2.31	7.45
Mauritania	3.1	3	53	2.9	42	13	64	1,026	0	38	0	277	175	3.5	0	0.42	1.11
Mauritius	1.2	600	72	0.8	16	7	44	2	53	4	8	1,871	1,677	581	0.02	1.18	3.03
Mexico	106.2	54	75	1.2	21	5	76	1,958	14	42	29	1,797	1,718	89	2.28	1.58	3.91
Micronesia, Fed. States	0.1	100	70	−0.1	25	5	30	0.7	51	16	0	1,490	220	170	–	–	–
Moldova	4.5	132	65	0.2	15	13	46	34	65	12	10	407	229	13	0.02	0.93	2.46
Mongolia	2.8	2	65	1.5	22	7	57	1,567	1	83	7	357	305	51	0.54	0.75	3.19
Morocco	32.7	73	71	1.6	22	6	59	447	21	47	7	478	298	87	0.01	0.36	1.1
Mozambique	19.4	24	40	1.5	36	21	38	802	6	56	39	50	36	5.1	0.12	0.13	0.09
Namibia	2.0	2	44	0.7	25	18	34	824	1	46	10	737	678	167	0.14	0.61	1.15
Nepal	27.7	196	60	2.2	32	9	16	147	23	12	27	51	21	7.2	0.02	0.06	0.11
Netherlands	16.4	390	79	0.5	11	9	67	42	28	29	11	15,409	17,872	564	3.98	6.01	16.07
New Zealand	4.0	15	79	1.0	14	8	86	271	13	52	30	4,943	4,963	994	4.51	5.49	9.91
Nicaragua	5.5	43	70	1.9	25	4	58	130	18	40	27	367	136	28	0.04	0.29	0.73
Niger	12.2	10	42	2.6	48	21	23	1,267	4	9	1	33	23	2.3	0.01	0.04	0.1
Nigeria	128.8	140	47	2.4	41	17	48	924	36	43	15	133	264	2	0.94	0.17	0.75
Norway	4.6	14	79	0.4	12	9	81	324	3	1	29	9,991	16,661	552	57.43	10.83	9.93
Oman	3.0	14	73	3.3	37	4	79	310	0	5	0	2,124	4,380	73	21.41	3.11	8.65
Pakistan	162.4	202	63	2.0	31	8	35	796	29	6	3	86	93	0.7	0.18	0.29	0.68
Panama	3.1	40	72	1.3	20	7	58	76	9	21	39	2,311	1,838	189	0.21	1.72	4.11
Papua New Guinea	5.5	12	65	2.3	30	7	13	463	2	0.2	68	246	443	0.9	0.59	0.21	0.46
Paraguay	6.3	15	75	2.5	30	5	59	407	8	55	59	529	466	10	1.97	1.59	0.61
Peru	27.9	22	70	1.4	21	6	75	1,285	3	21	51	344	441	33	0.37	0.52	1
Philippines	87.9	293	70	1.8	26	5	63	300	36	5	19			0.09	0.37	0.13	0.34	0.9
Poland	38.6	123	74	0.0	11	10	62	323	47	14	31	2,114	1,968	105	1.97	2.17	7.42
Portugal	10.6	115	78	0.4	11	10	56	89	29	16	40	4,915	3,555	654	0.23	2.57	6.18
Qatar	0.9	82	74	2.6	16	5	92	11	2	5	0	6,833	16,667	–	85.75	15.28	45.73

WEALTH						SOCIAL INDICATORS										COUNTRY
GNI (million US$)	GNI per capita (PPP US$)	Average annual growth in GDP per capita (%)	Agriculture (% of GDP)	Industry (% of GDP)	Services (% of GDP)	Human Develop. Index (HDI) value	Food intake (calories per capita per day)	Population per doctor	Adults living with HIV/AIDS (% 15–49 year olds)	Gender Develop. Index (GDI) value	Illiteracy rate (% adults)	Motor vehicles per thousand people	Internet usage per thousand people	Aid donated (−) /received (US$ per capita)	Military spending (% of GDP)	
2004	2004	1990–2002	2004	2004	2004	2002	2003	2003	2003	2002	2003	2002	2003	2002	2004	
26,945	4,140	1.3	22.7	19.5	57.9	0.649	2,219.1	917	1.1	0.635	29	61.8	33	17	0.8	Guatemala
3,681	2,130	1.7	25	38.2	36.8	0.425	2,408.9	7,692	3.2	–	64	2.4	5	39	1.7	Guinea
250	690	−2.2	62	12	26	0.350	2,024.2	5,882	10.0	0.329	58	–	15	82	3.1	Guinea-Bissau
765	4,110	4.1	38.3	19.9	41.8	0.719	2,691.7	3,846	2.5	0.715	1	100.8	142	361	0.9	Guyana
3,380	1,680	−3.0	30	20	50	0.463	2,086.2	4,000	5.6	0.458	47	19.3	18	16	0.9	Haiti
7,321	2,710	0.3	12.7	32.1	55.3	0.672	2,355.8	1,149	1.8	0.662	24	11.7	25	82	1.4	Honduras
83,315	15,620	2.4	3.3	31.4	65.3	0.848	3,483.2	282	0.1	0.847	1	305.2	232	25	1.8	Hungary
11,199	32,360	2.1	11.2	9.6	79.2	0.941	3,249.3	284	0.2	0.938	0	639.7	648	–	–	Iceland
674,580	3,100	4.0	23.6	28.4	48	0.595	2,459.0	1,961	0.8	0.572	40	12.9	17	3	2.5	India
248,007	3,460	2.1	14.6	45	40.4	0.692	2,903.9	6,250	0.1	0.685	11	27.6	38	12	3.0	Indonesia
153,984	7,550	2.2	11.2	40.9	48.7	0.732	3,084.9	–	0.1	0.713	21	25.8	72	6	3.3	Iran
–	–	–	13.6	58.6	27.8	–	2,197.0	–	0.1	–	60	47.2	1	32	–	Iraq
137,761	33,170	6.8	5	46	49	0.936	3,656.4	418	0.1	0.929	2	422.8	317	−71	0.9	Ireland
118,124	23,510	1.8	2.8	37.7	59.5	0.908	3,666.1	267	0.1	0.906	5	295.5	301	107	8.7	Israel
,503,562	27,860	1.5	2.3	28.8	68.9	0.920	3,670.6	165	0.4	0.914	1	641.1	337	−17	1.8	Italy
13,263	1,390	−0.1	27.8	19.4	52.8	0.399	2,630.6	11,111	7.0	0.379	49	6.6	14	58	1.2	Ivory Coast
7,738	3,630	−0.1	6.1	32.7	61.3	0.764	2,684.7	1,176	1.2	0.762	12	74.8	228	6	0.4	Jamaica
,749,910	30,040	1.0	1.3	24.7	74.1	0.938	2,760.9	495	0.1	0.932	1	566.8	483	−55	1.0	Japan
11,629	4,640	0.9	2.4	26	71.5	0.750	2,673.5	488	0.1	0.734	9	98.1	81	99	14.6	Jordan
33,780	6,980	−0.7	74	37.8	54.8	0.766	2,676.5	290	0.1	0.761	2	86.8	16	40	0.9	Kazakhstan
14,987	1,050	−0.6	193	18.5	62.4	0.488	2,090.1	7,143	6.7	0.486	15	16.7	13	14	1.3	Kenya
–	–	–	30.2	33.8	36	0.888	2,141.7	556	–	–	1	–	–	–	–	Korea, North
673,036	20,400	4.7	3.2	40.4	56.3	–	3,058.0	–	0.1	0.882	2	293.2	610	−4	2.8	Korea, South
43,052	19,510	−1.7	0.4	60.5	39.1	0.838	3,010.0	625	0.12	0.827	16	399.9	228	−4	5.3	Kuwait
2,050	1,840	−3.2	38.5	22.8	38.7	0.701	2,999.1	368	0.1	...	3	37.2	38	10	1.4	Kyrgyzstan
2,239	1,850	3.8	49.5	27.5	23	0.534	2,311.7	1,639	0.1	0.528	47	–	3	40	0.5	Laos
12,570	11,850	0.2	4.4	24.8	70.8	0.823	2,938.0	344	0.4	0.823	1	314.7	404	42	1.2	Latvia
22,668	5,380	3.1	12	21	67	0.758	3,195.9	365	0.1	0.755	13	416.5	117	230	3.1	Lebanon
1,336	3,210	2.4	15.2	43.9	40.9	0.493	2,638.3	14,286	28.9	0.483	15	–	10	22	2.3	Lesotho
391	130	–	76.9	5.4	17.7	–	1,899.8	781	5.9	–	42	9.7	0	28	0.2	Liberia
25,257	4,490	–	8.7	45.7	45.6	0.794	3,319.8	833	0.2	–	17	140.1	29	3	3.9	Libya
19,727	12,610	−0.3	6.1	33.4	60.5	0.842	3,324.5	248	0.1	0.841	1	375.7	202	63	1.9	Lithuania
25,302	61,220	3.7	0.5	16.3	83.1	0.933	3,701.0	394	0.2	0.926	0	746.9	370	−294	0.9	Luxembourg
4,855	6,480	−0.7	11.2	26	62.8	0.793	2,654.6	457	0.1	–	–	166.5	49	119	6.0	Macedonia (FYROM)
5,181	830	−0.9	29.3	16.7	54	0.469	2,004.6	11,111	1.7	0.462	31	4.9	4	20	1.2	Madagascar
1,922	620	1.1	54.8	19.2	26	0.388	2,154.6	–	14.2	0.374	37	6.9	3	45	0.7	Malawi
117,132	9,630	3.6	7.2	33.6	59.1	0.793	2,881.1	1,471	0.4	0.786	11	18.8	344	7	2.0	Malaysia
4,335	980	1.7	45	17	38	0.326	2,173.9	25,000	1.9	0.309	54	4.1	2	50	0.4	Mali
4,913	18,720	3.6	3	23	74	0.875	3,586.9	344	0.1	0.866	7	713.2	303	63	0.7	Malta
1,210	2,050	1.6	25	29	46	0.465	2,772.0	7,143	0.6	0.456	58	11.2	4	73	1.7	Mauritania
5,730	4,090	4.0	7.6	30	62.4	0.785	2,954.8	1,176	0.1	0.775	14	113.1	123	35	0.2	Mauritius
703,080	9,590	1.4	4	27.2	68.9	0.802	3,144.7	641	0.3	0.792	8	185.2	118	11	0.9	Mexico
252	590	−1.8	50	4	46	–	–	–	–	–	11	–	6	–	–	Micronesia, Fed. States
2,563	1,930	−6.9	22.4	24.8	52.8	0.681	2,806.0	369	0.2	0.678	1	64.3	80	23	0.4	Moldova
1,484	2,020	0.2	20.6	21.5	58	0.668	2,249.1	360	0.1	0.664	1	18	58	119	2.2	Mongolia
46,518	4,100	0.8	21.2	35.8	43	0.620	3,051.8	2,041	0.1	0.604	48	56.9	33	18	5.0	Morocco
4,710	1,160	4.5	21.1	32.1	46.9	0.354	2,078.9	50,000	12.2	0.339	52	8.7	3	34	2.2	Mozambique
4,813	6,960	0.9	11.3	30.8	57.9	0.607	2,277.5	3,448	21.3	0.602	16	38	34	80	3.1	Namibia
6,538	1,470	2.3	40	20	40	0.504	2,453.1	20,000	0.5	0.484	55	5.5	3	16	1.5	Nepal
515,148	31,220	2.2	2.4	24.5	73.1	0.942	3,362.3	305	0.2	0.938	1	438.6	522	−202	1.6	Netherlands
82,465	22,130	2.1	4.6	27.4	68	0.926	3,219.2	457	0.1	0.924	1	632.3	526	−25	1.0	New Zealand
4,452	3,300	1.5	20.7	24.7	54.6	0.667	2,298.0	1,613	0.2	0.66	32	36.5	17	133	0.7	Nicaragua
2,836	830	−0.8	39	17	44	0.292	2,130.4	33,333	1.2	0.278	82	8.9	1	30	1.1	Niger
53,983	930	−0.3	36.3	30.5	33.3	0.466	2,725.5	3,704	5.4	0.458	32	0.6	6	2	0.8	Nigeria
238,398	38,550	3.0	2.2	36.3	61.6	0.956	3,484.2	272	0.1	0.955	0	523.8	346	−304	1.9	Norway
20,508	13,250	0.9	3.1	41.1	55.8	0.770	–	730	0.1	0.747	24	191.6	71	26	11.4	Oman
90,663	2,160	1.1	22.6	24.1	53.3	0.497	2,418.8	1,471	0.1	0.471	54	11.1	10	5	4.9	Pakistan
13,468	6,870	2.5	7.2	13	79.8	0.791	2,271.7	826	0.9	0.785	7	96.3	62	66	1.1	Panama
3,262	2,300	0.5	34.5	34.7	30.8	0.542	2,175.0	16,667	0.6	0.536	34	20.6	14	74	1.4	Papua New Guinea
6,752	4,870	−0.5	25.3	24.9	49.8	0.751	2,565.3	2,041	0.5	0.736	6	66	20	14	0.9	Paraguay
65,043	5,370	2.2	8	27	65	0.752	2,570.9	971	0.5	0.736	9	50.1	104	33	1.4	Peru
96,930	4,890	1.1	14.8	31.9	53.2	0.753	2,379.3	870	0.1	0.751	4	34.3	44	14	1.0	Philippines
232,398	12,640	4.2	2.9	31.3	65.9	0.850	3,374.5	455	0.1	0.848	1	325.1	232	26	1.7	Poland
149,790	19,250	2.5	5.9	30.2	63.9	0.897	3,740.9	314	0.5	0.894	7	734.1	194	−26	2.3	Portugal
–	–	–	0.3	58.2	41.5	0.833	–	455	0.1	–	17	517.3	113	8	10.0	Qatar

COUNTRY	POPULATION							LAND & AGRICULTURE				TRADE, TOURISM & ENERGY					
	Total population (millions)	Population density (persons per km²)	Life expectancy (years)	Average annual population change (%)	Birth rate (births per thousand people)	Death rate (deaths per thousand people)	Urban population (% of total)	Land area (thousand km²)	Arable & permanent crops (% of land area)	Permanent pasture (% of land area)	Forest (% of land area)	Imports (US$ per capita)	Exports (US$ per capita)	Tourism receipts (US$ per capita)	Energy produced (tonnes of oil equiv. per capita)	Energy consumed (tonnes of oil equiv. per capita)	CO₂ emissions per capita (metric tonnes)
	2005	2005	2005	2005	2005	2005	2005	2002	2002	2000	2004	2004	2003	2002	2002	2003
Romania	22.3	94	71	−0.1	11	12	55	238	43	21	28	1,275	1,056	20	1.34	1.91	4.49
Russia	143.4	8	67	−0.4	10	15	73	17,075	7	5	50	648	1,133	31	7.94	4.78	11.21
Rwanda	8.4	323	47	2.4	41	16	22	26	55	19	12	31	8	3.7	0.01	0.04	0.11
St Lucia	0.2	200	74	1.3	20	5	31	0.5	30	3	15	1,335	330	1,410	0	0.63	2.38
Saudi Arabia	26.4	13	75	2.3	30	3	89	2,150	2	79	1	1,372	4,280	130	19.50	4.98	13.52
Senegal	11.7	60	57	2.5	35	11	51	197	13	29	32	182	117	16	0	0.15	0.45
Serbia & Montenegro†	10.8	106	75	0.0	12	10	52	102	37	18	2.8	883	300	14	1.06	1.60	4.75
Sierra Leone	5.9	82	73	2.2	43	21	40	72	8	31	67	45	8	10	0	0.06	0.19
Singapore	4.4	4,400	82	1.6	9	4	100	0.7	3	0	3	35,273	32,364	909	0	9.35	27.89
Slovak Republic	5.4	110	75	0.2	11	9	58	49	32	18	42	5,494	5,415	160	1.42	3.89	7.1
Slovenia	2.0	100	76	0.0	9	10	51	20	10	15	55	8,035	7,485	671	1.81	3.78	8.39
Solomon Is.	0.5	18	73	2.7	31	4	17	29	3	1	91	134	148	4	0	0.13	0.39
Somalia	8.6	13	48	3.4	46	17	36	638	2	69	12	40	9	–	0	0.03	0.09
South Africa	44.3	36	43	−0.3	18	21	58	1,221	13	69	7	890	947	96	3.22	2.66	9.13
Spain	40.3	80	80	0.2	10	10	77	498	38	23	29	5,509	4,280	1,037	0.81	3.64	8.27
Sri Lanka	20.1	305	73	0.8	16	6	21	66	29	7	30	361	264	21	0.04	0.24	0.61
Sudan	40.2	16	59	2.6	36	9	41	2,506	7	49	26	87	84	2.9	0.29	0.10	0.26
Suriname	0.4	2	69	0.3	18	7	77	163	0	0	90	1,510	1,238	10	2.39	2.41	3.94
Swaziland	1.1	65	36	0.3	28	25	24	17	11	71	30	1,036	818	24	0.12	0.32	1.25
Sweden	9.0	20	80	0.2	10	10	83	450	7	1	66	10,886	13,522	589	3.83	6.18	6.27
Switzerland	7.5	183	80	0.5	10	8	68	41	11	27	30	16,147	17,427	1,243	2.12	4.24	6
Syria	18.4	99	70	2.3	28	5	50	185	29	45	3	274	331	77	2.03	1.19	2.94
Taiwan	22.9	636	77	0.6	13	6	77	36	23	–	58	7,223	7,445	130	0.52	4.52	12.4
Tajikistan	7.2	50	65	2.2	33	8	24	143	7	23	3	181	157	0.3	0.54	0.82	1.03
Tanzania	36.8	39	45	1.8	38	17	38	945	6	40	44	54	34	12	0.02	0.05	0.1
Thailand	64.2	125	72	0.9	16	7	33	513	38	2	29	1,259	1,369	122	0.53	1.18	3.11
Togo	5.4	95	53	2.1	33	12	36	57	49	19	9	153	123	2.4	0	0.08	0.23
Trinidad & Tobago	1.0	200	69	−0.7	13	9	76	5	24	2	50	4,650	6,671	242	21.21	11.40	24.92
Tunisia	10.0	61	75	1.0	16	5	64	164	32	31	3	1,152	993	158	0.63	0.85	2.17
Turkey	69.7	89	72	1.1	17	6	67	775	37	17	13	1,356	997	189	0.34	1.12	2.86
Turkmenistan	5.0	10	61	1.8	30	9	46	488	4	65	8	570	800	–	12.17	3.01	8.83
Uganda	27.3	116	52	3.3	47	13	12	241	37	26	21	48	23	6.9	0.02	0.03	0.06
Ukraine	47.0	78	67	−0.6	10	16	67	604	55	13	17	669	700	20	1.86	3.43	7.13
United Arab Emirates	2.6	31	75	1.5	19	4	86	84	3	4	4	17,562	26,723	554	64.99	21.18	44.11
United Kingdom	60.4	247	78	0.3	11	10	89	242	24	46	11	7,275	5,748	377	4.50	3.97	9.53
USA	295.7	31	78	0.9	14	8	81	9,629	19	26	25	4,992	2,689	218	6.04	8.33	19.95
Uruguay	3.4	19	76	0.5	14	9	93	175	8	77	7	609	647	102	0.67	1.11	1.62
Uzbekistan	26.9	60	64	1.7	26	8	36	447	12	54	5	105	138	1.8	2.32	2.01	4.42
Venezuela	25.4	28	74	1.4	19	5	88	912	4	21	56	590	1,411	13	8.27	2.90	5.48
Vietnam	83.5	253	71	1.0	17	6	27	332	27	2	30	315	284	1	0.41	0.26	0.75
West Bank (OPT)*	2.4	400	73	3.1	32	4	–	6	–	–	–	625	85	1.7	–	–	–
Western Sahara	0.3	1	–	2.2	–	–	94	266	0	19	0	–	–	–	0	0.32	1.05
Yemen	20.7	39	62	3.5	43	9	26	528	3	30	1	180	216	6.7	1.16	0.19	0.5
Zambia	11.3	15	38	2.1	41	20	37	753	7	40	42	134	137	13	0.21	0.25	0.21
Zimbabwe	12.2	31	37	0.5	30	25	36	394	9	44	49	131	115	3.6	0.32	0.41	0.86

NOTES

SERBIA & MONTENEGRO†
Serbia & Montenegro became separate states in June 2006. Kosovo separated from Serbia in February 2008.

OPT*
Occupied Palestinian Territory.

PER CAPITA
An amount divided by the total population of a country or the amount per person.

PPP
Purchasing Power Parity (PPP) is a method used to enable real comparisons to be made between countries when measuring wealth. The UN International Comparison Programme gives estimates of the PPP for each country, so it can be used as an indicator of real price levels for goods and services rather than using currency exchange rates (see *GNI and GNI per capita*).

POPULATION TOTAL
These are estimates of the mid-year total in 2005.

POPULATION DENSITY
The total population divided by the land area (both are recorded in the table above).

LIFE EXPECTANCY
The average age that a child born today is expected to live to, if mortality levels of today last throughout its lifetime.

AVERAGE ANNUAL CHANGE
These are estimates of the percentage growth or decline of a country's population as a yearly average.

BIRTH/DEATH RATES
These are 2005 estimates from the *CIA World Factbook*.

URBAN POPULATION
The urban population shows the percentage of the total population living in towns and cities (each country will differ with regard to the size or type of town that is defined as an urban area).

LAND AREA
This is the total land area of a country, less the area of major lakes and rivers, in square kilometres.

ARABLE AND PERMANENT CROPS
These figures give a percentage of the total land area that is used for crops and fruit (including temporary fallow land or meadows).

PERMANENT PASTURE
This is the percentage of land area that has permanent forage crops for cattle or horses, cultivated or wild. Some land may be classified both as permanent pasture or as forest (see *Forest*), especially areas of scrub or savanna.

FOREST
Natural/planted trees including cleared land that will be reforested in the near future as a percentage of the land area.

IMPORTS AND EXPORTS
The total value of goods imported into a country and exported to other countries, given in US dollars ($) per capita.

TOURISM RECEIPTS
The total of income generated from tourism in US dollars per capita.

PRODUCTION AND CONSUMPTION OF ENERGY
The total amount of commercial energy produced or consumed in a country per capita (see *note*). It is expressed in metric tonnes of oil equivalent (an energy unit giving the heating value derived from one tonne of oil).

CARBON DIOXIDE EMISSIONS
The amount of carbon dioxide that each country produces per capita.

WEALTH						SOCIAL INDICATORS										COUNTRY
GNI (million US$)	GNI per capita (PPP US$)	Average annual growth in GDP per capita (%)	Agriculture (% of GDP)	Industry (% of GDP)	Services (% of GDP)	Human Develop. Index (HDI) value	Food intake (calories per capita per day)	Population per doctor	Adults living with HIV/AIDS (% 15–49 year olds)	Gender Develop. Index (GDI) value	Illiteracy rate (% adults)	Motor vehicles per thousand people	Internet usage per thousand people	Aid donated (–)/received (US$ per capita)	Military spending (% of GDP)	
2004	2004	1990–2002	2004	2004	2004	2002	2003	2003	2003	2002	2003	2002	2003	2002	2004	
63,910	8,190	0.1	13.1	33.7	53.2	0.778	3,454.6	529	0.1	0.775	2	166.2	184	17	2.5	Romania
487,335	9,620	–2.4	4.9	33.9	61.2	0.795	3,071.8	238	0.9	0.794	1	185.1	41	7	–	Russia
1,875	1,300	0.3	41.1	21.2	37.7	0.431	2,084.2	50,000	5.1	0.423	30	3.5	3	47	3.2	Rwanda
706	5,560	0.2	7	20	73	0.777	2,988.2	1,724	–	–	33	172.1	82	259	–	St Lucia
242,180	14,010	–0.6	4.2	67.2	28.6	0.768	2,844.5	654	0.1	0.739	21	372.2	67	–64	10.0	Saudi Arabia
6,967	1,720	1.2	15.9	21.4	62.7	0.437	2,279.5	10,000	0.8	0.429	60	28.3	22	33	1.5	Senegal
21,715	1,910	–	15.5	27.6	56.8	–	2,678.4	–	0.2	–	7	171.8	79	185	–	Serbia & Montenegro†
1,113	790	–5.9	49	30	21	0.273	1,936.0	11,111	7.0	–	69	7.9	2	17	1.7	Sierra Leone
104,994	26,590	3.8	0	32.6	67.4	0.902	–	714	0.2	0.884	7	134.9	509	0.3	4.9	Singapore
34,907	14,370	2.1	3.5	30.1	66.4	0.842	2,888.9	307	0.1	0.84	–	278.1	256	21	1.9	Slovak Republic
29,555	20,730	4.2	3	36	60	0.895	3,001.4	457	0.1	0.892	1	478.9	376	31	1.7	Slovenia
260	1,760	–2.4	42	11	47	0.624	2,264.9	7,692	–	–	–	–	5	56	–	Solomon Is.
–	–	–	65	10	25	–	1,628.0	–	1.0	–	62	1.4	9	7	0.9	Somalia
165,326	10,960	0.0	3.6	31.2	65.2	0.666	2,956.1	4,000	21.5	0.661	14	145.4	68	11	1.5	South Africa
875,817	25,070	2.3	3.5	28.5	68	0.922	3,370.6	304	0.5	0.916	2	545.9	239	–33	1.2	Spain
19,618	4,000	3.4	19.1	26.2	54.7	0.740	2,385.3	2,326	0.1	0.738	8	34	12	29	2.6	Sri Lanka
18,152	1,870	3.1	38.7	20.3	41	0.505	2,227.8	6,250	2.6	0.485	39	3.3	9	4	3.0	Sudan
997	1,990	0.5	13	22	65	0.780	2,652.1	2,000	1.2	–	7	203.5	42	108	0.7	Suriname
1,859	4,970	0.1	16.1	43.4	40.5	0.519	2,322.0	6,667	38.8	0.505	18	87.3	26	87	1.4	Swaziland
321,401	29,770	2.0	2	29	69	0.946	3,185.4	348	0.1	0.946	1	542.7	573	–189	1.7	Sweden
356,052	35,370	0.4	1.5	34	64.5	0.936	3,526.2	286	0.5	0.932	1	562.5	351	–147	1.0	Switzerland
21,125	3,550	1.8	25	31	44	0.710	3,038.0	704	0.1	0.689	23	32	13	11	5.9	Syria
–	–	–	1.7	30.9	67.4	–	–	–	–	–	14	–	–	–	2.6	Taiwan
1,779	1,150	–8.1	23.7	24.3	52	0.671	1,827.6	472	0.1	0.668	1	22	1	9	3.9	Tajikistan
11,560	660	0.7	43.2	17.2	39.6	0.407	1,974.9	25,000	8.8	0.401	22	3.8	7	33	0.2	Tanzania
158,703	8,020	2.9	9	44.3	46.7	0.768	2,467.3	3,333	1.5	0.766	4	126.1	111	2	1.8	Thailand
1,868	1,690	–0.7	39.5	20.4	40.1	0.495	2,345.4	16,667	4.1	0.477	39	16.2	42	14	1.9	Togo
11,360	11,180	2.9	2.7	47	50.3	0.801	2,732.4	1,333	3.2	0.795	2	219.8	106	22	0.6	Trinidad & Tobago
26,301	7,310	3.1	13.8	31.8	54.4	0.745	3,237.8	1,429	0.1	0.734	26	86.7	64	38	1.5	Tunisia
268,741	7,680	1.3	11.7	29.8	58.5	0.751	3,357.0	813	0.1	0.746	13	89.3	85	4	5.3	Turkey
6,615	6,910	–3.2	28.5	42.7	28.8	0.752	2,741.6	333	0.1	0.748	2	–	2	3	3.4	Turkmenistan
6,911	1,520	3.9	35.8	20.8	43.6	0.493	2,409.6	20,000	4.1	0.487	30	5.5	5	53	2.2	Uganda
60,297	6,250	–6.0	18	45.1	36.9	0.777	3,053.6	334	2	0.773	1	107.8	19	13	1.4	Ukraine
48,673	21,000	0.0	4	58.5	37.5	0.824	3,224.7	565	0.2	–	22	441.8	275	2	3.1	United Arab Emirates
2,016,393	31,460	2.4	1	26.3	72.7	0.936	3,412.2	610	0.1	0.934	1	497.9	423	–75	2.4	United Kingdom
2,150,931	39,710	2.0	0.9	19.7	79.4	0.939	3,774.1	358	0.6	0.936	3	800	551	–24	3.3	USA
13,414	9,070	1.4	7.9	27.4	64.8	0.833	2,828.0	258	0.3	0.829	2	217.3	119	7	2.0	Uruguay
11,860	1,860	–0.9	38	26.3	35.7	0.709	2,240.6	341	0.1	0.705	1	–	19	3	2.0	Uzbekistan
104,958	5,760	–1.0	0.1	46.5	53.4	0.778	2,336.3	500	0.5	0.77	7	100.2	60	3	1.5	Venezuela
45,082	2,700	5.9	21.8	40.1	38.1	0.691	2,566.2	1,852	0.4	0.689	6	0.7	43	34	2.5	Vietnam
3,771	1,110	–4.9	9	28	63	–	2,179.8	–	–	–	–	–	40	870	–	West Bank (OPT)*
–	–	–	–	–	40	–	–	–	–	–	–	–	–	–	–	Western Sahara
11,218	820	2.5	15.5	44.7	39.7	0.482	2,038.3	4,545	0.1	0.436	50	50.1	5	23	7.8	Yemen
4,748	890	–1.2	14.9	28.9	56.1	0.389	1,927.4	14,286	16.5	0.375	19	0.8	6	62	1.8	Zambia
6,165	2,180	–0.8	18.1	24.3	57.7	0.491	1,942.6	16,667	33.7	0.482	9	50.7	43	14	4.3	Zimbabwe

GNI
Gross National Income: this used to be referred to as GNP (Gross National Product) and is a good indication of a country's wealth. It is the income in US dollars from goods and services in a country for one year, including income from overseas.

GNI PER CAPITA
The GNI (see above) divided by the total population by using the PPP method (see note).

AVERAGE ANNUAL GROWTH IN GDP
The growth or decline of the Gross Domestic Product per capita (decline shown as a negative [–] number), as an average over the 12 years from 1990 to 2002. The GDP is the value of all goods and services made in a country in one year, but unlike GNI (see above) it does not include income gained from abroad.

AGRICULTURE, INDUSTRY AND SERVICES
The percentage contributions that each of these three sectors makes to a country's GDP (see note).

HUMAN DEVELOPMENT INDEX (HDI)
Produced by the UN Development Programme using indicators of life expectancy, knowledge and standards of living to give a value between 0 and 1 for each country. A high value shows a higher human development.

FOOD INTAKE
The amount of food (measured in calories) supplied, divided by the total population. Belgium and Luxembourg are shown as one country.

POPULATION PER DOCTOR
The total population divided by the number of qualified doctors.

ADULTS LIVING WITH HIV/AIDS
The percentage of all adults (aged 15–49) who have the Human Immunodeficiency Virus or the Acquired Immunodeficiency Syndrome. The total number of adults and children with HIV/AIDS in 2002 was 42 million.

GENDER DEVELOPMENT INDEX (GDI)
Like the HDI (see note), the GDI uses the same UNDP indicators but gives a value between 0 and 1 to measure the social and economic differences between men and women. The higher the value, the more equality exists between men and women.

ILLITERACY
The percentage of all adult men and women (over 15 years) who cannot read or write simple sentences.

MOTOR VEHICLES AND INTERNET USAGE
These are good indicators of a country's development wealth. They are shown in total numbers per 1,000 people.

AID DONATED AND RECEIVED
Aid defined here is Official Development Assistance (ODA) in US dollars per capita. The OECD Development Assistance Committee uses donations from donor countries and redistributes the money in the form of grants or loans to developing countries on their list of aid recipients. Donations are shown in the table with a negative (–) number. The money is given for economic development and welfare and not for military purposes.

MILITARY SPENDING
Government spending on the military or defence as a percentage of GDP.

Each topic list is divided into continents and within a continent the items are listed in order of size. The bottom part of many of the lists is selective in order to give examples from as many different countries as possible. The figures are rounded as appropriate.

World, Continents, Oceans

	km²	miles²	%
The World	509,450,000	196,672,000	–
Land	149,450,000	57,688,000	29.3
Water	360,000,000	138,984,000	70.7
Asia	44,500,000	17,177,000	29.8
Africa	30,302,000	11,697,000	20.3
North America	24,241,000	9,357,000	16.2
South America	17,793,000	6,868,000	11.9
Antarctica	14,100,000	5,443,000	9.4
Europe	9,957,000	3,843,000	6.7
Australia & Oceania	8,557,000	3,303,000	5.7
Pacific Ocean	155,557,000	60,061,000	46.4
Atlantic Ocean	76,762,000	29,638,000	22.9
Indian Ocean	68,556,000	26,470,000	20.4
Southern Ocean	20,327,000	7,848,000	6.1
Arctic Ocean	14,056,000	5,427,000	4.2

Ocean Depths

Atlantic Ocean	m	ft
Puerto Rico (Milwaukee) Deep	8,605	28,232
Cayman Trench	7,680	25,197
Gulf of Mexico	5,203	17,070
Mediterranean Sea	5,121	16,801
Black Sea	2,211	7,254
North Sea	660	2,165

Indian Ocean	m	ft
Java Trench	7,450	24,442
Red Sea	2,635	8,454

Pacific Ocean	m	ft
Mariana Trench	11,022	36,161
Tonga Trench	10,882	35,702
Japan Trench	10,554	34,626
Kuril Trench	10,542	34,587

Arctic Ocean	m	ft
Molloy Deep	5,608	18,399

Mountains

Europe		m	ft
Elbrus	*Russia*	5,642	18,510
Mont Blanc	*France/Italy*	4,807	15,771
Monte Rosa	*Italy/Switzerland*	4,634	15,203
Dom	Switzerland	4,545	14,911
Liskamm	*Switzerland*	4,527	14,852
Weisshorn	*Switzerland*	4,505	14,780
Taschorn	Switzerland	4,490	14,730
Matterhorn/Cervino	*Italy/Switzerland*	4,478	14,691
Mont Maudit	*France/Italy*	4,465	14,649
Dent Blanche	*Switzerland*	4,356	14,291
Nadelhorn	*Switzerland*	4,327	14,196
Grandes Jorasses	*France/Italy*	4,208	13,806
Jungfrau	*Switzerland*	4,158	13,642
Grossglockner	*Austria*	3,797	12,457
Mulhacén	*Spain*	3,478	11,411
Zugspitze	*Germany*	2,962	9,718
Olympus	*Greece*	2,917	9,570
Triglav	*Slovenia*	2,863	9,393
Gerlachovsky	*Slovak Republic*	2,655	8,711
Galdhøpiggen	*Norway*	2,469	8,100
Kebnekaise	*Sweden*	2,117	6,946
Ben Nevis	*UK*	1,342	4,403

Asia		m	ft
Everest	*China/Nepal*	8,850	29,035
K2 (Godwin Austen)	*China/Kashmir*	8,611	28,251
Kanchenjunga	*India/Nepal*	8,598	28,208
Lhotse	*China/Nepal*	8,516	27,939
Makalu	*China/Nepal*	8,481	27,824
Cho Oyu	*China/Nepal*	8,201	26,906
Dhaulagiri	*Nepal*	8,167	26,795
Manaslu	*Nepal*	8,156	26,758
Nanga Parbat	*Kashmir*	8,126	26,660
Annapurna	*Nepal*	8,078	26,502
Gasherbrum	*China/Kashmir*	8,068	26,469
Xixabangma	*China*	8,012	26,286
Kangbachen	*India/Nepal*	7,902	25,925
Trivor	*Pakistan*	7,720	25,328
Pik Kommunizma	*Tajikistan*	7,495	24,590
Demavend	*Iran*	5,604	18,386
Ararat	*Turkey*	5,165	16,945
Gunong Kinabalu	*Malaysia (Borneo)*	4,101	13,455
Fuji-San	*Japan*	3,776	12,388

Africa		m	ft
Kilimanjaro	*Tanzania*	5,895	19,340
Mt Kenya	*Kenya*	5,199	17,057
Ruwenzori	*Uganda/Congo (D.R.)*	5,109	16,762
Ras Dashen	*Ethiopia*	4,620	15,157
Meru	*Tanzania*	4,565	14,977
Karisimbi	*Rwanda/Congo (D.R.)*	4,507	14,787
Mt Elgon	*Kenya/Uganda*	4,321	14,176
Batu	*Ethiopia*	4,307	14,130
Toubkal	*Morocco*	4,165	13,665
Mt Cameroun	*Cameroon*	4,070	13,353

Oceania		m	ft
Puncak Jaya	*Indonesia*	5,029	16,499
Puncak Trikora	*Indonesia*	4,730	15,518
Puncak Mandala	*Indonesia*	4,702	15,427
Mt Wilhelm	*Papua New Guinea*	4,508	14,790
Mauna Kea	*USA (Hawaii)*	4,205	13,796
Mauna Loa	*USA (Hawaii)*	4,169	13,678
Aoraki Mt Cook	*New Zealand*	3,753	12,313
Mt Kosciuszko	*Australia*	2,228	7,309

North America		m	ft
Mt McKinley (Denali)	*USA (Alaska)*	6,194	20,321
Mt Logan	*Canada*	5,959	19,551
Pico de Orizaba	*Mexico*	5,610	18,405
Mt St Elias	*USA/Canada*	5,489	18,008
Popocatépetl	*Mexico*	5,452	17,887
Mt Foraker	*USA (Alaska)*	5,304	17,401
Iztaccihuatl	*Mexico*	5,286	17,342
Lucania	*Canada*	5,226	17,146
Mt Steele	*Canada*	5,073	16,644
Mt Bona	*USA (Alaska)*	5,005	16,420
Mt Whitney	*USA*	4,418	14,495
Tajumulco	*Guatemala*	4,220	13,845
Chirripó Grande	*Costa Rica*	3,837	12,589
Pico Duarte	*Dominican Rep.*	3,175	10,417

South America		m	ft
Aconcagua	*Argentina*	6,962	22,841
Bonete	*Argentina*	6,872	22,546
Ojos del Salado	*Argentina/Chile*	6,863	22,516
Pissis	*Argentina*	6,779	22,241
Mercedario	*Argentina/Chile*	6,770	22,211
Huascarán	*Peru*	6,768	22,204
Llullaillaco	*Argentina/Chile*	6,723	22,057
Nudo de Cachi	*Argentina*	6,720	22,047
Yerupaja	*Peru*	6,632	21,758
Sajama	*Bolivia*	6,520	21,391
Chimborazo	*Ecuador*	6,267	20,561
Pico Cristóbal Colón	*Colombia*	5,800	19,029
Pico Bolivar	*Venezuela*	5,007	16,427

Antarctica	m	ft
Vinson Massif	4,897	16,066
Mt Kirkpatrick	4,528	14,855

Rivers

Europe		km	miles
Volga	*Caspian Sea*	3,700	2,300
Danube	*Black Sea*	2,850	1,770
Ural	*Caspian Sea*	2,535	1,575
Dnieper	*Black Sea*	2,285	1,420
Kama	*Volga*	2,030	1,260
Don	*Volga*	1,990	1,240
Petchora	*Arctic Ocean*	1,790	1,110
Oka	*Volga*	1,480	920
Dniester	*Black Sea*	1,400	870
Vyatka	*Kama*	1,370	850
Rhine	*North Sea*	1,320	820
N. Dvina	*Arctic Ocean*	1,290	800
Elbe	*North Sea*	1,145	710

Asia		km	miles
Yangtze	*Pacific Ocean*	6,380	3,960
Yenisey–Angara	*Arctic Ocean*	5,550	3,445
Huang He	*Pacific Ocean*	5,464	3,395
Ob–Irtysh	*Arctic Ocean*	5,410	3,360
Mekong	*Pacific Ocean*	4,500	2,795
Amur	*Pacific Ocean*	4,442	2,760
Lena	*Arctic Ocean*	4,402	2,735
Irtysh	*Ob*	4,250	2,640
Yenisey	*Arctic Ocean*	4,090	2,540
Ob	*Arctic Ocean*	3,680	2,285
Indus	*Indian Ocean*	3,100	1,925
Brahmaputra	*Indian Ocean*	2,900	1,800
Syrdarya	*Aral Sea*	2,860	1,775
Salween	*Indian Ocean*	2,800	1,740
Euphrates	*Indian Ocean*	2,700	1,675
Amudarya	*Aral Sea*	2,540	1,575

Africa		km	miles
Nile	*Mediterranean*	6,670	4,140
Congo	*Atlantic Ocean*	4,670	2,900
Niger	*Atlantic Ocean*	4,180	2,595
Zambezi	*Indian Ocean*	3,540	2,200
Oubangi/Uele	*Congo (Dem. Rep.)*	2,250	1,400
Kasai	*Congo (Dem. Rep.)*	1,950	1,210
Shaballe	*Indian Ocean*	1,930	1,200
Orange	*Atlantic Ocean*	1,860	1,155
Cubango	*Okavango Delta*	1,800	1,120
Limpopo	*Indian Ocean*	1,770	1,100
Senegal	*Atlantic Ocean*	1,640	1,020

Australia		km	miles
Murray–Darling	*Southern Ocean*	3,750	2,330
Darling	*Murray*	3,070	1,905
Murray	*Southern Ocean*	2,575	1,600
Murrumbidgee	*Murray*	1,690	1,050

North America		km	miles
Mississippi–Missouri	*Gulf of Mexico*	5,971	3,710
Mackenzie	*Arctic Ocean*	4,240	2,630
Missouri	*Mississippi*	4,088	2,540
Mississippi	*Gulf of Mexico*	3,782	2,350
Yukon	*Pacific Ocean*	3,185	1,980
Rio Grande	*Gulf of Mexico*	3,030	1,880
Arkansas	*Mississippi*	2,340	1,450
Colorado	*Pacific Ocean*	2,330	1,445
Red	*Mississippi*	2,040	1,270
Columbia	*Pacific Ocean*	1,950	1,210
Saskatchewan	*Lake Winnipeg*	1,940	1,205

South America		km	miles
Amazon	*Atlantic Ocean*	6,450	4,010
Paraná–Plate	*Atlantic Ocean*	4,500	2,800
Purus	*Amazon*	3,350	2,080
Madeira	*Amazon*	3,200	1,990
São Francisco	*Atlantic Ocean*	2,900	1,800
Paraná	*Plate*	2,800	1,740
Tocantins	*Atlantic Ocean*	2,750	1,710
Orinoco	*Atlantic Ocean*	2,740	1,700
Paraguay	*Paraná*	2,550	1,580
Pilcomayo	*Paraná*	2,500	1,550
Araguaia	*Tocantins*	2,250	1,400

Lakes

Europe		km²	miles²
Lake Ladoga	*Russia*	17,700	6,800
Lake Onega	*Russia*	9,700	3,700
Saimaa system	*Finland*	8,000	3,100
Vänern	*Sweden*	5,500	2,100

Asia		km²	miles²
Caspian Sea	*Asia*	371,000	143,000
Lake Baikal	*Russia*	30,500	11,780
Aral Sea	*Kazakhstan/Uzbekistan*	28,687	11,086
Tonlé Sap	*Cambodia*	20,000	7,700
Lake Balqash	*Kazakhstan*	18,500	7,100

Africa		km²	miles²
Lake Victoria	*East Africa*	68,000	26,000
Lake Tanganyika	*Central Africa*	33,000	13,000
Lake Malawi/Nyasa	*East Africa*	29,600	11,430
Lake Chad	*Central Africa*	25,000	9,700
Lake Turkana	*Ethiopia/Kenya*	8,500	3,290
Lake Volta	*Ghana*	8,480	3,270

Australia		km²	miles²
Lake Eyre	*Australia*	8,900	3,400
Lake Torrens	*Australia*	5,800	2,200
Lake Gairdner	*Australia*	4,800	1,900

North America		km²	miles²
Lake Superior	*Canada/USA*	82,350	31,800
Lake Huron	*Canada/USA*	59,600	23,010
Lake Michigan	*USA*	58,000	22,400
Great Bear Lake	*Canada*	31,800	12,280
Great Slave Lake	*Canada*	28,500	11,000
Lake Erie	*Canada/USA*	25,700	9,900
Lake Winnipeg	*Canada*	24,400	9,400
Lake Ontario	*Canada/USA*	19,500	7,500
Lake Nicaragua	*Nicaragua*	8,200	3,200

South America		km²	miles²
Lake Titicaca	*Bolivia/Peru*	8,300	3,200
Lake Poopo	*Bolivia*	2,800	1,100

Islands

Europe		km²	miles²
Great Britain	*UK*	229,880	88,700
Iceland	*Atlantic Ocean*	103,000	39,800
Ireland	*Ireland/UK*	84,400	32,600
Novaya Zemlya (N.)	*Russia*	48,200	18,600
Sicily	*Italy*	25,500	9,800
Corsica	*France*	8,700	3,400

Asia		km²	miles²
Borneo	*South-east Asia*	744,360	287,400
Sumatra	*Indonesia*	473,600	182,860
Honshu	*Japan*	230,500	88,980
Celebes	*Indonesia*	189,000	73,000
Java	*Indonesia*	126,700	48,900
Luzon	*Philippines*	104,700	40,400
Hokkaido	*Japan*	78,400	30,300

Africa		km²	miles²
Madagascar	*Indian Ocean*	587,040	226,660
Socotra	*Indian Ocean*	3,600	1,400
Réunion	*Indian Ocean*	2,500	965

Oceania		km²	miles²
New Guinea	*Indonesia/Papua NG*	821,030	317,000
New Zealand (S.)	*Pacific Ocean*	150,500	58,100
New Zealand (N.)	*Pacific Ocean*	114,700	44,300
Tasmania	*Australia*	67,800	26,200
Hawaii	*Pacific Ocean*	10,450	4,000

North America		km²	miles²
Greenland	*Atlantic Ocean*	2,175,600	839,800
Baffin Is.	*Canada*	508,000	196,100
Victoria Is.	*Canada*	212,200	81,900
Ellesmere Is.	*Canada*	212,000	81,800
Cuba	*Caribbean Sea*	110,860	42,800
Hispaniola	*Dominican Rep./Haiti*	76,200	29,400
Jamaica	*Caribbean Sea*	11,400	4,400
Puerto Rico	*Atlantic Ocean*	8,900	3,400

South America		km²	miles²
Tierra del Fuego	*Argentina/Chile*	47,000	18,100
Falkland Is. (E.)	*Atlantic Ocean*	6,800	2,600

How to use the Index

The index contains the names of all the principal places and features shown on the maps. Each name is followed by an additional entry in italics giving the country or region within which it is located. The alphabetical order of names composed of two or more words is governed primarily by the first word and then by the second. This is an example of the rule:

Abbeville *France* 50°6N 1°49E **68** A4
Abbey Town *U.K.* 54°51N 3°17W **22** C2
Abbot Ice Shelf *Antarctica* 73°0S 92°0W **55** D16
Abbots Bromley *U.K.* 52°50N 1°52W **23** G5

Physical features composed of a proper name (Erie) and a description (Lake) are positioned alphabetically by the proper name. The description is positioned after the proper name and is usually abbreviated:

Erie, L. *N. Amer.* 42°15N 81°0W **112** D7

Where a description forms part of a settlement or administrative name, however, it is always written in full and put in its true alphabetical position:

Mount Isa *Australia* 20°42S 139°26E **98** E6

Names beginning with M' and Mc are indexed as if they were spelled Mac. Names beginning St. are alphabetized under Saint, but Santa and San are spelled in full and are alphabetized accordingly. If the same place name occurs two or more times in the index and all are in the same country, each is followed by the name of the administrative subdivision in which it is located.

The geographical co-ordinates that follow each name in the index give the latitude and longitude of each place. The first co-ordinate indicates latitude – the distance north or south of the Equator. The second co-ordinate indicates longitude – the distance east or west of the Greenwich Meridian. Both latitude and longitude are measured in degrees and minutes (there are 60 minutes in a degree).

The latitude is followed by N(orth) or S(outh) and the longitude by E(ast) or W(est).

The number in bold type that follows the geographical co-ordinates refers to the number of the map page where that feature or place will be found. This is usually the largest scale at which the place or feature appears.

The letter and figure that are immediately after the page number give the grid square on the map page, within which the feature is situated. The letter represents the latitude and the figure the longitude. A lower-case letter immediately after the page number refers to an inset map on that page.

In some cases the feature itself may fall within the specified square, while the name is outside. This is usually the case only with features that are larger than a grid square.

Rivers are indexed to their mouths or confluences, and carry the symbol → after their names. The following symbols are also used in the index: ■ country, ⊠ overseas territory or dependency, □ first-order administrative area, △ national park, ✈ (LHR) principal airport (and location identifier).

Abbreviations used in the Index

Afghan. – Afghanistan
Ala. – Alabama
Alta. – Alberta
Amer. – America(n)
Arch. – Archipelago
Ariz. – Arizona
Ark. – Arkansas
Atl. Oc. – Atlantic Ocean
B. – Baie, Bahía, Bay, Bucht, Bugt
B.C. – British Columbia
Bangla. – Bangladesh
C. – Cabo, Cap, Cape, Coast
C.A.R. – Central African Republic
Calif. – California
Cent. – Central
Chan. – Channel
Colo. – Colorado
Conn. – Connecticut
Cord. – Cordillera
Cr. – Creek
D.C. – District of Columbia
Del. – Delaware
Dom. Rep. – Dominican Republic
E. – East
El Salv. – El Salvador
Eq. Guin. – Equatorial Guinea
Fla. – Florida
Falk. Is. – Falkland Is.
G. – Golfe, Golfo, Gulf
Ga. – Georgia
Hd. – Head
Hts. – Heights
I.(s). – Île, Ilha, Insel, Isla, Island, Isle(s)
Ill. – Illinois
Ind. – Indiana
Ind. Oc. – Indian Ocean
Ivory C. – Ivory Coast
Kans. – Kansas
Ky. – Kentucky
L. – Lac, Lacul, Lago, Lagoa, Lake, Limni, Loch, Lough
La. – Louisiana
Lux. – Luxembourg
Madag. – Madagascar
Man. – Manitoba
Mass. – Massachusetts
Md. – Maryland
Me. – Maine
Mich. – Michigan
Minn. – Minnesota
Miss. – Mississippi
Mo. – Missouri
Mont. – Montana
Mozam. – Mozambique
Mt.(s) – Mont, Monte, Monti, Montaña, Mountain
N. – Nord, Norte, North, Northern,
N.B. – New Brunswick
N.C. – North Carolina
N. Cal. – New Caledonia
N. Dak. – North Dakota
N.H. – New Hampshire
N.J. – New Jersey
N. Mex. – New Mexico
N.S. – Nova Scotia
N.S.W. – New South Wales
N.W.T. – North West Territory
N.Y. – New York
N.Z. – New Zealand
Nat. Park – National Park
Nebr. – Nebraska
Neths. – Netherlands
Nev. – Nevada
Nfld. – Newfoundland and Labrador
Nic. – Nicaragua
Okla. – Oklahoma
Ont. – Ontario
Oreg. – Oregon
P.E.I. – Prince Edward Island
Pa. – Pennsylvania
Pac. Oc. – Pacific Ocean
Papua N.G. – Papua New Guinea
Pen. – Peninsula, Péninsule
Phil. – Philippines
Pk. – Peak
Plat. – Plateau
Prov. – Province, Provincial
Pt. – Point
Pta. – Ponta, Punta
Pte. – Pointe
Qué. – Québec
Queens. – Queensland
R. – Rio, River
R.I. – Rhode Island
Ra.(s) – Range(s)
Reg. – Region
Rep. – Republic
Res. – Reserve, Reservoir
S. – San, South
Si. Arabia – Saudi Arabia
S.C. – South Carolina
S. Dak. – South Dakota
Sa. – Serra, Sierra
Sask. – Saskatchewan
Scot. – Scotland
Sd. – Sound
Sib. – Siberia
St. – Saint, Sankt, Sint
Str. – Strait, Stretto
Switz. – Switzerland
Tas. – Tasmania
Tenn. – Tennessee
Tex. – Texas
Trin. & Tob.. – Trinidad & Tobago
U.A.E. – United Arab Emirates
U.K. – United Kingdom
U.S.A. – United States of America
Va. – Virginia
Vic. – Victoria
Vol. – Volcano
Vt. – Vermont
W. – West
W. Va. – West Virginia
Wash. – Washington
Wis. – Wisconsin

A

Aachen *Germany* 50°45N 6°6E **66** C4
Aalborg *Denmark* 57°2N 9°54E **63** F5
Aalst *Belgium* 50°56N 4°2E **65** D4
Aarau *Switz.* 47°23N 8°4E **66** E5
Aare → *Switz.* 47°33N 8°14E **66** E5
Aba *Nigeria* 5°10N 7°19E **94** G7
Abaco I. *Bahamas* 26°25N 77°10W **115** B9
Ābādān *Iran* 30°22N 48°20E **86** D7
Abaetetuba *Brazil* 1°40S 48°50W **120** C5
Abakan *Russia* 53°40N 91°10E **79** D11
Abancay *Peru* 13°35S 72°55W **120** D2
Abariringa *Kiribati* 2°50S 171°40W **99** A16
Abaya, L. *Ethiopia* 6°30N 37°50E **88** F2
Abbé, L. *Ethiopia* 11°8N 41°47E **88** E3
Abbeville *France* 50°6N 1°49E **68** A4
Abbey Town *U.K.* 54°51N 3°17W **22** C2
Abbot Ice Shelf *Antarctica* 73°0S 92°0W **55** D16
Abbots Bromley *U.K.* 52°50N 1°52W **23** G5
Abbotsbury *U.K.* 50°40N 2°37W **24** E3
Abéché *Chad* 13°50N 20°35E **95** F10
Abeokuta *Nigeria* 7°3N 3°19E **94** G6
Aberaeron *U.K.* 52°15N 4°15W **26** C5
Aberchirder *U.K.* 57°34N 2°37W **19** G12
Aberdare *U.K.* 51°43N 3°27W **26** D7
Aberdeen *U.K.* 57°9N 2°5W **19** H13
Aberdeen *S. Dak., U.S.A.* 45°28N 98°29W **110** A7
Aberdeen *Wash., U.S.A.* 46°59N 123°50W **110** A2
Aberdeenshire □ *U.K.* 57°17N 2°36W **19** H12
Aberdyfi *U.K.* 52°33N 4°3W **26** B5
Aberfeldy *U.K.* 56°37N 3°51W **21** A8
Aberfoyle *U.K.* 56°11N 4°23W **20** B7
Abergavenny *U.K.* 51°49N 3°1W **26** D7
Abergele *U.K.* 53°17N 3°35W **26** A6
Aberporth *U.K.* 52°8N 4°33W **26** C4
Abersoch *U.K.* 52°49N 4°30W **26** B5
Abersychan *U.K.* 51°44N 3°3W **26** D7
Abert, L. *U.S.A.* 42°38N 120°14W **110** B2
Abertillery *U.K.* 51°44N 3°8W **26** D7
Aberystwyth *U.K.* 52°25N 4°5W **26** C5
Abhā *Si. Arabia* 18°0N 42°34E **88** D3
Abidjan *Ivory C.* 5°26N 3°58W **94** G5
Abilene *U.S.A.* 32°28N 99°43W **110** D7
Abingdon *U.K.* 51°40N 1°17W **24** C6
Abitibi, L. *Canada* 48°40N 79°40W **109** E12
Abkhazia □ *Georgia* 43°12N 41°5E **73** F7
Abomey *Benin* 7°10N 2°5E **94** G6
Aboyne *U.K.* 57°4N 2°47W **19** H12
Absaroka Range *U.S.A.* 44°45N 109°50W **110** B5
Abu Dhabi *U.A.E.* 24°28N 54°22E **87** E8
Abu Hamed *Sudan* 19°32N 33°13E **95** E12
Abuja *Nigeria* 9°5N 7°32E **94** G7
Abunã *Brazil* 9°40S 65°20W **120** C3
Abunã → *Brazil* 9°41S 65°20W **120** C3
Acaponeta *Mexico* 22°30N 105°22W **114** C3
Acapulco *Mexico* 16°51N 99°55W **114** D5
Acarai, Serra *Brazil* 1°50N 57°50W **120** B4
Acarigua *Venezuela* 9°33N 69°12W **120** B3
Accomac *U.S.A.* 37°43N 75°40W **113** G10
Accra *Ghana* 5°35N 0°6W **94** G5
Accrington *U.K.* 53°45N 2°22W **23** E4
Aceh □ *Indonesia* 4°15N 97°30E **83** C1
Acharnes *Greece* 38°5N 23°44E **71** E10
Acheloos → *Greece* 38°19N 21°7E **71** E9
Achill Hd. *Ireland* 53°58N 10°15W **28** D1
Achill I. *Ireland* 53°58N 10°1W **28** D1
Acklins I. *Bahamas* 22°30N 74°0W **115** C10
Acle *U.K.* 52°39N 1°33E **25** A12
Aconcagua, Cerro *Argentina* 32°39S 70°0W **121** F3
Acre □ *Brazil* 9°1S 71°0W **120** C2
Acre → *Brazil* 8°45S 67°22W **120** C3
Acton Burnell *U.K.* 52°37N 2°41W **23** G3
Ad Dammām *Si. Arabia* 26°20N 50°5E **86** E7
Ad Dīwānīyah *Iraq* 32°0N 45°0E **86** D6
Adair, C. *Canada* 71°30N 71°34W **109** B12
Adak I. *U.S.A.* 51°45N 176°45W **108** D2
Adamawa Highlands *Cameroon* 7°20N 12°20E **95** G7
Adam's Bridge *Sri Lanka* 9°15N 79°40E **84** Q11
Adana *Turkey* 37°0N 35°16E **73** G6
Adare, C. *Antarctica* 71°0S 171°0E **55** D11
Addis Ababa *Ethiopia* 9°2N 38°42E **88** F2
Adelaide *Australia* 34°52S 138°30E **98** G6
Adelaide I. *Antarctica* 67°15S 68°30W **55** C17
Adelaide Pen. *Canada* 68°15N 97°30W **108** C10
Adélie, Terre *Antarctica* 68°0S 140°0E **55** C10
Aden *Yemen* 12°45N 45°0E **88** E4
Aden, G. of *Asia* 12°30N 47°30E **88** E4
Adige → *Italy* 45°9N 12°20E **70** B5
Adigrat *Ethiopia* 14°20N 39°26E **88** E2
Adirondack Mts. *U.S.A.* 44°0N 74°0W **113** D10
Adjuntas *Puerto Rico* 18°10N 66°43W **115** d
Admiralty Is. *Papua N. G.* 2°0S 147°0E **102** H6
Adour → *France* 43°32N 1°32W **68** E3
Adrar *Mauritania* 20°30N 7°30E **94** D3
Adrar des Iforas *Africa* 19°40N 1°40E **94** C5
Adrian *U.S.A.* 41°54N 84°2W **112** E5
Adriatic Sea *Medit. S.* 43°0N 16°0E **70** C6
Adwa *Ethiopia* 14°15N 38°52E **88** E2
Adwick le Street *U.K.* 53°34N 1°10W **23** E6
Adygea □ *Russia* 45°0N 40°0E **73** F7
Ægean Sea *Medit. S.* 38°30N 25°0E **71** E11
Aerhtai Shan *Mongolia* 46°40N 92°45E **80** B4
Afghanistan ■ *Asia* 33°0N 65°0E **87** C11
Africa 10°0N 20°0E **90** E6
Afyon *Turkey* 38°45N 30°33E **73** G5
Agadez *Niger* 16°58N 7°59E **94** E7
Agadir *Morocco* 30°28N 9°55W **94** B4
Agartala *India* 23°50N 91°23E **85** H17
Agen *France* 44°12N 0°38E **68** D4
Agra *India* 27°17N 77°58E **84** F10
Ağri *Turkey* 39°44N 43°3E **73** G7
Agrigento *Italy* 37°19N 13°34E **70** F5
Agua Prieta *Mexico* 31°18N 109°34W **114** A3
Aguadilla *Puerto Rico* 18°26N 67°10W **115** d
Aguascalientes *Mexico* 21°53N 102°18W **114** C4
Aguila, Punta *Puerto Rico* 17°57N 67°13W **115** d
Aguja, C. de la *Colombia* 11°18N 74°12W **116** B3
Agujereada, Pta. *Puerto Rico* 18°30N 67°8W **115** d
Agulhas, C. *S. Africa* 34°52S 20°0E **97** L4
Ahaggar *Algeria* 23°0N 6°30E **94** D76
Ahmadabad *India* 23°0N 72°40E **84** H8
Ahmadnagar *India* 19°7N 74°46E **84** K9
Ahmadpur *Pakistan* 29°12N 71°10E **84** E7
Ahvāz *Iran* 31°20N 48°40E **86** D7
Ahvenanmaa *Finland* 60°15N 20°0E **63** E8
Aḩwar *Yemen* 13°30N 46°40E **88** E4
Aihui *China* 50°10N 127°30E **81** A7
Ailsa Craig *U.K.* 55°15N 5°6W **20** D5
Aimorés *Brazil* 19°30S 41°4W **122** C2
Aïn Témouchent *Algeria* 35°16N 1°8W **94** A5
Ainsdale *U.K.* 53°37N 3°2W **23** E2
Aïr *Niger* 18°30N 8°0E **94** E7
Air Force I. *Canada* 67°58N 74°5W **109** C12
Aird, The *U.K.* 57°25N 4°33W **19** H8
Airdrie *Canada* 51°18N 114°2W **108** D8
Airdrie *U.K.* 55°52N 3°57W **21** C8
Aire → *U.K.* 53°43N 0°55W **23** E7
Aisgill *U.K.* 54°23N 2°21W **22** D4
Aisne → *France* 49°26N 2°50E **68** B5
Aix-en-Provence *France* 43°32N 5°27E **68** E6
Aix-les-Bains *France* 45°41N 5°53E **68** D6
Aizawl *India* 23°40N 92°44E **85** H18
Aizuwakamatsu *Japan* 37°30N 139°56E **82** E6
Ajaccio *France* 41°55N 8°40E **68** F8
Ajanta Ra. *India* 20°28N 75°50E **84** J9
Ajaria □ *Georgia* 41°30N 42°0E **73** F7
Ajdābiyā *Libya* 30°54N 20°4E **95** B10
'Ajmān *U.A.E.* 25°25N 55°30E **87** E8
Ajmer *India* 26°28N 74°37E **84** F9
Aketi *Dem. Rep. of the Congo* 2°38N 23°47E **96** D4
Akhisar *Turkey* 38°56N 27°48E **73** G4
Akimiski I. *Canada* 52°50N 81°30W **109** D11
Akita *Japan* 39°45N 140°7E **82** D7
'Akko *Israel* 32°55N 35°4E **86** C3
Aklavik *Canada* 68°12N 135°0W **108** C6
Akola *India* 20°42N 77°2E **84** J10
Akpatok I. *Canada* 60°25N 68°8W **109** C13
Akranes *Iceland* 64°19N 22°5W **63** B1
Akron *U.S.A.* 41°5N 81°31W **112** E7
Aksai Chin *China* 35°15N 79°55E **84** B11
Aksaray *Turkey* 38°25N 34°2E **73** G5
Akşehir Gölü *Turkey* 38°30N 31°25E **73** G5
Aksu *China* 41°5N 80°10E **80** B3
Aksum *Ethiopia* 14°5N 38°40E **88** E2
Akure *Nigeria* 7°15N 5°5E **94** G7
Akureyri *Iceland* 65°40N 18°6W **63** A2
Al 'Amārah *Iraq* 31°55N 47°15E **86** D6
Al 'Aqabah *Jordan* 29°31N 35°0E **86** D3
Al 'Aramah *Si. Arabia* 25°30N 46°0E **86** E6
Al 'Ayn *U.A.E.* 24°15N 55°45E **87** E8
Al Fallūjah *Iraq* 33°20N 43°55E **86** C5
Al Fāw *Iraq* 30°0N 48°30E **86** D7
Al Ḩadīthah *Iraq* 34°0N 41°13E **86** C5
Al Ḩillah *Iraq* 32°30N 44°25E **86** C6
Al Hoceïma *Morocco* 35°8N 3°58W **94** A5
Al Ḩudaydah *Yemen* 14°50N 43°0E **88** E3
Al Hufūf *Si. Arabia* 25°25N 49°45E **86** E7
Al Jahrah *Kuwait* 29°25N 47°40E **86** D6
Al Jawf *Libya* 24°10N 23°24E **95** D10
Al Jawf *Si. Arabia* 29°55N 39°40E **86** D4
Al Jubayl *Si. Arabia* 27°0N 49°50E **86** E7
Al Khalīl *West Bank* 31°32N 35°6E **86** D3
Al Khums *Libya* 32°40N 14°17E **95** B8
Al Kufrah *Libya* 24°17N 23°15E **95** D10
Al Kūt *Iraq* 32°30N 46°0E **86** C6
Al Manāmah *Bahrain* 26°10N 50°30E **87** E7
Al Mubarraz *Si. Arabia* 25°30N 49°40E **86** E7
Al Mukallā *Yemen* 14°33N 49°2E **88** E4
Al Musayyib *Iraq* 32°49N 44°20E **86** C6
Al Qāmishlī *Syria* 37°2N 41°14E **86** B5
Al Qaţīf *Si. Arabia* 26°35N 50°0E **86** E7
Al Qunfudhah *Si. Arabia* 19°3N 41°4E **88** D3
Alabama □ *U.S.A.* 33°0N 87°0W **111** D9
Alabama → *U.S.A.* 31°8N 87°57W **111** D9
Alagoas □ *Brazil* 9°0S 36°0W **122** A3
Alagoinhas *Brazil* 12°7S 38°20W **122** B3
Alai Range *Asia* 39°45N 72°0E **87** B13
Alamogordo *U.S.A.* 32°54N 105°57W **110** D5
Alamosa *U.S.A.* 37°28N 105°52W **110** C5
Åland = Ahvenanmaa *Finland* 60°15N 20°0E **63** E8
Alanya *Turkey* 36°38N 32°0E **73** G5
Alaşehir *Turkey* 38°23N 28°30E **73** G4
Alaska □ *U.S.A.* 64°0N 154°0W **108** C5
Alaska, G. of *Pac. Oc.* 58°0N 145°0W **108** D5
Alaska Peninsula *U.S.A.* 56°0N 159°0W **108** D4
Alaska Range *U.S.A.* 62°50N 151°0W **108** C4
Alba-Iulia *Romania* 46°8N 23°39E **67** E12
Albacete *Spain* 39°0N 1°50W **69** C5
Albanel, L. *Canada* 50°55N 73°12W **109** D12
Albania ■ *Europe* 41°0N 20°0E **71** D9
Albany *Australia* 35°1S 117°58E **98** H2
Albany *Ga., U.S.A.* 31°35N 84°10W **111** D10
Albany *N.Y., U.S.A.* 42°39N 73°45W **113** D11
Albany *Oreg., U.S.A.* 44°38N 123°6W **110** B2
Albany → *Canada* 52°17N 81°31W **109** D11
Albemarle Sd. *U.S.A.* 36°5N 76°0W **111** C11
Albert, L. *Africa* 1°30N 31°0E **96** D6
Albert Lea *U.S.A.* 43°39N 93°22W **111** B8
Albert Nile → *Uganda* 3°36N 32°2E **96** D6
Alberta □ *Canada* 54°40N 115°0W **108** D8
Albertville *France* 45°40N 6°22E **68** D7
Albi *France* 43°56N 2°9E **68** E5
Albion *U.S.A.* 42°15N 84°45W **112** D5
Albrighton *U.K.* 52°38N 2°16W **23** G4
Albuquerque *U.S.A.* 35°5N 106°39W **110** C5
Albury *Australia* 36°3S 146°56E **98** H8
Alcalá de Henares *Spain* 40°28N 3°22W **69** B4
Alcester *U.K.* 52°14N 1°52W **24** B5
Alchevsk *Ukraine* 48°30N 38°45E **73** E6
Alcoy *Spain* 38°43N 0°30W **69** C5
Aldabra Is. *Seychelles* 9°22S 46°28E **91** G8
Aldan *Russia* 58°40N 125°30E **79** D14

Aldan

Azamgarh

Azare   Bicester

Bicton   Burnham-on-Crouch

Burnham-on-Sea U.K. 51°14N 3°0W 24 D2
Burnie Australia 41°4S 145°56E 98 J8
Burnley U.K. 53°47N 2°14W 23 E4
Burnmouth U.K. 55°50N 2°4W 21 C11
Burns U.S.A. 43°35N 119°3W 110 B3
Burnside → Canada 66°51N 108°4W 108 C9
Burntisland U.K. 56°4N 3°13W 21 B9
Burqin China 47°43N 87°0E 80 B3
Burray U.K. 58°51N 2°54W 19 E12
Burren △ Ireland 53°1N 8°58W 30 B4
Burrow Hd. U.K. 54°41N 4°24W 20 E7
Burry Port U.K. 51°41N 4°15W 26 D5
Bursa Turkey 40°15N 29°5E 73 F4
Burstwick U.K. 53°44N 0°8W 23 E8
Burton U.K. 54°11N 2°43W 22 D3
Burton Agnes U.K. 54°4N 0°18W 22 D8
Burton Bradstock U.K. 50°42N 2°43W 24 E3
Burton Fleming U.K. 54°8N 0°20W 22 D8
Burton Latimer U.K. 52°22N 0°41W 25 B7
Burton upon Stather U.K. 53°39N 0°41W 23 E7
Burton upon Trent U.K. 52°48N 1°38W 23 G5
Buru Indonesia 3°30S 126°30E 83 D4
Burundi ■ Africa 3°15S 30°0E 96 E5
Burwash U.K. 50°59N 0°23E 25 E9
Burwell U.K. 52°17N 0°20E 25 B9
Burwick U.K. 58°45N 2°58W 19 E12
Bury U.K. 53°35N 2°17W 23 E4
Bury St. Edmunds U.K. 52°15N 0°43E 25 B10
Busan S. Korea 35°5N 129°0E 81 C7
Būshehr Iran 28°55N 50°55E 87 D7
Bushey U.K. 51°38N 0°22W 25 C8
Busto Arsízio Italy 45°37N 8°51E 70 B3
Buta Dem. Rep. of the Congo 2°50N 24°53E 96 D4
Butare Rwanda 2°31S 29°52E 96 E5
Butaritari Kiribati 3°30N 174°0E 102 G9
Bute U.K. 55°48N 5°2W 20 C5
Bute, Kyles of U.K. 55°55N 5°10W 20 C5
Butembo Dem. Rep. of the Congo 0°9N 29°18E 96 D5
Butha Qi China 48°0N 122°32E 81 B7
Butler U.S.A. 40°52N 79°54W 112 E8
Buton Indonesia 5°0S 122°45E 83 D4
Butte U.S.A. 46°0N 112°32W 110 A4
Buttermere U.K. 54°32N 3°16W 22 C2
Butterworth Malaysia 5°24N 100°23E 83 C2
Buttevant Ireland 52°14N 8°40W 30 D5
Butuan Phil. 8°57N 125°33E 83 C4
Buxton U.K. 53°16N 1°54W 23 F5
Buyant-Uhaa Mongolia 44°55N 110°11E 81 B6
Buzău Romania 45°10N 26°50E 67 F14
Buzuluk Russia 52°48N 52°12E 72 D9
Bydgoszcz Poland 53°10N 18°0E 67 B9
Byfield U.K. 52°10N 1°14W 24 B6
Bylot I. Canada 73°13N 78°34W 109 B12
Byrranga Ra. Russia 75°0N 100°0E 79 B12
Bytom Poland 50°25N 18°54E 67 C10

C

Ca Mau Vietnam 9°7N 105°8E 83 C2
Cabanatuan Phil. 15°30N 120°58E 83 B4
Cabedelo Brazil 7°0S 34°50W 120 C6
Cabimas Venezuela 10°23N 71°25W 120 A2
Cabinda Angola 5°33S 12°11E 96 F2
Cabinda □ Angola 5°0S 12°30E 96 F2
Cabo Frio Brazil 22°51S 42°3W 122 D2
Cabo San Lucas Mexico 22°53N 109°54W 114 C3
Cabonga, Réservoir Canada 47°20N 76°40W 109 E12
Cabora Bassa Dam Mozam. 15°20S 32°50E 97 H6
Cabot Str. Canada 47°15N 59°40W 109 E14
Čačak Serbia 43°54N 20°20E 71 C9
Cáceres Brazil 16°5S 57°40W 120 D4
Cáceres Spain 39°26N 6°23W 69 C2
Cachimbo, Serra do Brazil 9°30S 55°30W 120 C4
Cachoeira Brazil 12°30S 39°0W 122 B3
Cachoeira do Sul Brazil 30°3S 52°53W 121 F4
Cachoeiro de Itapemirim Brazil 20°51S 41°7W 122 D2
Cader Idris U.K. 52°42N 3°53W 26 B6
Cadillac U.S.A. 44°15N 85°24W 112 C5
Cádiz Spain 36°30N 6°20W 69 D2
Cádiz, G. de Spain 36°40N 7°0W 69 D2
Caen France 49°10N 0°22W 68 B3
Caenby Corner U.K. 53°24N 0°33W 23 F7
Caernarfon U.K. 53°8N 4°16W 26 A5
Caernarfon B. U.K. 53°4N 4°40W 26 A4
Caerphilly U.K. 51°35N 3°13W 27 D7
Caersws U.K. 52°31N 3°26W 26 B7
Caeté Brazil 19°55S 43°40W 122 C2
Caetité Brazil 13°50S 42°32W 122 B2
Cagayan de Oro Phil. 8°30N 124°40E 83 C4
Cágliari Italy 39°13N 9°7E 70 E3
Caguas Puerto Rico 18°14N 66°2W 115 d
Caha Mts. Ireland 51°45N 9°40W 30 E3
Caher Ireland 52°22N 7°56W 30 D7
Cahersiveen Ireland 51°56N 10°14W 30 E2
Cahore Pt. Ireland 52°33N 6°12W 31 C10
Cahors France 44°27N 1°27E 68 D4
Cairn Gorm U.K. 57°7N 3°39W 19 H10
Cairngorm Mts. U.K. 57°6N 3°42W 19 H10
Cairngorms △ U.K. 57°10N 3°50W 19 H10
Cairnryan U.K. 54°59N 5°1W 20 E5
Cairns Australia 16°57S 145°45E 98 D8
Cairnsmore of Fleet U.K. 54°59N 4°20W 20 E7
Cairo Egypt 30°2N 31°13E 95 B12
Cairo U.S.A. 37°0N 89°11W 112 G3
Caister-on-Sea U.K. 52°40N 1°43E 25 A12
Caistor U.K. 53°30N 0°18W 23 F8
Caithness U.K. 58°25N 3°35W 19 F10
Caithness, Ord of U.K. 58°8N 3°36W 19 F10
Caja de Muertos, I. Puerto Rico 17°54N 66°32W 115 d
Cajamarca Peru 7°5S 78°28W 120 C2
Calabar Nigeria 4°57N 8°20E 94 H7
Calábria □ Italy 39°0N 16°30E 70 E7
Calais France 50°57N 1°56E 68 A4
Calais U.S.A. 45°11N 67°17W 113 C14
Calama Chile 22°30S 68°55W 121 E3
Calamian Group Phil. 11°50N 119°55E 83 B3
Calanscio, Sarīr Libya 27°30N 21°30E 95 C10
Calapan Phil. 13°25N 121°7E 83 B4
Calbayog Phil. 12°4N 124°38E 83 B4
Calcutta = Kolkata India 22°34N 88°21E 85 H16
Caldbeck U.K. 54°45N 3°3W 22 C2
Calder → U.K. 53°44N 1°22W 23 E6
Calder Bridge U.K. 54°27N 3°29W 22 D2
Caldera Chile 27°5S 70°55W 121 E2
Caldew → U.K. 54°54N 2°56W 22 C3
Caldwell U.S.A. 43°40N 116°41W 110 B3
Caledonian Canal U.K. 57°29N 4°15W 19 H9
Calgary Canada 51°0N 114°10W 108 D8
Cali Colombia 3°25N 76°35W 120 B2
Calicut India 11°15N 75°43E 84 P9
California □ U.S.A. 37°30N 119°30W 110 C2
California, G. de Mexico 27°0N 111°0W 114 B2
Callan Ireland 52°32N 7°24W 31 C8
Callander U.K. 56°15N 4°13W 20 B7
Callao Peru 12°3S 77°8W 120 D2
Calne U.K. 51°26N 2°0W 24 D5
Calshot U.K. 50°48N 1°19W 24 E6
Calstock U.K. 50°30N 4°13W 27 F5
Caltanissetta Italy 37°29N 14°4E 70 F6
Calvi France 42°34N 8°45E 68 E8
Calvinia S. Africa 31°28S 19°45E 97 L3
Cam → U.K. 52°21N 0°16E 25 B9
Cam Ranh Vietnam 11°54N 109°12E 83 B2
Camagüey Cuba 21°20N 77°55W 115 C9
Camargue France 43°34N 4°34E 68 E6
Camberley U.K. 51°20N 0°44W 25 D7
Cambo U.K. 55°10N 1°57W 22 B5
Cambodia ■ Asia 12°15N 105°0E 83 B2
Camborne U.K. 50°12N 5°19W 27 G3
Cambrai France 50°11N 3°14E 68 A5
Cambrian Mts. U.K. 52°3N 3°57W 26 C6
Cambridge Jamaica 18°18N 77°54W 114 a
Cambridge U.K. 52°12N 0°8E 25 B9
Cambridge Mass., U.S.A. 42°23N 71°7W 113 D12
Cambridge Md., U.S.A. 38°34N 76°5W 113 F9
Cambridge Ohio, U.S.A. 40°2N 81°35W 112 E7
Cambridge Bay Canada 69°10N 105°0W 108 C9
Cambridgeshire □ U.K. 52°25N 0°7W 25 B8
Camden Ark., U.S.A. 33°35N 92°50W 111 D8
Camden N.J., U.S.A. 39°55N 75°7W 113 F10
Camden □ U.K. 51°32N 0°8W 25 C8
Camel → U.K. 50°31N 4°51W 27 F4
Camelford U.K. 50°37N 4°42W 27 F4
Cameroon ■ Africa 6°0N 12°30E 96 C2
Cameroun, Mt. Cameroon 4°13N 9°10E 96 D1
Cametá Brazil 2°12S 49°30W 120 C5
Camocim Brazil 2°55S 40°50W 120 C5
Campana, I. Chile 48°20S 75°20W 121 G2
Campánia □ Italy 41°0N 14°30E 70 D6
Campbell I. Pac. Oc. 52°30S 169°0E 102 N8
Campbell River Canada 50°5N 125°20W 108 D7
Campbellsville U.S.A. 37°21N 85°20W 112 G5
Campbellton Canada 47°57N 66°43W 109 E13
Campbeltown U.K. 55°26N 5°36W 20 D4
Campeche Mexico 19°51N 90°32W 114 D6
Campeche, Golfo de Mexico 19°30N 93°0W 114 D6
Campina Grande Brazil 7°20S 35°47W 120 C6
Campinas Brazil 22°50S 47°0W 122 D1
Campo Belo Brazil 20°52S 45°16W 122 D1
Campo Grande Brazil 20°25S 54°40W 120 E4
Campobasso Italy 41°34N 14°39E 70 D6
Campos Brazil 21°50S 41°20W 122 D2
Campos Belos Brazil 13°10S 47°3W 122 B1
Camrose Canada 53°0N 112°50W 108 D8
Can Tho Vietnam 10°2N 105°46E 83 B2
Canada ■ N. Amer. 60°0N 100°0W 108 D10
Canadian → U.S.A. 35°28N 95°3W 111 C7
Canadian Shield Canada 53°0N 75°0W 104 C9
Çanakkale Turkey 40°8N 26°24E 73 F4
Canandaigua U.S.A. 42°54N 77°17W 112 D9
Cananea Mexico 31°0N 110°18W 114 A2
Canaries St. Lucia 13°55N 61°4W 115 f
Canary Is. Atl. Oc. 28°30N 16°0W 94 C2
Canaveral, C. U.S.A. 28°27N 80°32W 111 E10
Canavieiras Brazil 15°39S 39°0W 122 C3
Canberra Australia 35°15S 149°8E 98 H8
Cancún Mexico 21°8N 86°44W 114 C7
Cangzhou China 38°19N 116°52E 81 C6
Caniapiscau → Canada 56°40N 69°30W 109 D13
Caniapiscau, L. de Canada 54°10N 69°55W 109 D13
Çankırı Turkey 40°40N 33°37E 73 F5
Canna U.K. 57°3N 6°33W 18 H4
Canna, Sd. of U.K. 57°1N 6°30W 18 H5
Cannanore India 11°53N 75°27E 84 P9
Cannes France 43°32N 7°1E 68 E7
Cannington U.K. 51°9N 3°4W 24 D2
Cannock U.K. 52°41N 2°1W 23 G4
Cannock Chase U.K. 52°44N 2°4W 23 G4
Canoas Brazil 29°56S 51°11W 121 E4
Cañon City U.S.A. 38°27N 105°14W 110 C5
Canonbie U.K. 55°5N 2°58W 21 D10
Canora Canada 51°40N 102°30W 108 D9
Canso Canada 45°20N 61°0W 113 C17
Cantabria □ Spain 43°10N 4°0W 69 A4
Cantábrica, Cordillera Spain 43°0N 5°10W 69 A3
Canterbury U.K. 51°16N 1°6E 25 D11
Canton = Guangzhou China 23°6N 113°13E 81 D6
Canton Ill., U.S.A. 40°33N 90°2W 112 E2
Canton N.Y., U.S.A. 44°36N 75°10W 113 C10
Canton Ohio, U.S.A. 40°48N 81°23W 112 E7
Canvey U.K. 51°31N 0°37E 25 C10
Cap-de-la-Madeleine Canada 46°22N 72°31W 113 B11
Cap-Haïtien Haiti 19°40N 72°20W 115 D10
Cap Pt. St. Lucia 14°7N 60°57W 115 f
Cape Breton I. Canada 46°0N 60°30W 113 C17
Cape Charles U.S.A. 37°16N 76°1W 113 G10
Cape Coast Ghana 5°5N 1°15W 94 G5
Cape Coral U.S.A. 26°33N 81°57W 111 E10
Cape Dorset Canada 64°14N 76°32W 109 C12
Cape Fear → U.S.A. 33°53N 78°1W 111 D11
Cape Girardeau U.S.A. 37°19N 89°32W 112 G3
Cape May U.S.A. 38°56N 74°56W 113 F10
Cape Town S. Africa 33°55S 18°22E 97 L3
Cape Verde Is. ■ Atl. Oc. 16°0N 24°0W 91 E1
Cape York Peninsula Australia 12°0S 142°30E 98 C7
Capela Brazil 10°30S 37°0W 122 B3
Capesterre-Belle-Eau Guadeloupe 16°4N 61°36W 114 b
Capesterre-de-Marie-Galante Guadeloupe 15°53N 61°14W 114 b
Capreol Canada 46°43N 80°56W 112 B7
Capri Italy 40°33N 14°14E 70 D6
Caprivi Strip Namibia 18°0S 23°0E 97 H4
Caquetá → Colombia 1°15S 69°15W 120 C3
Caracas Venezuela 10°30N 66°55W 120 A3
Caracol Brazil 9°15S 43°22W 122 A2
Carangola Brazil 20°44S 42°5W 122 D2
Caratasca, L. Honduras 15°20N 83°40W 115 D8
Caratinga Brazil 19°50S 42°10W 122 C2
Caravelas Brazil 17°45S 39°15W 122 C3
Caravelle, Presqu'île de la Martinique 14°46N 60°48W 114 c
Carbón, L. del Argentina 49°35S 68°21W 121 G3
Carbondale Ill., U.S.A. 37°44N 89°13W 112 G3
Carbondale Pa., U.S.A. 41°35N 75°30W 113 E10
Carbonear Canada 47°42N 53°13W 109 E14
Carcassonne France 43°13N 2°20E 68 E5
Carcross Canada 60°13N 134°45W 108 C6
Cardamon Hills India 9°30N 77°15E 84 Q10
Cárdenas Cuba 23°0N 81°30W 115 C8
Cardiff U.K. 51°29N 3°10W 27 E7
Cardigan U.K. 52°5N 4°40W 26 C4
Cardigan B. U.K. 52°30N 4°30W 26 B4
Cardington U.K. 52°6N 0°25W 25 B8
Cardston Canada 49°15N 113°20W 108 E8
Cariacica Brazil 20°16S 40°25W 122 D2
Caribbean Sea W. Indies 15°0N 75°0W 115 E10
Cariboo Mts. Canada 53°0N 121°0W 108 D7
Caribou U.S.A. 46°52N 68°1W 113 B13
Caribou Mts. Canada 59°12N 115°40W 108 D8
Carinhanha Brazil 14°15S 44°46W 122 B2
Carinhanha → Brazil 14°20S 43°47W 122 B2
Carinthia = Kärnten □ Austria 46°52N 13°30E 66 E8
Carisbrooke U.K. 50°41N 1°19W 24 E6
Cark U.K. 54°11N 2°58W 22 D3
Carleton Place Canada 45°8N 76°9W 113 C9
Carleton Rode U.K. 52°30N 1°7E 25 A11
Carlingford L. U.K. 54°3N 6°9W 29 C9
Carlinville U.S.A. 39°17N 89°53W 112 F3
Carlisle U.K. 54°54N 2°56W 22 C3
Carlisle U.S.A. 40°12N 77°12W 112 E9
Carlisle B. Barbados 13°5N 59°37W 115 g
Carlops U.K. 55°47N 3°20W 21 C9
Carlow Ireland 52°50N 6°56W 31 C9
Carlow □ Ireland 52°43N 6°50W 31 C9
Carlsbad U.S.A. 32°25N 104°14W 110 D6
Carlton U.K. 52°59N 1°5W 23 G6
Carlton Colville U.K. 52°27N 1°43E 25 B12
Carlton Miniott U.K. 54°12N 1°22W 22 D6
Carluke U.K. 55°45N 3°50W 21 C8
Carmacks Canada 62°5N 136°16W 108 C6
Carmarthen U.K. 51°52N 4°19W 26 D5
Carmarthen B. U.K. 51°40N 4°30W 26 D4
Carmarthenshire □ U.K. 51°55N 4°13W 26 D5
Carmaux France 44°3N 2°10E 68 D5
Carmi U.S.A. 38°5N 88°10W 112 F3
Carn Ban U.K. 57°7N 4°15W 19 H9
Carn Eige U.K. 57°17N 5°8W 18 H7
Carnarvon Australia 24°51S 113°42E 98 E1
Carnarvon S. Africa 30°56S 22°8E 97 L4
Carndonagh Ireland 55°16N 7°15W 29 A7
Carnegie, L. Australia 26°5S 122°30E 98 F3
Carnforth U.K. 54°7N 2°45W 22 D3
Carno U.K. 52°34N 3°30W 26 B6
Carnoustie U.K. 56°30N 2°42W 21 A10
Carnsore Pt. Ireland 52°10N 6°22W 31 D10
Caro U.S.A. 43°29N 83°24W 112 D6
Carolina Puerto Rico 18°23N 65°58W 115 d
Caroline I. Kiribati 9°58S 150°13W 103 H12
Caroline Is. Micronesia 8°0N 150°0E 102 G7
Carondelet Kiribati 5°33S 173°50E 99 B16
Caroni → Venezuela 8°21N 62°43W 120 B3
Carpathians Europe 49°30N 21°0E 67 D11
Carpentaria, G. of Australia 14°0S 139°0E 98 C6
Carpentras France 44°3N 5°2E 68 D6
Carpi Italy 44°47N 10°53E 70 B4
Carrara Italy 44°5N 10°6E 70 B4
Carrauntoohill Ireland 52°0N 9°45W 30 E3
Carrick-on-Shannon Ireland 53°57N 8°5W 28 D5
Carrick-on-Suir Ireland 52°21N 7°24W 31 D8
Carrickfergus U.K. 54°43N 5°49W 29 B10
Carrickmacross Ireland 53°59N 6°43W 29 D8
Carrollton U.S.A. 39°18N 90°24W 112 F2
Carron → U.K. 57°53N 4°22W 19 G9
Carron, L. U.K. 57°22N 5°35W 18 H6
Carson City U.S.A. 39°10N 119°46W 110 C3
Carson Sink U.S.A. 39°50N 118°25W 110 C3
Cartagena Colombia 10°25N 75°33W 120 A2
Cartagena Spain 37°38N 0°59W 69 D5
Cartago Colombia 4°45N 75°55W 120 B2
Carthage Tunisia 36°52N 10°20E 95 A8
Cartmel U.K. 54°12N 2°57W 22 D3
Cartwright Canada 53°41N 56°58W 109 D14
Caruaru Brazil 8°15S 35°55W 122 A3
Carúpano Venezuela 10°39N 63°15W 120 A3
Casa Grande U.S.A. 32°53N 111°45W 110 D4
Casablanca Morocco 33°36N 7°36W 94 B4
Cascade Ra. U.S.A. 47°0N 121°30W 110 A2
Cascavel Ceará, Brazil 4°7S 38°14W 120 C6
Cascavel Paraná, Brazil 24°57S 53°28W 121 E4
Caserta Italy 41°4N 14°20E 70 D6
Cashel Ireland 52°30N 7°53W 30 C7
Casiquiare → Venezuela 2°1N 67°7W 120 B3
Casper U.S.A. 42°51N 106°19W 110 B5
Caspian Depression Eurasia 47°0N 48°0E 73 E8
Caspian Sea Eurasia 43°0N 50°0E 73 F9
Cassiar Mts. Canada 59°30N 130°30W 108 D6
Castellammare di Stábia Italy 40°42N 14°29E 70 D6
Castelló de la Plana Spain 39°58N 0°3W 69 C5
Castelsarrasin France 44°2N 1°7E 68 E4
Castilla-La Mancha □ Spain 39°30N 3°30W 69 C4
Castilla y Leon □ Spain 42°0N 5°0W 69 B3
Castle Acre U.K. 52°42N 0°42E 25 A10
Castle Cary U.K. 51°6N 2°31W 24 D3
Castle Donington U.K. 52°51N 1°20W 23 G6
Castle Douglas U.K. 54°56N 3°56W 21 E8
Castlebar Ireland 53°52N 9°18W 28 D3
Castlebay U.K. 56°57N 7°31W 18 J2
Castleblaney Ireland 54°7N 6°44W 29 C8
Castlederg U.K. 54°42N 7°35W 28 B6
Castleford U.K. 53°43N 1°21W 23 E6
Castlemaine Harbour Ireland 52°8N 9°50W 30 D3
Castlepollard Ireland 53°41N 7°19W 28 D7
Castlerea Ireland 53°46N 8°29W 28 D5
Castleside U.K. 54°50N 1°52W 22 C5
Castleton Derby, U.K. 53°22N 1°46W 23 F5
Castleton N. Yorks., U.K. 54°28N 0°57W 22 D7
Castletown I. of Man 54°5N 4°38W 29 C12
Castletown Bearhaven Ireland 51°39N 9°55W 30 E3
Castres France 43°37N 2°13E 68 E5
Castries St. Lucia 14°2N 60°58W 115 f
Castro Chile 42°30S 73°50W 121 G2
Castro Alves Brazil 12°46S 39°33W 122 B3
Cat I. Bahamas 24°30N 75°30W 115 C9
Cataguases Brazil 21°23S 42°39W 122 D2
Catalão Brazil 18°10S 47°57W 122 C1
Cataluña □ Spain 41°40N 1°15E 69 B6
Catamarca Argentina 28°30S 65°50W 121 E3
Catanduanes □ Phil. 13°50N 124°20E 83 B4
Catanduva Brazil 21°5S 48°58W 122 D1
Catánia Italy 37°30N 15°6E 70 F6
Catanzaro Italy 38°54N 16°35E 70 E7
Catcleugh U.K. 55°20N 2°24W 22 B4
Caterham U.K. 51°15N 0°4W 25 D8
Catoche, C. Mexico 21°35N 87°5W 114 C7
Caton U.K. 54°5N 2°42W 22 D3
Catsfield U.K. 50°54N 0°28E 25 E9
Catskill U.S.A. 42°14N 73°52W 113 D11
Catskill Mts. U.S.A. 42°10N 74°25W 113 D10
Catterick U.K. 54°23N 1°37W 22 D5
Catterick Camp U.K. 54°22N 1°42W 22 D5
Catton U.K. 54°55N 2°15W 22 C4
Cauca → Colombia 8°54N 74°28W 120 B2
Caucaia Brazil 3°40S 38°35W 120 C6
Caucasus Mountains Eurasia 42°50N 44°0E 73 F7
Caulkerbush U.K. 54°54N 3°41W 21 E9
Caura → Venezuela 7°38N 64°53W 120 B3
Cauvery → India 11°9N 78°52E 84 P11
Cavan Ireland 54°0N 7°22W 28 D7
Cavan □ Ireland 54°1N 7°16W 29 C7
Caviana, I. Brazil 0°10N 50°10W 120 B4
Cawood U.K. 53°50N 1°8W 23 E6
Cawston U.K. 52°47N 1°9E 25 A11
Caxias Brazil 4°55S 43°20W 120 C5
Caxias do Sul Brazil 29°10S 51°10W 121 E4
Cayenne Fr. Guiana 5°5N 52°18W 120 B4
Cayey Puerto Rico 18°7N 66°10W 115 d
Cayman Is. ⊘ W. Indies 19°40N 80°30W 115 D8
Cayuga L. U.S.A. 42°41N 76°41W 112 D9
Ceananus Mor Ireland 53°44N 6°53W 29 D8
Ceará □ Brazil 5°0S 40°0W 120 C6
Cebu Phil. 10°18N 123°54E 83 B4
Cedar City U.S.A. 37°41N 113°4W 110 C4
Cedar L. Canada 53°10N 100°0W 108 D10
Cedar Rapids U.S.A. 41°59N 91°40W 111 B81
Cefalù Italy 38°2N 14°1E 70 E6
Cegléd Hungary 47°11N 19°47E 67 E10
Celaya Mexico 20°31N 100°37W 114 C4
Celebes Sea Indonesia 3°0N 123°0E 83 C4
Celina U.S.A. 40°33N 84°35W 112 E5
Cellar Hd. U.K. 58°25N 6°11W 18 F5
Celtic Sea Atl. Oc. 50°9N 9°34W 64 F2
Cemaes U.K. 53°24N 4°27W 26 A5
Central, Cordillera Colombia 5°0N 75°0W 116 C3
Central, Cordillera Puerto Rico 18°8N 66°35W 115 d
Central African Rep. ■ Africa 7°0N 20°0E 96 C4
Central Makran Range Pakistan 26°30N 64°15E 84 F4
Central Russian Uplands Europe 54°0N 36°0E 56 E13
Central Siberian Plateau Russia 65°0N 105°0E 74 B12
Centralia Ill., U.S.A. 38°32N 89°8W 112 F3
Centralia Wash., U.S.A. 46°43N 122°58W 110 A2
Cephalonia = Kefalonia Greece 38°15N 20°30E 71 E9
Ceredigion □ U.K. 52°16N 4°15W 26 C5
Cerignola Italy 41°17N 15°53E 70 D6
Cerne Abbas U.K. 50°49N 2°29W 24 E4
Cerrigydrudion U.K. 53°1N 3°35W 26 A6
Cesena Italy 44°8N 12°15E 70 B5
České Budějovice Czech Rep. 48°55N 14°25E 66 D8
Çeşme Turkey 38°20N 26°23E 73 G4
Ceuta N. Afr. 35°52N 5°18W 69 E3
Ceve-i-Ra Fiji 21°46S 174°31E 99 E13
Cévennes France 44°10N 3°50E 68 D5
Chacewater U.K. 50°15N 5°11W 27 G3
Chachapoyas Peru 6°15S 77°50W 120 C2
Chaco Austral S. Amer. 27°0S 61°30W 121 E3
Chaco Boreal S. Amer. 22°0S 60°0W 121 E4
Chaco Central S. Amer. 24°0S 61°0W 121 E3
Chad ■ Africa 15°0N 17°15E 95 F8
Chad, L. Chad 13°30N 14°30E 95 F8
Chadron U.S.A. 42°50N 103°0W 110 B6
Chagford U.K. 50°40N 3°50W 27 F6
Chaghcharān Afghan. 34°31N 65°15E 87 C11
Chagos Arch. ⊘ Ind. Oc. 6°0S 72°0E 75 J9
Chāh Gay Hills Afghan. 29°30N 64°0E 87 D10
Chakradharpur India 22°45N 85°40E 85 H14
Chaleur B. Canada 47°55N 65°30W 113 B15
Chalisgaon India 20°30N 75°10E 84 J9
Challenger Deep Pac. Oc. 11°30N 142°0E 102 F6
Chalon-sur-Saône France 46°48N 4°50E 68 C6
Châlons-en-Champagne France 48°58N 4°20E 68 B6
Chambal → India 26°29N 79°15E 84 F11
Chambersburg U.S.A. 39°56N 77°40W 112 F9
Chambéry France 45°34N 5°55E 68 D6
Chamonix-Mont Blanc France 45°55N 6°51E 68 D7
Champagne France 48°40N 4°20E 68 B6
Champaign U.S.A. 40°7N 88°15W 112 E3
Champlain, L. U.S.A. 44°40N 73°20W 113 C11
Chañaral Chile 26°23S 70°40W 121 E2
Chancery Lane Barbados 13°3N 59°30W 115 g
Chandigarh India 30°43N 76°47E 84 D10
Chandler's Ford U.K. 50°59N 1°22W 24 E6
Chandpur Bangla. 23°8N 90°45E 85 H17
Chandrapur India 19°57N 79°25E 84 K11
Changbai Shan China 42°20N 129°0E 81 B7
Changchun China 43°57N 125°17E 81 B7
Changde China 29°4N 111°35E 81 D6
Changhua Taiwan 24°2N 120°30E 81 D7
Changji China 44°1N 87°19E 80 B3
Changsha China 28°12N 113°0E 81 D6
Changzhi China 36°10N 113°6E 81 C6
Changzhou China 31°47N 119°58E 81 C6
Chania Greece 35°30N 24°4E 71 G11
Channel Is. U.K. 49°19N 2°24W 27 J9
Channel Is. U.S.A. 33°40N 119°15W 110 D2
Channel-Port aux Basques Canada 47°30N 59°9W 109 E14
Chantrey Inlet Canada 67°48N 96°20W 108 C10
Chaoyang China 41°35N 120°22E 81 B7
Chaozhou China 23°42N 116°32E 81 D6
Chapala, L. de Mexico 20°15N 103°0W 114 C4
Chapayevsk Russia 53°0N 49°40E 72 D8
Chapel en le Frith U.K. 53°20N 1°54W 23 F5
Chapel St. Leonards U.K. 53°13N 0°20E 23 F9
Chapleau Canada 47°50N 83°24W 109 E11
Charaña Bolivia 17°30S 69°25W 120 D3
Chard U.K. 50°52N 2°58W 24 E3
Chari → Chad 12°58N 14°31E 95 F8
Chārīkār Afghan. 35°0N 69°10E 87 C12
Charing U.K. 51°12N 0°49E 25 D10
Charlbury U.K. 51°53N 1°28W 24 C6
Charleroi Belgium 50°24N 4°27E 65 D4
Charles, C. U.S.A. 37°7N 75°58W 113 G10
Charles City U.S.A. 43°4N 92°41W 111 B81
Charleston Ill., U.S.A. 39°30N 88°10W 112 F3
Charleston Mo., U.S.A. 36°55N 89°21W 112 G3
Charleston S.C., U.S.A. 32°46N 79°56W 111 D11
Charleston W. Va., U.S.A. 38°21N 81°38W 112 F7
Charlestown Ireland 53°58N 8°48W 28 D4
Charlestown of Aberlour U.K. 57°28N 3°14W 19 H11
Charleville Australia 26°24S 146°15E 98 F8
Charleville-Mézières France 49°44N 4°40E 68 B6
Charlevoix U.S.A. 45°19N 85°16W 112 C5
Charlotte Mich., U.S.A. 42°34N 84°50W 112 D5
Charlotte N.C., U.S.A. 35°13N 80°50W 111 C10
Charlotte Amalie U.S. Virgin Is. 18°21N 64°56W 115 e
Charlotte Harbor U.S.A. 26°57N 82°4W 111 E10
Charlottesville U.S.A. 38°2N 78°30W 112 F8
Charlottetown Canada 46°14N 63°8W 113 B16
Charlton I. Canada 52°0N 79°20W 109 D12
Charlton Kings U.K. 51°53N 2°3W 24 C4
Charlwood U.K. 51°9N 0°13W 25 D8
Charminster U.K. 50°44N 2°28W 24 E4
Charmouth U.K. 50°44N 2°54W 24 E3
Charnwood Forest U.K. 52°44N 1°17W 23 G6
Charolles France 46°27N 4°16E 68 C6
Charters Towers Australia 20°5S 146°13E 98 E8
Chartham U.K. 51°14N 1°1E 25 D11
Chartres France 48°29N 1°30E 68 B4
Chascomús Argentina 35°30S 58°0W 121 F4
Châteaubriant France 47°43N 1°23W 68 C3
Châteaulin France 48°11N 4°8W 68 B1
Châteauroux France 46°50N 1°40E 68 C4
Châteaux, Pte. des Guadeloupe 16°15N 61°10W 114 b
Châtellerault France 46°50N 0°30E 68 C4
Chatham Canada 47°2N 65°28W 109 E13
Chatham U.K. 51°22N 0°32E 25 D10
Chatham Is. Pac. Oc. 44°0S 176°40W 99 J15
Chatham-Kent Canada 42°24N 82°11W 112 D6
Chattanooga U.S.A. 35°3N 85°19W 111 C9
Chatteris U.K. 52°28N 0°2E 25 B9
Chatton U.K. 55°35N 2°0W 22 A5
Chaumont France 48°7N 5°8E 68 B6
Chaykovskiy Russia 56°47N 54°9E 72 C9
Cheadle Gt. Man., U.K. 53°23N 2°12W 23 F4
Cheadle Staffs., U.K. 52°59N 1°58W 23 G5
Cheb Czech Rep. 50°9N 12°28E 66 C7
Cheboksary Russia 56°8N 47°12E 72 C8
Cheboygan U.S.A. 45°39N 84°29W 112 C5
Chech, Erg Africa 25°0N 2°15W 94 D5
Chechenia □ Russia 43°30N 45°29E 73 F8
Chedabucto B. Canada 45°25N 61°8W 113 C17
Cheddar U.K. 51°17N 2°46W 24 D3
Cheddleton U.K. 53°4N 2°2W 23 F4
Cheduba I. Burma 18°45N 93°40E 85 K18
Chegutu Zimbabwe 18°10S 30°14E 97 H6
Chelm Poland 51°8N 23°30E 67 C12
Chelmer → U.K. 51°44N 0°30E 25 C10
Chelmsford U.K. 51°44N 0°29E 25 C9
Cheltenham U.K. 51°54N 2°4W 24 C4
Chelyabinsk Russia 55°10N 61°24E 79 D8
Chelyuskin, C. Russia 77°30N 103°0E 79 B12
Chemnitz Germany 50°51N 12°54E 66 C7
Chenab → Pakistan 30°23N 71°2E 84 D7
Chengde China 40°59N 117°58E 81 B6
Chengdu China 30°38N 104°2E 80 C5
Chengjiang China 24°39N 103°0E 80 D5
Chennai India 13°8N 80°19E 84 N12
Chepstow U.K. 51°38N 2°41W 26 D8
Cher → France 47°21N 0°29E 68 C4
Cherbourg France 49°39N 1°40W 68 B3
Cherepovets Russia 59°5N 37°55E 72 C6
Chergui, Chott ech Algeria 34°21N 0°25E 94 B6
Cheriton U.K. 51°3N 1°8W 24 D6
Cheriton Fitzpaine U.K. 50°51N 3°35W 27 F6
Cherkasy Ukraine 49°27N 32°4E 73 E5
Cherkessk Russia 44°15N 42°5E 73 F7
Chernihiv Ukraine 51°28N 31°20E 72 D5
Chernivtsi Ukraine 48°15N 25°52E 67 D13

Cruz Bay   East Bengal

East Bergholt U.K. 51°59N 1°3E 25 C11
East Beskids Europe 49°20N 22°0E 67 D11
East Brent U.K. 51°15N 2°56W 24 D3
East C. = Dezhneva, Mys. Russia 66°5N 169°40W 79 C20
East China Sea Asia 30°0N 126°0E 81 D7
East Cowes U.K. 50°45N 1°16W 24 E6
East Falkland Falk. Is. 51°30S 58°30W 121 H4
East Fen U.K. 53°4N 0°5E 23 F9
East Grinstead U.K. 51°7N 0°0 25 D9
East Harling U.K. 52°26N 0°56E 25 B10
East Ilsley U.K. 51°31N 1°16W 24 C6
East Indies Asia 0°0 120°0E 74 J14
East Kilbride U.K. 55°47N 4°11W 20 C7
East Lansing U.S.A. 42°44N 84°29W 112 D5
East London S. Africa 33°0S 27°55E 97 L5
East Lothian □ U.K. 55°58N 2°44W 21 C10
East Markham U.K. 53°15N 0°53W 23 F7
East Moor U.K. 53°16N 1°34W 23 F5
East Pacific Rise Pac. Oc. 15°0S 110°0W 103 J17
East Pt. Br. Virgin Is. 18°40N 64°18W 115 e
East Pt. Canada 46°27N 61°58W 113 B17
East St. Louis U.S.A. 38°37N 90°9W 112 F2
East Sea = Japan, Sea of Asia 40°0N 135°0E 82 D4
East Siberian Sea Russia 73°0N 160°0E 79 B18
East Sussex □ U.K. 50°56N 0°19E 25 E9
East Timor ■ Asia 8°50S 126°0E 83 D4
East Wittering U.K. 50°46N 0°52W 25 E7
East Woodhay U.K. 51°21N 1°25W 24 D6
Eastbourne U.K. 50°46N 0°18E 25 E9
Eastchurch U.K. 51°24N 0°53E 25 D10
Eastern Ghats India 14°0N 78°50E 84 N11
Eastern Group Fiji 17°0S 178°30W 99 D15
Eastleigh U.K. 50°58N 1°21W 24 E6
Eastmain Canada 52°10N 78°30W 109 D12
Eastmain → Canada 52°27N 78°26W 109 D12
Eastnor U.K. 52°2N 2°23W 24 B4
Easton Dorset, U.K. 50°33N 2°26W 24 E4
Easton Northants., U.K. 52°37N 0°31W 25 A7
Easton Md., U.S.A. 38°47N 76°5W 113 F9
Easton Pa., U.S.A. 40°41N 75°13W 113 E10
Easton-in-Gordano U.K. 51°28N 2°42W 24 D3
Eastport U.S.A. 44°56N 67°0W 113 C14
Eastry U.K. 51°14N 1°19E 25 D11
Eastwood U.K. 53°1N 1°18W 23 F6
Eaton U.K. 52°51N 0°49W 23 G7
Eaton Socon U.K. 52°14N 0°17W 25 B8
Eau Claire U.S.A. 44°49N 91°30W 112 C2
Eau Claire, L. à l' Canada 56°10N 74°25W 109 D12
Ebberston U.K. 54°14N 0°37W 22 D7
Ebbw Vale U.K. 51°46N 3°12W 26 D7
Eberswalde-Finow Germany 52°50N 13°49E 66 B7
Ebetsu Japan 43°7N 141°34E 82 B7
Ebinur Hu China 44°55N 82°55E 80 B3
Ebolowa Cameroon 2°55N 11°10E 96 D2
Ebro → Spain 40°43N 0°54E 69 B6
Ecclefechan U.K. 55°4N 3°16W 21 D9
Eccleshall U.K. 52°52N 2°15W 23 G4
Ech Chéliff Algeria 36°10N 1°20E 94 A6
Echo Bay Canada 66°5N 117°55W 108 C8
Eckington U.K. 53°18N 1°22W 23 F6
Eclipse Sd. Canada 72°38N 79°0W 109 B12
Ecuador ■ S. Amer. 2°0S 78°0W 120 C2
Ed Damazin Sudan 11°46N 34°21E 95 F12
Edam Neths. 52°31N 5°3E 65 B5
Eday U.K. 59°11N 2°47W 19 D12
Eddrachillis B. U.K. 58°17N 5°14W 18 F7
Eddystone U.K. 50°11N 4°16W 27 G5
Eden → U.K. 54°57N 3°1W 22 C2
Edenbridge U.K. 51°12N 0°5E 25 D9
Edenderry Ireland 53°21N 7°4W 31 B8
Edge Hill U.K. 52°8N 1°26W 24 B6
Edinburgh U.K. 55°57N 3°13W 21 C9
Edinburgh ✕ (EDI) U.K. 55°54N 3°22W 21 C9
Edington U.K. 51°17N 2°5W 24 D4
Edirne Turkey 41°40N 26°34E 73 F4
Edmonton Canada 53°30N 113°30W 108 D8
Edmundbyers U.K. 54°50N 1°58W 22 C5
Edmundston Canada 47°23N 68°20W 109 E13
Edremit Turkey 39°34N 27°0E 86 B1
Edson Canada 53°35N 116°28W 108 D8
Edward, L. Africa 0°25S 29°40E 96 E5
Edward VII Land Antarctica 80°0S 150°0W 55 E13
Edwards Plateau U.S.A. 30°45N 101°20W 110 D6
Effingham U.S.A. 39°7N 88°33W 112 F3
Égadi, Ísole Italy 37°55N 12°16E 70 F5
Eganville Canada 45°32N 77°5W 112 C9
Eger Hungary 47°53N 20°27E 67 E11
Egham U.K. 51°25N 0°32W 25 D7
Eglinton I. Canada 75°48N 118°30W 109 B8
Egremont U.K. 54°29N 3°32W 22 D1
Eğridir Turkey 37°52N 30°51E 73 G5
Eğridir Gölü Turkey 37°53N 30°50E 73 G5
Egton U.K. 54°28N 0°44W 22 D7
Egypt ■ Africa 28°0N 31°0E 95 C12
Eifel Germany 50°15N 6°50E 66 C4
Eigg U.K. 56°54N 6°10W 18 J5
Eil, L. U.K. 56°51N 5°16W 18 J7
Eindhoven Neths. 51°26N 5°28E 65 C5
Eire = Ireland ■ Europe 53°50N 7°52W 64 E2
Eivissa Spain 38°54N 1°26E 69 C6
El Aaiún W. Sahara 27°9N 13°12W 94 C3
El 'Alamein Egypt 30°48N 28°58E 95 B11
El Centro U.S.A. 32°48N 115°34W 110 D3
El Djouf Mauritania 20°0N 9°0W 94 D4
El Dorado U.S.A. 33°12N 92°40W 111 D8
El Faiyûm Egypt 29°19N 30°50E 95 C12
El Fâsher Sudan 13°33N 25°26E 95 F11
El Fuerte Mexico 26°25N 108°39W 114 B3
El Geneina Sudan 13°27N 22°45E 95 F10
El Gezira □ Sudan 15°0N 33°0E 95 F12
El Gîza Egypt 30°0N 31°12E 95 C12
El Istiwa'iya Sudan 5°0N 28°0E 95 G11
El Jadida Morocco 33°11N 8°17W 94 B4
El Khârga Egypt 25°30N 30°33E 95 C12
El Mahalla el Kubra Egypt 31°0N 31°0E 95 B12
El Mansûra Egypt 31°0N 31°19E 95 B12
El Minyâ Egypt 28°7N 30°33E 95 C12
El Obeid Sudan 13°8N 30°10E 95 F12
El Oued Algeria 33°20N 6°58E 94 B7
El Paso U.S.A. 31°45N 106°29W 110 D5
El Puerto de Santa María Spain 36°36N 6°13W 69 D2
El Reno U.S.A. 35°32N 97°57W 110 C7
El Salvador ■ Cent. Amer. 13°50N 89°0W 114 E7
El Tigre Venezuela 8°44N 64°15W 120 B3
El Uqsur Egypt 25°41N 32°38E 95 C12
Elat Israel 29°30N 34°56E 86 D3
Elâzığ Turkey 38°37N 39°14E 73 G6
Elba Italy 42°46N 10°17E 70 C4
Elbasan Albania 41°9N 20°9E 71 D9
Elbe → Europe 53°50N 9°0E 66 B5
Elbert, Mt. U.S.A. 39°7N 106°27W 110 C5
Elbeuf France 49°17N 1°2E 68 B4
Elbląg Poland 54°10N 19°25E 67 A10
Elbrus Asia 43°21N 42°30E 73 F7
Elburz Mts. Iran 36°0N 52°0E 87 B8
Elche Spain 38°15N 0°42W 69 C5
Elda Spain 38°29N 0°47W 69 C5
Eldoret Kenya 0°30N 35°17E 96 D7
Elektrostal Russia 55°41N 38°32E 72 C6
Elemi Triangle Africa 5°0N 35°20E 96 D7
Elephant Butte Res. U.S.A. 33°9N 107°11W 110 D5
Elephant I. Antarctica 61°0S 55°0W 55 C18
Eleuthera Bahamas 25°0N 76°20W 115 C9
Elgin U.K. 57°39N 3°19W 19 G11
Elgin U.S.A. 42°2N 88°17W 112 D3
Elgon, Mt. Africa 1°10N 34°30E 96 D6
Elham U.K. 51°9N 1°8E 25 D11
Elishaw U.K. 55°15N 2°14W 22 B4
Elista Russia 46°16N 44°14E 73 E7
Elizabeth U.S.A. 40°39N 74°12W 113 E10
Elizabeth City U.S.A. 36°18N 76°14W 111 C11
Elizabethtown U.S.A. 37°42N 85°52W 112 G5
Elkhart U.S.A. 41°41N 85°58W 112 E5
Elkins U.S.A. 38°55N 79°51W 112 F8
Elko U.S.A. 40°50N 115°46W 110 B3
Elland U.K. 53°41N 1°50W 23 E5
Ellef Ringnes I. Canada 78°30N 102°2W 109 B9
Ellen → U.K. 54°44N 3°30W 22 C2
Ellensburg U.S.A. 46°59N 120°34W 110 A2
Ellerton Barbados 13°7N 59°33W 115 g
Ellesmere U.K. 52°55N 2°53W 23 G3
Ellesmere I. Canada 79°30N 80°0W 109 B12
Ellesmere Port U.K. 53°17N 2°54W 23 F3
Ellington U.K. 55°14N 1°33W 22 B5
Elliot Lake Canada 46°25N 82°35W 109 E11
Ellon U.K. 57°22N 2°4W 19 H13
Ellsworth Land Antarctica 76°0S 89°0W 55 D16
Elmalı Turkey 36°44N 29°56E 73 G4
Elmira U.S.A. 42°6N 76°48W 112 D9
Elmswell U.K. 52°15N 0°55E 25 B10
Eluru India 16°48N 81°8E 85 L12
Ely U.K. 52°24N 0°16E 25 B9
Ely U.S.A. 39°15N 114°54W 110 C4
Elyria U.S.A. 41°22N 82°7W 112 E6
Emāmrūd Iran 36°30N 55°0E 87 B8
Embarcación Argentina 23°10S 64°0W 121 E3
Embleton U.K. 55°29N 1°38W 22 B5
Emden Germany 53°21N 7°12E 66 B4
Emerald Australia 37°56S 145°29E 98 E8
Emmeloord Neths. 52°44N 5°46E 65 B5
Emmen Neths. 52°48N 6°57E 65 B6
Emmonak U.S.A. 62°47N 164°31W 108 C3
Empalme Mexico 27°58N 110°51W 114 B2
Empangeni S. Africa 28°50S 31°52E 97 K6
Empedrado Argentina 28°0S 58°46W 121 E4
Emperor Seamount Chain Pac. Oc. 40°0N 170°0E 102 D9
Emporia U.S.A. 38°25N 96°11W 111 C7
Emporium U.S.A. 41°31N 78°14W 112 E8
Empty Quarter = Rub' al Khālī Si. Arabia 19°0N 48°0E 88 D4
Ems → Germany 53°20N 7°12E 66 B4
En Nahud Sudan 12°45N 28°25E 95 F11
Enard B. U.K. 58°5N 5°20W 18 F7
Encarnación Paraguay 27°15S 55°50W 121 E4
Encounter B. Australia 35°45S 138°45E 98 H6
Ende Indonesia 8°45S 121°40E 83 D4
Enderbury I. Kiribati 3°8S 171°5W 102 H10
Enderby U.K. 52°36N 1°13W 23 G6
Enderby Land Antarctica 66°0S 53°0E 55 C5
Endicott U.S.A. 42°6N 76°4W 113 D9
Enewetak Atoll Marshall Is. 11°30N 162°15E 102 F8
Enez Turkey 40°45N 26°5E 73 F4
Enfer, Pte. d' Martinique 14°22N 60°54W 114 c
Enfield □ U.K. 51°38N 0°5W 25 C8
Engadin Switz. 46°45N 10°10E 66 E6
Engels Russia 51°28N 46°6E 73 D8
Enggano Indonesia 5°20S 102°40E 83 D2
England □ U.K. 53°0N 2°0W 64 E6
English → Canada 49°12N 91°5W 108 D10
English Channel Europe 50°0N 2°0W 64 F6
Enid U.S.A. 36°24N 97°53W 110 C7
Ennadai L. Canada 60°58N 101°20W 108 C9
Ennedi Chad 17°15N 22°0E 95 E10
Ennerdale Water U.K. 54°32N 3°24W 22 C2
Ennis Ireland 52°51N 8°59W 30 C5
Enniscorthy Ireland 52°30N 6°34W 31 D9
Enniskillen U.K. 54°21N 7°39W 28 C6
Ennistimon Ireland 52°57N 9°17W 30 C4
Enns → Austria 48°14N 14°32E 66 D8
Enschede Neths. 52°13N 6°53E 65 B6
Ensenada Mexico 31°52N 116°37W 114 A1
Enshi China 30°18N 109°29E 81 C5
Enstone U.K. 51°55N 1°27W 24 C6
Entebbe Uganda 0°4N 32°28E 96 D6
Entre Ríos □ Argentina 30°30S 58°30W 121 F4
Enugu Nigeria 6°30N 7°30E 94 G7
Éolie, Ís. Italy 38°30N 14°57E 70 E6
Épernay France 49°3N 3°56E 68 B5
Épinal France 48°10N 6°27E 68 B7
Epping U.K. 51°41N 0°7E 25 C9
Epping Forest U.K. 51°40N 0°5E 25 C9
Epsom U.K. 51°19N 0°16W 25 D8
Epworth U.K. 53°32N 0°48W 23 E7
Equatorial Guinea ■ Africa 2°0N 8°0E 96 D1
Er Rachidia Morocco 31°58N 4°20W 94 B5
Erciyaş Dağı Turkey 38°30N 35°30E 86 B3
Erdenet Mongolia 49°2N 104°5E 80 B5
Erebus, Mt. Antarctica 77°35S 167°0E 55 D11
Ereğli Konya, Turkey 37°31N 34°4E 73 G5
Ereğli Zonguldak, Turkey 41°15N 31°24E 73 F5
Erfurt Germany 50°58N 11°2E 66 C6
Ergeni Lowlands Russia 47°0N 44°0E 73 E7
Eriboll, L. U.K. 58°30N 4°42W 19 E8
Erie U.S.A. 42°8N 80°5W 112 D7
Erie, L. N. Amer. 42°15N 81°0W 112 D7
Eriskay U.K. 57°4N 7°18W 18 H3
Eritrea ■ Africa 14°0N 38°30E 88 D2
Erlangen Germany 49°36N 11°0E 66 D6
Ernakulam India 9°59N 76°22E 84 Q10
Erne → Ireland 54°30N 8°16W 28 C5
Erne, Lower L. U.K. 54°28N 7°47W 28 C6
Erne, Upper L. U.K. 54°14N 7°32W 28 C6
Erode India 11°24N 77°45E 84 P10
Erramala Hills India 15°30N 78°15E 84 M11
Errigal Ireland 55°2N 8°6W 28 A5
Erris Hd. Ireland 54°19N 10°0W 28 C1
Erromango Vanuatu 18°45S 169°5E 99 D12
Erzgebirge Germany 50°27N 12°55E 66 C7
Erzincan Turkey 39°46N 39°30E 73 G6
Erzurum Turkey 39°57N 41°15E 73 G7
Esbjerg Denmark 55°29N 8°29E 63 F5
Escada Brazil 8°22S 35°8W 122 A3
Escanaba U.S.A. 45°45N 87°4W 112 C4
Esch-sur-Alzette Lux. 49°32N 6°0E 65 E6
Escrick U.K. 53°53N 1°2W 23 E6
Escuinapa de Hidalgo Mexico 22°50N 105°50W 114 C3
Escuintla Guatemala 14°20N 90°48W 114 E6
Eşfahān Iran 32°39N 51°43E 87 C7
Esha Ness U.K. 60°29N 1°38W 18 B14
Esil → Russia 57°45N 71°10E 79 D9
Esk → Cumb., U.K. 54°20N 3°24W 22 D2
Esk → Dumf. & Gall., U.K. 54°58N 3°2W 21 E9
Esk → N. Yorks., U.K. 54°30N 0°37W 22 D7
Eskdale U.K. 55°12N 3°4W 21 D9
Esker Canada 53°53N 66°25W 109 D13
Eskilstuna Sweden 59°22N 16°32E 63 F7
Eskişehir Turkey 39°50N 30°30E 73 G5
Eslāmābād-e Gharb Iran 34°10N 46°30E 86 C6
Esperance Australia 33°45S 121°55E 98 G3
Esperanza Puerto Rico 18°6N 65°28W 115 d
Espinhaço, Serra do Brazil 17°30S 43°30W 122 C2
Espírito Santo □ Brazil 20°0S 40°45W 122 C2
Espíritu Santo Vanuatu 15°15S 166°50E 99 D12
Espoo Finland 60°12N 24°40E 63 E8
Essaouira Morocco 31°32N 9°42W 94 B4
Essen Germany 51°28N 7°2E 66 C4
Essequibo → Guyana 6°50N 58°30W 120 B4
Essex □ U.K. 51°54N 0°27E 25 C9
Esslingen Germany 48°44N 9°18E 66 D5
Estados, I. de Los Argentina 54°40S 64°30W 121 H3
Estância Brazil 11°16S 37°26W 122 B3
Estevan Canada 49°10N 102°59W 108 E9
Eston U.K. 54°34N 1°8W 22 C6
Estonia ■ Europe 58°30N 25°30E 63 F8
Estrela, Serra da Portugal 40°10N 7°45W 69 B2
Estrondo, Serra do Brazil 7°20S 48°0W 120 C5
Etawah India 26°48N 79°6E 84 F11
Etchingham U.K. 51°0N 0°26E 25 D9
eThekwini = Durban S. Africa 29°49S 31°1E 97 K6
Ethiopia ■ Africa 8°0N 40°0E 88 F3
Ethiopian Highlands Ethiopia 10°0N 37°0E 88 F2
Etive, L. U.K. 56°29N 5°10W 20 B5
Etna Italy 37°50N 14°55E 70 F6
Eton U.K. 51°30N 0°36W 25 D7
Etosha Pan Namibia 18°40S 16°30E 97 H3
Ettington U.K. 52°8N 1°35W 24 B5
Ettrick Forest U.K. 55°30N 3°0W 21 C9
Ettrick Water → U.K. 55°31N 2°55W 21 C10
Euclid U.S.A. 41°34N 81°32W 112 E7
Eugene U.S.A. 44°5N 123°4W 110 B2
Euphrates → Asia 31°0N 47°25E 86 D6
Eureka Canada 80°0N 85°56W 109 B11
Eureka U.S.A. 40°47N 124°9W 110 B2
Europa, Île Ind. Oc. 22°20S 40°22E 97 J8
Europa, Picos de Spain 43°10N 4°49W 69 A3
Europe 50°0N 20°0E 56 E10
Euxton U.K. 53°41N 2°41W 23 E3
Evanston Ill., U.S.A. 42°3N 87°40W 112 D4
Evanston Wyo., U.S.A. 41°16N 110°58W 110 B4
Evansville U.S.A. 37°58N 87°35W 112 G4
Evercreech U.K. 51°9N 2°30W 24 D4
Everest, Mt. Nepal 28°5N 86°58E 85 E15
Everett U.S.A. 47°59N 122°12W 110 A2
Everglades, The U.S.A. 25°50N 81°0W 111 E10
Evesham U.K. 52°6N 1°56W 24 B5
Evia Greece 38°30N 24°0E 71 E11
Évora Portugal 38°33N 7°57W 69 C2
Évreux France 49°3N 1°8E 68 B4
Evros → Greece 41°40N 26°34E 71 D12
Ewe, L. U.K. 57°49N 5°38W 18 G6
Ewell U.K. 51°20N 0°14W 25 D8
Ewhurst U.K. 51°9N 0°25W 25 D8
Exe → U.K. 50°41N 3°29W 27 F7
Exeter U.K. 50°43N 3°31W 27 F6
Exminster U.K. 50°40N 3°29W 27 F7
Exmoor U.K. 51°12N 3°45W 27 E6
Exmoor △ U.K. 51°8N 3°42W 27 E6
Exmouth U.K. 50°37N 3°25W 27 F7
Exton U.K. 52°42N 0°38W 23 G7
Extremadura □ Spain 39°30N 6°5W 69 C2
Eyam U.K. 53°17N 1°40W 23 F5
Eyasi, L. Tanzania 3°30S 35°0E 96 E6
Eye Cambs., U.K. 52°37N 0°11W 25 A8
Eye Suffolk, U.K. 52°19N 1°9E 25 B11
Eye Pen. U.K. 58°13N 6°10W 18 F5
Eyemouth U.K. 55°52N 2°5W 21 C11
Eynsham U.K. 51°47N 1°22W 24 C6
Eyre, L. Australia 29°30S 137°26E 98 F6
Eyre Pen. Australia 33°30S 136°17E 98 G6

F

F.Y.R.O.M. = Macedonia ■ Europe 41°53N 21°40E 71 D9
Faenza Italy 44°17N 11°53E 70 B4
Fair Hd. U.K. 55°14N 6°9W 29 A9
Fair Isle U.K. 59°32N 1°38W 18 C14
Fairbanks U.S.A. 64°51N 147°43W 108 C5
Fairfield U.S.A. 38°23N 88°22W 112 F3
Fairford U.K. 51°43N 1°46W 24 C5
Fairlight U.K. 50°52N 0°40E 25 E10
Fairmont U.S.A. 39°29N 80°9W 112 F7
Fairweather, Mt. U.S.A. 58°55N 137°32W 108 D6
Faisalabad Pakistan 31°30N 73°5E 84 D8
Faizabad India 26°45N 82°10E 85 F13
Fajardo Puerto Rico 18°20N 65°39W 115 d
Fakenham U.K. 52°51N 0°51E 25 A10
Falcon Res. U.S.A. 26°34N 99°10W 110 E7
Faldingworth U.K. 53°21N 0°24W 23 F8
Falkirk U.K. 56°0N 3°47W 21 C8
Falkland U.K. 56°16N 3°12W 21 B9
Falkland Is. ⊠ Atl. Oc. 51°30S 59°0W 121 H4
Fall River U.S.A. 41°43N 71°10W 113 E12
Falmouth Jamaica 18°30N 77°40W 114 a
Falmouth U.K. 50°9N 5°5W 27 G3
Falmouth B. U.K. 50°6N 5°5W 27 G3
Falstone U.K. 55°11N 2°26W 22 B4
Falun Sweden 60°37N 15°37E 63 E7
Famagusta Cyprus 35°8N 33°55E 86 C3
Fanad Hd. Ireland 55°17N 7°38W 28 A6
Fannich, L. U.K. 57°38N 4°59W 19 G8
Fano Italy 43°50N 13°1E 70 C5
Far East Asia 40°0N 130°0E 74 E14
Farāh Afghan. 32°20N 62°7E 87 C10
Farasān Si. Arabia 16°45N 41°55E 88 D3
Fareham U.K. 50°51N 1°11W 24 E6
Farewell C. Greenland 59°48N 43°55W 54 D5
Fargo U.S.A. 46°53N 96°48W 111 A7
Faridabad India 28°26N 77°19E 84 E10
Faringdon U.K. 51°39N 1°34W 24 C5
Farmington U.S.A. 36°44N 108°12W 110 C5
Farmville U.S.A. 37°18N 78°24W 112 G8
Farnborough U.K. 51°16N 0°45W 25 D7
Farne Is. U.K. 55°38N 1°37W 22 A5
Farnham U.K. 51°13N 0°47W 25 D7
Farnworth U.K. 53°34N 2°25W 23 E4
Faro Canada 62°11N 133°22W 108 C6
Faro Portugal 37°2N 7°55W 69 D2
Faroe Is. ⊠ Atl. Oc. 62°0N 7°0W 57 C4
Fārs □ Iran 29°30N 55°0E 87 D8
Fāryāb □ Afghan. 36°0N 65°0E 87 B11
Faslane U.K. 56°5N 4°49W 20 B6
Fataka Solomon Is. 11°55S 170°12E 99 C12
Fatehgarh India 27°25N 79°35E 84 F11
Fatehpur Raj., India 28°0N 74°40E 84 F9
Fatehpur Ut. P., India 25°56N 81°13E 85 G12
Fauldhouse U.K. 55°50N 3°43W 21 C8
Faversham U.K. 51°19N 0°56E 25 D10
Fawley U.K. 50°50N 1°20W 24 E6
Fayetteville Ark., U.S.A. 36°4N 94°10W 111 C8
Fayetteville N.C., U.S.A. 35°3N 78°53W 111 D11
Fazeley U.K. 52°37N 1°40W 23 G5
Fazilka India 30°27N 74°2E 84 D9
Fdérik Mauritania 22°40N 12°45W 94 D3
Feale → Ireland 52°27N 9°37W 30 D3
Fear, C. U.S.A. 33°50N 77°58W 111 D11
Fécamp France 49°45N 0°22E 68 B4
Fehmarn Germany 54°27N 11°7E 66 A6
Feira de Santana Brazil 12°15S 38°57W 122 B3
Felipe Carrillo Puerto Mexico 19°38N 88°3W 114 D7
Felixstowe U.K. 51°58N 1°23E 25 C11
Felton U.K. 55°18N 1°42W 22 B5
Feltwell U.K. 52°30N 0°32E 25 B10
Fenny Bentley U.K. 53°3N 1°45W 23 F5
Fenny Compton U.K. 52°10N 1°23W 24 B6
Fenny Stratford U.K. 52°0N 0°44W 25 C7
Fens, The U.K. 52°38N 0°2W 25 A8
Fenyang China 37°18N 111°48E 81 C6
Feodosiya Ukraine 45°2N 35°16E 73 E6
Fergus Falls U.S.A. 46°17N 96°4W 111 A7
Ferkéssédougou Ivory C. 9°35N 5°6W 94 G4
Fermanagh □ U.K. 54°21N 7°40W 28 C6
Fermont Canada 52°47N 67°5W 109 D13
Fermoy Ireland 52°9N 8°16W 30 D6
Fernhurst U.K. 51°3N 0°43W 25 D7
Ferrara Italy 44°50N 11°35E 70 B4
Ferret, C. France 44°38N 1°15W 68 D3
Ferrol Spain 43°29N 8°15W 69 A1
Ferryhill U.K. 54°41N 1°33W 22 C5
Fès Morocco 34°0N 5°0W 94 B5
Fethiye Turkey 36°36N 29°6E 73 G4
Fetlar U.K. 60°36N 0°52W 18 A16
Feuilles → Canada 58°47N 70°4W 109 D12
Feyzābād Afghan. 37°7N 70°33E 87 B12
Fezzan Libya 27°0N 13°0E 95 C8
Ffestiniog U.K. 52°57N 3°55W 26 B6
Fianarantsoa Madag. 21°26S 47°5E 97 J9
Fife □ U.K. 56°16N 3°1W 21 B9
Fife Ness U.K. 56°17N 2°35W 21 B10
Figeac France 44°37N 2°2E 68 D5
Figueres Spain 42°18N 2°58E 69 A7
Fiji ■ Pac. Oc. 17°20S 179°0E 99 D14
Filby U.K. 52°40N 1°39E 25 A12
Filey U.K. 54°12N 0°18W 22 D8
Filey B. U.K. 54°12N 0°15W 22 D8
Filton U.K. 51°30N 2°34W 24 C3
Fincham U.K. 52°38N 0°30E 25 A9
Findhorn → U.K. 57°38N 3°38W 19 G10
Findlay U.S.A. 41°2N 83°39W 112 E6
Finedon U.K. 52°21N 0°39W 25 B7
Finglas Ireland 53°23N 6°19W 31 B10
Finike Turkey 36°21N 30°10E 86 B2
Finland ■ Europe 63°0N 27°0E 63 E9
Finland, G. of Europe 60°0N 26°0E 63 F9
Finlay → Canada 57°0N 125°10W 108 D7
Finn → Ireland 54°51N 7°28W 28 B7
Firozabad India 27°10N 78°25E 84 F11
Firozpur India 30°55N 74°40E 84 D9
Fish → Namibia 28°7S 17°10E 97 K3
Fishguard U.K. 52°0N 4°58W 26 D4
Fishtoft U.K. 52°58N 0°1E 23 G9
Fisterra, C. Spain 42°50N 9°19W 69 A1
Fitchburg U.S.A. 42°35N 71°48W 113 D12
Flagstaff U.S.A. 35°12N 111°39W 110 C4
Flamborough U.K. 54°7N 0°7W 22 D8
Flamborough Hd. U.K. 54°7N 0°5W 22 D8
Flandre Europe 50°50N 2°30E 65 D2
Flathead L. U.S.A. 47°51N 114°8W 110 A4
Flattery, C. U.S.A. 48°23N 124°29W 110 A2
Fleet U.K. 51°17N 0°50W 25 D7
Fleetwood U.K. 53°55N 3°1W 23 E2
Flensburg Germany 54°47N 9°27E 66 A5
Flers France 48°47N 0°33W 68 B3
Flevoland □ Neths. 52°30N 5°30E 65 B5
Flimby U.K. 54°42N 3°30W 22 C2
Flin Flon Canada 54°46N 101°53W 108 D9
Flinders → Australia 17°36S 140°36E 98 D7
Flinders I. Australia 40°0S 148°0E 98 H8
Flinders Ranges Australia 31°30S 138°30E 98 G6
Flint U.K. 53°15N 3°8W 26 A7
Flint U.S.A. 43°1N 83°41W 112 D6
Flint → U.S.A. 30°57N 84°34W 111 D10
Flint I. Kiribati 11°26S 151°48W 103 J12
Flintshire □ U.K. 53°17N 3°17W 26 A7
Flitwick U.K. 52°0N 0°30W 25 C8
Flodden U.K. 55°37N 2°8W 22 A4
Flora U.S.A. 38°40N 88°29W 112 F3
Florence Italy 43°46N 11°15E 70 C4
Florence U.S.A. 34°12N 79°46W 111 D11
Florencia Colombia 1°36N 75°36W 120 B2
Flores Indonesia 8°35S 121°0E 83 D4
Flores Sea Indonesia 6°30S 120°0E 83 D4
Florianópolis Brazil 27°30S 48°30W 121 E5
Florida Uruguay 34°7S 56°10W 121 F4
Florida □ U.S.A. 28°0N 82°0W 111 E10
Florida, Straits of U.S.A. 25°0N 80°0W 115 C9
Florida Keys U.S.A. 24°40N 81°0W 111 F10
Florø Norway 61°35N 5°1E 63 E5
Fly → Papua N. G. 8°25S 143°0E 98 B7
Fochabers U.K. 57°37N 3°6W 19 G11
Focşani Romania 45°41N 27°15E 67 F14
Fóggia Italy 41°27N 15°34E 70 D6
Foix France 42°58N 1°38E 68 E4
Foligno Italy 42°57N 12°42E 70 C5
Folkestone U.K. 51°5N 1°12E 25 D11
Fond-du-Lac Canada 59°19N 107°12W 108 D9
Fond du Lac U.S.A. 43°47N 88°27W 112 D3
Fongafale Tuvalu 8°31S 179°13E 99 B14
Fontainebleau France 48°24N 2°40E 68 B5
Fontenay-le-Comte France 46°28N 0°48W 68 C3
Fordham U.K. 52°19N 0°23E 25 B9
Fordingbridge U.K. 50°56N 1°47W 24 E5
Forel, Mt. Greenland 66°52N 36°55W 54 C6
Forest Row U.K. 51°5N 0°3E 25 D9
Forfar U.K. 56°39N 2°53W 19 J12
Forli Italy 44°13N 12°3E 70 B5
Formartine U.K. 57°20N 2°15W 19 H13
Formby U.K. 53°34N 3°4W 23 E2
Formby Pt. U.K. 53°33N 3°6W 23 E2
Formentera Spain 38°43N 1°27E 69 C6
Formiga Brazil 20°27S 45°25W 122 D1
Formosa = Taiwan ■ Asia 23°30N 121°0E 81 D7
Formosa Argentina 26°15S 58°10W 121 E4
Formosa Brazil 15°32S 47°20W 122 C1
Forres U.K. 57°37N 3°37W 19 G10
Forsayth Australia 18°33S 143°34E 98 D7
Fort Albany Canada 52°15N 81°35W 109 D11
Fort Augustus U.K. 57°9N 4°42W 19 H8
Fort Chipewyan Canada 58°42N 111°8W 108 D8
Fort Collins U.S.A. 40°35N 105°5W 110 B5
Fort-Coulonge Canada 45°50N 76°45W 112 C9
Fort-de-France Martinique 14°36N 61°2W 114 c
Fort Dodge U.S.A. 42°30N 94°11W 111 B8
Fort Good Hope Canada 66°14N 128°40W 108 C7
Fort Kent U.S.A. 47°15N 68°36W 113 B13
Fort Lauderdale U.S.A. 26°7N 80°8W 111 E10
Fort Liard Canada 60°14N 123°30W 108 C7
Fort MacKay Canada 57°12N 111°41W 108 D8
Fort Macleod Canada 49°45N 113°30W 108 E8
Fort McMurray Canada 56°44N 111°7W 108 D8
Fort McPherson Canada 67°30N 134°55W 108 C6
Fort Morgan U.S.A. 40°15N 103°48W 110 B6
Fort Myers U.S.A. 26°39N 81°52W 111 E10
Fort Nelson Canada 58°50N 122°44W 108 D7
Fort Nelson → Canada 59°32N 124°0W 108 D7
Fort Peck L. U.S.A. 48°0N 106°26W 110 A5
Fort Providence Canada 61°3N 117°40W 108 C8
Fort Resolution Canada 61°10N 113°40W 108 C8
Fort St. John Canada 56°15N 120°50W 108 D7
Fort Scott U.S.A. 37°50N 94°42W 111 C8
Fort Shevchenko Kazakhstan 44°35N 50°23E 73 F9
Fort Simpson Canada 61°45N 121°15W 108 C7
Fort Smith Canada 60°0N 111°51W 108 B8
Fort Smith U.S.A. 35°23N 94°25W 111 C8
Fort Stockton U.S.A. 30°53N 102°53W 110 D6
Fort Wayne U.S.A. 41°4N 85°9W 112 E5
Fort William U.K. 56°49N 5°7W 18 J7
Fort Worth U.S.A. 32°43N 97°19W 111 D7
Fort Yukon U.S.A. 66°34N 145°16W 108 C5
Fortaleza Brazil 3°45S 38°35W 120 C6
Forth → U.K. 56°9N 3°50W 21 B8
Forth, Firth of U.K. 56°5N 2°55W 21 B10
Fortrose U.K. 57°35N 4°9W 19 G9
Foshan China 23°4N 113°5E 81 D6
Fostoria U.S.A. 41°10N 83°25W 112 E6
Fothergill U.K. 54°43N 3°29W 22 C2
Fotheringhay U.K. 52°32N 0°27W 25 A8
Fougères France 48°21N 1°14W 68 B3
Foula U.K. 60°10N 2°5W 64 A5
Foulness I. U.K. 51°36N 0°55E 25 C10
Foulness Pt. U.K. 51°37N 0°58E 25 C10
Foulsham U.K. 52°48N 0°59E 25 A10
Fountainhall U.K. 55°44N 2°53W 21 C10
Fouta Djallon Guinea 11°20N 12°10W 94 F3
Fovant U.K. 51°4N 2°0W 24 D5

Greenore

Hounslow

Hourn, L.

Kandalaksha, G. of

Kandanghaur

Lucan Ireland 53°22N 6°28W 31 B10
Lucania, Mt. Canada 61°1N 140°27W 108 C5
Lucca Italy 43°50N 10°29E 70 C4
Luce Bay U.K. 54°45N 4°48W 20 E6
Lucea Jamaica 18°27N 78°10W 114 a
Lucena Phil. 13°56N 121°37E 83 B4
Lucknow India 26°50N 81°0E 85 F12
Lüda = Dalian China 38°50N 121°40E 81 C7
Lüderitz Namibia 26°41S 15°8E 97 K3
Ludgershall U.K. 51°15N 1°37W 24 D5
Ludgvan U.K. 50°9N 5°30W 27 G2
Ludhiana India 30°57N 75°56E 84 D9
Ludington U.S.A. 43°57N 86°27W 112 D4
Ludlow U.K. 52°22N 2°42W 23 H3
Ludwigsburg Germany 48°53N 9°11E 66 D5
Ludwigshafen Germany 49°29N 8°26E 66 D5
Lufkin U.S.A. 31°21N 94°44W 111 D8
Luga Russia 58°40N 29°55E 72 C4
Lugano Switz. 46°1N 8°57E 66 E5
Lugansk Ukraine 48°38N 39°15E 73 E6
Lugnaquillia Ireland 52°58N 6°28W 31 C10
Lugo Spain 43°2N 7°35W 69 A2
Lugwardine U.K. 52°4N 2°39W 24 B3
Luing U.K. 56°14N 5°39W 20 B4
Luleå Sweden 65°35N 22°10E 63 D8
Luleälven → Sweden 65°35N 22°10E 63 D8
Lundy U.K. 51°10N 4°41W 27 E4
Lune → U.K. 54°0N 2°51W 23 D3
Lüneburger Heide Germany 53°10N 10°12E 66 B6
Lunéville France 48°36N 6°30E 68 B7
Luni → India 24°41N 71°14E 84 G7
Luofu Dem. Rep. of the Congo 0°10S 29°15E 96 E5
Luoyang China 34°40N 112°26E 81 C6
Luray U.S.A. 38°40N 78°28W 112 F8
Lurgan U.K. 54°28N 6°19W 29 C9
Lusaka Zambia 15°28S 28°16E 97 H5
Lūt, Dasht-e Iran 31°30N 58°0E 87 D9
Lutherstadt Wittenberg Germany 51°53N 12°39E 66 C7
Luton U.K. 51°53N 0°24W 25 C8
Łutselk'e Canada 62°24N 110°44W 108 C8
Lutsk Ukraine 50°50N 25°15E 67 C13
Lutterworth U.K. 52°28N 1°12W 23 H6
Luvua → Dem. Rep. of the Congo 6°50S 27°30E 90 G6
Luxembourg Lux. 49°37N 6°9E 65 E6
Luxembourg ■ Europe 49°45N 6°0E 65 E5
Luzern Switz. 47°3N 8°18E 66 E5
Luzhou China 28°52N 105°20E 80 D5
Luziânia Brazil 16°20S 48°0W 122 C1
Luzon Phil. 16°0N 121°0E 83 B4
Luzon Strait Asia 21°0N 120°40E 83 A4
Lvov Ukraine 49°50N 24°0E 67 D13
Lyakhov Is. Russia 73°40N 141°0E 79 B16
Lybster U.K. 58°18N 3°15W 19 F11
Lydd U.K. 50°57N 0°55E 25 E10
Lydford U.K. 50°38N 4°8W 27 F5
Lydham U.K. 52°31N 2°58W 23 G3
Lyme B. U.K. 50°42N 2°53W 24 E3
Lyme Regis U.K. 50°43N 2°57W 24 E3
Lyminge U.K. 51°7N 1°6E 25 D11
Lymington U.K. 50°45N 1°32W 24 E5
Lymm U.K. 53°23N 2°29W 23 F4
Lympne U.K. 51°4N 1°2E 25 D11
Lynchburg U.S.A. 37°25N 79°9W 112 G8
Lyndhurst U.K. 50°52N 1°35W 24 E5
Lyneham U.K. 51°30N 1°58W 24 C5
Lynmouth U.K. 51°13N 3°49W 27 E6
Lynn Lake Canada 56°51N 101°3W 108 D9
Lynton U.K. 51°13N 3°50W 27 E6
Lyonnais France 45°45N 4°15E 68 D6
Lyons France 45°46N 4°50E 68 D6
Lysva Russia 58°7N 57°49E 72 C10
Lysychansk Ukraine 48°55N 38°30E 73 E6
Lytchett Minster U.K. 50°44N 2°4W 24 E4
Lytham St. Anne's U.K. 53°45N 3°0W 23 E2
Lythe U.K. 54°31N 0°41W 22 C7
Lyubertsy Russia 55°40N 37°51E 72 C6

M

Ma-ubin Burma 16°44N 95°39E 85 L19
Ma'ān Jordan 30°12N 35°44E 86 D3
Ma'anshan China 31°44N 118°29E 81 C6
Maas → Neths. 51°45N 4°32E 65 C4
Maastricht Neths. 50°50N 5°40E 65 D5
Mablethorpe U.K. 53°20N 0°15E 23 F9
Macaé Brazil 22°20S 41°43W 122 D2
McAlester U.S.A. 34°56N 95°46W 111 D7
McAllen U.S.A. 26°12N 98°14W 110 E7
MacAlpine L. Canada 66°32N 102°45W 108 C9
Macapá Brazil 0°5N 51°4W 120 B4
Macau Brazil 5°15S 36°40W 120 C6
Macau China 22°12N 113°33E 81 D6
Macclesfield U.K. 53°15N 2°8W 23 F4
M'Clintock Chan. Canada 72°0N 102°0W 108 B9
M'Clure Str. Canada 75°0N 119°0W 109 B8
McComb U.S.A. 31°15N 90°27W 111 D8
McCook U.S.A. 40°12N 100°38W 110 B6
McDonald Is. Ind. Oc. 53°0S 73°0E 53 G13
MacDonnell Ranges Australia 23°40S 133°0E 98 E5
Macduff U.K. 57°40N 2°31W 19 G12
Macedonia □ Greece 40°39N 22°0E 71 D10
Macedonia ■ Europe 41°53N 21°40E 71 D9
Maceió Brazil 9°40S 35°41W 122 A3
Macgillycuddy's Reeks Ireland 51°58N 9°45W 30 E3
Mach Pakistan 29°50N 67°20E 84 E5
Machakos Kenya 1°30S 37°15E 96 E7
Machala Ecuador 3°20S 79°57W 120 C2
Machars, The U.K. 54°46N 4°30W 20 E6
Machias U.S.A. 44°43N 67°28W 113 C14
Machilipatnam India 16°12N 81°8E 85 L12
Machrihanish U.K. 55°25N 5°43W 20 D4
Machupicchu Peru 13°8S 72°30W 120 D2
Machynlleth U.K. 52°35N 3°50W 26 B6
Mackay Australia 21°8S 149°11E 98 E8
Mackay, L. Australia 22°30S 129°0E 98 E4
McKeesport U.S.A. 40°20N 79°51W 112 E8
Mackenzie Canada 55°20N 123°5W 108 D7
Mackenzie → Canada 69°10N 134°20W 108 C6
Mackenzie King I. Canada 77°45N 111°0W 109 B8
Mackenzie Mts. Canada 64°0N 130°0W 108 B6
Mackinaw City U.S.A. 45°47N 84°44W 112 C5
McKinley, Mt. U.S.A. 63°4N 151°0W 108 C4
McKinley Sea Arctic 82°0N 0°0 54 A7
McMinnville U.S.A. 45°13N 123°12W 110 A2
McMurdo Sd. Antarctica 77°0S 170°0E 55 D11
Macomb U.S.A. 40°27N 90°40W 112 E2
Mâcon France 46°19N 4°50E 68 C6
Macon U.S.A. 32°51N 83°38W 111 D10
McPherson U.S.A. 38°22N 97°40W 110 C7
Macquarie Is. Pac. Oc. 54°36S 158°55E 102 N7
Macroom Ireland 51°54N 8°57W 30 E5
Madagascar ■ Africa 20°0S 47°0E 97 J9
Madang Papua N. G. 5°12S 145°49E 98 B8
Madeira Atl. Oc. 32°50N 17°0W 94 B2
Madeira → Brazil 3°22S 58°45W 120 C4
Madeleine, Îs. de la Canada 47°30N 61°40W 113 B17
Madeley U.K. 53°0N 2°20W 23 F4
Madhya Pradesh □ India 22°50N 78°0E 84 H11
Madison Ind., U.S.A. 38°44N 85°23W 112 F5
Madison S. Dak., U.S.A. 44°0N 97°7W 111 B7
Madison Wis., U.S.A. 43°4N 89°24W 112 D3
Madisonville U.S.A. 37°20N 87°30W 112 G4
Madiun Indonesia 7°38S 111°32E 83 D3
Madley U.K. 52°2N 2°51W 24 B3
Madras = Chennai India 13°8N 80°19E 84 N12
Madre de Dios → Bolivia 10°59S 66°8W 120 D3
Madre de Dios, I. Chile 50°20S 75°10W 121 H2
Madre Occidental, Sierra Mexico 27°0N 107°0W 114 B3
Madre Oriental, Sierra Mexico 25°0N 100°0W 114 C5
Madrid Spain 40°24N 3°42W 69 B4
Madura Indonesia 7°30S 114°0E 83 D3
Madurai India 9°55N 78°10E 84 Q11
Maebashi Japan 36°24N 139°4E 82 E6
Maesteg U.K. 51°36N 3°40W 27 D6
Mafeking S. Africa 25°50S 25°38E 97 K5
Mafia I. Tanzania 7°45S 39°50E 96 F7
Magadan Russia 59°38N 150°50E 79 D17
Magallanes, Estrecho de Chile 52°30S 75°0W 121 H2
Magangué Colombia 9°14N 74°45W 120 B2
Magdalena → Colombia 11°6N 74°51W 120 A2
Magdeburg Germany 52°7N 11°38E 66 B6
Magee, I. U.K. 54°48N 5°43W 29 B10
Magelang Indonesia 7°29S 110°13E 83 D3
Magellan's Str. = Magallanes, Estrecho de Chile 52°30S 75°0W 121 H2
Maggiore, Lago Italy 45°57N 8°39E 70 B3
Maggotty Jamaica 18°9N 77°46W 114 a
Maghâgha Egypt 28°38N 30°50E 95 C12
Magherafelt U.K. 54°45N 6°37W 29 B8
Maghreb N. Afr. 32°0N 4°0W 90 C3
Maghull U.K. 53°31N 2°57W 23 E3
Magnetic Pole (North) Canada 82°42N 114°24W 54 A2
Magnetic Pole (South) Antarctica 64°8S 138°8E 55 C9
Magnitogorsk Russia 53°27N 59°4E 72 D10
Magog Canada 45°18N 72°9W 113 C11
Magwe Burma 20°10N 95°0E 85 J19
Mahābād Iran 36°50N 45°45E 86 B6
Mahajanga Madag. 15°40S 46°25E 97 H9
Mahakam → Indonesia 0°35S 117°17E 83 D3
Mahalapye Botswana 23°1S 26°51E 97 J5
Maḩallāt Iran 33°55N 50°30E 87 C7
Mahanadi → India 20°20N 86°25E 85 J15
Maharashtra □ India 20°30N 75°30E 84 J9
Mahdia Tunisia 35°28N 11°0E 95 A8
Mahesana India 23°39N 72°26E 84 H8
Mahilyow Belarus 53°55N 30°18E 67 B16
Mai-Ndombe, L. Dem. Rep. of the Congo 2°0S 18°20E 96 E3
Maiden Bradley U.K. 51°9N 2°17W 24 D4
Maiden Newton U.K. 50°46N 2°34W 24 E3
Maidenhead U.K. 51°31N 0°42W 25 C7
Maidstone U.K. 51°16N 0°32E 25 D10
Maiduguri Nigeria 12°0N 13°20E 95 F8
Maijdi Bangla. 22°48N 91°10E 85 H17
Main → Germany 50°0N 8°18E 66 C5
Main → U.K. 54°48N 6°18W 29 B9
Maine France 48°20N 0°15W 68 C3
Maine □ U.S.A. 45°20N 69°0W 113 C13
Maine → Ireland 52°9N 9°45W 30 D3
Mainland Orkney, U.K. 58°59N 3°8W 19 E11
Mainland Shet., U.K. 60°15N 1°22W 18 B15
Mainz Germany 50°1N 8°14E 66 C5
Maiquetía Venezuela 10°36N 66°57W 120 A3
Majorca = Mallorca Spain 39°30N 3°0E 69 C7
Makale Indonesia 3°6S 119°51E 83 D3
Makasar, Str. of Indonesia 1°0S 118°20E 83 D3
Makgadikgadi Salt Pans Botswana 20°40S 25°45E 97 J5
Makhachkala Russia 43°0N 47°30E 73 F8
Makhado S. Africa 23°1S 29°43E 97 J5
Makran Coast Range Pakistan 25°40N 64°0E 84 G4
Makurdi Nigeria 7°43N 8°35E 94 G7
Mal B. Ireland 52°50N 9°30W 30 C4
Malabar Coast India 11°0N 75°0E 84 P9
Malacca, Straits of Indonesia 3°0N 101°0E 83 C2
Málaga Spain 36°43N 4°23W 69 D3
Malahide Ireland 53°26N 6°9W 31 B10
Malaita Solomon Is. 9°0S 161°0E 99 B11
Malakâl Sudan 9°33N 31°40E 95 G12
Malakula Vanuatu 16°15S 167°30E 99 D12
Malang Indonesia 7°59S 112°45E 83 D3
Malanje Angola 9°36S 16°17E 96 F3
Mälaren Sweden 59°30N 17°10E 63 F7
Malatya Turkey 38°25N 38°20E 73 G6
Malawi ■ Africa 11°55S 34°0E 97 G6
Malawi, L. Africa 12°30S 34°30E 97 G6
Malay Pen. Asia 7°25N 100°0E 74 H12
Malāyer Iran 34°19N 48°51E 86 C7
Malaysia ■ Asia 5°0N 110°0E 83 C3
Malden U.S.A. 36°34N 89°57W 112 G3
Malden I. Kiribati 4°3S 155°1W 103 H12
Maldives ■ Ind. Oc. 5°0N 73°0E 75 H9
Maldon U.K. 51°44N 0°42E 25 C10
Maldonado Uruguay 34°59S 55°0W 121 F4
Malegaon India 20°30N 74°38E 84 J9
Malham Tarn U.K. 54°6N 2°10W 22 D4
Malheur L. U.S.A. 43°20N 118°48W 110 B3
Mali ■ Africa 17°0N 3°0W 94 E5
Malin Hd. Ireland 55°23N 7°23W 28 A7
Malin Pen. Ireland 55°20N 7°17W 29 A7
Malindi Kenya 3°12S 40°5E 96 E8
Mallaig U.K. 57°0N 5°50W 18 H6
Mallawi Egypt 27°44N 30°44E 95 C12
Mallorca Spain 39°30N 3°0E 69 C7
Mallow Ireland 52°8N 8°39W 30 D5
Malmesbury U.K. 51°35N 2°5W 24 C4
Malmö Sweden 55°36N 12°59E 63 F6
Malone U.S.A. 44°51N 74°18W 113 C10
Malpas U.K. 53°1N 2°45W 23 F3
Malpelo, I. de Colombia 4°3N 81°35W 103 G19
Malta ■ Europe 35°55N 14°26E 70 a
Maltby U.K. 53°25N 1°12W 23 F6
Malton U.K. 54°8N 0°49W 22 D7
Malvinas, Is. = Falkland Is. ◪ Atl. Oc. 51°30S 59°0W 121 H4
Mamoré → Bolivia 10°23S 65°53W 120 D3
Mamoudzou Mayotte 12°48S 45°14E 91 H8
Man Ivory C. 7°30N 7°40W 94 G4
Man, I. of U.K. 54°15N 4°30W 29 C12
Manacles, The U.K. 50°2N 5°4W 27 G3
Manado Indonesia 1°29N 124°51E 83 C4
Managua Nic. 12°6N 86°20W 114 E7
Manas China 44°17N 85°56E 80 B3
Manatí Puerto Rico 18°26N 66°29W 115 d
Manaus Brazil 3°0S 60°0W 120 C3
Manby U.K. 53°21N 0°6E 23 F9
Manchester U.K. 53°29N 2°12W 23 F4
Manchester U.S.A. 42°59N 71°28W 113 D12
Manchester Int. ✈ (MAN) U.K. 53°21N 2°17W 23 F4
Manchuria China 45°0N 125°0E 81 B7
Manchurian Plain China 47°0N 124°0E 74 D14
Mandal Norway 58°2N 7°25E 63 F5
Mandalay Burma 22°0N 96°4E 85 J20
Mandalgovĭ Mongolia 45°45N 106°10E 80 B5
Mandan U.S.A. 46°50N 100°54W 110 A6
Mandeville Jamaica 18°2N 77°31W 114 a
Mandla India 22°39N 80°30E 85 H12
Mandsaur India 24°3N 75°8E 84 G9
Mandvi India 22°51N 69°22E 84 H6
Manea U.K. 52°29N 0°10E 25 B9
Manfalût Egypt 27°20N 30°52E 95 C12
Manfredónia Italy 41°38N 15°55E 70 D6
Mangabeiras, Chapada das Brazil 10°0S 46°30W 122 B1
Mangalore India 12°55N 74°47E 84 N9
Mangnai China 37°52N 91°43E 80 C4
Mangole Indonesia 1°50S 125°55E 83 D4
Mangotsfield U.K. 51°29N 2°30W 24 D4
Manhattan U.S.A. 39°11N 96°35W 111 C7
Manhuaçu Brazil 20°15S 42°2W 122 D2
Manica Mozam. 18°58S 32°59E 97 H6
Manicoré Brazil 5°48S 61°16W 120 C3
Manicouagan → Canada 49°30N 68°30W 109 E13
Manicouagan, Rés. Canada 51°5N 68°40W 109 D13
Manihiki Cook Is. 10°24S 161°1W 103 J11
Manila Phil. 14°35N 120°58E 83 B4
Manipur □ India 25°0N 94°0E 85 G19
Manisa Turkey 38°38N 27°30E 73 G4
Manistee U.S.A. 44°15N 86°19W 112 C4
Manistee → U.S.A. 44°15N 86°21W 112 C4
Manistique U.S.A. 45°57N 86°15W 112 C4
Manitoba □ Canada 53°30N 97°0W 108 D10
Manitoba, L. Canada 51°0N 98°45W 108 D10
Manitou Is. U.S.A. 45°8N 86°0W 112 C4
Manitoulin I. Canada 45°40N 82°30W 112 C6
Manitowoc U.S.A. 44°5N 87°40W 112 C4
Manizales Colombia 5°5N 75°32W 120 B2
Mankato U.S.A. 44°10N 94°0W 111 B8
Mannar Sri Lanka 9°1N 79°54E 84 Q11
Mannar, G. of Asia 8°30N 79°0E 84 Q11
Mannheim Germany 49°29N 8°29E 66 D5
Manning Canada 56°53N 117°39W 108 D8
Manningtree U.K. 51°56N 1°5E 25 C11
Manokwari Indonesia 0°54S 134°0E 83 D5
Manosque France 43°49N 5°47E 68 E6
Manresa Spain 41°48N 1°50E 69 B6
Mansel I. Canada 62°0N 80°0W 109 C12
Mansfield U.K. 53°9N 1°11W 23 F6
Mansfield U.S.A. 40°45N 82°31W 112 E6
Mansfield Woodhouse U.K. 53°11N 1°12W 23 F6
Manta Ecuador 1°0S 80°40W 120 C1
Mantes-la-Jolie France 48°58N 1°41E 68 B4
Mantiqueira, Serra da Brazil 22°0S 44°0W 116 F6
Manton U.K. 52°38N 0°41W 23 G7
Manton U.S.A. 44°25N 85°24W 112 C5
Mántova Italy 45°9N 10°48E 70 B4
Manuel Alves → Brazil 11°19S 48°28W 122 B1
Manzai Pakistan 32°12N 70°15E 84 C7
Manzanillo Cuba 20°20N 77°31W 115 C9
Manzanillo Mexico 19°3N 104°20W 114 D4
Manzhouli China 49°35N 117°25E 81 B6
Maó Spain 39°53N 4°16E 69 C8
Maoming China 21°50N 110°54E 81 D6
Mapam Yumco China 30°45N 81°28E 80 C3
Maputo Mozam. 25°58S 32°32E 97 K6
Maputo B. Mozam. 25°50S 32°45E 90 J7
Maquinchao Argentina 41°15S 68°50W 121 G3
Maquoketa U.S.A. 42°4N 90°40W 112 D2
Mar U.K. 57°11N 2°53W 19 H12
Mar, Serra do Brazil 25°30S 49°0W 116 F6
Mar Chiquita, L. Argentina 30°40S 62°50W 121 F3
Mar del Plata Argentina 38°0S 57°30W 121 F4
Marabá Brazil 5°20S 49°5W 120 C5
Maracá, I. de Brazil 2°10N 50°30W 120 B4
Maracaibo Venezuela 10°40N 71°37W 120 A2
Maracaibo, L. de Venezuela 9°40N 71°30W 120 B2
Maracay Venezuela 10°15N 67°28W 120 A3
Maradi Niger 13°29N 7°20E 94 F7
Maragogipe Brazil 12°46S 38°55W 122 B3
Marajó, I. de Brazil 1°0S 49°30W 120 C5
Maranguape Brazil 3°55S 38°50W 120 C6
Maranhão □ Brazil 5°0S 46°0W 120 C5
Marañón → Peru 4°30S 73°35W 120 C2
Marazion U.K. 50°7N 5°29W 27 G3
Marbella Spain 36°30N 4°57W 69 D3
March U.K. 52°33N 0°5E 25 A9
Marche France 46°5N 1°20E 68 C4
Marcus I. Pac. Oc. 24°20N 153°58E 102 E7
Mardan Pakistan 34°20N 72°0E 84 B8
Marden U.K. 52°7N 2°42W 24 B3
Mardin Turkey 37°20N 40°43E 73 G7
Maree, L. U.K. 57°40N 5°26W 18 G7
Mareham le Fen U.K. 53°8N 0°4W 23 F8
Marfleet U.K. 53°45N 0°17W 23 E8
Margarita, I. de Venezuela 11°0N 64°0W 120 A3
Margate U.K. 51°23N 1°23E 25 D11
Marghilon Uzbekistan 40°27N 71°42E 87 A12
Māṟgow, Dasht-e Afghan. 30°40N 62°30E 87 D10
Mari El □ Russia 56°30N 48°0E 72 C8
Mariana Trench Pac. Oc. 13°0N 145°0E 102 F6
Marías, Is. Mexico 21°25N 106°28W 114 C3
Maribor Slovenia 46°36N 15°40E 66 E8
Marie Byrd Land Antarctica 79°30S 125°0W 55 D14
Marie-Galante Guadeloupe 15°56N 61°16W 114 b
Mariental Namibia 24°36S 18°0E 97 J3
Marietta U.S.A. 39°25N 81°27W 112 F7
Marília Brazil 22°13S 50°0W 120 E4
Marinette U.S.A. 45°6N 87°38W 112 C4
Marion Ill., U.S.A. 37°44N 88°56W 112 G3
Marion Ind., U.S.A. 40°32N 85°40W 112 E5
Marion Ohio, U.S.A. 40°35N 83°8W 112 E6
Mariupol Ukraine 47°5N 37°31E 73 E6
Markam China 29°42N 98°38E 80 D4
Market Bosworth U.K. 52°38N 1°24W 23 G6
Market Deeping U.K. 52°41N 0°19W 23 G8
Market Drayton U.K. 52°54N 2°29W 23 G4
Market Harborough U.K. 52°29N 0°55W 23 H7
Market Lavington U.K. 51°17N 1°58W 24 D5
Market Rasen U.K. 53°24N 0°20W 23 F8
Market Weighton U.K. 53°52N 0°40W 23 E7
Markfield U.K. 52°42N 1°17W 23 G6
Markham, Mt. Antarctica 83°0S 164°0E 55 E11
Marks Tey U.K. 51°52N 0°49E 25 C10
Marlborough U.K. 51°25N 1°43W 24 D5
Marlborough Downs U.K. 51°27N 1°53W 24 D5
Marlow U.K. 51°34N 0°46W 25 C7
Marmara, Sea of Turkey 40°45N 28°15E 73 F4
Marmaris Turkey 36°50N 28°14E 86 B2
Marmora Canada 44°28N 77°41W 112 C9
Marne → France 48°47N 2°29E 68 B5
Marnhull U.K. 50°57N 2°19W 24 E4
Maroua Cameroon 10°40N 14°20E 95 F8
Marple U.K. 53°24N 2°4W 23 F4
Marquette U.S.A. 46°33N 87°24W 112 B4
Marquis St. Lucia 14°2N 60°54W 115 f
Marquises, Îs. French Polynesia 9°30S 140°0W 103 H14
Marrakesh Morocco 31°9N 8°0W 94 B4
Marree Australia 29°39S 138°1E 98 F6
Marsá Matrûh Egypt 31°19N 27°9E 95 B11
Marsabit Kenya 2°18N 38°0E 96 D7
Marsala Italy 37°48N 12°26E 70 F5
Marseilles France 43°18N 5°23E 68 E6
Marsh I. U.S.A. 29°34N 91°53W 111 E8
Marshall U.S.A. 32°33N 94°23W 111 D8
Marshall Is. ■ Pac. Oc. 9°0N 171°0E 102 G9
Marshfield U.K. 51°28N 2°19W 24 D4
Marshfield U.S.A. 44°40N 90°10W 112 C2
Marske by the Sea U.K. 54°36N 1°0W 22 C7
Marston Moor U.K. 53°58N 1°17W 23 E6
Martaban Burma 16°30N 97°35E 85 L20
Martaban, G. of Burma 16°5N 96°30E 85 L20
Martapura Indonesia 3°22S 114°47E 83 D3
Martham U.K. 52°42N 1°37E 25 A12
Martha's Vineyard U.S.A. 41°25N 70°38W 113 E12
Martigues France 43°24N 5°4E 68 E6
Martinique ◪ W. Indies 14°40N 61°0W 114 c
Martin's Bay Barbados 13°12N 59°29W 115 g
Martinsburg U.S.A. 39°27N 77°58W 112 F9
Martinsville U.S.A. 39°26N 86°25W 112 F4
Martley U.K. 52°15N 2°21W 24 B4
Martock U.K. 50°58N 2°46W 24 E3
Marwar India 25°43N 73°45E 84 G8
Mary Turkmenistan 37°40N 61°50E 87 B10
Maryborough Australia 25°31S 152°37E 98 F9
Maryland □ U.S.A. 39°0N 76°30W 112 F9
Maryport U.K. 54°44N 3°28W 22 C2
Marystown Canada 47°10N 55°10W 109 E14
Marytavy U.K. 50°36N 4°7W 27 F5
Marzūq Libya 25°53N 13°57E 95 C8
Masai Steppe Tanzania 4°30S 36°30E 96 E7
Masan S. Korea 35°11N 128°32E 81 C7
Masandam, Ra's Oman 26°30N 56°30E 88 B6
Masaya Nic. 12°0N 86°7W 114 E7
Masbate Phil. 12°21N 123°36E 83 B4
Mascara Algeria 35°26N 0°6E 94 A6
Maseru Lesotho 29°18S 27°30E 97 K5
Masham U.K. 54°14N 1°39W 22 D5
Mashhad Iran 36°20N 59°35E 87 B9
Mashonaland Zimbabwe 16°30S 31°0E 97 H6
Maşīrah Oman 21°0N 58°50E 88 C6
Masjed Soleyman Iran 31°55N 49°18E 86 D7
Mask, L. Ireland 53°36N 9°22W 28 D3
Mason City U.S.A. 43°9N 93°12W 111 B8
Massa Italy 44°1N 10°9E 70 B4
Massachusetts □ U.S.A. 42°30N 72°0W 113 D11
Massawa Eritrea 15°35N 39°25E 88 D2
Massena U.S.A. 44°56N 74°54W 113 C10
Massiah Street Barbados 13°9N 59°29W 115 g
Massif Central France 44°55N 3°0E 68 D5
Massillon U.S.A. 40°48N 81°32W 112 E7
Masurian Lakes Poland 53°50N 21°0E 67 B11
Masvingo Zimbabwe 20°8S 30°49E 97 J6
Mata-Utu Wall. & F. Is. 13°17S 176°8W 99 C15
Matabeleland Zimbabwe 18°0S 27°0E 97 H5
Matadi Dem. Rep. of the Congo 5°52S 13°31E 96 F2
Matagalpa Nic. 13°0N 85°58W 114 E7
Matagami Canada 49°45N 77°34W 109 E12
Matagami, L. Canada 49°50N 77°40W 109 E12
Matagorda I. U.S.A. 28°15N 96°30W 111 E7
Matamoros Mexico 25°32N 103°15W 114 B5
Matane Canada 48°50N 67°33W 109 E13
Matanzas Cuba 23°0N 81°40W 115 C8
Matara Sri Lanka 5°58N 80°30E 84 S12
Mataró Spain 41°32N 2°29E 69 B7
Matehuala Mexico 23°39N 100°39W 114 C4
Mateke Hills Zimbabwe 21°48S 31°0E 97 J6
Matera Italy 40°40N 16°36E 70 D7
Mathura India 27°30N 77°40E 84 F10
Mati Phil. 6°55N 126°15E 83 C4
Matlock U.K. 53°9N 1°33W 23 F5
Mato Grosso □ Brazil 14°0S 55°0W 120 D4
Mato Grosso, Planalto do Brazil 15°0S 55°0W 120 D4
Mato Grosso do Sul □ Brazil 18°0S 55°0W 120 D4
Matopo Hills Zimbabwe 20°36S 28°20E 97 J5
Maţruḩ Oman 23°37N 58°30E 87 F9
Matsue Japan 35°25N 133°10E 82 F3
Matsumoto Japan 36°15N 138°0E 82 E6
Matsusaka Japan 34°34N 136°32E 82 F5
Matsuyama Japan 33°45N 132°45E 82 G3
Mattagami → Canada 50°43N 81°29W 109 D11
Mattancheri India 9°50N 76°15E 84 Q10
Mattawa Canada 46°20N 78°45W 112 B8
Matterhorn Switz. 45°58N 7°39E 66 F4
Matthew, Î. N. Cal. 22°29S 171°15E 99 E13
Mattoon U.S.A. 39°29N 88°23W 112 F3
Maturín Venezuela 9°45N 63°11W 120 B3
Maubeuge France 50°17N 3°57E 68 A6
Maudin Sun Burma 16°0N 94°30E 85 M19
Maui U.S.A. 20°48N 156°20W 110 H16
Maumee → U.S.A. 41°42N 83°28W 112 E6
Maumturk Mts. Ireland 53°32N 9°42W 28 D2
Maun Botswana 20°0S 23°26E 97 H4
Mauna Kea U.S.A. 19°50N 155°28W 110 J17
Mauna Loa U.S.A. 19°30N 155°35W 110 J17
Mauritania ■ Africa 20°50N 10°0W 94 E3
Mauritius ■ Ind. Oc. 20°0S 57°0E 91 J9
Mawgan U.K. 50°4N 5°13W 27 G3
Maxwellheugh U.K. 55°35N 2°26W 21 C11
May, I. of U.K. 56°11N 2°32W 21 B10
May Pen Jamaica 17°58N 77°15W 114 a
Mayaguana Bahamas 22°30N 72°44W 115 C10
Mayagüez Puerto Rico 18°12N 67°9W 115 d
Maybole U.K. 55°21N 4°42W 20 D6
Mayfield E. Sussex, U.K. 51°1N 0°17E 25 D9
Mayfield Staffs., U.K. 53°1N 1°47W 23 F5
Mayfield U.S.A. 36°44N 88°38W 112 G3
Maykop Russia 44°35N 40°10E 73 F7
Maynooth Ireland 53°23N 6°34W 31 B9
Mayo Canada 63°38N 135°57W 108 C6
Mayo □ Ireland 53°53N 9°3W 28 D3
Mayon Volcano Phil. 13°15N 123°41E 83 B4
Mayotte ◪ Ind. Oc. 12°50S 45°10E 97 G9
Maysville U.S.A. 38°39N 83°46W 112 F6
Māzandarān □ Iran 36°30N 52°0E 87 B8
Mazar China 36°32N 77°1E 80 C2
Mazār-e Sharīf Afghan. 36°41N 67°0E 87 B11
Mazaruni → Guyana 6°25N 58°35W 120 B4
Mazatlán Mexico 23°13N 106°25W 114 C3
Mazyr Belarus 51°59N 29°15E 72 D4
Mbabane Swaziland 26°18S 31°6E 97 K6
Mbaïki C.A.R. 3°53N 18°1E 96 D3
Mbala Zambia 8°46S 31°24E 96 F6
Mbale Uganda 1°8N 34°12E 96 D6
Mbandaka Dem. Rep. of the Congo 0°1N 18°18E 96 D3
Mbanza Ngungu Dem. Rep. of the Congo 5°12S 14°53E 96 F2
Mbeya Tanzania 8°54S 33°29E 96 F6
Mbour Senegal 14°22N 16°54W 94 F2
Mbuji-Mayi Dem. Rep. of the Congo 6°9S 23°40E 96 F4
Mdantsane S. Africa 32°56S 27°46E 97 L5
Mead, L. U.S.A. 36°0N 114°44W 110 C4
Meadow Lake Canada 54°10N 108°26W 108 D9
Meadville U.S.A. 41°39N 80°9W 112 E7
Meaford Canada 44°36N 80°35W 112 C7
Mealsgate U.K. 54°47N 3°13W 22 C2
Mearns, Howe of the U.K. 56°52N 2°26W 19 J13
Measham U.K. 52°43N 1°31W 23 G5
Meath □ Ireland 53°40N 6°57W 29 D8
Meaux France 48°58N 2°50E 68 B5
Mecca Si. Arabia 21°30N 39°54E 86 F4
Mechelen Belgium 51°2N 4°29E 65 C4
Mecklenburg Germany 53°33N 11°40E 66 B7
Mecklenburger Bucht Germany 54°20N 11°40E 66 A6
Medan Indonesia 3°40N 98°38E 83 C1
Médéa Algeria 36°12N 2°50E 94 A6
Medellín Colombia 6°15N 75°35W 120 B2
Medford Oreg., U.S.A. 42°19N 122°52W 110 B2
Medford Wis., U.S.A. 45°9N 90°20W 112 C2
Medicine Hat Canada 50°0N 110°45W 108 E8
Medina Si. Arabia 24°35N 39°52E 86 E4
Mediterranean Sea Europe 35°0N 15°0E 90 C5
Médoc France 45°10N 0°50W 68 D3
Medstead U.K. 51°8N 1°3W 24 D6
Medvezhyegorsk Russia 63°0N 34°25E 72 B5
Medway → U.K. 51°27N 0°46E 25 D10
Meekatharra Australia 26°32S 118°29E 98 F2
Meerut India 29°1N 77°42E 84 E10
Meghalaya □ India 25°50N 91°0E 85 G17
Meghna → Bangla. 22°50N 90°50E 85 H17
Megisti Greece 36°8N 29°34E 86 B2
Meighen I. Canada 80°0N 99°30W 109 B10
Meiktila Burma 20°53N 95°54E 85 J19
Meizhou China 24°16N 116°6E 81 D6
Mejillones Chile 23°10S 70°30W 121 E2
Mekele Ethiopia 13°33N 39°30E 88 E2
Mekhtar Pakistan 30°30N 69°15E 84 D6
Meknès Morocco 33°57N 5°33W 94 B4
Mekong → Asia 9°30N 106°15E 83 C2
Melaka Malaysia 2°15N 102°15E 83 C2

Melanesia · · · · · · · · Nanded

Nandurbar — Olsztyn

Olt

Placentia B.

Placetas *Cuba* 22°15N 79°44W **115** C9
Plainview *U.S.A.* 34°11N 101°43W **110** D6
Plata, Río de la → *S. Amer.* 34°45S 57°30W **121** F4
Platte → *U.S.A.* 39°16N 94°50W **111** C8
Plattsburgh *U.S.A.* 44°42N 73°28W **113** C11
Plauen *Germany* 50°30N 12°8E **66** C7
Plenty, B. of *N.Z.* 37°45S 177°0E **99** H14
Plessisville *Canada* 46°14N 71°47W **113** B12
Pleven *Bulgaria* 43°26N 24°37E **71** C11
Plock *Poland* 52°32N 19°40E **67** B10
Ploieşti *Romania* 44°57N 26°5E **67** F14
Plovdiv *Bulgaria* 42°8N 24°44E **71** C11
Plymouth *U.K.* 50°22N 4°10W **27** G5
Plymouth *Ind., U.S.A.* 41°21N 86°19W **112** E4
Plymouth *Wis., U.S.A.* 43°45N 87°59W **112** D4
Plympton *U.K.* 50°23N 4°5W **27** G5
Plymstock *U.K.* 50°21N 4°7W **27** G5
Plzeň *Czech Rep.* 49°45N 13°22E **66** D7
Po → *Italy* 44°57N 12°4E **70** B5
Pobedy, Pik *Kyrgyzstan* 42°0N 79°58E **80** B2
Pocatello *U.S.A.* 42°52N 112°27W **110** B4
Pocklington *U.K.* 53°56N 0°46W **23** E7
Poços de Caldas *Brazil* 21°50S 46°33W **122** D1
Podgorica *Montenegro* 42°30N 19°19E **71** C8
Podolsk *Russia* 55°25N 37°30E **72** C6
Pohnpei *Micronesia* 6°55N 158°10E **102** G7
Point Hope *U.S.A.* 68°21N 166°47W **108** C3
Point L. *Canada* 65°15N 113°4W **108** C8
Point Pleasant *U.S.A.* 38°51N 82°8W **112** F6
Pointe-à-Pitre *Guadeloupe* 16°10N 61°32W **114** b
Pointe-Noire *Congo* 4°48S 11°53E **96** E2
Pointe-Noire *Guadeloupe* 16°14N 61°47W **114** b
Poitiers *France* 46°35N 0°20E **68** C4
Poitou *France* 46°40N 0°10W **68** C3
Pokhara *Nepal* 28°14N 83°58E **85** E13
Poland ■ *Europe* 52°0N 20°0E **67** C10
Polatsk *Belarus* 55°30N 28°50E **72** C4
Polden Hills *U.K.* 51°7N 2°50W **24** D3
Polegate *U.K.* 50°49N 0°16E **25** E9
Polesworth *U.K.* 52°37N 1°36W **23** G5
Polevskoy *Russia* 56°26N 60°11E **72** C11
Polokwane *S. Africa* 23°54S 29°25E **97** J5
Polperro *U.K.* 50°20N 4°32W **27** G4
Polruan *U.K.* 50°19N 4°38W **27** G4
Poltava *Ukraine* 49°35N 34°35E **73** E5
Polynesia *Pac. Oc.* 10°0S 162°0W **103** F11
Ponca City *U.S.A.* 36°42N 97°5W **111** C7
Ponce *Puerto Rico* 18°1N 66°37W **115** d
Pond Inlet *Canada* 72°40N 77°0W **109** B12
Pondicherry *India* 11°59N 79°50E **84** P11
Ponferrada *Spain* 42°32N 6°35W **69** A2
Ponta Grossa *Brazil* 25°7S 50°10W **121** E4
Pontardawe *U.K.* 51°43N 3°51W **26** D6
Pontardulais *U.K.* 51°43N 4°3W **26** D5
Pontarlier *France* 46°54N 6°20E **68** C7
Pontchartrain, L. *U.S.A.* 30°5N 90°5W **111** D9
Ponte Nova *Brazil* 20°25S 42°54W **122** D2
Pontefract *U.K.* 53°42N 1°18W **23** E6
Ponteland *U.K.* 55°3N 1°45W **22** B5
Pontevedra *Spain* 42°26N 8°40W **69** A1
Pontiac *Ill., U.S.A.* 40°53N 88°38W **112** E3
Pontiac *Mich., U.S.A.* 42°38N 83°18W **112** D6
Pontianak *Indonesia* 0°3S 109°15E **83** D2
Pontine Mts. *Turkey* 41°0N 36°45E **73** F6
Pontivy *France* 48°5N 2°58W **68** B2
Pontrilas *U.K.* 51°56N 2°52W **24** C3
Pontypool *U.K.* 51°42N 3°2W **26** D7
Pontypridd *U.K.* 51°36N 3°20W **27** D7
Ponziane, Ísole *Italy* 40°55N 12°57E **70** D5
Poole *U.K.* 50°43N 1°59W **24** E5
Poole Harbour *U.K.* 50°41N 2°0W **24** E5
Pooley Bridge *U.K.* 54°37N 2°48W **22** C3
Poopó, L. de *Bolivia* 18°30S 67°35W **120** D3
Popayán *Colombia* 2°27N 76°36W **120** B2
Poplar Bluff *U.S.A.* 36°46N 90°24W **111** C81
Popocatépetl, Volcán *Mexico* 19°2N 98°38W **114** D5
Porbandar *India* 21°44N 69°43E **84** J6
Porcupine → *U.S.A.* 66°34N 145°19W **108** C5
Pori *Finland* 61°29N 21°48E **63** E8
Porlock *U.K.* 51°13N 3°35W **27** E6
Port Alberni *Canada* 49°14N 124°50W **108** E7
Port Antonio *Jamaica* 18°10N 76°26W **114** a
Port Arthur *U.S.A.* 29°54N 93°56W **111** E8
Port-au-Prince *Haiti* 18°40N 72°20W **115** D10
Port Augusta *Australia* 32°30S 137°50E **98** G6
Port Carlisle *U.K.* 54°57N 3°11W **22** C2
Port-Cartier *Canada* 50°2N 66°50W **109** D13
Port-de-Paix *Haiti* 19°50N 72°50W **115** D10
Port Elgin *Canada* 44°25N 81°25W **112** C7
Port Elizabeth *S. Africa* 33°58S 25°40E **97** L5
Port Ellen *U.K.* 55°38N 6°11W **20** C3
Port Erin *I. of Man* 54°5N 4°45W **29** C12
Port-Gentil *Gabon* 0°40S 8°50E **96** E1
Port Glasgow *U.K.* 55°56N 4°41W **20** C6
Port Harcourt *Nigeria* 4°40N 7°10E **94** H7
Port Hawkesbury *Canada* 45°36N 61°22W **109** E13
Port Hedland *Australia* 20°25S 118°35E **98** E2
Port Hope Simpson *Canada* 52°33N 56°18W **109** D14
Port Huron *U.S.A.* 42°58N 82°26W **112** D6
Port Isaac *U.K.* 50°35N 4°50W **27** F4
Port Isaac B. *U.K.* 50°36N 4°50W **27** F4
Port Laoise *Ireland* 53°2N 7°18W **31** B8
Port Lincoln *Australia* 34°42S 135°52E **98** G6
Port-Louis *Guadeloupe* 16°28N 61°32W **114** b
Port Louis *Mauritius* 20°10S 57°30E **91** H9
Port McNeill *Canada* 50°35N 127°6W **108** D7
Port Macquarie *Australia* 31°25S 152°25E **98** G9
Port Maria *Jamaica* 18°22N 76°54W **114** a
Port Morant *Jamaica* 17°54N 76°19W **114** a
Port Moresby *Papua N. G.* 9°24S 147°8E **98** B8
Port Nolloth *S. Africa* 29°17S 16°52E **97** K3
Port of Spain *Trin. & Tob.* 10°40N 61°31W **120** A3
Port Pirie *Australia* 33°10S 138°1E **98** G6
Port Said *Egypt* 31°16N 32°18E **95** B12
Port St. Lucie *U.S.A.* 27°18N 80°21W **111** E10
Port St. Mary *U.K.* 54°5N 4°44W **29** C12
Port Shepstone *S. Africa* 30°44S 30°28E **97** L6
Port Sudan *Sudan* 19°32N 37°9E **95** E13
Port Talbot *U.K.* 51°35N 3°47W **27** D6
Port Vila *Vanuatu* 17°45S 168°18E **99** D12
Port Washington *U.S.A.* 43°23N 87°53W **112** D4
Port William *U.K.* 54°46N 4°35W **20** E6
Portadown *U.K.* 54°25N 6°27W **29** C9
Portaferry *U.K.* 54°23N 5°33W **29** C10
Portage *U.S.A.* 43°33N 89°28W **112** D3
Portage la Prairie *Canada* 49°58N 98°18W **108** E10
Portarlington *Ireland* 53°9N 7°14W **31** B8
Porthcawl *U.K.* 51°29N 3°42W **27** E6
Porthleven *U.K.* 50°4N 5°19W **27** G3
Porthmadog *U.K.* 52°55N 4°8W **26** B5
Portishead *U.K.* 51°29N 2°46W **24** D3
Portknockie *U.K.* 57°42N 2°51W **19** G12
Portland *Maine, U.S.A.* 43°39N 70°16W **113** D12
Portland *Oreg., U.S.A.* 45°32N 122°37W **110** A2
Portland, I. of *U.K.* 50°33N 2°26W **24** E4
Portland Bight *Jamaica* 17°52N 77°5W **114** a
Portland Bill *U.K.* 50°31N 2°28W **27** F9
Portland Pt. *Jamaica* 17°42N 77°11W **114** a
Portmarnock *Ireland* 53°26N 6°8W **31** B10
Portmore *Jamaica* 17°53N 77°53W **114** a
Porto *Portugal* 41°8N 8°40W **69** B1
Pôrto Alegre *Brazil* 30°5S 51°10W **121** F4
Pôrto Esperança *Brazil* 19°37S 57°29W **120** D4
Pôrto Nacional *Brazil* 10°40S 48°30W **122** B1
Porto-Novo *Benin* 6°23N 2°42E **94** G6
Pôrto Seguro *Brazil* 16°26S 39°5W **122** C3
Porto Tórres *Italy* 40°50N 8°24E **70** D3
Porto-Vecchio *France* 41°35N 9°16E **68** F8
Pôrto Velho *Brazil* 8°46S 63°54W **120** C3
Porton *U.K.* 51°8N 1°43W **24** D5
Portpatrick *U.K.* 54°51N 5°7W **20** E5
Portree *U.K.* 57°25N 6°12W **18** H5
Portrush *U.K.* 55°12N 6°40W **29** A8
Portslade *U.K.* 50°50N 0°12W **25** E8
Portsmouth *U.K.* 50°48N 1°6W **24** E6
Portsmouth *N.H., U.S.A.* 43°5N 70°45W **113** D12
Portsmouth *Ohio, U.S.A.* 38°44N 82°57W **112** F6
Portsmouth *Va., U.S.A.* 36°58N 76°23W **111** C11
Portsoy *U.K.* 57°41N 2°41W **19** G12
Portstewart *U.K.* 55°11N 6°43W **29** A8
Porttipahdan tekojärvi *Finland* 68°5N 26°40E **63** D9
Portugal ■ *Europe* 40°0N 8°0W **69** C1
Portumna *Ireland* 53°6N 8°14W **30** B6
Posadas *Argentina* 27°30S 55°50W **121** E4
Posse *Brazil* 14°4S 46°18W **122** B1
Postmasburg *S. Africa* 28°18S 23°5E **97** K4
Potchefstroom *S. Africa* 26°41S 27°7E **97** K5
Potenza *Italy* 40°38N 15°48E **70** D6
Poti *Georgia* 42°10N 41°38E **73** F7
Potiskum *Nigeria* 11°39N 11°2E **95** F8
Potomac → *U.S.A.* 38°0N 76°23W **112** F9
Potosí *Bolivia* 19°38S 65°50W **120** D3
Potsdam *Germany* 52°23N 13°3E **66** B7
Potsdam *U.S.A.* 44°40N 74°59W **113** C10
Potter Heigham *U.K.* 52°42N 1°34E **25** A12
Potterne *U.K.* 51°20N 2°0W **24** D4
Potters Bar *U.K.* 51°42N 0°11W **25** C8
Potterspury *U.K.* 52°5N 0°52W **25** B7
Pottstown *U.S.A.* 40°15N 75°39W **113** E10
Pottsville *U.S.A.* 40°41N 76°12W **113** E9
Pottuvil *Sri Lanka* 6°55N 81°50E **84** R12
Poughkeepsie *U.S.A.* 41°42N 73°56W **113** E11
Poulaphouca Res. *Ireland* 53°8N 6°30W **31** B10
Poulton-le-Fylde *U.K.* 53°51N 2°58W **23** E3
Poundstock *U.K.* 50°44N 4°36W **27** F4
Pouso Alegre *Brazil* 22°14S 45°57W **122** D1
Powder → *U.S.A.* 46°45N 105°26W **110** A5
Powell, L. *U.S.A.* 36°57N 111°29W **110** C4
Powell River *Canada* 49°50N 124°35W **108** E7
Powers *U.S.A.* 45°41N 87°32W **112** C4
Powick *U.K.* 52°10N 2°14W **24** B4
Powys □ *U.K.* 52°20N 3°20W **26** C7
Poyang Hu *China* 29°5N 116°20E **81** D6
Poza Rica *Mexico* 20°33N 97°27W **114** C5
Poznań *Poland* 52°25N 16°55E **67** B9
Pozzuoli *Italy* 40°49N 14°7E **70** D6
Prado *Brazil* 17°20S 39°13W **122** C3
Prague *Czech Rep.* 50°4N 14°25E **66** C8
Praia *C. Verde Is.* 15°2N 23°34W **91** E1
Prairie du Chien *U.S.A.* 43°3N 91°9W **112** D2
Prata *Brazil* 19°25S 48°54W **122** C1
Prato *Italy* 43°53N 11°6E **70** C4
Pratt *U.S.A.* 37°39N 98°44W **110** C7
Prawle Pt. *U.K.* 50°12N 3°44W **27** G6
Praya *Indonesia* 8°39S 116°17E **83** D3
Prees *U.K.* 52°54N 2°40W **23** G3
Preesall *U.K.* 53°55N 2°57W **23** E3
Prescott *Canada* 44°45N 75°30W **113** C10
Prescott *U.S.A.* 34°33N 112°28W **110** D4
Presidencia Roque Saenz Peña *Argentina* 26°45S 60°30W **121** E3
Presidente Prudente *Brazil* 22°5S 51°25W **120** E4
Presidio *U.S.A.* 29°34N 104°22W **110** E6
Prespa, L. *Macedonia* 40°55N 21°0E **71** D9
Presque Isle *U.S.A.* 46°41N 68°1W **113** B13
Prestatyn *U.K.* 53°20N 3°24W **26** A7
Prestbury *U.K.* 51°54N 2°2W **24** C4
Presteigne *U.K.* 52°17N 3°0W **26** C7
Preston *Borders, U.K.* 55°49N 2°19W **21** C11
Preston *Dorset, U.K.* 50°38N 2°26W **24** E4
Preston *Lancs., U.K.* 53°46N 2°42W **23** E3
Preston *U.S.A.* 42°6N 111°53W **110** B4
Prestonpans *U.K.* 55°58N 2°58W **21** C10
Prestwich *U.K.* 53°32N 2°17W **23** E4
Prestwick *U.K.* 55°29N 4°37W **20** D6
Pretoria *S. Africa* 25°44S 28°12E **97** K5
Pribilof Is. *U.S.A.* 57°0N 170°0W **108** D2
Price *U.S.A.* 39°36N 110°49W **110** C4
Prieska *S. Africa* 29°40S 22°42E **97** K4
Prilep *Macedonia* 41°21N 21°32E **71** D9
Prince Albert *Canada* 53°15N 105°50W **108** D9
Prince Albert Pen. *Canada* 72°30N 116°0W **108** B8
Prince Albert Sd. *Canada* 70°25N 115°0W **108** B8
Prince Alfred, C. *Canada* 74°20N 124°40W **109** B7
Prince Charles I. *Canada* 67°47N 76°12W **109** C12
Prince Charles Mts. *Antarctica* 72°0S 67°0E **55** D6
Prince Edward I. □ *Canada* 46°20N 63°20W **113** B16
Prince Edward Is. *Ind. Oc.* 46°35S 38°0E **53** G11
Prince George *Canada* 53°55N 122°50W **108** D7
Prince Gustaf Adolf Sea *Canada* 78°30N 107°0W **109** B9
Prince of Wales I. *Canada* 73°0N 99°0W **108** B10
Prince of Wales I. *U.S.A.* 55°47N 132°50W **108** D6
Prince Patrick I. *Canada* 77°0N 120°0W **109** B8
Prince Rupert *Canada* 54°20N 130°20W **108** D6
Princes Risborough *U.K.* 51°43N 0°49W **25** C7
Princeton *Ill., U.S.A.* 41°23N 89°28W **112** E3
Princeton *Ind., U.S.A.* 38°21N 87°34W **112** F4
Princeton *Ky., U.S.A.* 37°7N 87°53W **112** G4
Princeton *W. Va., U.S.A.* 37°22N 81°6W **112** G7
Princetown *U.K.* 50°33N 4°0W **27** F5
Príncipe, I. de *Atl. Oc.* 1°37N 7°27E **90** F4
Pripet → *Europe* 51°20N 30°15E **67** C16
Pripet Marshes *Europe* 52°10N 28°10E **67** B15
Priština *Kosovo* 42°40N 21°13E **71** C9
Privas *France* 44°45N 4°37E **68** D6
Prizren *Kosovo* 42°13N 20°45E **71** C9
Probolinggo *Indonesia* 7°46S 113°13E **83** D3
Probus *U.K.* 50°17N 4°58W **27** G4
Progreso *Mexico* 21°20N 89°40W **114** C7
Prome *Burma* 18°49N 95°13E **85** K19
Propriá *Brazil* 10°13S 36°51W **122** B3
Provence *France* 43°40N 5°46E **68** E6
Providence *U.S.A.* 41°49N 71°24W **113** E12
Providencia, I. de *Colombia* 13°25N 81°26W **115** E8
Provins *France* 48°33N 3°15E **68** B5
Provo *U.S.A.* 40°14N 111°39W **110** B4
Prudhoe *U.K.* 54°57N 1°52W **22** C5
Prudhoe Bay *U.S.A.* 70°18N 148°22W **108** B5
Pruszków *Poland* 52°9N 20°49E **67** B11
Prut → *Romania* 45°28N 28°10E **67** F15
Pryluky *Ukraine* 50°30N 32°24E **73** D5
Przemyśl *Poland* 49°50N 22°45E **67** D12
Pskov *Russia* 57°50N 28°25E **72** C4
Puddletown *U.K.* 50°44N 2°20W **24** E4
Pudsey *U.K.* 53°47N 1°40W **23** E5
Puebla *Mexico* 19°3N 98°12W **114** D5
Pueblo *U.S.A.* 38°16N 104°37W **110** C6
Puerca, Pta. *Puerto Rico* 18°13N 65°36W **115** d
Puerto Aisén *Chile* 45°27S 73°0W **121** G2
Puerto Barrios *Guatemala* 15°40N 88°32W **114** D7
Puerto Cabello *Venezuela* 10°28N 68°1W **120** A3
Puerto Cabezas *Nic.* 14°0N 83°30W **115** E8
Puerto Carreño *Colombia* 6°12N 67°22W **120** B3
Puerto Cortés *Honduras* 15°51N 88°0W **114** D7
Puerto Deseado *Argentina* 47°55S 66°0W **121** G3
Puerto La Cruz *Venezuela* 10°13N 64°38W **120** A3
Puerto Madryn *Argentina* 42°48S 65°4W **121** G3
Puerto Maldonado *Peru* 12°30S 69°10W **120** D3
Puerto Montt *Chile* 41°28S 73°0W **121** G2
Puerto Plata *Dom. Rep.* 19°48N 70°45W **115** D10
Puerto Princesa *Phil.* 9°46N 118°45E **83** C3
Puerto Rico □ *W. Indies* 18°15N 66°45W **115** d
Puerto San Julián *Argentina* 49°18S 67°43W **121** G3
Puerto Suárez *Bolivia* 18°58S 57°52W **120** D4
Puerto Wilches *Colombia* 7°21N 73°54W **120** B2
Puertollano *Spain* 38°43N 4°7W **69** C3
Puffin I. *Ireland* 51°50N 10°24W **30** E2
Puget Sound *U.S.A.* 47°50N 122°30W **110** A2
Pukapuka *Cook Is.* 10°53S 165°49W **103** J11
Pula *Croatia* 44°54N 13°57E **70** B5
Pulacayo *Bolivia* 20°25S 66°41W **120** E3
Pulaski *U.S.A.* 37°3N 80°47W **111** C10
Pulborough *U.K.* 50°58N 0°30W **25** E8
Pulham Market *U.K.* 52°26N 1°13E **25** B11
Pulham St. Mary *U.K.* 52°26N 1°16E **25** B11
Pullman *U.S.A.* 46°44N 117°10W **110** A3
Pumlumon Fawr *U.K.* 52°28N 3°46W **26** C6
Pune *India* 18°29N 73°57E **84** K8
Punjab □ *India* 31°0N 76°0E **84** D10
Punjab □ *Pakistan* 32°0N 72°30E **84** E9
Puno *Peru* 15°55S 70°3W **120** D2
Punta, Cerro de *Puerto Rico* 18°10N 66°37W **115** d
Punta Arenas *Chile* 53°10S 71°0W **121** H2
Punxsatawney *U.S.A.* 40°57N 78°59W **112** E8
Purbeck, Isle of *U.K.* 50°39N 1°59W **24** E5
Purfleet *U.K.* 51°29N 0°16E **25** D9
Puri *India* 19°50N 85°58E **85** K14
Purley on Thames *U.K.* 51°29N 1°3W **24** D6
Purnia *India* 25°45N 87°31E **85** G15
Puruliya *India* 23°17N 86°24E **85** H15
Purus → *Brazil* 3°42S 61°28W **120** C3
Putian *China* 25°23N 119°0E **81** D6
Putorana *Russia* 69°0N 95°0E **79** C11
Puttalam *Sri Lanka* 8°1N 79°55E **84** Q11
Putumayo → *S. Amer.* 3°7S 67°58W **120** C3
Puvirnituq *Canada* 60°2N 77°10W **109** C12
Puy-de-Dôme *France* 45°46N 2°57E **68** D5
Pwllheli *U.K.* 52°53N 4°25W **26** B5
Pyatigorsk *Russia* 44°2N 43°6E **73** F7
Pyinmana *Burma* 19°45N 96°12E **85** K20
P'yŏngyang *N. Korea* 39°0N 125°30E **81** C7
Pyramid L. *U.S.A.* 40°1N 119°35W **110** C3
Pyrénées *Europe* 42°45N 0°18E **68** E4

Q

Qaanaaq *Greenland* 77°40N 69°0W **54** B4
Qā'emshahr *Iran* 36°30N 52°53E **87** B8
Qaidam Basin *China* 37°0N 95°0E **80** C4
Qandahār *Afghan.* 31°32N 65°43E **87** D11
Qaqortoq *Greenland* 60°43N 46°0W **54** C5
Qarqan He → *China* 39°30N 88°30E **80** C3
Qarshi *Uzbekistan* 38°53N 65°48E **87** B11
Qatar ■ *Asia* 25°30N 51°15E **87** E7
Qattâra Depression *Egypt* 29°30N 27°30E **95** C11
Qazvīn *Iran* 36°15N 50°0E **86** B7
Qena *Egypt* 26°10N 32°43E **95** C12
Qeqertarsuaq *Greenland* 69°15N 53°38W **54** C5
Qeshm *Iran* 26°55N 56°10E **87** E9
Qiemo *China* 38°8N 85°32E **80** C3
Qijiaojing *China* 43°28N 91°36E **80** B4
Qikiqtarjuaq *Canada* 67°33N 63°0W **109** C13
Qilian Shan *China* 38°30N 96°0E **80** C4
Qingdao *China* 36°5N 120°20E **81** C7
Qinghai □ *China* 36°0N 98°0E **80** C4
Qinghai Hu *China* 36°40N 100°10E **80** C5
Qinhuangdao *China* 39°56N 119°30E **81** C6
Qinzhou *China* 21°58N 108°38E **80** D5
Qiqihar *China* 47°26N 124°0E **81** B7
Qira *China* 37°0N 80°48E **80** C3
Qitai *China* 44°2N 89°35E **80** B3
Qom *Iran* 34°40N 51°0E **87** C7
Qondūz *Afghan.* 36°50N 68°50E **87** B12
Quadring *U.K.* 52°54N 0°10W **23** G8
Quang Ngai *Vietnam* 15°13N 108°58E **83** B2
Quantock Hills *U.K.* 51°8N 3°10W **24** D2
Quanzhou *China* 24°55N 118°34E **81** D6
Quaqtaq *Canada* 60°55N 69°40W **109** C13
Quartu Sant'Élena *Italy* 39°15N 9°10E **70** E3
Québec *Canada* 46°52N 71°13W **113** B12
Québec □ *Canada* 48°0N 74°0W **109** E12
Queen Charlotte Is. *Canada* 53°20N 132°10W **108** D6
Queen Charlotte Sd. *Canada* 51°0N 128°0W **108** D7
Queen Elizabeth Is. *Canada* 76°0N 95°0W **109** B10
Queen Maud G. *Canada* 68°15N 102°30W **108** C9
Queenborough *U.K.* 51°25N 0°46E **25** D10
Queensbury *U.K.* 53°46N 1°50W **23** E5
Queensland □ *Australia* 22°0S 142°0E **98** E7
Queenstown *N.Z.* 45°1S 168°40E **99** K12
Queenstown *S. Africa* 31°52S 26°52E **97** L5
Queimadas *Brazil* 11°0S 39°38W **122** B3
Quelimane *Mozam.* 17°53S 36°58E **97** H7
Quendale, B. of *U.K.* 59°53N 1°20W **18** C15
Querétaro *Mexico* 20°36N 100°23W **114** C4
Quesnel *Canada* 53°0N 122°30W **108** D7
Quesnel L. *Canada* 52°30N 121°20W **108** D7
Quetta *Pakistan* 30°15N 66°55E **84** D5
Quezaltenango *Guatemala* 14°50N 91°30W **114** E6
Quezon City *Phil.* 14°37N 121°2E **83** B4
Qui Nhon *Vietnam* 13°40N 109°13E **83** B2
Quibdo *Colombia* 5°42N 76°40W **120** B2
Quilán, C. *Chile* 43°15S 74°30W **121** G2
Quilon *India* 8°50N 76°38E **84** Q10
Quilpie *Australia* 26°35S 144°11E **98** F7
Quimper *France* 48°0N 4°9W **68** B1
Quincy *Ill., U.S.A.* 39°56N 91°23W **111** C81
Quincy *Mass., U.S.A.* 42°14N 71°0W **113** D12
Quinte West *Canada* 44°10N 77°34W **112** C9
Quito *Ecuador* 0°15S 78°35W **120** C2
Qŭnghirot *Uzbekistan* 43°2N 58°50E **87** A9
Quorndon *U.K.* 52°46N 1°10W **23** G6
Qŭqon *Uzbekistan* 40°31N 70°56E **87** A12
Quseir *Egypt* 26°7N 34°16E **95** C12
Quzhou *China* 28°57N 118°54E **81** D6

R

Raahe *Finland* 64°40N 24°28E **63** E8
Raasay *U.K.* 57°25N 6°4W **18** H5
Raasay, Sd. of *U.K.* 57°30N 6°8W **18** H5
Raba *Indonesia* 8°36S 118°55E **83** D3
Rabat *Morocco* 34°2N 6°48W **94** B4
Rābigh *Si. Arabia* 22°50N 39°5E **88** C2
Race, C. *Canada* 46°40N 53°5W **109** E14
Rach Gia *Vietnam* 10°5N 105°5E **83** B2
Racine *U.S.A.* 42°44N 87°47W **112** D4
Rackheath *U.K.* 52°40N 1°22E **25** A11
Radcliffe *U.K.* 53°34N 2°18W **23** E4
Radcliffe-on-Trent *U.K.* 52°57N 1°2W **23** G6
Radford *U.S.A.* 37°8N 80°34W **112** G7
Radley *U.K.* 51°41N 1°14W **24** C6
Radnor Forest *U.K.* 52°17N 3°10W **26** C7
Radom *Poland* 51°23N 21°12E **67** C11
Radstock *U.K.* 51°17N 2°26W **24** D4
Rae *Canada* 62°50N 116°3W **108** C8
Rae Bareli *India* 26°18N 81°20E **85** F12
Rae Isthmus *Canada* 66°40N 87°30W **109** C11
Rafaela *Argentina* 31°10S 61°30W **121** F3
Rafsanjān *Iran* 30°30N 56°5E **87** D9
Ragusa *Italy* 36°55N 14°44E **70** F6
Rahimyar Khan *Pakistan* 28°30N 70°25E **84** E7
Raichur *India* 16°10N 77°20E **84** L10
Raigarh *India* 21°56N 83°25E **85** J13
Rainbow Lake *Canada* 58°30N 119°23W **108** D8
Rainham *U.K.* 51°22N 0°37E **25** D10
Rainier, Mt. *U.S.A.* 46°52N 121°46W **110** A2
Rainworth *U.K.* 53°7N 1°7W **23** F6
Rainy L. *Canada* 48°42N 93°10W **108** E10
Raipur *India* 21°17N 81°45E **85** J12
Raj Nandgaon *India* 21°5N 81°5E **85** J12
Rajahmundry *India* 17°1N 81°48E **85** L12
Rajapalaiyam *India* 9°25N 77°35E **84** Q10
Rajasthan □ *India* 26°45N 73°30E **84** F8
Rajkot *India* 22°15N 70°56E **84** H7
Rajshahi *Bangla.* 24°22N 88°39E **85** G16
Rajshahi □ *Bangla.* 25°0N 89°0E **85** G16
Raleigh *U.S.A.* 35°47N 78°39W **111** C11
Rame Head *U.K.* 50°19N 4°13W **27** G5
Ramgarh *India* 23°40N 85°35E **85** H14
Ramna Stacks *U.K.* 60°35N 1°24W **18** A15
Râmnicu Vâlcea *Romania* 45°9N 24°21E **67** F13
Rampside *U.K.* 54°6N 3°9W **22** D2
Rampur *India* 28°50N 79°5E **84** E11
Ramree I. *Burma* 19°0N 93°40E **85** K19
Ramsbottom *U.K.* 53°38N 2°19W **23** E4
Ramsbury *U.K.* 51°26N 1°36W **24** D5
Ramsey *I. of Man* 54°20N 4°22W **29** C13
Ramsey *Cambs., U.K.* 52°27N 0°7W **25** B8
Ramsey *Essex, U.K.* 51°55N 1°13E **25** C11
Ramsgate *U.K.* 51°20N 1°25E **25** D11
Rancagua *Chile* 34°10S 70°50W **121** F2
Ranchi *India* 23°19N 85°27E **85** H14
Randalstown *U.K.* 54°45N 6°19W **29** B9
Randers *Denmark* 56°29N 10°1E **63** F6
Rangoon *Burma* 16°45N 96°20E **85** L20
Rangpur *Bangla.* 25°42N 89°22E **85** G16
Rankin Inlet *Canada* 62°30N 93°0W **108** C10
Rannoch *U.K.* 56°40N 4°20W **19** J9
Rannoch, L. *U.K.* 56°41N 4°20W **19** J9
Rannoch Moor *U.K.* 56°38N 4°48W **19** J8
Rantoul *U.S.A.* 40°19N 88°9W **112** E3
Rapa *French Polynesia* 27°35S 144°20W **103** K13
Rapallo *Italy* 44°21N 9°14E **70** B3
Raper, C. *Canada* 69°44N 67°6W **109** C13
Rapid City *U.S.A.* 44°5N 103°14W **110** B6
Rarotonga *Cook Is.* 21°30S 160°0W **103** K12
Ra's al Khaymah *U.A.E.* 25°50N 55°59E **87** E9
Rasht *Iran* 37°20N 49°40E **86** B7
Rat Islands *U.S.A.* 52°0N 178°0E **108** D1
Ratangarh *India* 28°5N 74°35E **84** E9
Rath Luirc *Ireland* 52°21N 8°40W **30** D5
Rathcoole *Ireland* 53°17N 6°29W **31** B10
Rathdrum *Ireland* 52°56N 6°14W **31** C10
Rathkeale *Ireland* 52°32N 8°56W **30** C5
Rathlin I. *U.K.* 55°18N 6°14W **29** A9
Rathmelton *Ireland* 55°2N 7°38W **28** A6
Ratlam *India* 23°20N 75°0E **84** H9
Ratnagiri *India* 16°57N 73°18E **84** L8
Raton *U.S.A.* 36°54N 104°24W **110** C6
Rattray Hd. *U.K.* 57°38N 1°50W **19** G14
Rauma *Finland* 61°10N 21°30E **63** E8
Raunds *U.K.* 52°21N 0°32W **25** B7
Raurkela *India* 22°14N 84°50E **85** H14
Ravenglass *U.K.* 54°22N 3°24W **22** D2
Ravenna *Italy* 44°25N 12°12E **70** B5
Ravenstonedale *U.K.* 54°26N 2°25W **22** D4
Ravi → *Pakistan* 30°35N 71°49E **84** D7
Rawalpindi *Pakistan* 33°38N 73°8E **84** C8
Rawāndūz *Iraq* 36°40N 44°30E **86** B6
Rawlins *U.S.A.* 41°47N 107°14W **110** B5
Rawmarsh *U.K.* 53°27N 1°21W **23** F6
Rawson *Argentina* 43°15S 65°5W **121** G3
Rawtenstall *U.K.* 53°42N 2°17W **23** E4
Ray, C. *Canada* 47°33N 59°15W **109** E14
Rayleigh *U.K.* 51°36N 0°37E **25** C10
Rayong *Thailand* 12°40N 101°20E **83** B2
Raz, Pte. du *France* 48°2N 4°47W **68** C1
Razazah, L. *Iraq* 32°40N 43°35E **86** C5
Ré, Î. de *France* 46°12N 1°30W **68** C3
Reading *U.K.* 51°27N 0°58W **25** D7
Reading *U.S.A.* 40°20N 75°56W **113** E10
Reay Forest *U.K.* 58°22N 4°55W **19** F8
Rebiana Desert *Libya* 24°30N 21°0E **95** D10
Recife *Brazil* 8°0S 35°0W **122** A3
Reconquista *Argentina* 29°10S 59°45W **121** E4
Red → *U.S.A.* 31°1N 91°45W **111** D8
Red Bluff *U.S.A.* 40°11N 122°15W **110** B2
Red Deer *Canada* 52°20N 113°50W **108** D8
Red Dial *U.K.* 54°49N 3°10W **22** C2
Red L. *U.S.A.* 48°8N 94°45W **111** A8
Red Lake *Canada* 51°3N 93°49W **108** D10
Red Oak *U.S.A.* 41°1N 95°14W **111** B7
Red River of the North → *N. Amer.* 49°0N 97°15W **108** D10
Red Sea *Asia* 25°0N 36°0E **88** C2
Red Wing *U.S.A.* 44°34N 92°31W **111** B81
Redbridge □ *U.K.* 51°35N 0°7E **25** C9
Redcar *U.K.* 54°37N 1°4W **22** C6
Redding *U.S.A.* 40°35N 122°24W **110** B2
Redditch *U.K.* 52°18N 1°55W **24** B5
Rede → *U.K.* 55°9N 2°13W **22** B4
Redesmouth *U.K.* 55°8N 2°13W **22** B4
Redhill *U.K.* 51°14N 0°9W **25** D8
Redlynch *U.K.* 50°59N 1°41W **24** E5
Redmile *U.K.* 52°55N 0°48W **23** G7
Redmire *U.K.* 54°19N 1°55W **22** D5
Redon *France* 47°40N 2°6W **68** C2
Redruth *U.K.* 50°14N 5°14W **27** G3
Ree, L. *Ireland* 53°35N 8°0W **28** D6
Reedham *U.K.* 52°34N 1°34E **25** A12
Reepham *U.K.* 52°46N 1°6E **25** A11
Reese → *U.S.A.* 40°48N 117°4W **110** B3
Reeth *U.K.* 54°23N 1°56W **22** D5
Regensburg *Germany* 49°1N 12°6E **66** D7
Réggio di Calábria *Italy* 38°6N 15°39E **70** E6
Réggio nell'Emilia *Italy* 44°43N 10°36E **70** B4
Regina *Canada* 50°27N 104°35W **108** D9
Reichenbach *Germany* 50°37N 12°17E **66** C7
Reigate *U.K.* 51°14N 0°12W **25** D8
Reims *France* 49°15N 4°1E **68** B6
Reina Adelaida, Arch. *Chile* 52°20S 74°0W **121** H2
Reindeer L. *Canada* 57°15N 102°15W **108** D9
Remscheid *Germany* 51°11N 7°12E **65** C7
Renfrew *Canada* 45°30N 76°40W **112** C9
Renfrew *U.K.* 55°52N 4°24W **20** C7
Rennell *Solomon Is.* 11°40S 160°10E **99** C11
Rennes *France* 48°7N 1°41W **68** B3
Reno *U.S.A.* 39°31N 119°48W **110** C3
Repton *U.K.* 52°50N 1°33W **23** G5
Republican → *U.S.A.* 39°4N 96°48W **111** C7
Repulse Bay *Canada* 66°30N 86°30W **109** C11
Resistencia *Argentina* 27°30S 59°0W **121** E4
Resolute *Canada* 74°42N 94°54W **109** B10
Resolution I. *Canada* 61°30N 65°0W **109** C13
Reston *U.K.* 55°51N 2°10W **21** C11
Retford *U.K.* 53°19N 0°56W **23** F7
Rethimno *Greece* 35°18N 24°30E **71** G11
Réunion □ *Ind. Oc.* 21°0S 56°0E **91** J9
Reus *Spain* 41°10N 1°5E **69** B6
Reutlingen *Germany* 48°29N 9°12E **66** D5
Revda *Russia* 56°48N 59°57E **72** C10
Revelstoke *Canada* 51°0N 118°10W **108** D8
Revillagigedo, Is. de *Pac. Oc.* 18°40N 112°0W **114** D2
Rewa *India* 24°33N 81°25E **85** G12
Rexburg *U.S.A.* 43°49N 111°47W **110** B4
Rey Malabo *Eq. Guin.* 3°45N 8°50E **96** D1
Reykjavík *Iceland* 64°10N 21°57W **63** B1
Reynosa *Mexico* 26°7N 98°18W **114** B5
Rēzekne *Latvia* 56°30N 27°17E **63** F9
Rhayader *U.K.* 52°18N 3°29W **26** C7
Rheidol → *U.K.* 52°25N 4°5W **26** C5
Rheine *Germany* 52°17N 7°26E **66** B4
Rheinland-Pfalz □ *Germany* 50°0N 7°0E **66** C4
Rhine → *Europe* 51°52N 6°2E **65** C6
Rhinelander *U.S.A.* 45°38N 89°25W **112** C3
Rhinns Pt. *U.K.* 55°40N 6°29W **20** C3
Rhins, The *U.K.* 54°52N 5°3W **20** E5
Rhode Island □ *U.S.A.* 41°40N 71°30W **113** E12
Rhodes *Greece* 36°15N 28°10E **71** F13

Rhodope Mts. Bulgaria 41°40N 24°20E 71 D11
Rhondda U.K. 51°39N 3°31W 26 D6
Rhône → France 43°28N 4°42E 68 E6
Rhosllanerchrugog U.K. 53°1N 3°3W 26 A7
Rhossili U.K. 51°34N 4°17W 27 D5
Rhossili B. U.K. 51°32N 4°14W 27 D5
Rhum U.K. 57°0N 6°20W 18 J5
Rhum, Sound of U.K. 56°55N 6°14W 18 J5
Rhyl U.K. 53°20N 3°29W 26 A7
Rhymney U.K. 51°46N 3°17W 26 D7
Riau, Kepulauan Indonesia 0°30N 104°20E 83 C2
Ribble → U.K. 53°52N 2°25W 23 E4
Ribeirão Prêto Brazil 21°10S 47°50W 122 D1
Riberalta Bolivia 11°0S 66°0W 120 D3
Riccall U.K. 53°50N 1°3W 23 E6
Rice Lake U.S.A. 45°30N 91°44W 112 C2
Richards Bay S. Africa 28°48S 32°6E 97 K6
Richfield U.S.A. 38°46N 112°5W 110 C4
Richland U.S.A. 46°17N 119°18W 110 A3
Richland Center U.S.A. 43°21N 90°23W 112 D2
Richlands U.S.A. 37°6N 81°48W 112 G7
Richmond U.K. 54°25N 1°43W 22 D5
Richmond Ind., U.S.A. 39°50N 84°53W 112 F5
Richmond Ky., U.S.A. 37°45N 84°18W 112 G5
Richmond Va., U.S.A. 37°33N 77°27W 112 G9
Richmond-upon-Thames □ U.K. 51°27N 0°17W 25 D8
Rickmansworth U.K. 51°38N 0°29W 25 C8
Ridgecrest U.S.A. 35°38N 117°40W 110 C3
Ridgway U.S.A. 41°25N 78°44W 112 E8
Ridsdale U.K. 55°9N 2°9W 22 B4
Rievaulx U.K. 54°16N 1°7W 22 D6
Rift Valley Africa 7°0N 30°0E 90 G7
Rīga Latvia 56°53N 24°8E 63 F8
Riga, G. of Latvia 57°40N 23°45E 63 F8
Rīgestān Afghan. 30°15N 65°0E 87 D11
Rigolet Canada 54°10N 58°23W 109 D14
Rijeka Croatia 45°20N 14°21E 70 B6
Rillington U.K. 54°9N 0°42W 22 D7
Rimini Italy 44°3N 12°33E 70 B5
Rimouski Canada 48°27N 68°30W 109 E13
Ringmer U.K. 50°53N 0°5E 25 E9
Ringwood U.K. 50°50N 1°47W 24 E5
Rio Branco Brazil 9°58S 67°49W 120 C3
Rio Claro Brazil 22°19S 47°35W 122 D1
Río Cuarto Argentina 33°10S 64°25W 121 F3
Rio de Janeiro Brazil 22°54S 43°12W 122 D2
Rio de Janeiro □ Brazil 22°50S 43°0W 122 D2
Río Gallegos Argentina 51°35S 69°15W 121 H3
Rio Grande Brazil 32°0S 52°20W 121 F4
Río Grande Nic. 12°54N 83°33W 115 E8
Río Grande Puerto Rico 18°23N 65°50W 115 d
Rio Grande → N. Amer. 25°58N 97°9W 111 E7
Rio Grande de Santiago → Mexico 21°36N 105°26W 114 C3
Rio Grande do Norte □ Brazil 5°40S 36°0W 120 C6
Rio Grande do Sul □ Brazil 30°0S 53°0W 121 E4
Rio Largo Brazil 9°28S 35°50W 122 A3
Río Muni □ Eq. Guin. 1°30N 10°0E 96 D2
Riohacha Colombia 11°33N 72°55W 120 A2
Ripley Derby, U.K. 53°3N 1°24W 23 F6
Ripley N. Yorks., U.K. 54°3N 1°34W 22 D5
Ripon U.K. 54°9N 1°31W 22 D5
Ripon U.S.A. 43°51N 88°50W 112 D3
Risca U.K. 51°37N 3°5W 27 D7
Rishton U.K. 53°46N 2°26W 23 E4
Rivera Uruguay 31°0S 55°50W 121 F4
Riverhead U.S.A. 40°55N 72°40W 113 E11
Riverside U.S.A. 33°59N 117°22W 110 D3
Riverton U.S.A. 43°2N 108°23W 110 B5
Rivière-du-Loup Canada 47°50N 69°30W 109 E13
Rivière-Pilote Martinique 14°26N 60°53W 114 c
Rivière-Salée Martinique 14°31N 61°0W 114 c
Rivne Ukraine 50°40N 26°10E 67 C14
Riyadh Si. Arabia 24°41N 46°42E 86 E6
Rize Turkey 41°0N 40°30E 73 F7
Rizhao China 35°25N 119°30E 81 C6
Road Town Br. Virgin Is. 18°27N 64°37W 115 e
Roade U.K. 52°9N 0°53W 25 B7
Roanne France 46°3N 4°4E 68 C6
Roanoke U.S.A. 37°16N 79°56W 112 G8
Roanoke → U.S.A. 35°57N 76°42W 111 C11
Roberton U.K. 55°25N 2°54W 21 D10
Roberval Canada 48°32N 72°15W 109 E12
Robin Hood's Bay U.K. 54°27N 0°32W 22 D7
Robson, Mt. Canada 53°10N 119°10W 108 D8
Roca, C. da Portugal 38°40N 9°31W 69 C1
Rocester U.K. 52°57N 1°50W 23 G5
Rocha Uruguay 34°30S 54°25W 121 F4
Rochdale U.K. 53°38N 2°9W 23 E4
Roche U.K. 50°24N 4°50W 27 G4
Rochefort France 45°56N 0°57W 68 D3
Rochester Medway, U.K. 51°23N 0°31E 25 D10
Rochester Northumberland, U.K. 55°17N 2°17W 22 B4
Rochester Ind., U.S.A. 41°4N 86°13W 112 E4
Rochester Minn., U.S.A. 44°1N 92°28W 111 B81
Rochester N.H., U.S.A. 43°18N 70°59W 113 D12
Rochester N.Y., U.S.A. 43°10N 77°37W 112 D9
Rochford U.K. 51°34N 0°43E 25 C10
Rock Hill U.S.A. 34°56N 81°1W 111 D10
Rock Island U.S.A. 41°30N 90°34W 112 E2
Rock Springs U.S.A. 41°35N 109°14W 110 B5
Rockall Atl. Oc. 57°37N 13°42W 56 D3
Rockcliffe U.K. 54°57N 3°0W 22 C3
Rockford U.S.A. 42°16N 89°6W 112 D3
Rockhampton Australia 23°22S 150°32E 98 E9
Rockingham U.K. 52°31N 0°43W 25 A7
Rockingham Forest U.K. 52°29N 0°42W 25 B7
Rockland U.S.A. 44°6N 69°7W 113 C13
Rocky Mount U.S.A. 35°57N 77°48W 111 C11
Rocky Mts. N. Amer. 49°0N 115°0W 108 D7
Rodez France 44°21N 2°33E 68 D5
Roding → U.K. 51°31N 0°6E 25 C9
Rodriguez Ind. Oc. 19°45S 63°20E 53 E13
Roe → U.K. 55°6N 6°59W 29 A8
Roermond Neths. 51°12N 6°0E 65 C6
Roes Welcome Sd. Canada 65°0N 87°0W 109 C11
Roeselare Belgium 50°57N 3°7E 65 D3
Rogans Seat U.K. 54°26N 2°7W 22 D4
Rogate U.K. 51°0N 0°50W 25 D7
Rogers City U.S.A. 45°25N 83°49W 112 C6
Rohri Pakistan 27°45N 68°51E 84 F6
Rojo, C. Mexico 21°33N 97°20W 114 C5
Rolla U.S.A. 37°57N 91°46W 111 C81
Roma Australia 26°32S 148°49E 98 F8
Romaine → Canada 50°18N 63°47W 109 D13
Romania ■ Europe 46°0N 25°0E 67 F12
Romans-sur-Isère France 45°3N 5°3E 68 D6
Rome Italy 41°54N 12°28E 70 D5
Rome Ga., U.S.A. 34°15N 85°10W 111 D9
Rome N.Y., U.S.A. 43°13N 75°27W 113 D10
Romney U.S.A. 39°21N 78°45W 112 F8
Romney Marsh U.K. 51°2N 0°54E 25 D10
Romorantin-Lanthenay France 47°21N 1°45E 68 C4
Romsey U.K. 51°0N 1°29W 24 E6
Rona U.K. 57°34N 5°59W 18 G6
Roncador, Serra do Brazil 12°30S 52°30W 120 D4
Rondônia □ Brazil 11°0S 63°0W 120 D3
Rondonópolis Brazil 16°28S 54°38W 120 D4
Ronge, L. la Canada 55°6N 105°17W 108 D9
Ronne Ice Shelf Antarctica 77°30S 60°0W 55 D18
Ronse Belgium 50°45N 3°35E 65 D3
Roosendaal Neths. 51°32N 4°29E 65 C4
Roosevelt → Brazil 7°35S 60°20W 120 C3
Roosevelt I. Antarctica 79°30S 162°0W 55 D12
Ropsley U.K. 52°54N 0°30W 23 G8
Roquetas de Mar Spain 36°46N 2°36W 69 D4
Roraima □ Brazil 2°0N 61°30W 120 B3
Roraima, Mt. Venezuela 5°10N 60°40W 120 B3
Rosario Argentina 33°0S 60°40W 121 F3
Rosario Mexico 22°58N 105°53W 114 C3
Rosario de la Frontera Argentina 25°50S 65°0W 121 E3
Roscommon Ireland 53°38N 8°11W 28 D5
Roscommon □ Ireland 53°49N 8°23W 28 D5
Roscrea Ireland 52°57N 7°49W 30 C7
Roseau Dominica 15°17N 61°24W 115 D12
Roseburg U.S.A. 43°13N 123°20W 110 B2
Rosedale Abbey U.K. 54°21N 0°52W 22 D7
Rosehearty U.K. 57°42N 2°7W 19 G13
Rosenheim Germany 47°51N 12°7E 66 E7
Rosetown Canada 51°35N 107°59W 108 D9
Roseville U.S.A. 38°45N 121°17W 110 C2
Roslavl Russia 53°57N 32°55E 72 D5
Ross Ice Shelf Antarctica 80°0S 180°0E 55 E12
Ross-on-Wye U.K. 51°54N 2°34W 24 C3
Ross River Canada 62°30N 131°30W 108 C6
Ross Sea Antarctica 74°0S 178°0E 55 D11
Rossall Pt. U.K. 53°55N 3°3W 23 E2
Rossan Pt. Ireland 54°42N 8°47W 28 B4
Rosses, The Ireland 55°2N 8°20W 28 A5
Rossignol L. Canada 44°12N 65°10W 113 C15
Rosslare Ireland 52°17N 6°24W 31 D10
Rosslare Harbour Ireland 52°15N 6°20W 31 D10
Rossosh Russia 50°15N 39°28E 73 D6
Rostock Germany 54°5N 12°8E 66 A7
Rostov Russia 47°15N 39°45E 73 E6
Roswell Ga., U.S.A. 34°2N 84°22W 111 D10
Roswell N. Mex., U.S.A. 33°24N 104°32W 110 D6
Rothbury U.K. 55°19N 1°58W 22 B5
Rothbury Forest U.K. 55°19N 1°50W 22 B5
Rother → U.K. 50°59N 0°45E 25 E10
Rotherham U.K. 53°26N 1°20W 23 F6
Rothes U.K. 57°32N 3°13W 19 G11
Rothesay U.K. 55°50N 5°3W 20 C5
Rothwell Northants., U.K. 52°25N 0°48W 25 B7
Rothwell W. Yorks., U.K. 53°45N 1°28W 23 E6
Roti Indonesia 10°50S 123°0E 83 E4
Rotorua N.Z. 38°9S 176°16E 99 H14
Rotterdam Neths. 51°55N 4°30E 65 C4
Rottingdean U.K. 50°48N 0°4W 25 E8
Rotuma Fiji 12°25S 177°5E 99 C14
Roubaix France 50°40N 3°10E 68 A5
Rouen France 49°27N 1°4E 68 B4
Round Mt. Australia 30°26S 152°16E 98 G9
Rousay U.K. 59°10N 3°2W 19 D11
Roussillon France 42°30N 2°35E 68 E5
Rouyn-Noranda Canada 48°20N 79°0W 109 E12
Rovaniemi Finland 66°29N 25°41E 63 D9
Rovigo Italy 45°4N 11°47E 70 B4
Rowanburn U.K. 55°5N 2°55W 21 D10
Roxas Phil. 11°36N 122°49E 83 B4
Roxburgh U.K. 55°35N 2°28W 21 C11
Roxby U.K. 53°38N 0°38W 23 E7
Royal Canal Ireland 53°30N 7°13W 31 B8
Royal Leamington Spa U.K. 52°18N 1°31W 24 B5
Royal Tunbridge Wells U.K. 51°7N 0°16E 25 D9
Royale, Isle U.S.A. 48°0N 88°54W 112 B3
Royan France 45°37N 1°2W 68 D3
Royston U.K. 52°3N 0°0 25 B8
Royton U.K. 53°34N 2°8W 23 E4
Rub' al Khālī Si. Arabia 19°0N 48°0E 88 D4
Rubery U.K. 52°24N 2°1W 24 B4
Rubh a' Mhail U.K. 55°56N 6°8W 20 C3
Rubha Hunish U.K. 57°42N 6°20W 18 G5
Ruby L. U.S.A. 40°10N 115°28W 110 B3
Rudston U.K. 54°6N 0°20W 22 D8
Ruffling Pt. Br. Virgin Is. 18°44N 64°27W 115 e
Rufford U.K. 53°38N 2°50W 23 E3
Rufiji → Tanzania 7°50S 39°15E 96 F7
Rugby U.K. 52°23N 1°16W 24 B6
Rugeley U.K. 52°46N 1°55W 23 G5
Rügen Germany 54°22N 13°24E 66 A7
Ruhr → Germany 51°27N 6°43E 66 C4
Ruki → Dem. Rep. of the Congo 0°5N 18°17E 96 E3
Rukwa, L. Tanzania 8°0S 32°20E 96 F6
Rumania = Romania ■ Europe 46°0N 25°0E 67 F12
Rumford U.S.A. 44°33N 70°33W 113 C12
Runaway Bay Jamaica 18°27N 77°20W 114 a
Runcorn U.K. 53°21N 2°44W 23 F3
Rundu Namibia 17°52S 19°43E 97 H3
Rungwe Tanzania 9°11S 33°32E 90 G7
Ruoqiang China 38°55N 88°10E 80 C3
Rupert U.S.A. 42°37N 113°41W 110 B4
Rupert → Canada 51°29N 78°45W 109 D12
Ruse Bulgaria 43°48N 25°59E 71 C12
Rush Ireland 53°31N 6°6W 31 A10
Rushden U.K. 52°18N 0°35W 25 B7
Rushville Ill., U.S.A. 40°7N 90°34W 112 E2
Rushville Ind., U.S.A. 39°37N 85°27W 112 F5
Ruskington U.K. 53°3N 0°22W 23 F8
Russellville U.S.A. 35°17N 93°8W 111 C8
Russia ■ Eurasia 62°0N 105°0E 79 C12
Rustavi Georgia 41°30N 45°0E 73 F8
Rustenburg S. Africa 25°41S 27°14E 97 K5
Rutherglen U.K. 55°49N 4°13W 20 C7
Ruthin U.K. 53°6N 3°19W 26 A7
Ruthwell U.K. 55°0N 3°25W 21 E9
Rutog China 33°27N 79°42E 80 C2
Ruvuma → Tanzania 10°29S 40°28E 96 G8
Ruwenzori Africa 0°30N 29°55E 96 D5
Rwanda ■ Africa 2°0S 30°0E 96 E5
Ryan, L. U.K. 55°0N 5°2W 20 E5
Ryazan Russia 54°40N 39°40E 72 D6
Rybachi Pen. Russia 69°43N 32°0E 72 A5
Rybinsk Russia 58°5N 38°50E 72 C6
Rybinsk Res. Russia 58°30N 38°25E 72 C6
Rydal U.K. 54°27N 2°59W 22 D3
Ryde U.K. 50°43N 1°9W 24 E6
Rye U.K. 50°57N 0°45E 25 E10
Rye → U.K. 54°11N 0°44W 22 D7
Rye Bay U.K. 50°52N 0°49E 25 E10
Ryhope U.K. 54°53N 1°21W 22 C6
Ryton U.K. 52°22N 1°25W 24 B6
Ryukyu Is. Japan 26°0N 126°0E 81 D7
Rzeszów Poland 50°5N 21°58E 67 C11
Rzhev Russia 56°20N 34°20E 72 C5

S

Saale → Germany 51°56N 11°54E 66 C6
Saar → Europe 49°41N 6°32E 65 E6
Saarbrücken Germany 49°14N 6°59E 66 D4
Saaremaa Estonia 58°30N 22°30E 63 F8
Sabadell Spain 41°28N 2°7E 69 B7
Sabah □ Malaysia 6°0N 117°0E 83 C3
Sabará Brazil 19°55S 43°46W 122 C2
Sabhā Libya 27°9N 14°29E 95 C8
Sabinas Mexico 27°51N 101°7W 114 B4
Sabinas Hidalgo Mexico 26°30N 100°10W 114 B4
Sabine → U.S.A. 29°59N 93°47W 111 E8
Sable, C. Canada 43°29N 65°38W 113 D15
Sable, C. U.S.A. 25°9N 81°8W 111 E10
Sable I. Canada 44°0N 60°0W 109 E14
Sachsen □ Germany 50°55N 13°10E 66 C7
Sachsen-Anhalt □ Germany 52°0N 12°0E 66 C7
Saco U.S.A. 43°30N 70°27W 113 D12
Sacramento U.S.A. 38°35N 121°29W 110 C2
Sacramento → U.S.A. 38°3N 121°56W 110 C2
Sacramento Mts. U.S.A. 32°30N 105°30W 110 D5
Sado Japan 38°0N 138°25E 82 D6
Safford U.S.A. 32°50N 109°43W 110 D5
Saffron Walden U.K. 52°1N 0°16E 25 B9
Safi Morocco 32°18N 9°20W 94 B4
Saga Japan 33°15N 130°16E 82 G2
Sagaing Burma 21°52N 95°59E 85 J19
Sagar India 23°50N 78°44E 84 H11
Saginaw U.S.A. 43°26N 83°56W 112 D6
Saginaw B. U.S.A. 43°50N 83°40W 112 D6
Sagua la Grande Cuba 22°50N 80°10W 115 C8
Saguenay → Canada 48°22N 71°0W 113 A12
Sagunt Spain 39°42N 0°18W 69 C5
Sahara Africa 23°0N 5°0E 94 D6
Saharan Atlas Algeria 33°30N 1°0E 94 B6
Saharanpur India 29°58N 77°33E 84 E10
Sahel Africa 16°0N 5°0E 94 E5
Sahiwal Pakistan 30°45N 73°8E 84 D8
Saidpur Bangla. 25°48N 89°0E 85 G16
St. Abb's Head U.K. 55°55N 2°8W 21 C11
St. Agnes Corn., U.K. 50°19N 5°13W 27 G3
St. Agnes Corn., U.K. 49°54N 6°21W 27 H1
St. Agnes Hd. U.K. 50°19N 5°15W 27 G3
St. Albans U.K. 51°45N 0°19W 25 C8
St. Albans Vt., U.S.A. 44°49N 73°5W 113 C11
St. Albans W. Va., U.S.A. 38°23N 81°50W 112 F7
St. Alban's Head U.K. 50°34N 2°4W 24 E4
St. Andrews U.K. 56°20N 2°47W 21 B10
St. Ann's U.K. 55°14N 3°28W 21 D9
St. Ann's Bay Jamaica 18°26N 77°12W 114 a
St. Anthony Canada 51°22N 55°35W 109 D14
St. Asaph U.K. 53°15N 3°27W 26 A7
St-Augustin Canada 51°13N 58°38W 109 D14
St. Augustine U.S.A. 29°54N 81°19W 111 E10
St. Austell U.K. 50°20N 4°47W 27 G4
St. Bees U.K. 54°30N 3°35W 22 C1
St. Bees Hd. U.K. 54°31N 3°38W 22 C1
St. Blazey U.K. 50°22N 4°43W 27 G4
St. Brides B. U.K. 51°49N 5°9W 26 D3
St-Brieuc France 48°30N 2°46W 68 B2
St. Buryan U.K. 50°4N 5°37W 27 G2
St. Catharines Canada 43°10N 79°15W 112 D8
St. Catherine's Pt. U.K. 50°34N 1°18W 24 E6
St. Charles U.S.A. 38°47N 90°29W 112 F2
St. Clair, L. N. Amer. 42°27N 82°39W 112 D6
St. Clears U.K. 51°49N 4°31W 26 D4
St. Cloud U.S.A. 45°34N 94°10W 111 A8
St. Columb Major U.K. 50°26N 4°58W 27 G4
St. Croix U.S. Virgin Is. 17°45N 64°45W 115 D12
St. David's U.K. 51°53N 5°16W 26 D3
St. David's Head U.K. 51°54N 5°19W 26 D3
St-Denis France 48°56N 2°20E 68 B5
St. Dennis U.K. 50°23N 4°53W 27 G4
St-Dizier France 48°38N 4°56E 68 B6
St. Dominick U.K. 50°29N 4°16W 27 G5
St. Elias, Mt. U.S.A. 60°18N 140°56W 108 C5
St. Elias Mts. N. Amer. 60°33N 139°28W 108 D6
St. Enoder U.K. 50°22N 4°59W 27 G4
St. Erth U.K. 50°9N 5°26W 27 G3
St-Étienne France 45°27N 4°22E 68 D6
St-Félicien Canada 48°40N 72°25W 113 A11
St-Flour France 45°2N 3°6E 68 D5
St. Gallen Switz. 47°26N 9°22E 66 E5
St-Gaudens France 43°6N 0°44E 68 E4
St. George U.S.A. 37°6N 113°35W 110 C4
St-Georges Canada 46°8N 70°40W 113 B12
St. George's Grenada 12°5N 61°43W 115 E12
St. George's Channel Europe 52°0N 6°0W 31 E11
St. Germans U.K. 50°23N 4°19W 27 G5
St. Helena Atl. Oc. 15°58S 5°42W 52 E9
St. Helens U.K. 53°27N 2°44W 23 F3
St. Helens, Mt. U.S.A. 46°12N 122°12W 110 A2
St. Helier U.K. 49°10N 2°7W 27 J9
St-Hyacinthe Canada 45°40N 72°58W 109 E12
St. Ignace U.S.A. 45°52N 84°44W 112 C5
St. Issey U.K. 50°30N 4°57W 27 G4
St. Ives Cambs., U.K. 52°20N 0°4W 25 B8
St. Ives Corn., U.K. 50°12N 5°30W 27 G3
St. Ives B. U.K. 50°13N 5°27W 27 G3
St-Jean, L. Canada 48°40N 72°0W 113 A12
St-Jérôme Canada 45°47N 74°0W 113 C11
St. John Canada 45°20N 66°8W 109 E13
St. John I. U.S. Virgin Is. 18°20N 64°42W 115 e
St. John's Antigua & B. 17°6N 61°51W 115 D12
St. John's Canada 47°35N 52°40W 109 E14
St. Johns U.S.A. 43°0N 84°33W 112 D5
St. Johns → U.S.A. 30°24N 81°24W 111 D10
St. Johns Chapel U.K. 54°44N 2°10W 22 C4
St. John's Pt. Ireland 54°34N 8°27W 28 B5
St. Johnsbury U.S.A. 44°25N 72°1W 113 C11
St-Joseph Martinique 14°39N 61°4W 114 c
St. Joseph Mich., U.S.A. 42°6N 86°29W 112 D4
St. Joseph Mo., U.S.A. 39°46N 94°50W 111 C8
St. Joseph, L. Canada 51°10N 90°35W 109 D10
St. Just U.K. 50°7N 5°42W 27 G2
St. Keverne U.K. 50°3N 5°6W 27 G3
St. Kilda U.K. 57°49N 8°34W 64 C2
St. Kitts & Nevis ■ W. Indies 17°20N 62°40W 115 D12
St. Lawrence → Canada 49°30N 66°0W 109 E13
St. Lawrence, Gulf of Canada 48°25N 62°0W 109 E13
St. Lawrence I. U.S.A. 63°30N 170°30W 108 C3
St. Levan U.K. 50°2N 5°41W 27 G2
St-Lô France 49°7N 1°5W 68 B3
St-Louis Guadeloupe 15°56N 61°19W 114 b
St. Louis Senegal 16°8N 16°27W 94 E2
St. Louis U.S.A. 38°37N 90°11W 112 F2
St. Lucia ■ W. Indies 14°0N 60°57W 115 f
St. Mabyn U.K. 50°30N 4°47W 27 F4
St. Magnus B. U.K. 60°25N 1°35W 18 B14
St-Malo France 48°39N 2°1W 68 B2
St-Marc Haiti 19°10N 72°41W 115 D10
St. Margaret's-at-Cliffe U.K. 51°9N 1°23E 25 D11
St-Martin ☒ W. Indies 18°0N 63°0W 115 D12
St-Martin, C. Martinique 14°52N 61°14W 114 c
St. Martins Barbados 13°5N 59°28W 115 g
St. Martin's U.K. 49°58N 6°17W 27 H1
St. Mary Bourne U.K. 51°15N 1°24W 24 D6
St. Mary's Corn., U.K. 49°55N 6°18W 27 H1
St. Mary's Orkney, U.K. 58°54N 2°54W 19 E12
St. Marys U.S.A. 41°26N 78°34W 112 E8
St. Mary's Sd. U.K. 49°54N 6°20W 27 H1
St. Matthew I. U.S.A. 60°24N 172°42W 108 C2
St. Mawes U.K. 50°10N 5°2W 27 G3
St. Merryn U.K. 50°32N 5°1W 27 F3
St. Michael's Mount U.K. 50°7N 5°29W 27 G3
St. Minver U.K. 50°33N 4°53W 27 F4
St. Moritz Switz. 46°30N 9°51E 66 E5
St-Nazaire France 47°17N 2°12W 68 C2
St. Neots U.K. 52°14N 0°15W 25 B8
St-Niklaas Belgium 51°10N 4°8E 65 C4
St-Omer France 50°45N 2°15E 68 A5
St. Osyth U.K. 51°47N 1°5E 25 C11
St. Paul U.S.A. 44°56N 93°5W 111 B8
St. Paul, I. Ind. Oc. 38°55S 77°34E 53 F13
St. Peter Port U.K. 49°26N 2°33W 27 J8
St. Petersburg Russia 59°55N 30°20E 72 C5
St. Petersburg U.S.A. 27°46N 82°40W 111 E10
St-Pierre Martinique 14°45N 61°10W 114 c
St-Pierre-et-Miquelon ☒ N. Amer. 46°55N 56°10W 109 E14
St-Quentin France 49°50N 3°16E 68 B5
St. Stephen Canada 45°16N 67°17W 113 C14
St. Stephen U.K. 50°21N 4°53W 27 G4
St. Teath U.K. 50°35N 4°45W 27 F4
St. Thomas Canada 42°45N 81°10W 112 D7
St. Thomas I. U.S. Virgin Is. 18°20N 64°55W 115 e
St-Tropez France 43°17N 6°38E 68 E7
St. Tudy U.K. 50°33N 4°45W 27 F4
St. Vincent, G. Australia 35°0S 138°0E 98 G6
St. Vincent & the Grenadines ■ W. Indies 13°0N 61°10W 115 E12
Ste-Anne Guadeloupe 16°13N 61°24W 114 b
Ste. Genevieve U.S.A. 37°59N 90°2W 112 G2
Ste-Marie Canada 46°26N 71°0W 113 B12
Ste-Marie Martinique 14°48N 61°1W 114 c
Ste-Rose Guadeloupe 16°20N 61°45W 114 b
Saintes France 45°45N 0°37W 68 D3
Saintes, Îs. des Guadeloupe 15°50N 61°35W 114 b
Saintfield U.K. 54°28N 5°49W 29 C10
Saintonge France 45°40N 0°50W 68 D3
Saipan N. Marianas 15°12N 145°45E 102 F6
Sajama Bolivia 18°7S 69°0W 120 D3
Sakakawea, L. U.S.A. 47°30N 101°25W 110 A6
Sakarya Turkey 40°48N 30°25E 73 F5
Sakata Japan 38°55N 139°50E 82 D6
Sakhalin Russia 51°0N 143°0E 79 D16
Sala Sweden 59°58N 16°35E 63 F7
Sala-y-Gómez Pac. Oc. 26°28S 105°28W 103 K17
Salado → La Pampa, Argentina 37°30S 67°0W 121 F3
Salado → Santa Fe, Argentina 31°40S 60°41W 121 F3
Salālah Oman 16°56N 53°59E 88 D5
Salamanca Spain 40°58N 5°39W 69 B3
Salamanca U.S.A. 42°10N 78°43W 112 D8
Salar de Uyuni Bolivia 20°30S 67°45W 120 E3
Salavat Russia 53°21N 55°55E 72 D10
Salaverry Peru 8°15S 79°0W 120 C2
Salayar Indonesia 6°7S 120°30E 83 D4
Salcombe U.K. 50°14N 3°47W 27 G6
Saldanha S. Africa 33°0S 17°58E 97 L3
Sale Australia 38°6S 147°6E 98 H8
Salé Morocco 34°3N 6°48W 94 B4
Sale U.K. 53°26N 2°19W 23 F4
Salekhard Russia 66°30N 66°35E 79 C8
Salem India 11°40N 78°11E 84 P11
Salem Ind., U.S.A. 38°36N 86°6W 112 F4
Salem Mass., U.S.A. 42°31N 70°53W 113 D12
Salem Ohio, U.S.A. 40°54N 80°52W 112 E7
Salem Oreg., U.S.A. 44°56N 123°2W 110 B2
Salem Va., U.S.A. 37°18N 80°3W 112 G7
Salerno Italy 40°41N 14°47E 70 D6
Salford U.K. 53°30N 2°18W 23 F4
Salford Priors U.K. 52°10N 1°53W 24 B5
Salida U.S.A. 38°32N 106°0W 110 C5
Salina U.S.A. 38°50N 97°37W 110 C7
Salina Cruz Mexico 16°10N 95°12W 114 D5
Salinas Ecuador 2°10S 80°58W 120 C1
Salinas U.S.A. 36°40N 121°39W 110 C2
Salinas → U.S.A. 36°45N 121°48W 110 C2
Salinas Grandes Argentina 30°0S 65°0W 121 E3
Salisbury U.K. 51°4N 1°47W 24 D5
Salisbury U.S.A. 38°22N 75°36W 113 F10
Salisbury I. Canada 63°30N 77°0W 109 C12
Salisbury Plain U.K. 51°14N 1°55W 24 D5
Salmon U.S.A. 45°11N 113°54W 110 A4
Salmon → U.S.A. 45°51N 116°47W 110 A3
Salmon Arm Canada 50°40N 119°15W 108 D8
Salmon River Mts. U.S.A. 44°50N 115°30W 110 B4
Salon-de-Provence France 43°39N 5°6E 68 E6
Salsk Russia 46°28N 41°30E 73 E7
Salt → U.S.A. 33°23N 112°19W 110 D4
Salt Lake City U.S.A. 40°45N 111°53W 110 B4
Salta Argentina 24°57S 65°25W 121 E3
Saltash U.K. 50°24N 4°14W 27 G5
Saltburn by the Sea U.K. 54°35N 0°58W 22 C7
Saltcoats U.K. 55°38N 4°47W 20 C6
Saltee Is. Ireland 52°7N 6°37W 31 D9
Saltfleet U.K. 53°25N 0°11E 23 F9
Saltfleetby U.K. 53°23N 0°10E 23 F9
Saltillo Mexico 25°25N 101°0W 114 B4
Salton Sea U.S.A. 33°15N 115°45W 110 D3
Saltwood U.K. 51°4N 1°2E 25 D11
Salvador Brazil 13°0S 38°30W 122 B3
Salvador, El ■ Cent. Amer. 13°50N 89°0W 114 E7
Salween → Burma 16°31N 97°37E 85 L20
Salyan Azerbaijan 39°33N 48°59E 73 G8
Salzburg Austria 47°48N 13°2E 66 E7
Salzgitter Germany 52°9N 10°19E 66 B6
Samangān □ Afghan. 36°15N 68°3E 87 B12
Samar Phil. 12°0N 125°0E 83 B4
Samara Russia 53°8N 50°6E 72 D9
Samarinda Indonesia 0°30S 117°9E 83 D3
Samarkand Uzbekistan 39°40N 66°55E 87 B11
Sambalpur India 21°28N 84°4E 85 J14
Sambhal India 28°35N 78°37E 84 E11
Sambhar India 26°52N 75°6E 84 F9
Samoa ■ Pac. Oc. 14°0S 172°0W 99 C16
Samos Greece 37°45N 26°50E 71 F12
Samothraki Greece 40°28N 25°28E 71 D11
Sampford Courtenay U.K. 50°47N 3°58W 27 F6
Samsun Turkey 41°15N 36°22E 73 F6
Samui, Ko Thailand 9°30N 100°0E 83 C2
San → Poland 50°45N 21°51E 67 C11
San Ambrosio Pac. Oc. 26°28S 79°53W 103 K20
San Andrés, I. de Caribbean 12°42N 81°46W 115 E8
San Andres Mts. U.S.A. 33°0N 106°30W 110 D5
San Andrés Tuxtla Mexico 18°27N 95°13W 114 D5
San Angelo U.S.A. 31°28N 100°26W 110 D6
San Antonio Chile 33°40S 71°40W 121 F2
San Antonio U.S.A. 29°25N 98°29W 110 E7
San Antonio → U.S.A. 28°30N 96°54W 111 E7
San Antonio Oeste Argentina 40°40S 65°0W 121 G3
San Bernardino U.S.A. 34°7N 117°19W 110 D3
San Bernardino Str. Phil. 13°0N 125°0E 83 B4
San Bernardo Chile 33°40S 70°50W 121 F2
San Blas, C. U.S.A. 29°40N 85°21W 111 E9
San Carlos Phil. 10°29N 123°25E 83 B4
San Carlos de Bariloche Argentina 41°10S 71°25W 121 G2
San Carlos de Bolívar Argentina 36°15S 61°6W 121 F3
San Cristóbal Argentina 30°20S 61°10W 121 F3
San Cristóbal Solomon Is. 10°30S 161°0E 99 C11
San Cristóbal Venezuela 7°46N 72°14W 120 B2
San Cristóbal de las Casas Mexico 16°45N 92°38W 114 D6
San Diego U.S.A. 32°42N 117°9W 110 D3
San Felipe Venezuela 10°20N 68°44W 120 A3
San Félix Pac. Oc. 26°23S 80°0W 103 K20
San Fernando Chile 34°30S 71°0W 121 F2
San Fernando Spain 36°28N 6°17W 69 D2
San Fernando de Apure Venezuela 7°54N 67°15W 120 B3
San Francisco U.S.A. 37°46N 122°23W 110 C2
San Francisco, C. de Colombia 6°18N 77°29W 116 C3
San Francisco de Macorís Dom. Rep. 19°19N 70°15W 115 D10
San German Puerto Rico 18°4N 67°4W 115 d
San Gottardo, P. del Switz. 46°33N 8°33E 66 E5
San Ignacio Bolivia 16°20S 60°55W 120 D3
San Joaquin → U.S.A. 38°4N 121°51W 110 C2
San Jorge, G. Argentina 46°0S 66°0W 121 G3
San José Costa Rica 9°55N 84°2W 115 F8
San Jose Phil. 12°27N 121°4E 83 B4
San Jose U.S.A. 37°20N 121°53W 110 C2
San Jose → U.S.A. 34°25N 106°45W 110 D5
San José de Chiquitos Bolivia 17°53S 60°50W 120 D3
San José de Jáchal Argentina 30°15S 68°46W 121 F3
San José de Mayo Uruguay 34°27S 56°40W 121 F4
San Juan Argentina 31°30S 68°30W 121 F3
San Juan Dom. Rep. 18°49N 71°12W 115 D10
San Juan Puerto Rico 18°28N 66°7W 115 d
San Juan → Nic. 10°56N 83°42W 115 E8
San Juan → U.S.A. 37°16N 110°26W 110 C4
San Juan de los Morros Venezuela 9°55N 67°21W 120 B3
San Juan Mts. U.S.A. 37°30N 107°0W 110 C5
San Lorenzo, Mte. Argentina 47°40S 72°20W 121 G2
San Lucas, C. Mexico 22°52N 109°53W 114 C3
San Luis Argentina 33°20S 66°20W 121 F3

San Luis Obispo   Skeleton Coast

Skellefteå — Talgarth

Taliabu

Tuticorin

Tutuila   Wells

Wells-next-the-Sea   Zwickau